The Twentieth Century is the first volume to appear in the Laurel British Drama series, which will present the outstanding plays of that country from medieval times to the present. In this volume the significant plays of our century have been collected. Included also are essays on each by noted critics or by the authors themselves, which give fresh insight into the works.

Robert W. Corrigan is Professor of Dramatic Literature and Director of the Program in the Arts at New York University. He has taught drama at several colleges, including Carnegie Institute of Technology where he was Andrew Mellon Professor and Head of the Department of Drama. Professor Corrigan was the founder and first editor of the TULANE DRAMA REVIEW, and has also edited numerous books on the theatre including THE MODERN THEATRE, THEATRE IN THE 20TH CENTURY, CHEKHOV: SIX PLAYS, THE LAUREL CLASSICAL DRAMA SERIES (5 vols. Dell), and the NEW THEATRE OF EUROPE (2 vols. Delta).

Forthcoming titles in the Laurel British Drama series:

LAUREL BRITISH DRAMA:

The Twentieth Century

Edited, with an Introduction by

Robert W. Corrigan

Published by DELL PUBLISHING CO., INC.

750 Third Avenue, New York 17, N.Y.

© *Copyright, 1965, by Dell Publishing Co., Inc.*

Laurel ® *TM 674623, Dell Publishing Co., Inc.*

First printing: September, 1965

Printed in U.S.A.

DEDICATION: *For Phil Gelb*

ACKNOWLEDGMENTS:

Heartbreak House: "Notes for a Production of *Heartbreak House*" by Harold Clurman, THE TULANE DRAMA REVIEW, Vol. 5, No. 3 (March, 1961). Copyright ©, 1961, THE TULANE DRAMA REVIEW. Reprinted by permission of Mr. Clurman.
  Heartbreak House by George Bernard Shaw. Reprinted by permission of the Public Trustee and The Society of Authors.

Loyalties: "Some Platitudes Concerning Drama" is reprinted with the permission of Charles Scribner's Sons from THE INN OF TRANQUILITY by John Galsworthy. Copyright 1912, Charles Scribner's Sons; renewal copyright 1940 by Ada Galsworthy.
  Loyalties (Copyright 1922, Charles Scribner's Sons; renewal copyright 1950, Ada Galsworthy) is reprinted by permission of Charles Scribner's Sons.
  CAUTION: Professionals and amateurs are hereby warned that *Loyalties* by John Galsworthy is fully protected under the Copyright Laws of the United States of America, the British Commonwealth and Empire, including the Dominion of Canada, and in all other countries of the Universal Copyright Convention and under other Copyright Treaties and Conventions in force. Inquiries regarding dramatic rights must be addressed to A. J. P. Sellar, c/o Halsay, Lightly & Hemsley, 32 St. James Place, London, S. W. 1, England.

Private Lives: "Noel Coward: An Appreciation of His Work in the Theatre" by Terence Rattigan from THE THEATRICAL COMPANION TO COWARD by Raymond Mander and Joe Michenson. Copyright 1957 by Rockliff Publishing Corporation, London. Reprinted by permission of Terence Rattigan.
  Private Lives by Noel Coward. Copyright 1930 by Doubleday & Company, Inc. Reprinted by permission of the publisher.

Contents

The British Drama
in the Twentieth Century

It is somewhat disturbing to realize that it is possible to trace the development of the British drama in the twentieth century by dividing it into three distinct periods, and not be too guilty of either journalistic inaccuracy or pedantic oversimplification. The first thirty years were dominated by Shaw; the next twenty-five can only be described as a fallow period; and finally, beginning with the opening of John Osborne's *Look Back in Anger* in May of 1956, it moved into what has come to be known as the "anger" period, a time that many commentators have hailed as the renaissance of the British theatre. Of course, all one has to do is set up such tidy divisions, and all of their limitations—not to mention the numerous exceptions—immediately come to the surface. For instance: what about the plays of Barrie, Galsworthy, and Maugham? Can writers like Eliot, Coward, Rattigan, and Fry be glibly dismissed as so much alfalfa? We all appreciate the critic's rage for order, but how can anyone in his right mind place playwrights so diverse in tone, style, and attitude as Osborne, Pinter, Bolt, Arden, Whiting, Wesker, and Simpson under the banner of the "angry generation." Such objections are valid and fairly raised; nonetheless, after considering them, I believe these three divisions are still pretty descriptive of the uneven way the British theatre has developed in our century.

Certainly, no twentieth-century British playwright (we have intentionally excluded the distinctly Irish writers Yeats, Synge, and O'Casey) has ever achieved a stature comparable to Shaw's, and those writing while G.B.S. was at his dramatic best seem like midgets when placed beside him. The great gulf that exists between Shaw and Barrie and Galsworthy, the other major dramatists of the first quarter of the century, becomes immediately apparent when we remember that *Man and Superman* and *The Admirable Crichton* were both completed in 1903, or recall that *Loyalties* and *Back to*

Methuselah were first produced in 1922, and that *Saint Joan* came a year later.

Some people may well protest that to describe the years from 1930 to 1956 as a dormant period in the drama is to be too harsh, if not completely wrong-headed. But today, even the greatest achievements of those years seem to have either lost most of their lustre or remain as isolated monuments that were never repeated and that had little or no influence over the succeeding generation of playwrights. *Murder in the Cathedral* (1935) is a great play, but even Mr. Eliot himself considered it a museum piece, and his more recent plays have had, at best, only partial success in the theatre and have failed to match the first in language, design, or dramatic impact. Priestley is now hopelessly out of date. We still enjoy Mr. Coward's delightful, quick, almost parthenogenetic wit, but his plays are, after all, essentially a part of the century-old tradition of English drawing-room comedy. This is a noble tradition and not to be slighted, but Coward has certainly not brought anything new into the English theatre. I, for one, had great hopes that Christopher Fry would be instrumental in revitalizing the British drama. *A Lady's Not for Burning* and *A Sleep of Prisoners* have admirable qualities, and the latter still ranks as one of the most important plays written in England since the second World War. But Fry has never been able to subordinate his undisputed lyric powers to the service of a dramatic action, and it is probably significant that in recent years he has been more successful as a translator than as a playwright in his own name. As for Terence Rattigan, there is no doubt that he is a master craftsman, and plays such as *The Winslow Boy* and *Separate Tables* were, and will continue to be, a staple in the commercial theatre. But Rattigan has not led the theatre in any new directions nor do we expect him to. Each of these writers—not to mention others active during this period—have a record of solid achievement in the theatre, but they lacked the sustained creativity and vital inventiveness (characteristics that Eliot had as a poet) that makes the theatre come alive and become a meaningful force in the cultural life of a nation or the world.

Then in the mid-1950's something new began to happen in the English theatre. Playwrights popped up everywhere, and their plays were so different in tone, theme, and form that the change could only be described as revolutionary. Interestingly enough, it was Kenneth Tynan, who was to become the spokesman-critic of the new breed, who chronicled the mid-century death and rebirth of the London stage. Within the same month he reviewed the opening of Enid Bagnold's *The Chalk Garden* (which was significantly first produced in New York) and John Osborne's *Look Back in Anger*. Of the former, he wrote:

> On Wednesday night a wonder happened: the West End theatre justified its existence. One had thought it an anachronism, wilfully preserving a formal, patrician acting style for which the modern drama had no use, a style as remote from reality as a troop of cavalry in an age of turbo-jets. One was shamefully wrong. On Wednesday night, superbly caparisoned, the cavalry went into action and gave a display of theatrical equitation which silenced all grumblers. This engagement completed, the brigade may have to be disbanded. But at least it went out with a flourish, its banners resplendent in the last rays of the sun.

Ten days later he was to write:

> *Look Back in Anger* is likely to remain a minority taste. What matters, however, is the size of the minority. I estimate it at roughly 6,733,000, which is the number of people in this country between the ages of twenty and thirty. And this figure will doubtless be swelled by refugees from other age-groups who are curious to know precisely what the contemporary young pup is thinking and feeling. I doubt if I could love anyone who did not wish to see *Look Back in Anger*. It is the best young play of its decade.

As Tynan predicted, this minority was important and within four years London had become the most vital center of the theatre in the world. There have been many attempts to explain why this radical change took place: the emergence of the lower-middle class as a political force, the changes made in British life by the postwar Labor government, the effect of national television, the rise of Joan Littlewood as a dominant force in the English theatre. All of these explanations are at least partially true, but the more important fact remains: England once again had a theatre! Osborne was soon followed by Behan (Irish, but first produced by

Littlewood at the Royal Court), Delaney, Pinter, Wesker, Kops, Arden, Bolt, a new John Whiting, Simpson, and most recently Ann Jellicoe. Now, no one will ever try to argue that all of these playwrights are alike or are members of some "new school" of the theatre. But what links writers as different as N. F. Simpson and Robert Bolt is their willingness to try new things in the theatre. At first glance, *A Man for All Seasons* seems like a traditional British play in the heroic mode of the old dispensation. But as his Preface makes clear, Bolt is approaching his subject in a totally new way (for one thing the influence of Brecht is readily apparent), with the result that the play's form and meaning have a quality of forcefulness that this kind of play had been lacking for so long. It is a willingness to try new things, and the insistence that the theatre must deal with different subjects if it is to be relevant to its audiences that characterize the drama of "Anger and After." We are still too close to this theatre to judge adequately its accomplishments, but of the fact that it is different, there can be no doubt.

And now to the plays and playwrights represented in this book.

Our aim in each of the volumes in this series is to provide the reader with a sampling of plays that we believe are representative of each period in the British theatre from medieval times to the present. In this volume we have wanted to show the rich diversity of the British drama in the twentieth century. To this end we have chosen two plays from each of the three periods described above, which would demonstrate the extreme achievements of that period as well as its essential common qualities. Such an approach makes it difficult, if not impossible, to discuss each of the plays included in this volume with some kind of omnibus essay on a single theme. Instead, I shall comment briefly on the plays in an attempt to show how it is representative of its author's work, and also to indicate its place in the British drama of our century.

> Heartbreak House is not merely the name of the play which follows this preface. It is cultured, leisured Europe before the war. . . .

With these words George Bernard Shaw begins his Preface to *Heartbreak House*. The rest of the preface is a description of how the basic assumptions of the Western World were all too rapidly disintegrating and how they were finally destroyed in the first World War. The most important of these assumptions to go was that the rational rather than the irrational is the dominant mode of human existence. Shaw, though he fought the good fight, was of that legion of iconoclasts who realized that man is not so much a creature of reason as a victim of irrational and unconscious forces. It is in *Heartbreak House* that he first came to grips without equivocation with those questions which had haunted Ibsen, Strindberg, and Chekhov before him. How is one to live in an irrational world? How is one to give meaning to life in a world where one doesn't know the rules? How are human relationships to be maintained meaningfully when one cannot be sure of his feelings and when one's feelings can change without one's knowing it? How can man live without being destroyed when irreconcilable conflict is the central fact of all life?

The world of *Heartbreak House* is one that has permanently misplaced the life, vitality, and victory of *Major Barbara*. The people who whirl before us in this mad "dance of death" rapidly lose whatever veneer of virtue they may have had and stand revealed as vain, insipid, blind, and vapid men and women who have made their society into "an economic, political, and as far as practical, a moral vacuum. . . ." In the years between these two plays the world was radically changed by the war, and Shaw—always sensitive to changes in moral climate—was certainly not immune to it. In postwar Europe man seems to have lost his faith in himself, and without this faith there can be no truth. This is the theme of *Heartbreak House* as it has been the theme of so many of Shaw's plays: How does man find a faith in himself that will lead to the truth? The big difference between this play and those written before it is that man not only does not succeed in *Heartbreak House*, but the possibility of his ever succeeding is flatly rejected. In the first act (written before the war) there still seems to be the possibility of salvation, but in the remaining two acts man's stupidity and evil—the nothingness of the characters and their philosophy, their inability to live in the modern world, their unworthiness to be preserved—are revealed. But here the Shavian "true believer" will rise up in Godly wrath and cry, "Nay, 'tis not so! It is easy enough to dismiss Mangan, Mazzini, Hector, Lady Utterword, and even Hesione, but have you forgotten that magnificent old man, Captain Shotover and our Ellie, so fine and true? How can you condemn them along with all the rest? It is they who will save the world. They are our hope." Captain Shotover, delightful as he is, cannot be a candidate for the man to whom one could say: "What must we do to be saved?" First of all, his life has been spent and he has accomplished little for his fellowman. His philosophy of life, in his own words, is one of self-interest above all: "A man's interest in the world is only the overflow from his interest in himself." His main activity is working out a means of destroying his fellowmen with a dynamite that explodes by thought. He, in fact, cancels out the hope some have found in *Major Barbara.* "You are going to let the fear of poverty govern your life; and your reward will be that you will eat, but you will not live." Undershaft's solution will not work in Shotover's world. Money will not save men—not even Ellie. Shotover not only sees clearly what Heartbreak House has become, he knows that it has already been judged. And he has been judged most severely, although he has found an escape of sorts. "I cannot bear men and women," he says. "I have to run away. I must run away now." There is no tranquility in his old age. "I can't remember what I really am. I feel nothing but the accursed happiness I have dreaded all my life: the happiness that comes as life goes, the happiness of yielding and dreaming instead of resisting and doing, the sweetness of fruit that is going rotten." Shaw has denied this society even the hope of a peaceful old age that can await a heavenly home. The Captain fears and hates sleep, so he drinks to keep awake and away from death.

Captain Shotover does, however, do one thing no one else in the play can do: he speaks the truth. In this he is an essential partner for Ellie. The two of them must provide the answers no matter how despairing they may be. Ellie turns to him for guidance from the first. She is that person in each of us who asks the eternal questions: "What is truth and reality? How can I exist in this futile world?" In the beginning we feel that perhaps she will find the answer, but gradually as more and more deception, cruelty, and emptiness are revealed to her, she too becomes embittered. "What a vile world it is!" she cries. But Captain Shotover only replies: "It doesn't concern me. I'm nearly out of it!" Ellie comes to realize that the things she had first looked for in Heartbreak House cannot be found—even in the Captain. She turns to him as the best of those available, but her attitude in doing so is negative: ". . . I feel now as if there was nothing I could do, because I want nothing." Captain Shotover understands that she is clinging to something that does not exist. When she says, "Your own spirit is not dead," he replies "Echoes: nothing but echoes. The last shot was fired years ago." And clinging to the old man, Ellie moves further and further from any solution to her questions, until at the end of the play she is lost—callously disappointed at the shortness of the bombing attack. Her future is the most despairing of all, for when Hesione says: "But what a glorious experience; I hope they'll come again tomorrow night." Ellie [*radiant at the prospect*] answers, "Oh, I hope so." Is this Shaw's answer? Could there be anything more ironical than his choice of words—"radiant" and "I hope"—as symbols of future salvation applied to a request for more war and death. Nothing is left—nothing is real or true in Heartbreak House. Ellie states her own failure and that of those around her.

> There seems to be nothing in the world except my father and Shakespeare. Marcus's tigers are false; Mr. Mangan's millions are false; there is nothing really strong and true about Hesione but her beautiful black hair; and Lady Utterword's too pretty to be real. The only thing that was left to me was the Captain's seventh degree of concentration; and that turns out to be . . .
>
> CAPTAIN SHOTOVER: Rum!

No one has ever questioned that *Heartbreak House* is one of Shaw's masterpieces, but today, as we look back on his career as a dramatist, this play takes on a new significance: it is clearly a pivotal play. The staunch believer in the life force has come to believe that the laws of navigation can never be learned. In all the plays up to, and including, *Major Barbara*, Shaw seemed to insist that salvation was possible if only we are bold of heart and clear in mind. But with *Heartbreak House* that hard-won optimism disappears never again to return. The optimism of the later plays is, as Joseph Wood Krutch put it, "more a matter of temperament than of philosophical conviction." With *Heartbreak House* the British theatre entered the continental mainstream and the only difference between Shaw and the Ibsen, Strindberg, and Chekhov he so admired is that he was able to take the loss of hope more cheerfully.

Today, when we read one of John Galsworthy's plays we cannot help but feel that he must have been a very fine and distinguished gentleman whom it would have been a great privilege to know. As a playwright, however, he seems terribly old-fashioned. In fact, to read a play like *Loyalties,* which is certainly one of Galsworthy's best, is to be reminded of just how limited and limiting the carefully constructed, elaborately plotted problem play can be. But unlike so many of our contemporary Galsworthys, he was a humble man who had few pretensions about his abilities as a dramatist. He even admits to being inarticulate. In one of his prefaces, he compares his plays to Shaw's: "About Shaw's plays one might say that they contain characters who express emotions which they do not possess. About mine one might say that they contain characters who possess emotions which they cannot express." He was talking about his characters here, but even a brief examination of his dramatic techniques will reveal that he could have been talking about his plays as well. Shaw was so imaginative that his plays always seem on the verge of breaking the limits of dramatic art. In Galsworthy everything is under control.

Control! That is the key to a Galsworthy play. There are no climactic curtains, well-calculated to achieve an artificial emotional response. In his attempts to view the action with "wise" impartiality, he gives both sides their say in a continuous series of parallel scenes. There are no villains or heroes, nor is there any tendency to judge his characters. Being trained as a lawyer, Galsworthy tried to present matters as they would be handled in the perfect court—if such a Platonic institution could ever exist. To us, his plots appear to be triumphs of the obvious: the planted lines, the impossible coincidences, the clichéd warnings. But in all fairness, these devices are not used because Galsworthy was lazy or believed in cheap theatrical tricks, but rather because he insisted on the importance of logical development in the writing of a play. And this kind of development does create a kind of detective-story suspense in his plays. A similar explanation can be given for the absence of any real character conflicts in the plays. He takes a situation and seeks to reveal how people act when they are in it. The characters react to the situation, not to each other. In everything, Galsworthy desperately sought to avoid any kind of artificiality or theatrical dishonesty. And he succeeded! Unfortunately, he never seemed to know that the theatre is a dishonest medium, with the ironic result that his plays seem extremely wooden and completely artificial.

But for all its limitations, *Loyalties* is a significant play. It is even a courageous one. With a daring surpassed in the English theatre of his time only by Shaw, Galsworthy dealt with an important theme: prejudice against the Jews. We feel his results are superficial and melodramatic, but this is not because he failed to draw some dramatic conclusions (à la *Gentlemen's Agreement*). Molière, after all, didn't try to solve the problem of hypocrisy in *Tartuffe;* he was concerned with showing us hypocrisy in many of its forms. If today we judge Galsworthy as a failure, it is not because of his choice of subject matter or his refusal to resolve his actions and pass judgments on his characters; rather we must attribute it to his inability to "feel" the nature of the theatre. The theatre is not a courtroom (although the two have much in common), nor is it a novel (although both use narrative techniques). Galsworthy, for all his wisdom, never seemed to understand these distinctions.

However, while we may dismiss Galsworthy today, we should do so with the full knowledge that in rejecting him we also reject one of the staples of the American theatre: the popular "dramatic" play. *A Case of Libel, The Desperate Hours, Inherit the Wind,* or *Witness for the Prosecution* may be more up-to-date, but in reality they are a Galsworthy play in mid-twentieth-century dress. There are many reasons (several of them good) that the theatre embraces such plays, even at a time when it is riding the crest of so many new waves. How much more impressive, then, is Galsworthy's achievement to have written what he did at a time when the British theatre was at ebb tide.

Mention of Noel Coward's name invariably evokes controversy. Some, including the judicious Desmond Mac-Carthy, hold him up on high as one of the few renaissance men of the twentieth-century theatre. He can do anything —write, compose, act, direct, dance, and even design—and do it with perfect grace and an adroit tact that enables him to be sentimental without ever being dull. For these admirers he is a master stage chef who prepares amazing dishes that satisfy the palates of even the most demanding gourmets. Others dismiss him as nothing more than a clever and facile manipulator who concocts a theatrical froth as nourishing as a mound of canned whipped cream. The fact is, both sides are right and this explains why the dispute, which has been going on since his first successes in the 1920's, erupts anew each time one of his plays is revived. No one can deny the charm of his effervescent sophistication and sparkling wit, but we must also remember that the gourmet's taste is jaded by satiety and that subtle delicacies—whether at the Mayfair or Maxim's—are enjoyed by most of us only on rare and special occasions.

There are many people who believe that a large Coward revival is on the verge of taking place. I think they may be right. But not for the same reasons that originally brought him to the pinnacle of popularity. I doubt if there is much interest today in the glamour and elegance of high society. That kind of society, as Cleveland Amory tells us, is pretty nearly dead, and our fascination for its naughty hijinks has been transferred to celebrities who are in no one class. We may also be impressed by the serpentine grace of Coward's style and the sharpness of his dialogue and repartee, but this, too, is not enough to prompt much of a revival. Its cause, if it does take place, will be probably more significant. In 1947, Harold Clurman quite correctly observed that "all of Coward's plays reveal a state of mind in which contempt and indifference to the world have been accepted as a sort of aristocratic privilege." The aristocracy may be dead, but we still seek to assume its privileges. In a time dominated by the fear of nuclear war, the tension of cold-war diplomacy, and the insecurity of a defense economy, we all understandably find ourselves reaching out for ways to escape, rise above, or forget our anxieties. And Coward's smart-set indifference and smirking contempt is an attractive—albeit immature—alternative to *Angst*. When we see a Coward play we can believe, if only for an hour or two, that there is no reason to be at our wit's end; for in Coward's world wit always carries the day, and oftentimes the night as well.

Private Lives is one of Coward's best plays. It is by no means profound, but it is a superb acting piece and is a brilliant example of a play in which wit seems to outpoint anxiety. Why worry about being neurotic? After all, "very few people are completely normal really, deep down in their private lives." In an age when God is dead, there is a new dispensation: "Chance rules our lives," so "be nice to everyone and always be gay." In a world where everything is so uncertain, laughter is the only truth so "let's savour the delight of the moment." *Carpe diem* is an old saw, but it has never been more alluring than it is today. Such defenses of the spirit are not usually very effective, but there is no denying their attractiveness. We all know that to enjoy a Coward play (like all of the arts of diversion) in the "Age of the Bomb" is like whistling in the dark while walking through a graveyard. But, then, Mr. Coward, in addition to his many other talents, also whistles very well.

Gerald Weales' penetrating essay on *The Chalk Garden*, which precedes Enid Bagnold's play in this volume, deals with most of the critical issues raised by the play, and I have little to add to his remarks except to say that I agree with nearly everything he has written. I also share the enthusiasm that my colleagues Harold Clurman, Eric Bentley, and Kenneth Tynan have for the play. ("The best new English play in London"—Clurman; "I believe that, all in all, *The Chalk Garden*, by Enid Bagnold, is the best new play of the 1955–56 season, a very brilliant piece of composition, one of the most skillfully *built* plays of recent years, with a good subject, and an honorable theme."—Bentley; ". . . may well be the finest artificial comedy to have flowed from an English (as opposed to an Irish) pen since the death of Congreve. . . . In this production (by Sir John Gielgud) we see English actors doing perfectly what few actors on earth can do at all: reproduce in the theatre the spirited elegance of a Mozart quintet."—Tynan.) It is one of the finest and most delicately beautiful plays written in England in this century. However, I should like to develop one point that Mr. Weales touched upon, but seemed reluctant to pursue too far: the play's religious dimension. More than anything else, I believe *The Chalk Garden* is about the power of Grace and the possibility of salvation. As a character, Miss Madrigal—"The East Wind"—embodies everything that affirms love and life. But she does so as a mediator. The play is not about her or her life (she is not quietistic, indeed she's most assertive, but she has no needs of her own. As she says: "I am burnt out, white—like the moon, lunar!"), but about how she transforms the spirit and quality of all the life around her. Mrs. St. Maugham is a suppliant and Miss Madrigal answers her call for aid. The St. Maugham household gets more from Miss Madrigal than it bargained for, but not more than it needs. Working with a mysterious power that theologians probably understand better than drama critics, she saves Laura, revitalizes Olivia's capacity to love, rejuvenates Maitland's spirit and strengthens his will, restores the judge's sense of justice, hastens the death of Pinkbell (who is referred to as the Devil on several occasions), and, most important, she agrees to help Mrs. St. Maugham onto Salvation's road. The play is by no means homiletical, however. When Miss Madrigal states that for the remainder of her life she will "continue to explore—the astonishment of living," we know she will do so not as a questing Dante but as a guiding Virgil. Thus the end of the play is a new beginning as well, and as Miss Madrigal and Mrs. St. Maugham begin to revive the chalk garden (not the Garden of Eden) I feel that they would both agree on the aptness to their enterprise of these lines by Christopher Fry:

> The human heart can go to the lengths of God.
> Dark and cold we may be, but this
> Is no winter now. The frozen misery
> Of centuries breaks, cracks, begins to move,
> The thunder is the thunder of the floes,
> The thaw, the flood, the upstart Spring.
> Thank God our time is now when wrong
> Comes up to face us everywhere,
> Never to leave us till we take
> The longest stride of soul men ever took.
> Affairs are now soul size.
> The enterprise
> Is exploration into God,
> Where no nation's foot has ever trodden yet.
>
> —*A Sleep of Prisoners*

Robert Bolt's *A Man for All Seasons* [1] is one of the finest achievements of the modern theatre. It is a history play dealing with the life of the famous sixteenth-century statesman and churchman, Sir Thomas More. But like all great history plays, it is more about the time *in* which it is written than the time *about* which it is written.

---

1 Since I have already written about this play in some detail in my introduction to *The New Theatre of Europe* I (Delta Books), what follows are those remarks in a somewhat modified form.

Bolt sees very clearly the effects that industrialization and collectivism have had upon the individual in the twentieth century. In his preface to the play he describes how in our time we have lost all conception of ourselves as individual men, and how, as a result, we have increasingly come to see ourselves in the third person. As this happens we are less and less able to deal with life's psychic, social, and spiritual collisions. Thomas More does not see himself in this way; he is "a man with an adamantine sense of his own self. He knew where he began and left off," and the action of the play is best described as a series of collisions between More and a group of powerful and able adversaries who would have him deny his selfhood to serve the wishes of his king. It is not my purpose here to describe the plot of the play, but briefly, King Henry VIII wanted his marriage to Catherine of Spain, who had not given him a son, annulled by the Pope so he could marry Anne Boleyn. Sir Thomas, although he could sympathize with the King, and even willingly stepped into the background so as not to be an obstruction in the King's divorce proceedings, refused to swear an oath that what the King was doing was right. Because of More's stature in society, the King would be content with nothing less. The play is the struggle of More, who had a tremendous love of life and a great capacity for it, to keep alive and still maintain his integrity, i.e., not make the oath. He is finally executed after a young man, whom he had helped earlier in the play, testified falsely that More was guilty of treason. But More could go to the gallows calmly, serenely, and able to say in all honesty: "I am the King's true subject, and pray for him and all the realm. . . . I do none harm, I say none harm, I think none harm. And if this be not enough to keep a man alive, in good faith I long not to live."

The matter of the oath is the crucial issue of the play. In a collective society the individual tends to become an equivocal commodity, and when we think of ourselves in this way we lose all sense of our own identity. More's refusal to take the oath is Bolt's way of asserting that even under the greatest of pressures man can exist unequivocally; that it is possible to live in the modern world without "selling out." "A man takes an oath," Bolt says in the preface, "only when he wants to commit himself quite exceptionally to the statement, when he wants to make an identity between the truth of it and his own virtue; he offers himself as a guar-

antee." Such a commitment implies a self to guarantee.
Because of his inviolable sense of himself, Sir Thomas More
cannot take an oath that would in effect deny his whole
being. For, as he says to his daughter, "When a man takes
an oath, Meg, he's holding his own self in his own hands.
Like water [*cups hands*] and if he opens his fingers *then*—
he needn't hope to find himself again. Some men aren't
capable of this, but I'd be loath to think your father one of
them." He is capable of it, and as a result has a nobility of
character that is rarely found in the modern theatre.

But such triumphs are not easily won. For Bolt only those
conflicts between real alternatives are meaningful; and, therefore, More's antagonists are not straw men. King Henry is
a giant of man; he has a keen intellect, a sharp wit, a pleasing disposition (except when he is crossed), taste and sensitivity, and a gluttonous thirst for life. Only in the realm of
ethics is this mercurial personality deficient. Cromwell is
also a man of great power; historically, he was a successful
administrator and was largely responsible for shaping much
of present-day English law. His success was based on his
shrewd understanding of what people wanted and his ability
to manipulate persons and events to his own ends. More may
have despised Cromwell as a pragmatist and an opportunist,
but he never underestimated him. Norfolk, too, has significance as an antagonist. He lacked moral and intellectual
courage, but he was a good friend. And the claims of friendship can sometimes be a more dangerous foe to integrity
than open opposition. But if the claims of friendship are
difficult to withstand, those of love are almost impossible.
In this regard, More's faithful wife and family must also be
considered powerful threats to his selfhood. His family life
was the most meaningful part of More's existence, and his
stand against the King meant poverty, pain, and disgrace
(not to mention their lack of understanding and partial
rejection) for those closest to him. Only great spiritual courage, and the realization that his own self-respect was the
foundation of these cherished relationships, made it possible for him to resist their claims. And, finally, there is
More's strongest antagonist: the Common Man, that "plain
simple man" who just wants "to keep out of trouble." Quite
rightly, More cries out passionately, "Oh, Sweet Jesus! These
plain, simple men!" For it is the Common Man—sentimental, faithless, and concerned only for his own safety and
welfare—who, out of his own sense of inadequacy, ulti-

mately judges and executes the heroes of selfhood.

Sir Thomas More did not believe the natural end of man was martyrdom, and as the forces of opposition began closing in on him, this end was no temptation for him. In a moving speech to his daughter and son-in-law, he says:

> Now listen. . . . God made the *angels* to show him splendor—as He made animals for innocence and plants for their simplicity. But Man He made to serve him wittily, in the tangle of his mind! If he suffers us to fall to such a case that there is no escaping, then we may stand to our tackle as best we can, and yes, Will, then we may clamor like champions . . . if we have the spittle for it. And no doubt it delights God to see splendor where He looked for complexity. But it's God's part, not our own, to bring ourselves to that extremity! Our natural business lies in escaping—so let's get home and study this Bill.

The law, then, was More's defense, and although Bolt has no illusions about the sufficiency of human law, he does see it as the only defense man can create to fight against the forces of evil. ("The law is a causeway upon which so long as he keeps to it a citizen may walk safely.") Ultimately, because men and their laws are corruptible, More cannot escape that fatal web that has ensnared him; but he dies knowing that his soul is his own, and "a man's soul is his self." He died, as he lived, with full consciousness and pure respect for his own selfhood and the selfhood of all men.

In a time when social and economic forces tend to destroy individual integrity and the courage to accept the Destiny of our own identity, many people have lost faith in the power and the possibility of heroism. Robert Bolt has not! His hero, Sir Thomas More, is able to look the modern world straight in the face and say:

> If we lived in a State where virtue was profitable, common sense would make us good, and greed would make us saintly. And we'd live like animals or angels in the happy land that *needs* no heroes. But since in fact we see that avarice, anger, envy, pride, sloth, lust, and stupidity commonly profit far beyond humility, chastity, fortitude, justice, and thought, and have to choose, to be human at all . . . why then perhaps we *must* stand fast a little—even at the risk of being heroes.

Nothing demonstrates the vitality and rich diversity of the postwar British theatre (and justifies the use of such a grand term as "renaissance") more vividly than the pairing of Bolt's play with Ann Jellicoe's *The Knack*. It would be difficult to pick two plays—both extremely successful—so completely different in tone, style, construction, and language. One is a serious drama, the other slapstick farce; Bolt's play contains some of the most powerful dramatic language written in our century, while Miss Jellicoe achieves equally dramatic effects with dialogue that is monosyllabic and barren; *A Man for All Seasons* is heavy with significance, *The Knack* so light in spirit that it bobs about like a pretty red balloon on a breezy afternoon, but both plays have the power to jolt audiences.

In a way, there is nothing for the critic to say about *The Knack*. As a literary text the script is insignificant. What do you say about a text that says "ping" for two pages to the tune of "The Blue Danube," or about a main character who shouts little more than "rape" throughout most of the last act? *The Knack* is not a literary experience (and is, therefore, immune to the techniques of literary criticism), but it is a theatrical experience of rare power. More so than most plays, it must be visualized rather than read. Miss Jellicoe has written a play for actors not readers, and in this regard the play is symptomatic of a great revolution that is presently going on in the theatre.

We have heard so much about the so-called theatre of the absurd in the last few years that one hesitates to mention it again. Most of the discussions of this form of the avantgarde get tangled up in such things as Camus and Kierkegaard, despair and solitude, and black comedy and gray tragedy. The critics so caught up with these weighty concerns don't seem to realize that what the "absurdist" playwrights are really revolting against is the tyranny of words in the modern theatre. In each of their plays there is an insistent demand that the gestures of pantomime are the theatre's most appropriate and valuable means of expression, the insistence that the mimetic gesture precedes the spoken word and that the gesture is the true expression of what we feel, while words only *describe* what we feel. The real aesthetic of this theatre is to be found in Artaud's *The Theatre and Its Double*. Artaud's basic premise is that it is a mistake in the theatre to assume that "in the beginning was the Word." The theatre is *not* a branch of literature, and a play is not a performed text! As Artaud put it: "The stage is a concrete physical place which must speak its own language—a language that goes deeper than spoken language, a language that speaks directly to our senses rather than primarily to the mind as is the case with the language of words."

This is the most significant thing about the so-called avant-garde theatre: it is a theatre of gesture. "In the beginning was the Gesture!" Gesture is not a decorative addition that accompanies words; rather it is the source, cause, and director of language, and insofar as language is dramatic it is gestural. The famous director, Meyerhold, was striving to achieve this in his attempts to restore vitality to the Russian theatre at the turn of the century. With the exception of Chekhov—and the affinity of Chekhov to the avant-garde is greater than is commonly supposed—most of the playwrights of that time were trying to transform literature for reading into literature for the theatre. Meyerhold correctly saw that these playwrights were in fact novelists who thought that by reducing the number of descriptive passages and, for the liveliness of the story, increasing the characters' dialogue, a play would result. Then this novelist-playwright would invite his reader to pass from the library into the auditorium. As Meyerhold put it in his essay, "Farce":

> Does the novelist need the services of mime? Of course not. The readers themselves can come onto the stage, assume parts, and read aloud to the audience the dialogue of their favorite novelist. This is called "a harmoniously performed play." A name is quickly given to the reader-transformed-into-actor, and a new term, "an intelligent actor," is coined. The same dead silence reigns in the auditorium as in the library. The public is dozing. Such immobility and solemnity is appropriate only in a library.

There is a bit of intentional overstatement in this passage. Obviously, it is not a matter of suppressing speech in the theatre. It is not that language is unimportant in the theatre; it is rather a matter of changing its role. Since the theatre is really concerned only with the way feelings and passions conflict with each other, the language of the theatre must be considered as something more than a means of conducting human characters to external ends. It must capture the turbulence of experience. To change the role of speech in the theatre is to make use of it in a concrete and spatial sense, combining it with everything else on the stage. This is what these playwrights of revolt mean when they insist that the language of the theatre must always be gestural: it must grow out of the gesture, must always act and can never be only descriptive.

Ironically, no one has discussed the nature of gestural language more intelligently than a literary critic. R. P. Blackmur, in his now famous essay, "Language as Gesture," defines what is meant when we say that language is gestural. He sees beyond the simple distinction that language is made of words and gesture is made of motion, to the reverse distinction: "Words are made of motion, made of action or response, at whatever remove; and gesture is made of language—made of the language beneath or beyond or alongside of the language of words." Working from this premise it is possible for Mr. Blackmur to consider that notion which is so important for anyone writing for the theatre: "When the language of words most succeeds it becomes gesture in its words." He sees that gesture is not only native to language, but that it precedes it, and must be, as it were, carried into language whenever the context is imaginative or dramatic. Without a gestural quality in language there can be no drama. This is so since "the great part of our knowledge of life and nature—perhaps all our knowledge of their play and interplay (their drama)—comes to us as gesture, and we are masters of the skill of that knowledge before we can ever make a rhyme or a pun, or even a simple sentence." Blackmur then goes on to define what he means by gesture in language:

> Gesture, in language, is the outward and dramatic play of inward and imaged meaning. It is that play of meaningfulness among words which cannot be defined in the formulas in the dictionary, but which is defined in their use together; gesture is that meaningfulness which is moving, in every sense of that word: what moves the words and what moves us.

This is the quality in words that the playwrights of the new revolt are trying to express when they write for actors. It is this quality, more than anything else, which makes Sophocles, Shakespeare and Molière great dramatists. Now,

I don't believe Ann Jellicoe is the next Molière, but *The Knack* is a significant play, significant because it indicates that the theatre is beginning the process of stripping away the non-theatrical verbiage. This is the necessary first step if we are ever to have a theatre in our time that can rival the great theatrical ages of the past. To the "literary" minded this may sound like sacrilege, but we should remember that while each week a new play of great literary merit opens, only to close shortly thereafter, a play like *The Knack* keeps running to full and delighted houses.

ROBERT W. CORRIGAN

New York City
Autumn 1964

George Bernard Shaw **Heartbreak House**

A FANTASIA IN THE RUSSIAN MANNER ON ENGLISH THEMES

Notes for a Production
of Heartbreak House

BY HAROLD CLURMAN

[*One of the highlights of the 1959–60 New York season
was the revival of Shaw's* Heartbreak House *starring
Maurice Evans, Pamela Brown, Sam Levene, Diana Wyn-
yard, Diane Cilento, and Dennis Price. The production was
directed by Harold Clurman.*]

FIRST NOTES.

This *crazy house* is a truth house—for adults.

There is a certain "childishness" in this play.

The play of a bunch of brilliant kids not as old as the
people they impersonate—much wiser and gayer and more
crackingly articulate than such people would "normally"
(naturalistically!) be.

A charming, surprising *harlequinade.* (An intellectual
vaudeville.)

Make them funnier—"nuttier"—than Shavian "realism"
(or literalism) usually permits.

"The house is full of surprises" the Nurse says. The Captain's whistle, the sudden entrances and exits are Shaw's
clues to this.

Another character says "something odd about this house."

The style tends toward a bright-minded whackiness. A
puppet show! (Shaw jokes about bowings, introductions,
greetings, etc.)

"We are under the dome of heaven."—The garden outside should be very much part of the first act "interior."
(Variable nonrealistic lighting.)

Sound—"a sort of splendid drumming in the air." Later
the air raid is compared to Beethoven. Ideally the air raid
should be orchestrated—use musical instruments—on a
Beethoven annunciatory theme—but not the motto of the
5th!

SECOND NOTES (*on further reading*).

Shaw's characters are ideas—conceptions of people, theatrically and comically colored. The adverse criticism of certain critics who say that Shaw's characters are merely puppets spouting ideas should be made a positive element of the production style.

They may be made as puppet-like as the nature of the play's dramatic structure and the audience's taste will allow.

Mangan says he wants to get "to hell out of this house." Everyone in the play wants somehow to escape his or her condition. All are dissatisfied with it . . . it's a crazy house, driving them crazy!

All in a sense are "crazy," not true to themselves, not what he or she seems or pretends to be. So that everyone is somehow odd, a *clown*—disguised, masked. Outside is "the wide earth, the high seas, the spacious skies"—waiting.

"In this house," says Hector, "everybody poses." "The Trick is to find the man under the pose."

This is the director's job as well:
  a. What is the pose?
  b. What is the man or woman under the pose?

MORE RANDOM NOTES (*after still further readings*).

These English in *Heartbreak House* do not behave as English people do: an Irishman has rendered them! They are more impish, more extrovert, more devilish, devilishly *comic*.

Hesione is a "serpent"—she has mischief in her—not a "proper" lady. She's the cat who swallowed the canary, an intelligent minx. Mentally speaking she *winks*.

An element of "ballet-extravaganza" throughout—as if everyone were "high."

The audience is to enjoy: ideas as color, comedy, and "show," or intelligence as clowning.

They are all aware that they are living in a looney world, which' they are expected to take seriously—but can't. As they progress they become aware of the need to act mad in order to approximate reality. To achieve their liberation— their world must be destroyed.

Some of the madness demands that they hide it—which is the greatest madness. Thus they speak of "form," of not making scenes—while they are always making scenes. (Lady Utterword.)

They want to burst the bonds of the old times—convention—"to get the hell out." Thus the comic outbursts. (Prelude to England's "angry young men.")

RANDOM NOTES CONTINUED.

Shotover roars.

The world's askew (the set to begin with).

They are all flying off the handle: the "handle" being the old steady values, the desire to get the hell out of a situation which no longer supports anybody. The "handle" supplies the form—which these people no longer can grip. Lady Utterword still wants to hold on with her unseen husband Hastings Utterword. (A "wooden" handle!)

The movement of the play is not placid, polite (or Chekhovian!). It is rapid, hectic, almost "wild." (The actors are asked by Shaw to sit on tables, etc.)

Mangan "not able-bodied." Has aches and pains—presses his liver when he is irritated.

Randall—curly hair ("lovelocks"—like the fop in the film of *Kipps*).

SPINE (*or Main Action*).

To get the hell out of this place.

This "hell" suggests some of the explosive quality desired in the playing—the element of *opera-bouffe* involved.

THE CHARACTERS.

Shotover: The Sage of Heartbreak House.

This "sage" has fed himself on rum, worked hard with his body, his fists, and his wits. The rugged person on whose hard work and tough life the house was built. But this sage has a mask—a Pose—as important for the actor as his wisdom—indeed more important. It is the mask of the Drinking Devil—almost the "debauchee" with his West Indian Black wife.

Bluff, gruff, hardy—also shut off from anything but his own thoughts and "ways." (Modern England was built by such men: born 1818 . . . in their prime in 1865.)

His dismissal of everything secondary comes from his urge to get at fundamental reality—to run the ship—to find the means to set the boat on its due course. This requires the "seventh degree of concentration."

To drive toward *that* goal (the seventh degree, etc.) is his spine—his prime motive or action. (To scare people into doing what he wants, or to be free of their nonsense, their blather.)

He wants to go on with his quest; his energy is great enough to do so, but at 88 he knows it's late. Therefore he's wistful too. Despite himself he has to relax into a resignation which is a sort of "happiness." This is his pathetic side.

(The clearing and cleaning up necessary to achieve the "seventh degree" will entail a certain amount of destruction —dynamite. He is prepared for that too.)

He moves with nervous energy, sudden shifts of pace, to absolute quiet or concentrated energy—as when he sits down to work on his drawing board.

I'd rather he looked like old Walt Whitman than Shaw!

Ellie: The new life or youth in Heartbreak House.

She wants to find Port. (A goal for her life.)

The Pose is the Sweet Young Thing: the well-bred ingenue.

The real person is eager, intelligent, with a strong will and capacity to fight.

The House is bewildering, heartbreaking: all the facts she learns are upsetting. . . . She encounters hidden or masked wisdom in the Devil—the ogre Shotover. So she ends bravely in a sort of exaltation—"greater than happiness."

In the transition between these two aspects of her character she is miserable, hard, calculating.

Then she "falls in love"—differently—with life itself, in all its danger in the person or symbol of Shotover.

This is the Education of Ellie.

Shotover's dreams and ravings—his wisdom and idealism —are the most real things in the world to her—new blood.

She knows her strength (the last curtain), so she *looks forward* to another air raid . . . as toward the prospect of a new world, a fresh start!

Hesione: Heartbreak House is *her* house.

The Eternal Womanly! (And an "actress" by nature.)

She wants to make life beautiful, to keep it romantically beautiful.

She wants to get out of the house too (they all do) because she knows its madness . . . yet she likes it here—the adventure, the uncertainty, the fun . . . like an actress who understands the theatre's absurdity and deception but at the same time enjoys its warm charm.

She is loving but so intelligent that she occasionally is sharp—in the face of hypocrisy, or stuffiness.

Hushabye (the Soother!). She loves company, the "menagerie." She sees through her husband, admires and laughs at him. . . .

She is active . . . yet "lazy" . . . likes to fall asleep when unoccupied because she enjoys all agreeable sensations and experiences. She is not a particularly good housekeeper . . . not thrifty . . . not very neat (show this through "business" at the very outset) . . . the maid takes care of "all that."

She likes to gossip . . . so she's socially endearing. Frank, open, *Enthusiastic*, likes to tease affectionately.

She's a flirt—for fun. It is also gracious, it keeps things "interesting."

Something of the improvident Bohemian—with very little care for money.

"You are your father's daughter, Hesione." (She's got the Devil in her too.)

She has temperament and temper too—like an actress!

She is changeable—with swift alternations of mood.

Lady Utterword (Addy): The Fine Lady of Horseback Hall.

Conventionality is her mask and protection—the sense of "form" in the "Colonel's lady" manner.

Her reality beneath the mask is a hunger for experience . . . her desire to escape the prison of her class convention. This expresses itself secretly, stealthily, unobserved . . . except in unguarded moments of hysteria.

"The first impression is one of comic silliness." She has the English "twitter."

Her "form" makes her appear more stagey than Hesione (who is real theatre!). Addy is what we call theatrical theatre of the old *very* English school (1910).

She swishes quite a bit.

Her way out of Heartbreak House is to run off to India, to the garden, to tea, to fashionable behavior.

She wants to cultivate, hold on to the "manner" which

"saves" her and perhaps gives her the best of both worlds—that of feeling and that of decorum: the one utterly private, the other a "style."

A consciously picturesque *flirt* . . . but her flirtatiousness rarely goes any further than that—titillation plus elegance, and a slight touch of danger.

When all is said and done she is very practical: she sticks by her husband, Hastings—the "enduring" Englishman.

Hector: The Intelligent Man without Employment in Heartbreak House.

He wants *to get* out—*somehow* . . . but there's no place to go. He cannot see the goal. Therefore he wants everything destroyed! He has no task. For this reason he dreams up exploits, philanders, plays "parts," dresses up (in "crazy" costumes), becomes decorative . . . even in his intelligence.

Like Ellie he's trying to find—port, but he knows of none, foresees none.

"I am deliberately playing the fool," but not out of worthlessness, out of aimlessness.

He's a dilettante—forced to be one—yet he has the energy and intelligence to be something more.

Debonair and cool like a practical madman. A bit of a show-off. This gives him an identity. . . .

But this is his pose . . . the real man is dissatisfied, unhappy.

A pretty woman is a challenge to him: it leads to an activity of flirtation, the semblance of impressive action. He is telling the truth—or part of it—when he says he doesn't like being attracted—for it arouses him without leading anywhere. He is a civilized person, not a lecher. Thus he is a romantic without a cause.

He sees futility in all positions and arguments—even that of the anarchist . . . he hasn't even the confidence to feel superior to anyone.

He curses women because they are the only thing left for him to deal with . . . yet he knows they are only distractions to him.

He wants "beauty, bravery on earth." But he cannot find it around him or in him—except as a senseless activity.

The "saddest" character in the play and he behaves like an ass and a liar . . . though he often speaks honestly and even wisely.

Mangan: The "Strong Man" of Heartbreak House ("Not a well man").

He wants to get in everywhere—and to get the hell out, too.

The big "capitalist"; the sharper, the practical man, the man who counts in business and in politics. All of this is the Pose.

The real man is wistful, twisted, rather frightened and a somewhat resentful child . . . the most "cheated" or frustrated person in the house.

He's "aggressive" . . . yet he is always caught off guard. He's sure an aggressive manner is the way to success, but he becomes unsure when his success is challenged or his aggressiveness doesn't impress.

Except in a very limited sphere, he's always out of his element, shaky—unhappy.

So he's always *forced* to pose—except when he believes it's particularly clever of him to tell the truth about himself.

"I don't quite understand my position here"—is the keynote. He never does—anywhere outside his office.

In the end he has a "presentiment" (of death) because he's insecure, a "worrier."

Afraid of women—gullible—an easy prey for them. Shy with Ellie, mooney with Hesione.

Like all lower-class folk who have arrived at the upper middle class he has an excessive sense of propriety—or priggishness.

He's full of unaccountable resentments (a source of comedy in this)—secret and almost ludicrous hostilities. He gets sore and vindictive in spurts. One can hardly discern the source of his irritations.

The craziness (or "unusual circumstances") of this house bursts the bubble of his pose . . . he collapses into tears, a hurt boy.

Mazzini Dunn: The Ineffectual Intellectual in Heartbreak House.

To be helpful to all (in Heartbreak House) is the "spine." Mazzini has "moist eyes," always smiling—except for moments of total consternation, and even then there's a little smile. He is obliging to everybody.

He feels a bit inferior, insufficient, guilty. Thus he wants to make up for it by being helpful. He regards everyone as somehow better, cleverer, stronger than he. He admires everyone.

(From the actor's standpoint: a sweet zany.) Shy and

modest because of all this. But sweet: there is nothing cring-
ing or undignified about him. He accepts his humble position.

He loves his wife as he does Ellie but he feels indebted to
them—as to everyone else.

He is credulous, gullible . . . the world is always a surprise
to him; he smiles with wonder and admiration. He really
doesn't understand evil.

He thinks all one has to have are the right influences and
inspirations to become good, loyal, strong.

(Key lines: "How distressing! Can I do anything I wonder?" "Think of the risk those people up there are taking"—
in reference to the bombers in the air raid. "And the poor
clergyman will have to get a new house.")

Randall.

To act as if he were the one proper—immovable—person.
The "imperturbably," the superb English gentleman. Orna-
ment of all diplomatic circles.

That is the Pose. Unruffled, exquisite, the last word in
smoothness. Narcissistic.

The real man: a bundle of ragged nerves, a spoiled almost
hysterical baby.

He believes himself a romantic character, so impressive in
bearing that no matter what he does he must somehow appear dashing and right.

He's always play-acting till his "hat" is knocked off . . .
then he screams like a helpless kid.

The most absurd of all the characters . . . the most
"typically" British—in the old-fashioned comic sense. A
"cultured" dandy, super-sophisticated. He will still look and
be a kid at sixty-five.

His nerves will always show through his *sang-froid*.

His eyelids flutter . . . a bit effeminate.

He has no real passions or convictions. Therefore he needs
his adoration for Lady Utterword. All his convictions have
been absorbed in his pose—which is his class pattern.

Billy Dunn.

He reverses all values in *Heartbreak House.*

To get out, make out—any way he can.

Shaw's intention with this character is to illustrate the total
topsy-turvydom of Heartbreak House. A sense of guilt
hovers over Heartbreak House. Its inhabitants no longer
believe in the old justice. The criminal no longer believes in

his crime: it's just another way of earning a living.

Because of all this Dunn behaves like a clown—now contrite, now shrewd, now crooked, now pious, now immoral, now joking: for all these poses serve him. (A "ham" actor.)

The real man is the poor bloke who couldn't make it either in Heartbreak House or in Horseback Hall, and therefore preys on both—preferably on the former, since he would simply be given a tanning in the latter.

He ends in a terrified attempt to escape—in vain.

Nurse Guinness: The Leveller.

To wait it out—with a minimum of worry.

She's an "anarchist"—she doesn't care because she does get along.

"Quite unconcerned," says Shaw. She's quietly brazen.

A CONCLUDING STATEMENT [1]

Sitting at the back of the auditorium at a Washington performance of *Heartbreak House,* I was delighted to hear a spectator whisper to his neighbor, "Shaw certainly wrote wonderful gags." Why "delighted," why not dismayed? Shaw a gag writer: blasphemy! But I *was* delighted because the spontaneous remark in ordinary American meant that the person who had made it was glad to be attending a "laugh show."

Everyone nowadays refers glibly to Shavian wit. But in relation to *Heartbreak House*—less known because infrequently performed—there is a tendency to become solemn. Shaw himself is largely responsible for this, first, because he called his play a Fantasia in the Russian Manner on English Themes, and, second, because in his Preface he cited Chekhov's plays as models.

In directing the play the first thing I told the actors was that both the phrase "Russian manner" and the name Chekhov were to be disregarded in connection with *Heartbreak House:* they were altogether misleading. True, the name *Heartbreak House* signifies in Shaw's words "cultured, leisured Europe before the (First World) War" and Chekhov's plays deal with the educated middle class of the late nineteenth century. It is also true that in Russia Chekhov's plays—despite their melancholy—are construed as com-

---

[1] Published in the Souvenir Program sold in the theatre a few days after the opening.

edies, but there most of the resemblance between *Heartbreak House* and Chekhov ends.

The only other parallel between the work of the two playwrights is that Chekhov's world was destroyed by the Revolution of 1917 and the folk in *Heartbreak House* drifted into the First World War and if not destroyed were terribly shaken. Also the emphasis in this Shaw play—as in those of Chekhov—is not on the plot but on character and atmosphere.

What makes *Heartbreak House* utterly different from Chekhov is its unique style. Shaw's play is extravagant, full of capering humor which verges on the farcical. One of the characters refers to the environment he finds himself in as "a crazy house" in which one's mind "might as well be a football." The fact that this "crazy house" is also a truth house—a sort of distorting mirror which exaggerates the features of the people who enter it—gives the play its human and social relevance but it does not distract from the topsy-turvy fun that my Washington playgoer enjoyed so much.

Years ago when there was still some resistance to Shaw—as we all know the greatest playwrights of our time encountered resistance as they came on the scene—certain critics complained that Shaw's characters were not people but puppets. There is no need to deny this. Shaw's characters *are* puppets—unnatural only in the sense that they reveal the truth about themselves more directly, more pointedly, more eloquently, more wittily than people in life are able to.

The director's task then was to combine the "fun" aspect of the play—its arch frivolousness—with its basic intent. The setting had not only to disclose a place but make a comment —smilingly suggestive of the author's mood. The clothes had to be costumes. The characterizations had to be tipped from realism to a kind of gay picturesqueness. Gravity had to be avoided—except as fleeting reminders that we were still dealing with a truth about life—our lives. This slight duality —a sort of "gayed up" seriousness—part game, part prophecy—is only a reflection of the text itself, which begins as a comedy of mad manners and ends with an air raid by an enemy never named or even hinted at throughout the course of the play.

What was Shaw's purpose and why did he write *Heartbreak House* in this peculiar way? The play exemplifies a typical Shavian "trick." *Heartbreak House* is all carefree talk and horseplay—apparently devoid of dark portent; then it bursts for a moment into a scene of shock and ends ironically on a note of almost languid peace. "Nothing will happen," one of the guests says. Something does happen and something more fatal may yet happen—expected, almost hoped for, by certain of the characters.

These "charming people, most advanced, unprejudiced, frank, humane, unconventional, free thinking and everything that is delightful," are content to drift. No matter what inner qualms they may have, no matter what emptiness or discontent they occasionally experience, they have settled for the happiness of dreams and daily pastimes. For all his sharp teasing, Shaw is tolerant with them. Only, says he, in earnest jest, if you go on like this without "navigation"—that is without plan, purpose and preparative action—your ship will "strike and sink and split."

The thought or warning which informs the play—stated in a frolic of entertaining words and postures—is wholly appropriate to our day and our theatre. Though the people of *Heartbreak House* are English it is not merely a play about a certain class or a certain country. Time has turned it into a play about practically all of us, everyone.

CHARACTERS

(*In order of appearance*)
Nurse Guinness
Ellie Dunn
Captain Shotover
Lady Utterword
Mrs Hushabye
Mazzini Dunn
Hector Hushabye
Boss Mangan
Randall Utterword
The Burglar

The hilly country in the middle of the north edge of Sussex, looking very pleasant on a fine evening at the end of September, is seen through the windows of a room which has been built so as to resemble the after part of an old-fashioned high-pooped ship with a stern gallery; for the windows are ship built with heavy timbering, and run right across the room as continuously as the stability of the wall allows. A row of lockers under the windows provides an unupholstered window-seat interrupted by twin glass doors, respectively halfway between the stern post and the sides. Another door strains the illusion a little by being apparently in the ship's port side, and yet leading, not to the open sea, but to the entrance hall of the house. Between this door and the stern gallery are bookshelves. There are electric light switches beside the door leading to the hall and the glass doors in the stern gallery. Against the starboard wall is a carpenter's bench. The vice has a board in its jaws; and the floor is littered with shavings, overflowing from a waste-paper basket. A couple of planes and a centrebit are on the bench. In the same wall, between the bench and the windows, is a narrow doorway with a half door, above which a glimpse of the room beyond shews that it is a shelved pantry with bottles and kitchen crockery.

On the starboard side, but close to the middle, is a plain oak drawing-table with drawing-board, T-square, straight-edges, set squares, mathematical instruments, saucers of water color, a tumbler of discolored water, Indian ink, pencils, and brushes on it. The drawingboard is set so that the draughtsman's chair has the window on its left hand. On the floor at the end of the table, on his right, is a ship's fire bucket. On the port side of the room, near the bookshelves, is a sofa with its back to the windows. It is a sturdy mahogany article, oddly upholstered in sailcoth, including the

*bolster, with a couple of blankets hanging over the back.
Between the sofa and the drawing-table is a big wicker chair,
with broad arms and a low sloping back, with its back to the
light. A small but stout table of teak, with a round top and
gate legs, stands against the port wall between the door and
the bookcase. It is the only article in the room that suggests
(not at all convincingly) a woman's hand in the furnishing.
The uncarpeted floor of narrow boards is caulked and holy-
stoned like a deck.*

*The garden to which the glass doors lead dips to the south
before the landscape rises again to the hills. Emerging from
the hollow is the cupola of an observatory. Between the observatory and the house is a flagstaff on a little esplanade,
with a hammock on the east side and a long garden seat on
the west.*

*A young lady, gloved and hatted, with a dust coat on, is
sitting in the window-seat with her body twisted to enable
her to look out at the view. One hand props her chin: the
other hangs down with a volume of the Temple Shakespear
in it, and her finger stuck in the page she has been reading.*

A clock strikes six.

*The young lady turns and looks at her watch. She rises
with an air of one who waits and is almost at the end of her
patience. She is a pretty girl, slender, fair, and intelligent
looking, nicely but not expensively dressed, evidently not a
smart idler.*

*With a sigh of weary resignation she comes to the
draughtsman's chair; sits down; and begins to read Shakespear. Presently the book sinks to her lap; her eyes close;
and she dozes into a slumber.*

*An elderly womanservant comes in from the hall with
three unopened bottles of rum on a tray. She passes through
and disappears in the pantry without noticing the young
lady. She places the bottles on the shelf and fills her tray
with empty bottles. As she returns with these, the young lady
lets her book drop, awakening herself, and startling the
womanservant so that she all but lets the tray fall.*

The Womanservant. God bless us! [*The young lady picks
up the book and places it on the table.*] Sorry to wake

you, miss, I'm sure; but you are a stranger to me. What might you be waiting here for now?

The Young Lady. Waiting for somebody to shew some signs of knowing that I have been invited here.

The Womanservant. Oh, you're invited are you? And has nobody come? Dear! dear!

The Young Lady. A wild-looking old gentleman came and looked in at the window; and I heard him calling out "Nurse: there is a young and attractive female waiting in the poop. Go and see what she wants." Are you the nurse?

The Womanservant. Yes, miss: I'm Nurse Guinness. That was old Captain Shotover, Mrs Hushabye's father. I heard him roaring; but I thought it was for something else. I suppose it was Mrs Hushabye that invited you, ducky?

The Young Lady. I understood her to do so. But really I think I'd better go.

Nurse Guinness. Oh, dont think of such a thing, miss. If Mrs Hushabye has forgotten all about it, it will be a pleasant surprise for her to see you, wont it?

The Young Lady. It has been a very unpleasant surprise to me to find that nobody expects me.

Nurse Guinness. Youll get used to it, miss: this house is full of surprises for them that dont know our ways.

Captain Shotover [*looking in from the hall suddenly: an ancient but still hardy man with an immense white beard, in a reefer jacket with a whistle hanging from his neck*]. Nurse: there is a hold-all and a handbag on the front steps for everybody to fall over. Also a tennis racquet. Who the devil left them there?

The Young Lady. They are mine, I'm afraid.

The Captain [*advancing to the drawing-table*]. Nurse: who is this misguided and unfortunate young lady?

Nurse Guinness. She says Miss Hessy invited her, sir.

The Captain. And had she no friend, no parents, to warn her against my daughter's invitations? This is a pretty sort of house, by heavens! A young and attractive lady is invited here. Her luggage is left on the steps for hours; and she herself is deposited in the poop and abandoned, tired and starving. This is our hospitality. These are our manners. No room ready. No hot water.

No welcoming hostess. Our visitor is to sleep in the toolshed, and to wash in the duckpond.

Nurse Guinness. Now it's all right, Captain: I'll get the lady some tea; and her room shall be ready before she has finished it. [*To the young lady.*] Take off your hat, ducky; and make yourself at home. [*She goes to the door leading to the hall.*]

The Captain [*as she passes him*]. Ducky! Do you suppose, woman, that because this young lady has been insulted and neglected, you have the right to address her as you address my wretched children, whom you have brought up in ignorance of the commonest decencies of social intercourse?

Nurse Guinness. Never mind him, doty. [*Quite unconcerned, she goes out into the hall on her way to the kitchen.*]

The Captain. Madam: will you favor me with your name? [*He sits down in the big wicker chair.*]

The Young Lady. My name is Ellie Dunn.

The Captain. Dunn! I had a boatswain whose name was Dunn. He was originally a pirate in China. He set up as a ship's chandler with stores which I have every reason to believe he stole from me. No doubt he became rich. Are you his daughter?

Ellie [*indignant*]. No: certainly not. I am proud to be able to say that though my father has not been a successful man, nobody has ever had one word to say against him. I think my father is the best man I have ever known.

The Captain. He must be greatly changed. Has he attained the seventh degree of concentration?

Ellie. I dont understand.

The Captain. But how could he, with a daughter? I, madam, have two daughters. One of them is Hesione Hushabye, who invited you here. I keep this house: she upsets it. I desire to attain the seventh degree of concentration: she invites visitors and leaves me to entertain them. [*Nurse Guinness returns with the tea-tray, which she places on the teak table.*] I have a second daughter who is, thank God, in a remote part of the Empire with her numskull of a husband. As a child she thought the figure-head of my ship, the Dauntless, the most beautiful thing on earth. He resembled it. He had the same expression: wooden yet enterprising. She married him, and will never set foot in this house again.

Nurse Guinness [*carrying the table, with the tea-things on it, to Ellie's side*]. Indeed you never were more mistaken. She is in England this very moment. You have been told three times this week that she is coming home for a year for her health. And very glad you should be to see your own daughter again after all these years.

The Captain. I am not glad. The natural term of the affection of the human animal for its offspring is six years. My daughter Ariadne was born when I was forty-six. I am now eighty-eight. If she comes, I am not at home. If she wants anything, let her take it. If she asks for me, let her be informed that I am extremely old, and have totally forgotten her.

Nurse Guinness. Thats no talk to offer to a young lady. Here, ducky, have some tea; and dont listen to him. [*She pours out a cup of tea.*]

The Captain [*rising wrathfully*]. Now before high heaven they have given this innocent child Indian tea: the stuff they tan their own leather insides with. [*He seizes the cup and the tea-pot and empties both into the leathern bucket.*]

Ellie [*almost in tears*]. Oh, please! I am so tired. I should have been glad of anything.

Nurse Guinness. Oh, what a thing to do! The poor lamb is ready to drop.

The Captain. You shall have some of my tea. Do not touch that fly-blown cake: nobody eats it here except the dogs. [*He disappears into the pantry.*]

Nurse Guinness. Theres a man for you! They say he sold himself to the devil in Zanzibar before he was a captain; and the older he grows the more I believe them.

A Woman's Voice [*in the hall*]. Is anyone at home? Hesione! Nurse! Papa! Do come, somebody; and take in my luggage.

[*Thumping heard, as of an umbrella, on the wainscot.*]

Nurse Guinness. My gracious! It's Miss Addy, Lady Utterword, Mrs Hushabye's sister: the one I told the Captain about. [*Calling.*] Coming, miss, coming.

[*She carries the table back to its place by the door, and is hurrying out when she is intercepted by Lady Utterword, who bursts in much flustered. Lady Utterword, a blonde, is very handsome, very well dressed, and so precipitate in speech and action that the first impression (erroneous) is one of comic silliness.*]

Lady Utterword. Oh, is that you, Nurse? How are you? You
dont look a day older. Is nobody at home? Where is
Hesione? Doesnt she expect me? Where are the servants? Whose luggage is that on the steps? Where's
papa? Is everybody asleep? [*Seeing Ellie.*] Oh! I beg
your pardon. I suppose you are one of my nieces.
[*Approaching her with outstretched arms.*] Come and
kiss your aunt, darling.

Ellie. I'm only a visitor. It is my luggage on the steps.

Nurse Guinness. I'll go get you some fresh tea, ducky. [*She
takes up the tray.*]

Ellie. But the old gentleman said he would make some himself.

Nurse Guinness. Bless you! he's forgotten what he went for
already. His mind wanders from one thing to another.

Lady Utterword. Papa, I suppose?

Nurse Guinness. Yes, miss.

Lady Utterword [*vehemently*]. Dont be silly, Nurse. Dont
call me miss.

Nurse Guinness [*placidly*]. No, lovey. [*She goes out with
the tea-tray.*]

Lady Utterword [*sitting down with a flounce on the sofa*].
I know what you must feel. Oh, this house, this house!
I come back to it after twenty-three years; and it is just
the same: the luggage lying on the steps, the servants
spoilt and impossible, nobody at home to receive anybody, no regular meals, nobody ever hungry because
they are always gnawing bread and butter or munching
apples, and, what is worse, the same disorder in ideas,
in talk, in feeling. When I was a child I was used to it:
I had never known anything better, though I was unhappy, and longed all the time—oh, how I longed!—to
be respectable, to be a lady, to live as others did, not to
have to think of everything for myself. I married at
nineteen to escape from it. My husband is Sir Hastings
Utterword, who has been governor of all the crown
colonies in succession. I have always been the mistress
of Government House. I have been so happy: I had
forgotten that people could live like this. I wanted to
see my father, my sister, my nephews and nieces (one
ought to, you know), and I was looking forward to it.
And now the state of the house! the way I'm received!
the casual impudence of that woman Guinness, our old

nurse! really Hesione might at least have been here:
some preparation might have been made for me. You
must excuse my going on in this way; but I am really
very much hurt and annoyed and disillusioned: and if
I had realized it was to be like this, I wouldnt have
come. I have a great mind to go away without another
word. [*She is on the point of weeping.*]

Ellie [*also very miserable*]. Nobody has been here to receive
me either. I thought I ought to go away too. But how
can I, Lady Utterword? My luggage is on the steps; and
the station fly has gone.

[*The Captain emerges from the pantry with a tray of
Chinese lacquer and a very fine tea-set on it. He rests
it provisionally on the end of the table; snatches away
the drawing-board, which he stands on the floor against
the table legs; and puts the tray in the space thus
cleared. Ellie pours out a cup greedily.*]

The Captain. Your tea, young lady. What! another lady! I
must fetch another cup. [*He makes for the pantry.*]

Lady Utterword [*rising from the sofa, suffused with emotion*]. Papa! Don't you know me? I'm your daughter.

The Captain. Nonsense! my daughter's upstairs asleep. [*He
vanishes through the half door.*]

[*Lady Utterword retires to the window to conceal her tears.*]

Ellie [*going to her with the cup*]. Dont be so distressed.
Have this cup of tea. He is very old and very strange:
he has been just like that to me. I know how dreadful
it must be: my own father is all the world to me. Oh,
I'm sure he didnt mean it.

[*The Captain returns with another cup.*]

The Captain. Now we are complete. [*He places it on the
tray.*]

Lady Utterword [*hysterically*]. Papa: you cant have forgotten me. I am Ariadne. I'm little Paddy Patkins.
Wont you kiss me? [*She goes to him and throws her
arms round his neck.*]

* *The Captain* [*woodenly enduring her embrace*]. How can
you be Ariadne? You are a middle-aged woman: well-
preserved, madam, but no longer young.

Lady Utterword. But think of all the years and years I have
been away, papa. I have had to grow old, like other
people.

The Captain [*disengaging himself*]. You should grow out of
  kissing strange men: they may be striving to attain the
  seventh degree of concentration.

Lady Utterword. But I'm your daughter. You havnt seen
  me for years.

The Captain. So much the worse! When our relatives are
  at home, we have to think of all their good points or it
  would be impossible to endure them. But when they
  are away, we console ourselves for their absence by
  dwelling on their vices. That is how I have come to
  think my absent daughter Ariadne a perfect fiend; so
  do not try to ingratiate yourself here by impersonating
  her. [*He walks firmly away to the other side of the
  room.*]

Lady Utterword. Ingratiating myself indeed! [*With dignity.*]
  Very well, papa. [*She sits down at the drawing-table
  and pours out tea for herself.*]

The Captain. I am neglecting my social duties. You remember Dunn? Billy Dunn?

Lady Utterword. Do you mean that villainous sailor who
  robbed you?

The Captain [*introducing Ellie*]. His daughter. [*He sits
  down on the sofa.*]

Ellie [*protesting*]. No—

[*Nurse Guinness returns with fresh tea.*]

The Captain. Take that hogwash away. Do you hear?

Nurse. Youve actually remembered about the tea! [*To Ellie.*]
  O, miss, he didnt forget you after all! You *have* made
  an impression.

The Captain [*gloomily*]. Youth! beauty! novelty! They are
  badly wanted in this house. I am excessively old.
  Hesione is only moderately young. Her children are not
  youthful.

Lady Utterword. How can children be expected to be youthful in this house? Almost before we could speak we were
  filled with notions that might have been all very well
  for pagan philosophers of fifty, but were certainly quite
  unfit for respectable people of any age.

Nurse. You were always for respectability, Miss Addy.

Lady Utterword. Nurse: will you please remember that I
  am Lady Utterword, and not Miss Addy, nor lovey,
  nor darling, nor doty? Do you hear?

Nurse. Yes, ducky: all right. I'll tell them all they must call you my lady. [*She takes her tray out with undisturbed placidity.*]

Lady Utterword. What comfort? what sense is there in having servants with no manners?

Ellie [*rising and coming to the table to put down her empty cup*]. Lady Utterword: do you think Mrs Hushabye really expects me?

Lady Utterword. Oh, dont ask me. You can see for yourself that Ive just arrived; her only sister, after twenty-three years absence! and it seems that *I* am not expected.

The Captain. What does it matter whether the young lady is expected or not? She is welcome. There are beds: there is food. I'll find a room for her myself. [*He makes for the door.*]

Ellie [*following him to stop him*]. Oh please— [*He goes out.*] Lady Utterword: I dont know what to do. Your father persists in believing that my father is some sailor who robbed him.

Lady Utterword. You had better pretend not to notice it. My father is a very clever man; but he always forgot things; and now that he is old, of course he is worse. And I must warn you that it is sometimes very hard to feel quite sure that he really forgets.

[*Mrs Hushabye bursts into the room tempestuously, and embraces Ellie. She is a couple of years older than Lady Utterword, and even better looking. She has magnificent black hair, eyes like the fishpools of Heshbon, and a nobly modelled neck, short at the back and low between her shoulders in front. Unlike her sister she is uncorseted and dressed anyhow in a rich robe of black pile that shews off her white skin and statuesque contour.*]

Mrs Hushabye. Ellie, my darling, my pettikins [*Kissing her.*]: how long have you been here? Ive been at home all the time: I was putting flowers and things in your room; and when I just sat down for a moment to try how comfortable the armchair was I went off to sleep. Papa woke me and told me you were here. Fancy your finding no one, and being neglected and abandoned. [*Kissing her again.*] My poor love! [*She deposits Ellie on the sofa. Meanwhile Ariadne has left the table and come over to claim her share of attention.*] Oh! youve brought someone with you. Introduce me.

Lady Utterword. Hesione: is it possible that you dont know me?

Mrs Hushabye [*conventionally*]. Of course I remember your face quite well. Where have we met?

Lady Utterword. Didnt papa tell you I was here? Oh! this is really too much. [*She throws herself sulkily into the big chair.*]

Mrs Hushabye. Papa!

Lady Utterword. Yes: Papa. Our papa, you unfeeling wretch. [*Rising angrily.*] I'll go straight to a hotel.

Mrs Hushabye [*seizing her by the shoulders*]. My goodness gracious goodness, you dont mean to say that youre Addy!

Lady Utterword. I certainly am Addy; and I dont think I can be so changed that you would not have recognized me if you had any real affection for me. And papa didnt think me even worth mentioning!

Mrs Hushabye. What a lark! Sit down. [*She pushes her back into the chair instead of kissing her, and posts herself behind it.*] You do look a swell. Youre much handsomer than you used to be. Youve made the acquaintance of Ellie, of course. She is going to marry a perfect hog of a millionaire for the sake of her father, who is as poor as a church mouse; and you must help me to stop her.

Ellie. Oh *please,* Hesione.

Mrs Hushabye. My pettikins, the man's coming here today with your father to begin persecuting you; and everybody will see the state of the case in ten minutes; so whats the use of making a secret of it?

Ellie. He is not a hog, Hesione. You dont know how wonderfully good he was to my father, and how deeply grateful I am to him.

Mrs Hushabye [*to Lady Utterword*]. Her father is a very remarkable man, Addy. His name is Mazzini Dunn. Mazzini was a celebrity of some kind who knew Ellie's grandparents. They were both poets, like the Brownings; and when her father came into the world Mazzini said "Another soldier born for freedom!" So they christened him Mazzini; and he has been fighting for freedom in his quiet way ever since. Thats why he is so poor.

Ellie. I am proud of his poverty.

Mrs Hushabye. Of course you are, pettikins. Why not leave him in it, and marry someone you love?

Lady Utterword [*rising suddenly and explosively*]. Hesione: are you going to kiss me or are you not?

Mrs Hushabye. What do you want to be kissed for?

Lady Utterword. I *dont* want to be kissed; but I do want you to behave properly and decently. We are sisters. We have been separated for twenty-three years. You *ought* to kiss me.

Mrs Hushabye. To-morrow morning, dear, before you make up. I hate the smell of powder.

Lady Utterword. Oh! you unfeeling— [*She is interrupted by the return of the Captain.*]

The Captain [*to Ellie*]. Your room is ready. [*Ellie rises.*] The sheets were damp; but I have changed them. [*He makes for the garden door on the port side.*]

Lady Utterword. Oh! What about my sheets?

The Captain [*halting at the door*]. Take my advice: air them; or take them off and sleep in blankets. You shall sleep in Ariadne's old room.

Lady Utterword. Indeed I shall do nothing of the sort. That little hole! I am entitled to the best spare room.

The Captain [*continuing unmoved*]. She married a numskull. She told me she would marry anyone to get away from home.

Lady Utterword. You are pretending not to know me on purpose. I will leave the house.

[*Mazzini Dunn enters from the hall. He is a little elderly man with bulging credulous eyes and earnest manners. He is dressed in a blue serge jacket suit with an unbuttoned mackintosh over it, and carries a soft black hat of clerical cut.*]

Ellie. At last! Captain Shotover: here is my father.

The Captain. This! Nonsense! not a bit like him. [*He goes away through the garden, shutting the door sharply behind him.*]

Lady Utterword. I will not be ignored and pretended to be somebody else. I will have it out with papa now, this instant. [*To Mazzini.*] Excuse me. [*She follows the Captain out, making a hasty bow to Mazzini, who returns it.*]

Mrs Hushabye [*hospitably, shaking hands*]. How good of you to come, Mr Dunn! You dont mind papa, do you? He is as mad as a hatter, you know, but quite harmless, and extremely clever. You will have some delightful talks with him.

Mazzini. I hope so. [*To Ellie.*] So here you are, Ellie, dear. [*He draws her arm affectionately through his.*] I must thank you, Mrs Hushabye, for your kindness to my daughter. I'm afraid she would have had no holiday if you had not invited her.

Mrs Hushabye. Not at all. Very nice of her to come and attract young people to the house for us.

Mazzini [*smiling*]. I'm afraid Ellie is not interested in young men, Mrs Hushabye. Her taste is on the graver, solider side.

Mrs Hushabye [*with a sudden rather hard brightness in her manner*]. Wont you take off your overcoat, Mr Dunn? You will find a cupboard for coats and hats and things in the corner of the hall.

Mazzini [*hastily releasing Ellie*]. Yes—thank you—I had better— [*He goes out.*]

Mrs Hushabye [*emphatically*]. The old brute!

Ellie. Who?

Mrs Hushabye. Who! Him. He. It. [*Pointing after Mazzini.*] "Graver, solider tastes," indeed!

Ellie [*aghast*]. You dont mean that you were speaking like that of my father!

Mrs Hushabye. I was. You know I was.

Ellie [*with dignity*]. I will leave your house at once. [*She turns to the door.*]

Mrs Hushabye. If you attempt it, I'll tell your father why.

Ellie [*turning again*]. Oh! How can you treat a visitor like this, Mrs Hushabye?

Mrs Hushabye. I thought you were going to call me Hesione.

Ellie. Certainly not now?

Mrs Hushabye. Very well: I'll tell your father.

Ellie [*distressed*]. Oh!

Mrs Hushabye. If you turn a' hair—if you take his part against me and against your own heart for a moment, I'll give that born soldier of freedom a piece of my mind that will stand him on his selfish old head for a week.

Ellie. Hesione! My father selfish! How little you know—
[*She is interrupted by Mazzini, who returns, excited and perspiring.*]

Mazzini. Ellie: Mangan has come: I thought youd like to know. Excuse me, Mrs Hushabye: the strange old gentleman—

Mrs Hushabye. Papa. Quite so.

Mazzini. Oh, I beg your pardon: of course: I was a little
     confused by his manner. He is making Mangan help
     him with something in the garden; and he wants me to—
[*A powerful whistle is heard.*]

The Captain's Voice. Bosun ahoy! [*The whistle is repeated.*]

Mazzini [*flustered*]. Oh dear! I believe he is whistling for me.
[*He hurries out.*]

Mrs Hushabye. Now my father is a wonderful man if you
     like.

Ellie. Hesione: listen to me. You dont understand. My
     father and Mr Mangan were boys together. Mr Ma—

Mrs Hushabye. I dont care what they were: we must sit
     down if you are going to begin as far back as that. [*She
     snatches at Ellie's waist, and makes her sit down on the
     sofa beside her.*] Now, pettikins: tell me all about Mr
     Mangan. They call him Boss Mangan, dont they? He is
     a Napoleon of industry and disgustingly rich, isnt he?
     Why isnt your father rich?

Ellie. My poor father should never have been in business.
     His parents were poets; and they gave him the noblest
     ideas; but they could not afford to give him a profession.

Mrs Hushabye. Fancy your grandparents, with their eyes in
     fine frenzy rolling! And so your poor father had to go
     into business. Hasnt he succeeded in it?

Ellie. He always used to say he could succeed if he only had
     some capital. He fought his way along, to keep a roof
     over our heads and bring us up well; but it was always a
     struggle: always the same difficulty of not having capi-
     tal enough. I dont know how to describe it to you.

Mrs Hushabye. Poor Ellie! I know. Pulling the devil by the
     tail.

Ellie [*hurt*]. Oh no. Not like that. It was at least dignified.

Mrs Hushabye. That made it all the harder, didnt it? *I*
     shouldn't have pulled the devil by the tail with dignity.
     I should have pulled hard—[*Between her teeth.*] *hard*.
     Well? Go on.

Ellie. At last it seemed that all our troubles were at an end.
     Mr Mangan did an extraordinarily noble thing out of
     pure friendship for my father and respect for his char-
     acter. He asked him how much capital he wanted,
     and gave it to him. I dont mean that he lent it to him, or
     that he invested it in his business. He just simply made
     him a present of it. Wasnt that splendid of him?

Mrs Hushabye. On condition that you married him?

Ellie. Oh no, no, no. This was when I was a child. He had never even seen me: he never came to our house. It was absolutely disinterested. Pure generosity.

Mrs Hushabye. Oh! I beg the gentleman's pardon. Well, what became of the money?

Ellie. We all got new clothes and moved into another house. And I went to another school for two years.

Mrs Hushabye. Only two years?

Ellie. That was all; for at the end of two years my father was utterly ruined.

Mrs Hushabye. How?

Ellie. I dont know. I never could understand. But it was dreadful. When we were poor my father had never been in debt. But when he launched out into business on a large scale, he had to incur liabilities. When the business went into liquidation he owed more money than Mr Mangan had given him.

Mrs Hushabye. Bit off more than he could chew, I suppose.

Ellie. I think you are a little unfeeling about it.

Mrs Hushabye. My pettikins: you mustnt mind my way of talking. I was quite as sensitive and particular as you once; but I have picked up so much slang from the children that I am really hardly presentable. I suppose your father had no head for business, and made a mess of it.

Ellie. Oh, that just shews how entirely you are mistaken about him. The business turned out a great success. It now pays forty-four per cent after deducting the excess profits tax.

Mrs Hushabye. Then why arent you rolling in money?

Ellie. I dont know. It seems very unfair to me. You see, my father was made bankrupt. It nearly broke his heart, because he had persuaded several of his friends to put money into the business. He was sure it would succeed; and events proved that he was quite right. But they all lost their money. It was dreadful. I dont know what we should have done but for Mr Mangan.

Mrs Hushabye. What! Did the Boss come to the rescue again, after all his money being thrown away?

Ellie. He did indeed, and never uttered a reproach to my father. He bought what was left of the business—the buildings and the machinery and things—from the official trustee for enough money to enable my father to pay six and eightpence in the pound and get his discharge. Everyone pitied papa so much, and saw so plainly that he was an honorable man, that they let him off at six and eightpence instead of ten shillings. Then Mr Mangan started a company to take up the business, and made my father a manager in it to save us from starvation; for I wasnt earning anything then.

Mrs Hushabye. Quite a romance. And when did the Boss develop the tender passion?

Ellie. Oh, that was years after, quite lately. He took the chair one night at a sort of people's concert. I was singing there. As an amateur, you know: half a guinea for expenses and three songs with three encores. He was so pleased with my singing that he asked might he walk home with me. I never saw anyone so taken aback as he was when I took him home and introduced him to my father: his own manager. It was then that my father told me how nobly he had behaved. Of course it was considered a great chance for me, as he is so rich. And —and—we drifted into a sort of understanding—I suppose I should call it an engagement— [*She is distressed and cannot go on.*]

Mrs Hushabye [*rising and marching about*]. You may have drifted into it; but you will bounce out of it, my pettikins, if I am to have anything to do with it.

Ellie [*hopelessly*]. No: it's no use. I am bound in honor and gratitude. I will go through with it.

Mrs Hushabye [*behind the sofa, scolding down at her*]. You know, of course, that it's not honorable or grateful to marry a man you dont love. Do you love this Mangan man?

Ellie. Yes. At least—

Mrs Hushabye. I dont want to know about "the least": I want to know the worst. Girls of your age fall in love with all sorts of impossible people, especially old people.

Ellie. I like Mr Mangan very much; and I shall always be—

Mrs Hushabye [*impatiently completing the sentence and prancing away intolerantly to starboard*]. —grateful to him for his kindness to dear father. I know. Anybody else?

Ellie. What do you mean?

Mrs Hushabye. Anybody else? Are you in love with anybody else?

Ellie. Of course not.

Mrs Hushabye. Humph! [*The book on the drawing-table catches her eye. She picks it up, and evidently finds the title very unexpected. She looks at Ellie, and asks, quaintly.*] Quite sure youre not in love with an actor?

Ellie. No, no. Why? What put such a thing into your head?

Mrs Hushabye. This is yours, isnt it? Why else should you be reading *Othello*?

Ellie. My father taught me to love Shakespear.

Mrs Hushabye [*flinging the book down on the table*]. Really! your father does seem to be about the limit.

Ellie [*naïvely*]. Do you never read Shakespear, Hesione? That seems to me so extraordinary. I like *Othello*.

Mrs Hushabye. Do you indeed? He was jealous, wasnt he?

Ellie. Oh, not that. I think all the part about jealousy is horrible. But dont you think it must have been a wonderful experience for Desdemona, brought up so quietly at home, to meet a man who had been out in the world doing all sorts of brave things and having terrible adventures, and yet finding something in her that made him love to sit and talk with her and tell her about them?

Mrs Hushabye. Thats your idea of romance, is it?

Ellie. Not romance, exactly. It might really happen.

[*Ellie's eyes shew that she is not arguing, but in a daydream. Mrs Hushabye, watching her inquisitively, goes deliberately back to the sofa and resumes her seat beside her.*]

Mrs Hushabye. Ellie darling: have you noticed that some of those stories that Othello told Desdemona couldnt have happened?

Ellie. Oh no. Shakespear thought they could have happened.

Mrs Hushabye. Hm! Desdemona thought they could have happened. But they didnt.

Ellie. Why do you look so enigmatic about it? You are such a sphinx: I never know what you mean.

Mrs Hushabye. Desdemona would have found him out if she had lived, you know. I wonder was that why he strangled her!

Ellie. Othello was not telling lies.

Mrs Hushabye. How do you know?

Ellie. Shakespear would have said if he was. Hesione: there are men who have done wonderful things: men like Othello, only, of course, white, and very handsome, and—

Mrs Hushabye. Ah! Now we're coming to it. Tell me all about him. I knew there must be somebody, or youd never have been so miserable about Mangan: youd have thought it quite a lark to marry him.

Ellie [*blushing vividly*]. Hesione: you are dreadful. But I dont want to make a secret of it, though of course I dont tell everybody. Besides, I dont know him.

Mrs Hushabye. Dont know him! What does that mean?

Ellie. Well, of course I know him to speak to.

Mrs Hushabye. But you want to know him ever so much more intimately, eh?

Ellie. No no: I know him quite—almost intimately.

Mrs Hushabye. You dont know him; and you know him almost intimately. How lucid!

Ellie. I mean that he does not call on us. I—I got into conversation with him by chance at a concert.

Mrs Hushabye. You seem to have rather a gay time at your concerts, Ellie.

Ellie. Not at all: we talk to everyone in the greenroom waiting for our turns. I thought he was one of the artists: he looked so splendid. But he was only one of the committee. I happened to tell him that I was copying a picture at the National Gallery. I make a little money that way. I cant paint much; but as it's always the same picture I can do it pretty quickly and get two or three pounds for it. It happened that he came to the National Gallery one day.

Mrs Hushabye. One student's day. Paid sixpence to stumble about through a crowd of easels, when he might have come in next day for nothing and found the floor clear! Quite by accident?

Ellie [*triumphantly*]. No. On purpose. He liked talking to me. He knows lots of the most spendid people. Fashionable women who are all in love with him. But he ran away from them to see me at the National Gallery and persuade me to come with him for a drive round Richmond Park in a taxi.

Mrs Hushabye. My pettikins, you have been going it. It's wonderful what you good girls can do without anyone saying a word.

Ellie. I am not in society, Hesione. If I didn't make acquaintances in that way I shouldnt have any at all.

Mrs Hushabye. Well, no harm if you know how to take care of yourself. May I ask his name?

Ellie [*slowly and musically*]. Marcus Darnley.

Mrs Hushabye [*echoing the music*]. Marcus Darnley! What a splendid name!

Ellie. Oh, I'm so glad you think so. I think so too; but I was afraid it was only a silly fancy of my own.

Mrs Hushabye. Hm! Is he one of the Aberdeen Darnleys?

Ellie. Nobody knows. Just fancy! He was found in an antique chest—

Mrs Hushabye. A what?

Ellie. An antique chest, one summer morning in a rose garden, after a night of the most terrible thunderstorm.

Mrs Hushabye. What on earth was he doing in the chest? Did he get into it because he was afraid of the lightning?

Ellie. Oh no, no: he was a baby. The name Marcus Darnley was embroidered on his babyclothes. And five hundred pounds in gold.

Mrs Hushabye [*looking hard at her*]. Ellie!

Ellie. The garden of the Viscount—

Mrs Hushabye. —de Rougemont?

Ellie [*innocently*]. No: de Larochejaquelin. A French family. A vicomte. His life has been one long romance. A tiger—

Mrs Hushabye. Slain by his own hand?

Ellie. Oh no: nothing vulgar like that. He saved the life of the tiger from a hunting party: one of King Edward's hunting parties in India. The King was furious: that was why he never had his military services properly recognized. But he doesnt care. He is a Socialist and despises rank, and has been in three revolutions fighting on the barricades.

Mrs Hushabye. How can you sit there telling me such lies? You, Ellie, of all people! And I thought you were a perfectly simple, straightforward, good girl.

Ellie [*rising, dignified but very angry*]. Do you mean to say you dont believe me?

Mrs Hushabye. Of course I dont believe you. Youre inventing every word of it. Do you take me for a fool?

[*Ellie stares at her. Her candor is so obvious that Mrs Hushabye is puzzled.*]

Ellie. Goodbye, Hesione. I'm very sorry. I see now that it sounds very improbable as I tell it. But I cant stay if you think that way about me.

Mrs Hushabye [*catching her dress*]. You shant go. I couldnt be so mistaken: I know too well what liars are like. Somebody has really told you all this.

Ellie [*flushing*]. Hesione: dont say that you dont believe him. I couldn't bear that.

Mrs Hushabye [*soothing her*]. Of course I believe him, dearest. But you should have broken it to me by degrees. [*Drawing her back to her seat.*] Now tell me all about him. Are you in love with him?

Ellie. Oh no. I'm not so foolish. I dont fall in love with people. I'm not so silly as you think.

Mrs Hushabye. I see. Only something to think about—to give some interest and pleasure to life.

Ellie. Just so. Thats all, really.

Mrs Hushabye. It makes the hours go fast, doesnt it? No tedious waiting to go to sleep at nights and wondering whether you will have a bad night. How delightful it makes waking up in the morning! How much better than the happiest dream! All life transfigured! No more wishing one had an interesting book to read, because life is so much happier than any book! No desire but to be alone and not to have to talk to anyone: to be alone and just think about it.

Ellie [*embracing her*]. Hesione: you are a witch. How do you know? Oh, you are the most sympathetic woman in the world.

Mrs Hushabye [*caressing her*]. Pettikins, my pettikins: how I envy you! and how I pity you!

Ellie. Pity me! Oh, why?

[*A very handsome man of fifty, with mousquetaire moustaches, wearing a rather dandified curly brimmed hat, and carrying an elaborate walking-stick, comes into the room from the hall, and stops short at sight of the women on the sofa.*]

Ellie [*seeing him and rising in glad surprise*]. Oh! Hesione: this is Mr Marcus Darnley.

Mrs Hushabye [*rising*]. What a lark! He is my husband.

Ellie. But how— [*She stops suddenly; then turns pale and sways.*]

Mrs Hushabye [*catching her and sitting down with her on the sofa.*] Steady, my pettikins.

The Man [*with a mixture of confusion and effrontery, depositing his hat and stick on the teak table*]. My real name, Miss Dunn, is Hector Hushabye. I leave you to judge whether that is a name any sensitive man would care to confess to. I never use it when I can possibly help it. I have been away for nearly a month; and I had no idea you knew my wife, or that you were coming here. I am none the less delighted to find you in our little house.

Ellie [*in great distress*]. I dont know what to do. Please, may I speak to papa? Do leave me. I cant bear it.

Mrs Hushabye. Be off, Hector.

Hector. I—

Mrs Hushabye. Quick, quick. Get out.

Hector. If you think it better— [*He goes out, taking his hat with him but leaving the stick on the table.*]

Mrs Hushabye [*laying Ellie down at the end of the sofa*]. Now, pettikins, he is gone. Theres nobody but me. You can let yourself go. Dont try to control yourself. Have a good cry.

Ellie [*raising her head*]. Damn!

Mrs Hushabye. Splendid! Oh, what a relief! I thought you were going to be broken-hearted. Never mind me. Damn him again.

Ellie. I am not damning him: I am damning myself for being such a fool. [*Rising.*] How could I let myself be taken in so? [*She begins prowling to and fro, her bloom gone, looking curiously older and harder.*]

Mrs Hushabye [*cheerfully*]. Why not, pettikins? Very few young women can resist Hector. I couldn't when I was your age. He is really rather splendid, you know.

Ellie [*turning on her*]. Splendid! Yes: splendid looking, of course. But how can you love a liar?

Mrs Hushabye. I dont know. But you can, fortunately. Otherwise there wouldnt be much love in the world.

Ellie. But to lie like that! To be a boaster! a coward!

Mrs Hushabye [*rising in alarm*]. Pettikins: none of that, if you please. If you hint the slightest doubt of Hector's courage, he will go straight off and do the most horribly dangerous things to convince himself that he isnt a coward. He has a dreadful trick of getting out of one third-floor window and coming in at another, just to test his nerve. He has a whole drawerful of Albert Medals for saving people's lives.

Ellie. He never told me that.

Mrs Hushabye. He never boasts of anything he really did: he cant bear it; and it makes him shy if anyone else does. All his stories are made-up stories.

Ellie [*coming to her*]. Do you mean that he is really brave, and really has adventures, and yet tells lies about things that he never did and that never happened?

Mrs Hushabye. Yes, pettikins, I do. People dont have their virtues and vices in sets: they have them anyhow: all mixed.

Ellie [*staring at her thoughtfully*]. Theres something odd about this house, Hesione, and even about you. I dont know why I'm talking to you so calmly. I have a horrible fear that my heart is broken, but that heartbreak is not like what I thought it must be.

Mrs Hushabye [*fondling her*]. It's only life educating you, pettikins. How do you feel about Boss Mangan now?

Ellie [*disengaging herself with an expression of distaste*]. Oh, how can you remind me of him, Hesione?

Mrs Hushabye. Sorry, dear. I think I hear Hector coming back. You dont mind now, do you, dear?

Ellie. Not in the least. I'm quite cured.

[*Mazzini Dunn and Hector come in from the hall.*]

Hector [*as he opens the door and allows Mazzini to pass in*]. One second more, and she would have been a dead woman!

Mazzini. Dear! dear! what an escape! Ellie, my love: Mr Hushabye has just been telling me the most extraordinary—

Ellie. Yes: Ive heard it. [*She crosses to the other side of the room.*]

Hector [*following her*]. Not this one. I'll tell it to you after dinner. I think youll like it. The truth is, I made it up for you, and was looking forward to the pleasure of telling it to you. But in a moment of impatience at being turned out of the room, I threw it away on your father.

Ellie [*turning at bay with her back to the carpenter's bench, scornfully self-possessed*]. It was not thrown away. He believes it. I should not have believed it.

Mazzini [*benevolently*]. Ellie is very naughty, Mr Hushabye. Of course she does not really think that. [*He goes to the bookshelves, and inspects the titles of the volumes.*]

[*Boss Mangan comes in from the hall, followed by the Captain. Mangan, carefully frock-coated as for church or for a directors' meeting, is about fifty-five, with a careworn, mistrustful expression, standing a little on an entirely imaginary dignity, with a dull complexion,*] *straight, lustreless hair, and features so entirely commonplace that it is impossible to describe them.*]

Captain Shotover [*to Mrs Hushabye, introducing the newcomer*]. Says his name is Mangan. Not ablebodied.

Mrs Hushabye [*graciously*]. How do you do, Mr Mangan?

Mangan [*shaking hands*]. Very pleased.

Captain Shotover. Dunn's lost his muscle, but recovered his nerve. Men seldom do after three attacks of delirium tremens. [*He goes into the pantry.*]

Mrs. Hushabye. I congratulate you, Mr Dunn.

Mazzini [*dazed*]. I am a lifelong teetotaler.

Mrs. Hushabye. You will find it far less trouble to let papa have his own way than try to explain.

Mazzini. But three attacks of delirium tremens, really!

Mrs Hushabye [*to Mangan*]. Do you know my husband, Mr Mangan? [*She indicates Hector.*]

Mangan [*going to Hector, who meets him with outstretched hand*]. Very pleased. [*Turning to Ellie.*] I hope, Miss Ellie, you have not found the journey down too fatiguing. [*They shake hands.*]

Mrs Hushabye. Hector: shew Mr Dunn his room.

Hector. Certainly. Come along, Mr Dunn. [*He takes Mazzini out.*]

Ellie. You havnt shewn me my room yet, Hesione.

Mrs Hushabye. How stupid of me! Come along. Make yourself quite at home, Mr Mangan. Papa will entertain you. [*She calls to the Captain in the pantry.*] Papa: come and explain the house to Mr Mangan.

[*She goes out with Ellie. The Captain comes from the pantry.*]

Captain Shotover. Youre going to marry Dunn's daughter. Dont. Youre too old.

Mangan [*staggered*]. Well! Thats fairly blunt, Captain.

Captain Shotover. It's true.

Mangan. She doesnt think so.

Captain Shotover. She does.

Mangan. Older men than I have—

Captain Shotover [*finishing the sentence for him*].—made fools of themselves. That, also, is true.

Mangan [*asserting himself*]. I dont see that this is any business of yours.

Captain Shotover. It is everybody's business. The stars in their courses are shaken when such things happen.

Mangan. I'm going to marry her all the same.

Captain Shotover. How do you know?

Mangan [*playing the strong man*]. I intend to. I mean to. See? I never made up my mind to do a thing yet that I didnt bring it off. Thats the sort of man I am; and there will be a better understanding between us when you make up your mind to that, Captain.

Captain Shotover. You frequent picture palaces.

Mangan. Perhaps I do. Who told you?

Captain Shotover. Talk like a man, not like a movy. You mean that you make a hundred thousand a year.

Mangan. I dont boast. But when I meet a man that makes a hundred thousand a year, I take off my hat to that man, and stretch out my hand to him and call him brother.

Captain Shotover. Then you also make a hundred thousand a year, hey?

Mangan. No. I cant say that. Fifty thousand, perhaps.

Captain Shotover. His half brother only. [*He turns away from Mangan with his usual abruptness, and collects the empty tea-cups on the Chinese tray*.]

Mangan [*irritated*]. See here, Captain Shotover. I dont quite understand my position here. I came here on your daughter's invitation. Am I in her house or in yours?

Captain Shotover. You are beneath the dome of heaven, in the house of God. What is true within these walls is true outside them. Go out on the seas; climb the mountains; wander through the valleys. She is still too young.

Mangan [*weakening*]. But I'm very little over fifty.

Captain Shotover. You are still less under sixty. Boss Mangan: you will not marry the pirate's child. [*He carries the tray away into the pantry*.]

Mangan [*following him to the half door*]. What pirate's child? What are you talking about?

Captain Shotover [*in the pantry*]. Ellie Dunn. You will not marry her.

Mangan. Who will stop me?

Captain Shotover [*emerging*]. My daughter. [*He makes for the door leading to the hall*.]

Mangan [*following him*]. Mrs Hushabye! Do you mean to say she brought me down here to break it off?

Captain Shotover [*stopping and turning on him*]. I know nothing more than I have seen in her eye. She will break it off. Take my advice: marry a West Indian negress: they make excellent wives. I was married to one myself for two years.

Mangan. Well, I am damned!

Captain Shotover. I thought so. I was, too, for many years. The negress redeemed me.

Mangan [*feebly*]. This is queer. I ought to walk out of this house.

Captain Shotover. Why?

Mangan. Well, many men would be offended by your style of talking.

Captain Shotover. Nonsense! It's the other sort of talking that makes quarrels. Nobody ever quarrels with me.

[*A gentleman, whose firstrate tailoring and frictionless manners proclaim the wellbred West Ender, comes in from the hall. He has an engaging air of being young and unmarried, but on close inspection is found to be at least over forty.*]

The Gentleman. Excuse my intruding in this fashion; but there is no knocker on the door; and the bell does not seem to ring.

Captain Shotover. Why should there be a knocker? Why should the bell ring? The door is open.

The Gentleman. Precisely. So I ventured to come in.

Captain Shotover. Quite right. I will see about a room for you. [*He makes for the door.*]

The Gentleman [*stopping him*]. But I'm afraid you dont know who I am.

Captain Shotover. Do you suppose that at my age I make distinctions between one fellowcreature and another? [*He goes out. Mangan and the newcomer stare at one another.*]

Mangan. Strange character, Captain Shotover, sir.

The Gentleman. Very.

Captain Shotover [*shouting outside*]. Hesione: another person has arrived and wants a room. Man about town, well dressed, fifty.

The Gentleman. Fancy Hesione's feelings! May I ask are you a member of the family?

Mangan. No.

The Gentleman. I am. At least a connexion.

[*Mrs Hushabye comes back.*]

Mrs Hushabye. How do you do? How good of you to come!

The Gentleman. I am very glad indeed to make your acquaintance, Hesione. [*Instead of taking her hand he kisses her. At the same moment the Captain appears*

in the doorway.] You will excuse my kissing your
daughter, Captain, when I tell you that—

Captain Shotover. Stuff! Everyone kisses my daughter. Kiss
her as much as you like. [*He makes for the pantry.*]

The Gentleman. Thank you. One moment, Captain. [*The
Captain halts and turns. The gentleman goes to him
affably.*] Do you happen to remember—but probably
you dont, as it occurred many years ago—that your
younger daughter married a numskull?

Captain Shotover. Yes. She said she'd marry anybody to get
away from this house. I should not have recognized
you: your head is no longer like a walnut. Your aspect
is softened. You have been boiled in bread and milk
for years and years, like other married men. Poor devil!
[*He disappears into the pantry.*]

Mrs Hushabye [*going past Mangan to the gentleman and
scrutinizing him.*] I dont believe you are Hastings Utterword.

The Gentleman. I am not.

Mrs Hushabye. Then what business had you to kiss me?

The Gentleman. I thought I would like to. The fact is, I am
Randall Utterword, the unworthy younger brother of
Hastings. I was abroad diplomatizing when he was
married.

Lady Utterword [*dashing in*]. Hesione: where is the key of
the wardrobe in my room? My diamonds are in my
dressing-bag: I must lock it up— [*Recognizing the
stranger with a shock.*] Randall: how dare you? [*She
marches at him past Mrs Hushabye, who retreats and
joins Mangan near the sofa.*]

Randall. How dare I what? I am not doing anything.

Lady Utterword. Who told you I was here?

Randall. Hastings. You had just left when I called on you
at Claridge's; so I followed you down here. You are
looking extremely well.

Lady Utterword. Dont presume to tell me so.

Mrs Hushabye. What is wrong with Mr Randall, Addy?

Lady Utterword [*recollecting herself*]. Oh, nothing. But he
has no right to come bothering you and papa without
being invited. [*She goes to the window-seat and sits
down, turning away from them ill-humoredly and looking into the garden where Hector and Ellie are now
seen strolling together.*]

Mrs Hushabye. I think you have not met Mr Mangan, Addy.

Lady Utterword [*turning her head and nodding coldly to Mangan*]. I beg your pardon. Randall: you have flustered me so: I made a perfect fool of myself.

Mrs. Hushabye. Lady Utterword. My sister. My younger sister.

Mangan [*bowing*]. Pleased to meet you, Lady Utterword.

Lady Utterword [*with marked interest*]. Who is that gentleman walking in the garden with Miss Dunn?

Mrs Hushabye. I dont know. She quarrelled mortally with my husband only ten minutes ago; and I didnt know anyone else had come. It must be a visitor. [*She goes to the window to look.*] Oh, it is Hector. Theyve made it up.

Lady Utterword. Your husband! That handsome man?

Mrs Hushabye. Well, why shouldnt my husband be a handsome man?

Randall [*joining them at the window*]. One's husband never is, Ariadne. [*He sits by Lady Utterword, on her right.*]

Mrs Hushabye. One's sister's husband always is, Mr Randall.

Lady Utterword. Dont be vulgar, Randall. And you, Hesione, are just as bad.

[*Ellie and Hector come in from the garden by the starboard door. Randall rises. Ellie retires into the corner near the pantry. Hector comes forward; and Lady Utterword rises looking her very best.*]

Mrs Hushabye. Hector: this is Addy.

Hector [*apparently surprised*]. Not this lady.

Lady Utterword [*smiling*]. Why not?

Hector [*looking at her with a piercing glance of deep but respectful admiration, his moustache bristling*]. I thought —[*Pulling himself together.*] I beg your pardon, Lady Utterword. I am extremely glad to welcome you at last under our roof. [*He offers his hand with grave courtesy.*]

Mrs Hushabye. She wants to be kissed, Hector.

Lady Utterword. Hesione! [*But she still smiles.*]

Mrs Hushabye. Call her Addy; and kiss her like a good brother-in-law; and have done with it. [*She leaves them to themselves.*]

Hector. Behave yourself, Hesione. Lady Utterword is entitled not only to hospitality but to civilization.

Lady Utterword [*gratefully*]. Thank you, Hector. [*They shake hands cordially.*]

[*Mazzini Dunn is seen crossing the garden from starboard to port.*]

Captain Shotover [*coming from the pantry and addressing Ellie.*] Your father has washed himself.

Ellie [*quite self-possessed*]. He often does, Captain Shotover.

Captain Shotover. A strange conversion! I saw him through the pantry window.

[*Mazzini Dunn enters through the port window door, newly washed and brushed, and stops, smiling benevolently, between Mangan and Mrs Hushabye.*]

Mrs Hushabye [*introducing*]. Mr Mazzini Dunn, Lady Ut— oh, I forgot: youve met. [*Indicating Ellie.*] Miss Dunn.

Mazzini [*walking across the room to take Ellie's hand, and beaming at his own naughty irony*]. I have met Miss Dunn also. She is my daughter. [*He draws her arm through his caressingly.*]

Mrs Hushabye. Of course: how stupid! Mr Utterword, my sister's—er—

Randall [*shaking hands agreeably*]. Her brother-in-law, Mr Dunn. How do you do?

Mrs Hushabye. This is my husband.

Hector. We have met, dear. Dont introduce us any more. [*He moves away to the big chair, and adds:*] Wont you sit down, Lady Utterword? [*She does so very graciously.*]

Mrs Hushabye. Sorry. I hate it: it's like making people shew their tickets.

Mazzini [*sententiously*]. How little it tells us, after all! The great question is, not who we are, but what we are.

Captain Shotover. Ha! What are you?

Mazzini [*taken aback*]. What am I?

Captain Shotover. A thief, a pirate, and a murderer.

Mazzini. I assure you you are mistaken.

Captain Shotover. An adventurous life; but what does it end in? Respectability. A ladylike daughter. The language and appearance of a city missionary. Let it be a warning to all of you. [*He goes out through the garden.*]

Dunn. I hope nobody here believes that I am a thief, a pirate, or a murderer. Mrs Hushabye: will you excuse me a moment? I must really go and explain. [*He follows the Captain.*]

Mrs Hushabye [*as he goes*]. It's no use. Youd really better
— [*But Dunn has vanished.*] We had better all go out
and look for some tea. We never have regular tea;
but you can always get some when you want: the servants keep it stewing all day. The kitchen veranda is
the best place to ask. May I shew you? [*She goes to the
starboard door.*]

Randall [*going with her*]. Thank you, I dont think I'll take
any tea this afternoon. But if you will shew me the
garden—?

Mrs Hushabye. Theres nothing to see in the garden except
papa's observatory, and a gravel pit with a cave where
he keeps dynamite and things of that sort. However, it's
pleasanter out of doors; so come along.

Randall. Dynamite! Isnt that rather risky?

Mrs Hushabye. Well, we dont sit in the gravel pit when
theres a thunderstorm.

Lady Utterword. Thats something new. What is the dynamite for?

Hector. To blow up the human race if it goes too far. He
is trying to discover a psychic ray that will explode all
the explosives at the will of a Mahatma.

Ellie. The Captain's tea is delicious, Mr Utterword.

Mrs Hushabye [*stopping in the doorway*]. Do you mean
to say that youve had some of my father's tea? that you
got round him before you were ten minutes in the
house?

Ellie. I did.

Mrs Hushabye. You little devil! [*She goes out with Randall.*]

Mangan. Wont you come, Miss Ellie?

Ellie. I'm too tired. I'll take a book up to my room and rest
a little. [*She goes to the bookshelf.*]

Mangan. Right. You cant do better. But I'm disappointed.
[*He follows Randall and Mrs Hushabye.*]

[*Ellie, Hector, and Lady Utterword are left. Hector is close
to Lady Utterword. They look at Ellie, waiting for her
to go.*]

Ellie [*looking at the title of a book.*] Do you like stories of
adventure, Lady Utterword?

Lady Utterword [*patronizingly*]. Of course, dear.

Ellie. Then I'll leave you to Mr Hushabye. [*She goes out
through the hall.*]

Hector. That girl is mad about tales of adventure. The lies
I have to tell her!

Lady Utterword [*not interested in Ellie*]. When you saw me what did you mean by saying that you thought, and then stopping short? What did you think?

Hector [*folding his arms and looking down at her magnetically*]. May I tell you?

Lady Utterword. Of course.

Hector. It will not sound very civil. I was on the point of saying "I thought you were a plain woman."

Lady Utterword. Oh for shame, Hector! What right had you to notice whether I am plain or not?

Hector. Listen to me, Ariadne. Until today I have seen only photographs of you; and no photograph can give the strange fascination of the daughters of that supernatural old man. There is some damnable quality in them that destroys men's moral sense, and carries them beyond honor and dishonor. You know that, dont you?

Lady Utterword. Perhaps I do, Hector. But let me warn you once for all that I am a rigidly conventional woman. You may think because I'm a Shotover that I'm a Bohemian, because we are all so horribly Bohemian. But I'm not. I hate and loathe Bohemianism. No child brought up in a strict Puritan household ever suffered from Puritanism as I suffered from our Bohemianism.

Hector. Our children are like that. They spend their holidays in the houses of their respectable schoolfellows.

Lady Utterword. I shall invite them for Christmas.

Hector. Their absence leaves us both without our natural chaperons.

Lady Utterword. Children are certainly very inconvenient sometimes. But intelligent people can always manage, unless they are Bohemians.

Hector. You are no Bohemian; but you are no Puritan either: your attraction is alive and powerful. What sort of woman do you count yourself?

Lady Utterword. I am a woman of the world, Hector; and I can assure you that if you will only take the trouble always to do the perfectly correct thing, and to say the perfectly correct thing, you can do just what you like. An ill-conducted, careless woman gets simply no chance. An ill-conducted, careless man is never allowed within arms length of any woman worth knowing.

Hector. I see. You are neither a Bohemian woman nor a Puritan woman. You are a dangerous woman.

Lady Utterword. On the contrary, I am a safe woman.

Hector. You are a most accursedly attractive woman. Mind: I am not making love to you. I do not like being attracted. But you had better know how I feel if you are going to stay here.

Lady Utterword. You are an exceedingly clever ladykiller, Hector. And terribly handsome. I am quite a good player, myself, at that game. Is it quite understood that we are only playing?

Hector. Quite. I am deliberately playing the fool, out of sheer worthlessness.

Lady Utterword [*rising brightly*]. Well, you are my brother-in-law. Hesione asked you to kiss me. [*He seizes her in his arms, and kisses her strenuously.*] Oh! that was a little more than play, brother-in-law. [*She pushes him suddenly away.*] You shall not do that again.

Hector. In effect, you got your claws deeper into me than I intended.

Mrs Hushabye [*coming in from the garden*]. Dont let me disturb you: I only want a cap to put on daddiest. The sun is setting; and he'll catch cold. [*She makes for the door leading to the hall.*]

Lady Utterword. Your husband is quite charming, darling. He has actually condescended to kiss me at last. I shall go into the garden: it's cooler now. [*She goes out by the port door.*]

Mrs Hushabye. Take care, dear child. I dont believe any man can kiss Addy without falling in love with her. [*She goes into the hall.*]

Hector [*striking himself on the chest*]. Fool! Goat!

[*Mrs Hushabye comes back with the Captain's cap.*]

Hector. Your sister is an extremely enterprising old girl. Wheres Miss Dunn!

Mrs Hushabye. Mangan says she has gone up to her room for a nap. Addy wont let you talk to Ellie: she has marked you for her own.

Hector. She has the diabolical family fascination. I began making love to her automatically. What am I to do? I cant fall in love; and I cant hurt a woman's feelings by telling her so when she falls in love with me. And as women are always falling in love with my moustache I get landed in all sorts of tedious and terrifying flirtations in which I'm not a bit in earnest.

Mrs Hushabye. Oh, neither is Addy. She has never been in love in her life, though she has always been trying to fall in head over ears. She is worse than you, because you had one real go at least, with me.

Hector. That was a confounded madness. I cant believe that such an amazing experience is common. It has left its mark on me. I believe that is why I have never been able to repeat it.

Mrs Hushabye [*laughing and caressing his arm*]. We were frightfully in love with one another, Hector. It was such an enchanting dream that I have never been able to grudge it to you or anyone else since. I have invited all sorts of pretty women to the house on the chance of giving you another turn. But it has never come off.

Hector. I dont know that I want it to come off. It was damned dangerous. You fascinated me; but I loved you; so it was heaven. This sister of yours fascinates me; but I hate her; so it is hell. I shall kill her if she persists.

Mrs Hushabye. Nothing will kill Addy: she is as strong as a horse. [*Releasing him.*] Now *I* am going off to fascinate somebody.

Hector. The Foreign Office toff? Randall?

Mrs Hushabye. Goodness gracious, no! Why should I fascinate him?

Hector. I presume you dont mean the bloated capitalist, Mangan?

Mrs Hushabye. Hm! I think he had better be fascinated by me than by Ellie. [*She is going into the garden when the Captain comes in from it with some sticks in his hand.*] What have you got there, daddiest?

Captain Shotover. Dynamite.

Mrs Hushabye. Youve been to the gravel pit. Dont drop it about the house: theres a dear. [*She goes into the garden, where the evening light is now very red.*]

Hector. Listen, O sage. How long dare you concentrate on a feeling without risking having it fixed in your consciousness all the rest of your life?

Captain Shotover. Ninety minutes. An hour and a half. [*He goes into the pantry.*]

[*Hector, left alone, contracts his brows, and falls into a daydream. He does not move for some time. Then he folds his arms. Then, throwing his hands behind him, and gripping one with the other, he strides tragically once to and fro. Suddenly he snatches his walking-stick from the teak table, and draws it; for it is a sword-stick. He fights a desperate duel with an imaginary antagonist,*

*and after many vicissitudes runs him through the body
up to the hilt. He sheathes his sword and throws it on
the sofa, falling into another reverie as he does so. He
looks straight into the eyes of an imaginary woman,
seizes her by the arms; and says in a deep and thrilling
tone* "Do you love me!" *The Captain comes out of the
pantry at this moment; and Hector, caught with his
arms stretched out and his fists clenched, has to account for his attitude by going through a series of
gymnastic exercises.*]

Captain Shotover. That sort of strength is no good. You will
never be as strong as a gorilla.

Hector. What is the dynamite for?

Captain Shotover. To kill fellows like Mangan.

Hector. No use. They will always be able to buy more
dynamite than you.

Captain Shotover. I will make a dynamite that he cannot
explode.

Hector. And that you can, eh?

Captain Shotover. Yes: when I have attained the seventh
degree of concentration.

Hector. Whats the use of that? You never do attain it.

Captain Shotover. What then is to be done? Are we to be
kept for ever in the mud by these hogs to whom the
universe is nothing but a machine for greasing their
bristles and filling their snouts?

Hector. Are Mangan's bristles worse than Randall's lovelocks?

Captain Shotover. We must win powers of life and death
over them both. I refuse to die until I have invented
the means.

Hector. Who are we that we should judge them?

Captain Shotover. What are they that they should judge us?
Yet they do, unhesitatingly. There is enmity between
our seed and their seed. They know it and act on it,
strangling our souls. They believe in themselves. When
we believe in ourselves, we shall kill them.

Hector. It is the same seed. You forget that your pirate has
a very nice daughter. Mangan's son may be a Plato:
Randall's a Shelley. What was my father?

Captain Shotover. The damndest scoundrel I ever met. [*He
replaces the drawing-board; sits down at the table; and
begins to mix a wash of color.*]

Hector. Precisely. Well, dare you kill his innocent grand-children?

Captain Shotover. They are mine also.

Hector. Just so. We are members one of another. [*He throws himself carelessly on the sofa.*] I tell you I have often thought of this killing of human vermin. Many men have thought of it. Decent men are like Daniel in the lion's den: their survival is a miracle; and they do not always survive. We live among the Mangans and Randalls and Billy Dunns as they, poor devils, live among the disease germs and the doctors and the law-yers and the parsons and the restaurant chefs and the tradesmen and the servants and all the rest of the para-sites and blackmailers. What are our terrors to theirs? Give me the power to kill them; and I'll spare them in sheer—

Captain Shotover [*cutting in sharply*]. Fellow feeling?

Hector. No. I should kill myself if I believed that. I must believe that my spark, small as it is, is divine, and that the red light over their door is hell fire. I should spare them in simple magnanimous pity.

Captain Shotover. You cant spare them until you have the power to kill them. At present they have the power to kill you. There are millions of blacks over the water for them to train and let loose on us. Theyre going to do it. Theyre doing it already.

Hector. They are too stupid to use their power.

Captain Shotover [*throwing down his brush and coming to the end of the sofa*]. Do not deceive yourself: they do use it. We kill the better half of ourselves every day to propitiate them. The knowledge that these people are there to render all our aspirations barren prevents us having the aspirations. And when we are tempted to seek their destruction they bring forth demons to delude us, disguised as pretty daughters, and singers and poets and the like, for whose sake we spare them.

Hector [*sitting up and leaning towards him*]. May not Hes-ione be such a demon, brought forth by you lest I should slay you?

Captain Shotover. That is possible. She has used you up, and left you nothing but dreams, as some women do.

Hector. Vampire women, demon women.

Captain Shotover. Men think the world well lost for them,

and lose it accordingly. Who are the men that do things? The husbands of the shrew and of the drunkard, the men with the thorn in the flesh. [*Walking distractedly away towards the pantry.*] I must think these things out. [*Turning suddenly.*] But I go on with the dynamite none the less. I will discover a ray mightier than any X-ray: a mind ray that will explode the ammunition in the belt of my adversary before he can point his gun at me. And I must hurry. I am old: I have no time to waste in talk. [*He is about to go into the pantry, and Hector is making for the hall, when Hesione comes back.*]

Mrs Hushabye. Daddiest: you and Hector must come and help me to entertain all these people. What on earth were you shouting about?

Hector [*stopping in the act of turning the door handle*]. He is madder than usual.

Mrs Hushabye. We all are.

Hector. I must change. [*He resumes his door opening.*]

Mrs Hushabye. Stop, stop. Come back, both of you. Come back. [*They return, reluctantly.*] Money is running short.

Hector. Money! Where are my April dividends?

Mrs Hushabye. Where is all the snow that fell last year?

Captain Shotover. Where is all the money you had for that patent lifeboat I invented?

Mrs Hushabye. Five hundred pounds; and I have made it last since Easter!

Captain Shotover. Since Easter! Barely four months! Monstrous extravagance! I could live for seven years on £500.

Mrs Hushabye. Not keeping open house as we do here, daddiest.

Captain Shotover. Only £500 for that lifeboat! I got twelve thousand for the invention before that.

Mrs Hushabye. Yes, dear; but that was for the ship with the magnetic keel that sucked up submarines. Living at the rate we do, you cannot afford life-saving inventions. Cant you think of something that will murder half Europe at one bang?

Captain Shotover. No. I am ageing fast. My mind does not dwell on slaughter as it did when I was a boy. Why doesnt your husband invent something? He does nothing but tell lies to women.

Hector. Well, that is a form of invention, is it not? However, you are right: I ought to support my wife.

Mrs Hushabye. Indeed you shall do nothing of the sort: I should never see you from breakfast to dinner. I want my husband.

Hector [*bitterly*]. I might as well be your lapdog.

Mrs Hushabye. Do you want to be my breadwinner, like the other poor husbands?

Hector. No, by thunder! What a damned creature a husband is anyhow!

Mrs Hushabye [*to the Captain*]. What about that harpoon cannon?

Captain Shotover. No use. It kills whales, not men.

Mrs Hushabye. Why not? You fire the harpoon out of a cannon. It sticks in the enemy's general; you wind him in; and there you are.

Hector. You are your father's daughter, Hesione.

Captain Shotover. There is something in it. Not to wind in generals: they are not dangerous. But one could fire a grapnel and wind in a machine gun or even a tank. I will think it out.

Mrs Hushabye [*squeezing the Captain's arm affectionately*]. Saved! You are a darling, daddiest. Now we must go back to these dreadful people and entertain them.

Captain Shotover. They have had no dinner. Dont forget that.

Hector. Neither have I. And it is dark: it must be all hours.

Mrs Hushabye. Oh, Guinness will produce some sort of dinner for them. The servants always take jolly good care that there is food in the house.

Captain Shotover [*raising a strange wail in the darkness*]. What a house! What a daughter!

Mrs Hushabye [*raving*]. What a father!

Hector [*following suit*]. What a husband!

Captain Shotover. Is there no thunder in heaven?

Hector. Is there no beauty, no bravery, on earth?

Mrs Hushabye. What do men want? They have their food, their firesides, their clothes mended, and our love at the end of the day. Why are they not satisfied? Why do they envy us the pain with which we bring them into the world, and make strange dangers and torments for themselves to be even with us?

Captain Shotover [*weirdly chanting*].

I built a house for my daughters, and opened the
>   doors thereof,
That men might come for their choosing, and their
>   betters spring from their love;
But one of them married a numskull;

Hector [*taking up the rhythm*].

>   The other a liar wed;

Mrs Hushabye [*completing the stanza*].

And now must she lie beside him, even as she made her
>   bed.

Lady Utterword [*calling from the garden*]. Hesione! Hes-
>   ione! Where are you?

Hector. The cat is on the tiles.

Mrs Hushabye. Coming, darling, coming. [*She goes quickly
>   into the garden.*]

[*The Captain goes back to his place at the table.*]

Hector [*going into the hall*]. Shall I turn up the lights for
>   you?

Captain Shotover. No. Give me deeper darkness. Money is
>   not made in the light.

The same room, with the lights turned up and the curtains drawn. Ellie comes in, followed by Mangan. Both are dressed for dinner. She strolls to the drawing-table. He comes between the table and the wicker chair.

Mangan. What a dinner! I dont call it a dinner: I call it a meal.

Ellie. I am accustomed to meals, Mr Mangan, and very lucky to get them. Besides, the Captain cooked some macaroni for me.

Mangan [*shuddering liverishly*]. Too rich: I cant eat such things. I suppose it's because I have to work so much with my brain. Thats the worst of being a man of business: you are always thinking, thinking, thinking. By the way, now that we are alone, may I take the opportunity to come to a little understanding with you?

Ellie [*settling into the draughtsman's seat*]. Certainly. I should like to.

Mangan [*taken aback*]. Should you? That surprises me; for I thought I noticed this afternoon that you avoided me all you could. Not for the first time either.

Ellie. I was very tired and upset. I wasn't used to the ways of this extraordinary house. Please forgive me.

Mangan. Oh, thats all right: I dont mind. But Captain Shotover has been talking to me about you. You and me, you know.

Ellie [*interested*]. The captain! What did he say?

Mangan. Well, he noticed the difference between our ages.

Ellie. He notices everything.

Mangan. You dont mind, then?

Ellie. Of course I know quite well that our engagement—

Mangan. Oh! you call it an engagement.

Ellie. Well, isnt it?

Mangan. Oh, yes, yes: no doubt it is if you hold to it. This is the first time youve used the word; and I didnt quite know where we stood: thats all. [*He sits down in the wicker chair; and resigns himself to allow her to lead the conversation.*] You were saying——?

Ellie. Was I? I forget. Tell me. Do you like this part of the country? I heard you ask Mr Hushabye at dinner whether there are any nice houses to let down here.

Mangan. I like the place. The air suits me. I shouldnt be surprised if I settled down here.

Ellie. Nothing would please me better. The air suits me too. And I want to be near Hesione.

Mangan [*with growing uneasiness*]. The air may suit us; but the question is, should we suit one another? Have you thought about that?

Ellie. Mr Mangan: we must be sensible, mustnt we? Its no use pretending that we are Romeo and Juliet. But we can get on very well together if we choose to make the best of it. Your kindness of heart will make it easy for me.

Mangan [*leaning forward, with the beginning of something like deliberate unpleasantness in his voice.*] Kindness of heart, eh? I ruined your father, didnt I?

Ellie. Oh, not intentionally.

Mangan. Yes I did. Ruined him on purpose.

Ellie. On purpose!

Mangan. Not out of ill-nature, you know. And youll admit that I kept a job for him when I had finished with him. But business is business; and I ruined him as a matter of business.

Ellie. I dont understand how that can be. Are you trying to make me feel that I need not be grateful to you, so that I may choose freely?

Mangan [*rising aggressively*]. No. I mean what I say.

Ellie. But how could it possibly do you any good to ruin my father? The money he lost was yours.

Mangan [*with a sour laugh*]. Was mine! It is mine, Miss Ellie, and all the money the other fellows lost too. [*He shoves his hands into his pockets and shews his teeth.*] I just smoked them out like a hive of bees. What do you say to that? A bit of a shock, eh?

Ellie. It would have been, this morning. Now! you cant think how little it matters. But it's quite interesting. Only, you must explain it to me. I dont understand it. [*Propping her elbows on the drawing-board, chin in hand, she composes herself to listen with a combination of conscious curiosity with unconscious contempt which provokes him to more and more unpleasantness, and an attempt at patronage of her ignorance.*]

Mangan. Of course you dont understand: what do you know about business? You just listen and learn. Your father's business was a new business; and I dont start new businesses: I let other fellows start them. They put all their money and their friends' money into starting them. They wear out their souls and bodies trying to make a success of them. Theyre what you call enthusiasts. But the first dead lift of the thing is too much for them; and they havnt enough financial experience. In a year or so they have either to let the whole show go bust, or sell out to a new lot of fellows for a few deferred ordinary shares: that is, if theyre lucky enough to get anything at all. As likely as not the very same thing happens to the new lot. They put in more money and a couple of years more work; and then perhaps they have to sell out to a third lot. If it's really a big thing the third lot will have to sell out too, and leave their work and their money behind them. And thats where the real business man comes in: where I come in. But I'm cleverer than some: I dont mind dropping a little money to start the process. I took your father's measure. I saw that he had a sound idea, and that he would work himself silly for it if he got the chance. I saw that he was a child in business, and was dead certain to outrun his expenses and be in too great a hurry to wait for his market. I knew that the surest way to ruin a man who doesnt know how to handle money is to give him some. I explained my idea to some friends in the city, and they found the money; for I take no risks in ideas, even when theyre my own. Your father and the friends that ventured their money with him were no more to me than a heap of squeezed lemons. Youve been wasting your gratitude: my kind heart is all rot. I'm sick of it. When I see your father beaming at me with his moist, grateful eyes, regularly wallowing in gratitude, I sometimes feel I must tell him the truth or burst. What stops me is that I know he wouldnt believe me. He'd think it was my modesty, as you did just now. He'd think anything rather than the truth, which is that he's a blamed fool, and I am a man that knows how to take care of himself. [*He throws himself back into the big chair with large self-approval.*] Now what do you think of me, Miss Ellie?

Ellie [*dropping her hands*]. How strange! that my mother, who knew nothing at all about business, should have been quite right about you! She always said—not before papa, of course, but to us children—that you were just that sort of man.

Mangan [*sitting up, much hurt*]. Oh! did she? And yet she'd have let you marry me.

Ellie. Well, you see, Mr Mangan, my mother married a very good man—for whatever you may think of my father as a man of business, he is the soul of goodness —and she is not at all keen on my doing the same.

Mangan. Anyhow, you dont want to marry me now, do you?

Ellie [*very calmly*]. Oh, I think so. Why not?

Mangan [*rising aghast*]. Why not!

Ellie. I dont see why we shouldnt get on very well together.

Mangan. Well, but look here, you know— [*He stops, quite at a loss.*]

Ellie [*patiently*]. Well?

Mangan. Well, I thought you were rather particular about people's characters.

Ellie. If we women were particular about men's characters, we should never get married at all, Mr Mangan.

Mangan. A child like you talking of "we women"! What next! Youre not in earnest?

Ellie. Yes I am. Arent you?

Mangan. You mean to hold me to it?

Ellie. Do you wish to back out of it?

Mangan. Oh no. Not exactly back out of it.

Ellie. Well?

[*He has nothing to say. With a long whispered whistle, he drops into the wicker chair and stares before him like a beggared gambler. But a cunning look soon comes into his face. He leans over towards her on his right elbow, and speaks in a low steady voice.*]

Mangan. Suppose I told you I was in love with another woman!

Ellie [*echoing him*]. Suppose I told you I was in love with another man!

Mangan [*bouncing angrily out of his chair*]. I'm not joking.

Ellie. Who told you *I* was?

Mangan. I tell you I'm serious. Youre too young to be serious; but youll have to believe me. I want to be near your friend Mrs Hushabye. I'm in love with her. Now the murder's out.

Ellie. I want to be near your friend Mr Hushabye. I'm in
love with him. [*She rises and adds with a frank air:*]
Now we are in one another's confidence, we shall be
real friends. Thank you for telling me.

Mangan [*almost beside himself*]. Do you think I'll be made
a convenience of like this?

Ellie. Come, Mr Mangan! You made a business convenience
of my father. Well, a woman's business is marriage.
Why shouldnt I make a domestic convenience of you?

Mangan. Because I dont choose, see? Because I'm not a
silly gull like your father. Thats why.

Ellie [*with serene contempt*]. You are not good enough to
clean my father's boots, Mr Mangan; and I am paying
you a great compliment in condescending to make a
convenience of you, as you call it. Of course you are
free to throw over our engagement if you like; but, if
you do, youll never enter Hesione's house again: I will
take care of that.

Mangan [*gasping*]. You little devil, youve done me. [*On the
point of collapsing into the big chair again he recovers
himself.*] Wait a bit, though: youre not so cute as you
think. You cant beat Boss Mangan as easy as that. Suppose I go straight to Mrs Hushabye and tell her that
youre in love with her husband.

Ellie. She knows it.

Mangan. You told her!!!

Ellie. She told me.

Mangan [*clutching at his bursting temples*]. Oh, this is a
crazy house. Or else I'm going clean off my chump. Is
she making a swop with you—she to have your husband and you to have hers?

Ellie. Well, you dont want us both, do you?

Mangan [*throwing himself into the chair distractedly*]. My
brain wont stand it. My head's going to split. Help!
Help me to hold it. Quick: hold it: squeeze it. Save me.
[*Ellie comes behind his chair; clasps his head hard for
a moment; then begins to draw her hands from his
forehead back to his ears.*] Thank you. [*Drowsily.*]
Thats very refreshing. [*Waking a little.*] Don't you hypnotize me, though. Ive seen men made fools of by
hypnotism.

Ellie [*steadily*]. Be quiet. Ive seen men made fools of without
hypnotism.

Mangan [*humbly*]. You dont dislike touching me, I hope.

You never touched me before, I noticed.

Ellie. Not since you fell in love naturally with a grown-up nice woman, who will never expect you to make love to her. And I will never expect him to make love to me.

Mangan. He may, though.

Ellie [*making her passes rhythmically*]. Hush. Go to sleep. Do you hear? You are to go to sleep, go to sleep, go to sleep; be quiet, deeply deeply quiet; sleep, sleep, sleep, sleep, sleep.

[*He falls asleep. Ellie steals away; turns the light out; and goes into the garden. Nurse Guinness opens the door and is seen in the light which comes in from the hall.*]

Guinness [*speaking to someone outside*]. Mr Mangan's not here, ducky: theres no one here. It's all dark.

Mrs Hushabye [*without*]. Try the garden. Mr Dunn and I will be in my boudoir. Shew him the way.

Guinness. Yes, ducky. [*She makes for the garden door in the dark; stumbles over the sleeping Mangan; and screams.*] Ahoo! Oh Lord, sir! I beg your pardon, I'm sure: I didnt see you in the dark. Who is it? [*She goes back to the door and turns on the light.*] Oh, Mr Mangan, sir, I hope I havent hurt you plumping into your lap like that. [*Coming to him.*] I was looking for you, sir. Mrs Hushabye says will you please— [*Noticing that he remains quite insensible.*] Oh, my good Lord, I hope I havnt killed him. Sir! Mr Mangan! Sir! [*She shakes him; and he is rolling inertly off the chair on the floor when she holds him up and props him against the cushion.*] Miss Hessy! Miss Hessy! Quick, doty darling. Miss Hessy! [*Mrs Hushabye comes in from the hall, followed by Mazzini Dunn.*] Oh, Miss Hessy, Ive been and killed him.

[*Mazzini runs round the back of the chair to Mangan's right hand, and sees that the nurse's words are apparently only too true.*]

Mazzini. What tempted you to commit such a crime, woman?

Mrs Hushabye [*trying not to laugh*]. Do you mean you did it on purpose?

Guinness. Now is it likely I'd kill any man on purpose? I fell over him in the dark; and I'm a pretty tidy weight. He never spoke nor moved until I shook him; and then he would have dropped dead on the floor. Isnt it tiresome?

Mrs. Hushabye [*going past the nurse to Mangan's side, and inspecting him less credulously than Mazzini*]. Non-

sense! he is not dead: he is only asleep. I can see him
breathing.

Guinness. But why wont he wake?

Mazzini [*speaking very politely into Mangan's ear*]. Mangan!
My dear Mangan! [*He blows into Mangan's ear.*]

Mrs Hushabye. Thats no good. [*She shakes him vigorously.*]
Mr Mangan: wake up. Do you hear? [*He begins to
roll over.*] Oh! Nurse, nurse: he's falling: help me.

[*Nurse Guinness rushes to the rescue. With Mazzini's assistance, Mangan is propped safely up again.*]

Guinness [*behind the chair; bending over to test the case with
her nose*]. Would he be drunk, do you think, pet?

Mrs Hushabye. Had he any of papa's rum?

Mazzini. It cant be that: he is most abstemious. I am afraid
he drank too much formerly, and has to drink too
little now. You know, Mrs Hushabye, I really think he
has been hypnotized.

Guinness. Hip no what, sir?

Mazzini. One evening at home, after we had seen a hypno-
tizing performance, the children began playing at it;
and Ellie stroked my head. I assure you I went off dead
asleep; and they had to send for a professional to wake
me up after I had slept eighteen hours. They had to
carry me upstairs; and as the poor children were not
very strong, they let me slip; and I rolled right down
the whole flight and never woke up [*Mrs Hushabye
splutters*]. Oh, you may laugh, Mrs Hushabye; but I
might have been killed.

Mrs Hushabye. I couldnt have helped laughing even if you
had been, Mr Dunn. So Ellie has hypnotized him. What
fun!

Mazzini. Oh no, no, no. It was such a terrible lesson to her:
nothing would induce her to try such a thing again.

Mrs Hushabye. Then who did it? *I* didnt.

Mazzini. I thought perhaps the Captain might have done it
unintentionally. He is so fearfully magnetic: I feel
vibrations whenever he comes close to me.

Guinness. The Captain will get him out of it anyhow, sir:
I'll back him for that. I'll go fetch him. [*She makes for
the pantry.*]

Mrs Hushabye. Wait a bit. [*To Mazzini.*] You say he is all
right for eighteen hours?

Mazzini. Well, *I* was asleep for eighteen hours.

Mrs Hushabye. Were you any the worse for it?

Mazzini. I dont quite remember. They had poured brandy down my throat, you see; and—

Mrs Hushabye. Quite. Anyhow, you survived. Nurse, darling: go and ask Miss Dunn to come to us here. Say I want to speak to her particularly. You will find her with Mr Hushabye probably.

Guinness. I think not, ducky: Miss Addy is with him. But I'll find her and send her to you. [*She goes out into the garden.*]

Mrs Hushabye [*calling Mazzini's attention to the figure on the chair*]. Now, Mr Dunn, look. Just look. Look hard. Do you still intend to sacrifice your daughter to that thing?

Mazzini [*troubled*]. You have completely upset me, Mrs Hushabye, by all you have said to me. That anyone could imagine that I—I, a consecrated soldier of freedom, if I may say so—could sacrifice Ellie to anybody or anyone, or that I should ever have dreamed of forcing her inclinations in any way, is a most painful blow to my—well, I suppose you would say to my good opinion of myself.

Mrs Hushabye [*rather stolidly*]. Sorry.

Mazzini [*looking forlornly at the body*]. What is your objection to poor Mangan, Mrs Hushabye? He looks all right to me. But then I am so accustomed to him.

Mrs Hushabye. Have you no heart? Have you no sense? Look at the brute! Think of poor weak innocent Ellie in the clutches of this slavedriver, who spends his life making thousands of rough violent workmen bend to his will and sweat for him: a man accustomed to have great masses of iron beaten into shape for him by steam-hammers! to fight with women and girls over a halfpenny an hour ruthlessly! a captain of industry, I think you call him, dont you? Are you going to fling your delicate, sweet, helpless child into such a beast's claws just because he will keep her in an expensive house and make her wear diamonds to shew how rich he is?

Mazzini [*staring at her in wide-eyed amazement*]. Bless you, dear Mrs Hushabye, what romantic ideas of business you have! Poor dear Mangan isnt a bit like that.

Mrs Hushabye [*scornfully*]. Poor dear Mangan indeed!

Mazzini. But he doesnt know anything about machinery. He never goes near the men: he couldnt manage them: he is afraid of them. I never can get him to take the least interest in the works: he hardly knows more about them than you do. People are cruelly unjust to Mangan: they think he is all rugged strength just because his manners are bad.

Mrs Hushabye. Do you mean to tell me he isnt strong enough to crush poor little Ellie?

Mazzini. Of course it's very hard to say how any marriage will turn out; but speaking for myself, I should say that he wont have a dog's chance against Ellie. You know, Ellie has remarkable strength of character. I think it is because I taught her to like Shakespear when she was very young.

Mrs Hushabye [*contemptuously*]. Shakespear! The next thing you will tell me is that you could have made a great deal more money than Mangan. [*She retires to the sofa, and sits down at the port end of it in the worst of humors.*]

Mazzini [*following her and taking the other end*]. No: I'm no good at making money. I dont care enough for it, somehow. I'm not ambitious! that must be it. Mangan is wonderful about money: he thinks of nothing else. He is so dreadfully afraid of being poor. I am always thinking of other things: even at the works I think of the things we are doing and not of what they cost. And the worst of it is, poor Mangan doesnt know what to do with his money when he gets it. He is such a baby that he doesnt know even what to eat and drink: he has ruined his liver eating and drinking the wrong things; and now he can hardly eat at all. Ellie will diet him splendidly. You will be surprised when you come to know him better: he is really the most helpless of mortals. You get quite a protective feeling towards him.

Mrs Hushabye. Then who manages his business, pray?

Mazzini. I do. And of course other people like me.

Mrs Hushabye. Footling people, you mean.

Mazzini. I suppose youd think us so.

Mrs Hushabye. And pray why dont you do without him if youre all so much cleverer?

Mazzini. Oh, we couldnt: we should ruin the business in a year. I've tried; and I know. We should spend too much on everything. We should improve the quality of the goods and make them too dear. We should be sentimental about the hard cases among the workpeople. But

Mangan keeps us in order. He is down on us about every extra halfpenny. We could never do without him. You see, he will sit up all night thinking of how to save sixpence. Wont Ellie make him jump, though, when she takes his house in hand!

Mrs Hushabye. Then the creature is a fraud even as a captain of industry!

Mazzini. I am afraid all the captains of industry are what you call frauds, Mrs Hushabye. Of course there are some manufacturers who really do understand their own works; but they dont make as high a rate of profit as Mangan does. I assure you Mangan is quite a good fellow in his way. He means well.

Mrs Hushabye. He doesnt look well. He is not in his first youth, is he?

Mazzini. After all, no husband is in his first youth for very long, Mrs Hushabye. And men cant afford to marry in their first youths nowadays.

Mrs Hushabye. Now if *I* said that, it would sound witty. Why cant you say it wittily? What on earth is the matter with you? Why dont you inspire everybody with confidence? with respect?

Mazzini [*humbly*]. I think that what is the matter with me is that I am poor. You dont know what that means at home. Mind: I dont say they have ever complained. Theyve all been wonderful: theyve been proud of my poverty. Theyve even joked about it quite often. But my wife has had a very poor time of it. She has been quite resigned—

Mrs Hushabye [*shuddering involuntarily*]!!

Mazzini. There! You see, Mrs Hushabye. I dont want Ellie to live on resignation.

Mrs Hushabye. Do you want her to have to resign herself to living with a man she doesnt love?

Mazzini [*wistfully*]. Are you sure that would be worse than living with a man she did love, if he was a footling person?

Mrs Hushabye [*relaxing her contemptuous attitude, quite interested in Mazzini now*]. You know, I really think you must love Ellie very much; for you become quite clever when you talk about her.

Mazzini. I didnt know I was so very stupid on other subjects.

Mrs Hushabye. You are, sometimes.

Mazzini [*turning his head away; for his eyes are wet*]. I have learnt a good deal about myself from you, Mrs Hushabye; and I'm afraid I shall not be the happier for your plain speaking. But if you thought I needed it to make me think of Ellie's happiness you were very much mistaken.

Mrs Hushabye [*leaning towards him kindly*]. Have I been a beast?

Mazzini [*pulling himself together*]. It doesnt matter about me, Mrs Hushabye. I think you like Ellie; and that is enough for me.

Mrs Hushabye. I'm beginning to like you a little. I perfectly loathed you at first. I thought you the most odious, self-satisfied, boresome elderly prig I ever met.

Mazzini [*resigned, and now quite cheerful*]. I daresay I am all that. I never have been a favorite with gorgeous women like you. They always frighten me.

Mrs Hushabye [*pleased*]. Am I a gorgeous woman, Mazzini? I shall fall in love with you presently.

Mazzini [*with placid gallantry*]. No you wont, Hesione. But you would be quite safe. Would you believe it that quite a lot of women have flirted with me because I am quite safe? But they get tired of me for the same reason.

Mrs Hushabye [*mischievously*]. Take care. You may not be so safe as you think.

Mazzini. Oh yes, quite safe. You see, I have been in love really: the sort of love that only happens once. [*Softly.*] Thats why Ellie is such a lovely girl.

Mrs Hushabye. Well, really, you are coming out. Are you quite sure you wont let me tempt you into a second grand passion?

Mazzini. Quite. It wouldnt be natural. The fact is, you dont strike on my box, Mrs Hushabye; and I certainly dont strike on yours.

Mrs Hushabye. I see. Your marriage was a safety match.

Mazzini. What a very witty application of the expression I used. I should never have thought of it.

[*Ellie comes in from the garden, looking anything but happy.*]

Mrs Hushabye [*rising*]. Oh! here is Ellie at last. [*She goes behind the sofa.*]

Ellie [*on the threshold of the starboard door*]. Guinness said you wanted me: you and papa.

Mrs Hushabye. You have kept us waiting so long that it almost came to—well, never mind. Your father is a

very wonderful man [*She ruffles his hair affectionately*]:
the only one I ever met who could resist me when I
made myself really agreeable. [*She comes to the big
chair, on Mangan's left.*] Come here. I have something
to shew you. [*Ellie strolls listlessly to the other side of
the chair.*] Look.

Ellie [*contemplating Mangan without interest*]. I know. He
is only asleep. We had a talk after dinner; and he fell
asleep in the middle of it.

Mrs Hushabye. You did it, Ellie. You put him asleep.

Mazzini [*rising quickly and coming to the back of the chair*].
Oh, I hope not. Did you, Ellie?

Ellie [*wearily*]. He asked me to.

Mazzini. But it's dangerous. You know what happened to me.

Ellie [*utterly indifferent*]. Oh, I daresay I can wake him.
If not, somebody else can.

Mrs Hushabye. It doesnt matter, anyhow, because I have
at last persuaded your father that you dont want to
marry him.

Ellie [*suddenly coming out of her listlessness, much vexed*].
But why did you do that, Hesione? I do want to marry
him. I fully intend to marry him.

Mazzini. Are you quite sure, Ellie? Mrs Hushabye has made
me feel that I may have been thoughtless and selfish
about it.

Ellie [*very clearly and steadily*]. Papa. When Mrs Hushabye
takes it on herself to explain to you what I think or dont
think, shut your ears tight; and shut your eyes too.
Hesione knows nothing about me: she hasnt the least
notion of the sort of person I am, and never will. I
promise you I wont do anything I dont want to do and
mean to do for my own sake.

Mazzini. You are quite, quite sure?

Ellie. Quite, quite sure. Now you must go away and leave
me to talk to Mrs Hushabye.

Mazzini. But I should like to hear. Shall I be in the way?

Ellie [*inexorable*]. I had rather talk to her alone.

Mazzini [*affectionately*]. Oh, well, I know what a nuisance
parents are, dear. I will be good and go. [*He goes to the
garden door.*] By the way, do you remember the address
of that professional who woke me up? Dont you think
I had better telegraph to him?

Mrs Hushabye [*moving towards the sofa*]. It's too late to
telegraph tonight.

Mazzini. I suppose so. I do hope he'll wake up in the course of the night. [*He goes out into the garden.*]

Ellie [*turning vigorously on Hesione the moment her father is out of the room.*] Hesione: what the devil do you mean by making mischief with my father about Mangan?

Mrs Hushabye [*promptly losing her temper*]. Dont you dare speak to me like that, you little minx. Remember that you are in my house.

Ellie. Stuff! Why dont you mind your own business? What is it to you whether I choose to marry Mangan or not?

Mrs Hushabye. Do you suppose you can bully me, you miserable little matrimonial adventurer?

Ellie. Every woman who hasnt any money is a matrimonial adventurer. It's easy for you to talk: you have never known what it is to want money; and you can pick up men as if they were daisies. I am poor and respectable——

Mrs Hushabye [*interrupting*]. Ho! respectable! How did you pick up Mangan? How did you pick up my husband? You have the audacity to tell me that I am a——a——a——

Ellie. A siren. So you are. You were born to lead men by the nose: if you werent, Marcus would have waited for me, perhaps.

Mrs Hushabye [*suddenly melting and half laughing*]. Oh, my poor Ellie, my pettikins, my unhappy darling! I am so sorry about Hector. But what can I do? It's not my fault: I'd give him to you if I could.

Ellie. I dont blame you for that.

Mrs Hushabye. What a brute I was to quarrel with you and call you names! Do kiss me and say youre not angry with me.

Ellie [*fiercely*]. Oh, dont slop and gush and be sentimental. Dont you see that unless I can be hard—as hard as nails—I shall go mad? I dont care a damn about your calling me names: do you think a woman in my situation can feel a few hard words?

Mrs Hushabye. Poor little woman! Poor little situation!

Ellie. I suppose you think youre being sympathetic. You are just foolish and stupid and selfish. You see me getting a smasher right in the face that kills a whole part of my life: the best part that can never come again; and you think you can help me over it by a little coaxing and kissing. When I want all the strength I can get to lean on: something iron, something stony, I dont care how cruel it is, you go all mushy and want to slobber over me. I'm not angry; I'm not unfriendly; but for God's sake do pull yourself together; and dont think that because youre on velvet and always have been, women who are in hell can take it as easily as you.

Mrs Hushabye [*shrugging her shoulders*]. Very well. [*She sits down on the sofa in her old place.*] But I warn you that when I am neither coaxing and kissing nor laughing, I am just wondering how much longer I can stand living in this cruel, damnable world. You object to the siren: well, I drop the siren. You want to rest your wounded bosom against a grindstone. Well [*Folding her arms.*], here is the grindstone.

Ellie [*sitting down beside her, appeased*]. Thats better: you really have the trick of falling in with everyone's mood; but you dont understand, because you are not the sort of woman for whom there is only one man and only one chance.

Mrs Hushabye. I certainly dont understand how your marrying that object [*Indicating Mangan.*] will console you for not being able to marry Hector.

Ellie. Perhaps you dont understand why I was quite a nice girl this morning, and am now neither a girl nor particularly nice.

Mrs Hushabye. Oh yes, I do. It's because you have made up your mind to do something despicable and wicked.

Ellie. I dont think so, Hesione. I must make the best of my ruined house.

Mrs Hushabye. Pooh! Youll get over it. Your house isnt ruined.

Ellie. Of course I shall get over it. You dont suppose I'm going to sit down and die of a broken heart, I hope, or be an old maid living on a pittance from the Sick and Indigent Roomkeepers' Association. But my heart is broken, all the same. What I mean by that is that I know that what has happened to me with Marcus will not happen to me ever again. In the world for me there is Marcus and a lot of other men of whom one is just the same as another. Well, if I cant have love, thats no reason why I should have poverty. If Mangan has nothing else, he has money.

Mrs Hushabye. And are there no young men with money?

Ellie. Not within my reach. Besides, a young man would have the right to expect love from me, and would perhaps leave me when he found I could not give it to him. Rich young men can get rid of their wives, you know, pretty cheaply. But this object, as you call him, can expect nothing more from me than I am prepared to give him.

Mrs Hushabye. He will be your owner, remember. If he buys you, he will make the bargain pay him and not you. Ask your father.

Ellie [*rising and strolling to the chair to contemplate their subject*]. You need not trouble on that score, Hesione. I have more to give Boss Mangan than he has to give me: it is I who am buying him, and at a pretty good price too, I think. Women are better at that sort of bargain than men. I have taken the Boss's measure; and ten Boss Mangans shall not prevent me doing far more as I please as his wife than I have ever been able to do as a poor girl. [*Stooping to the recumbent figure.*] Shall they, Boss? I think not. [*She passes on to the drawing-table, and leans against the end of it, facing the windows.*] I shall not have to spend most of my time wondering how long my gloves will last, anyhow.

Mrs Hushabye [*rising superbly*]. Ellie: you are a wicked sordid little beast. And to think that I actually condescended to fascinate that creature there to save you from him! Well, let me tell you this: if you make this disgusting match, you will never see Hector again if I can help it.

Ellie [*unmoved*]. I nailed Mangan by telling him that if he did not marry me he should never see you again. [*She lifts herself on her wrists and seats herself on the end of the table.*]

Mrs Hushabye [*recoiling*]. Oh!

Ellie. So you see I am not unprepared for your playing that trump against me. Well, you just try it: thats all. I should have made a man of Marcus, not a household pet.

Mrs Hushabye [*flaming*]. You dare!

Ellie [*looking almost dangerous*]. Set him thinking about me if you dare.

Mrs Hushabye. Well, of all the impudent little fiends I ever met! Hector says there is a certain point at which the only answer you can give to a man who breaks all the rules is to knock him down. What would you say if I were to box your ears?

Ellie [*calmly*]. I should pull your hair.

Mrs Hushabye [*mischievously*]. That wouldnt hurt me. Perhaps it comes off at night.

Ellie [*so taken aback that she drops off the table and runs to her*]. Oh, you dont mean to say, Hesione, that your beautiful black hair is false?

Mrs Hushabye [*patting it*]. Dont tell Hector. He believes in it.

Ellie [*groaning*]. Oh! Even the hair that ensnared him false! Everything false!

Mrs Hushabye. Pull it and try. Other women can snare men in their hair; but I can swing a baby on mine. Aha! You cant do that, Goldylocks.

Ellie [*heartbroken*]. No. You have stolen my babies.

Mrs Hushabye. Pettikins: dont make me cry. You know, what you said about my making a household pet of him is a little true. Perhaps he ought to have waited for you. Would any other woman on earth forgive you?

Ellie. Oh, what right had you to take him all for yourself! [*Pulling herself together.*] There! You couldnt help it: neither of us could help it. He couldnt help it. No: dont say anything more: I cant bear it. Let us wake the object. [*She begins stroking Mangan's head, reversing the movement with which she put him to sleep.*] Wake up, do you hear? You are to wake up at once. Wake up, wake up, wake—

Mangan [*bouncing out of the chair in a fury and turning on them*]. Wake up! So you think Ive been asleep, do you? [*He kicks the chair violently back out of his way, and gets between them.*] You throw me into a trance so that I cant move hand or foot—I might have been buried alive! it's a mercy I wasnt—and then you think I was only asleep. If youd let me drop the two times you rolled me about, my nose would have been flattened for life against the floor. But Ive found you all out, anyhow. I know the sort of people I'm among now. Ive heard every word youve said, you and your precious father, and [*To Mrs Hushabye.*] you too. So I'm an object, am I? I'm a thing, am I? I'm a fool that hasnt sense enough to feed myself properly, am I? I'm afraid of the men that would starve if it weren't for the wages I give them, am I? I'm nothing but a disgusting old skinflint to be made a convenience of by designing women and fool managers of my works, am I? I'm—

Mrs Hushabye [*with the most elegant aplomb*]. Sh-sh-sh-
sh-sh! Mr Mangan: you are bound in honor to obliter-
ate from your mind all you heard while you were pretending to be asleep. It was not meant for you to hear.

Mangan. Pretending to be asleep! Do you think if I was only
pretending that I'd have sprawled there helpless, and
listened to such unfairness, such lies, such injustice and
plotting and backbiting and slandering of me, if I could
have up and told you what I thought of you! I wonder I
didnt burst.

Mrs Hushabye [*sweetly*]. You dreamt it all, Mr Mangan. We
were only saying how beautifully peaceful you looked
in your sleep. That was all, wasnt it, Ellie? Believe me,
Mr Mangan, all those unpleasant things came into your
mind in the last half second before you woke. Ellie
rubbed your hair the wrong way; and the disagreeable
sensation suggested a disagreeable dream.

Mangan [*doggedly*]. I believe in dreams.

Mrs Hushabye. So do I. But they go by contraries, dont they?

Mangan [*depths of emotion suddenly welling up in him*]. I
shant forget, to my dying day, that when you gave me
the glad eye that time in the garden, you were making a
fool of me. That was a dirty low mean thing to do. You
had no right to let me come near you if I disgusted you.
It isnt my fault if I'm old and havnt a moustache like a
bronze candlestick as your husband has. There are
things no decent woman would do to a man—like a man
hitting a woman in the breast.

[*Hesione, utterly shamed, sits down on the sofa and covers
her face with her hands. Mangan sits down also on his
chair and begins to cry like a child. Ellie stares at them.
Mrs Hushabye, at the distressing sound he makes, takes
down her hands and looks at him. She rises and runs
to him.*]

Mrs Hushabye. Dont cry: I cant bear it. Have I broken your
heart? I didnt know you had one. How could I?

Mangan. I'm a man aint I?

Mrs Hushabye [*half coaxing, half rallying, altogether tenderly*]. Oh no: not what I call a man. Only a Boss: just
that and nothing else. What business has a Boss with a
heart?

Mangan. Then youre not a bit sorry for what you did, nor
ashamed?

Mrs Hushabye. I was ashamed for the first time in my life

when you said that about hitting a woman in the breast,
and I found out what I'd done. My very bones blushed
red. Youve had your revenge, Boss. Arent you satisfied?

Mangan. Serve you right! Do you hear? Serve you right!
Youre just cruel. Cruel.

Mrs Hushabye. Yes: cruelty would be delicious if one could
only find some sort of cruelty that didnt really hurt. By
the way [*Sitting down beside him on the arm of the
chair.*], whats your name? It's not really Boss, is it?

Mangan [*shortly*]. If you want to know, my name's Alfred.

Mrs Hushabye [*springing up*]. Alfred! Ellie: he was christened after Tennyson!!!

Mangan [*rising*]. I was christened after my uncle, and never
had a penny from him, damn him! What of it?

Mrs. Hushabye. It comes to me suddenly that you are a real
person: that you had a mother, like anyone else. [*Putting her hands on his shoulders and surveying him.*]
Little Alf!

Mangan. Well, you have a nerve.

Mrs Hushabye. And you have a heart, Alfy, a whimpering
little heart, but a real one. [*Releasing him suddenly.*]
Now run and make it up with Ellie. She has had time to
think what to say to you, which is more than I had.
[*She goes out quickly into the garden by the port door.*]

Mangan. That woman has a pair of hands that go right
through you.

Ellie. Still in love with her, in spite of all we said about you?

Mangan. Are all women like you two? Do they never think
of anything about a man except what they can get out
of him? You werent even thinking that about me. You
were only thinking whether your gloves would last.

Ellie. I shall not have to think about that when we are
married.

Mangan. And you think I am going to marry you after what
I heard there!

Ellie. You heard nothing from me that I did not tell you
before.

Mangan. Perhaps you think I cant do without you.

Ellie. I think you would feel lonely without us all now, after
coming to know us so well.

Mangan [*with something like a yell of despair*]. Am I never
to have the last word?

Captain Shotover [*appearing at the starboard garden door*].
There is a soul in torment here. What is the matter?

Mangan. This girl doesnt want to spend her life wondering how long her gloves will last.

Captain Shotover [*passing through*]. Dont wear any. I never do. [*He goes into the pantry.*]

Lady Utterword [*appearing at the port garden door, in a handsome dinner dress*]. Is anything the matter?

Ellie. This gentleman wants to know is he never to have the last word?

Lady Utterword [*coming forward to the sofa*]. I should let him have it, my dear. The important thing is not to have the last word, but to have your own way.

Mangan. She wants both.

Lady Utterword. She wont get them, Mr Mangan. Providence always has the last word.

Mangan [*desperately*]. Now you are going to come religion over me. In this house a man's mind might as well be a football. I'm going. [*He makes for the hall, but is stopped by a hail from the Captain, who has just emerged from his pantry.*]

Captain Shotover. Whither away, Boss Mangan?

Mangan. To hell out of this house: let that be enough for you and all here.

Captain Shotover. You were welcome to come: you are free to go. The wide earth, the high seas, the spacious skies are waiting for you outside.

Lady Utterword. But your things, Mr Mangan. Your bags, your comb and brushes, your pyjamas—

Hector [*who has just appeared in the port doorway in a handsome Arab costume*]. Why should the escaping slave take his chains with him?

Mangan. Thats right, Hushabye. Keep the pyjamas, my lady; and much good may they do you.

Hector [*advancing to Lady Utterword's left hand*]. Let us all go out into the night and leave everything behind us.

Mangan. You stay where you are, the lot of you. I want no company, especially female company.

Ellie. Let him go. He is unhappy here. He is angry with us.

Captain Shotover. Go, Boss Mangan; and when you have found the land where there is happiness and where there are no women, send me its latitude and longitude; and I will join you there.

Lady Utterword. You will certainly not be comfortable without your luggage, Mr Mangan.

Ellie [*impatient*]. Go, go; why dont you go? It is a heavenly

night: you can sleep on the heath. Take my waterproof
   to lie on: it is hanging up in the hall.

Hector. Breakfast at nine, unless you prefer to breakfast with
   the Captain at six.

Ellie. Good night, Alfred.

Hector. Alfred! [*He runs back to the door and calls into the
   garden.*] Randall: Mangan's Christian name is Alfred.

Randall [*appearing in the starboard doorway in evening
   dress*]. Then Hesione wins her bet.

[*Mrs Hushabye appears in the port doorway. She throws her
   left arm round Hector's neck; draws him with her to the
   back of the sofa; and throws her right arm round Lady
   Utterword's neck.*]

Mrs Hushabye. They wouldnt believe me, Alf.

[*They contemplate him.*]

Mangan. Is there any more of you coming in to look at me,
   as if I was the latest thing in a menagerie?

Mrs Hushabye. You are the latest thing in this menagerie.

[*Before Mangan can retort, a fall of furniture is heard from
   upstairs; then a pistol shot, and a yell of pain. The
   staring group breaks up in consternation.*]

Mazzini's Voice [*from above*]. Help! A burglar! Help!

Hector [*his eyes blazing*]. A burglar!!!

Mrs Hushabye. No, Hector: youll be shot. [*But it is too late:
   he has dashed out past Mangan, who hastily moves towards the bookshelves out of his way.*]

Captain Shotover [*blowing his whistle*]. All hands aloft! [*He
   strides out after Hector.*]

Lady Utterword. My diamonds! [*She follows the Captain.*]

Randall [*rushing after her*]. No, Ariadne. Let me.

Ellie. Oh, is papa shot? [*She runs out.*]

Mrs Hushabye. Are you frightened, Alf?

Mangan. No. It aint my house, thank God.

Mrs Hushabye. If they catch a burglar, shall we have to go
   into court as witnesses, and be asked all sorts of questions about our private lives?

Mangan. You wont be believed if you tell the truth.

[*Mazzini, terribly upset, with a duelling pistol in his hand,
   comes from the hall, and makes his way to the drawing-
   table.*]

Mazzini. Oh, my dear Mrs Hushabye, I might have killed
   him. [*He throws the pistol on the table and staggers
   round to the chair.*] I hope you wont believe I really
   intended to.

[*Hector comes in, marching an old and villainous looking man before him by the collar. He plants him in the middle of the room and releases him. Ellie follows, and immediately runs across to the back of her father's chair and pats his shoulders.*]

Randall [*entering with a poker*]. Keep your eye on this door, Mangan. I'll look after the other. [*He goes to the starboard door and stands on guard there.*]

[*Lady Utterword comes in after Randall and goes between Mrs Hushabye and Mangan. Nurse Guinness brings up the rear, and waits near the door, on Mangan's left.*]

Mrs Hushabye. What has happened?

Mazzini. Your housekeeper told me there was somebody upstairs, and gave me a pistol that Mr Hushabye had been practising with. I thought it would frighten him; but it went off at a touch.

The Burglar. Yes, and took the skin off my ear. Precious near took the top off my head. Why dont you have a proper revolver instead of a thing like that, that goes off if you as much as blow on it?

Hector. One of my duelling pistols. Sorry.

Mazzini. He put his hands up and said it was a fair cop.

The Burglar. So it was. Send for the police.

Hector. No, by thunder! It was not a fair cop. We were four to one.

Mrs Hushabye. What will they do to him?

The Burglar. Ten years. Beginning with solitary. Ten years off my life. I shant serve it all: I'm too old. It will see me out.

Lady Utterword. You should have thought of that before you stole my diamonds.

The Burglar. Well, youve got them back, lady: havent you? Can you give me back the years of my life you are going to take from me?

Mrs Hushabye. Oh, we cant bury a man alive for ten years for a few diamonds.

The Burglar. Ten little shining diamonds! Ten long black years!

Lady Utterword. Think of what it is for us to be dragged through the horrors of a criminal court, and have all our family affairs in the papers! If you were a native, and Hastings could order you a good beating and send you away, I shouldnt mind; but here in England there is no real protection for any respectable person.

The Burglar. I'm too old to be give a hiding, lady. Send for the police and have done with it. It's only just and right you should.

Randall [*who has relaxed his vigilance on seeing the burglar so pacifically disposed, and comes forward swinging the poker between his fingers like a well-folded umbrella*]. It is neither just nor right that we should be put to a lot of inconvenience to gratify your moral enthusiasm, my friend. You had better get out, while you have the chance.

The Burglar [*inexorably*]. No. I must work my sin off my conscience. This has come as a sort of call to me. Let me spend the rest of my life repenting in a cell. I shall have my reward above.

Mangan [*exasperated*]. The very burglars cant behave naturally in this house.

Hector. My good sir: you must work out your salvation at somebody else's expense. Nobody here is going to charge you.

The Burglar. Oh, you wont charge me, wont you?

Hector. No. I'm sorry to be inhospitable; but will you kindly leave the house?

The Burglar. Right. I'll go to the police station and give myself up. [*He turns resolutely to the door; but Hector stops him.*]

Hector.
Randall. } Oh no. You mustnt do that.
No, no. Clear out, man, cant you; and dont be a fool.
Mrs Hushabye. } Dont be so silly. Cant you repent at home?

Lady Utterword. You will have to do as you are told.

The Burglar. It's compounding a felony, you know.

Mrs Hushabye. This is utterly ridiculous. Are we to be forced to prosecute this man when we dont want to?

The Burglar. Am I to be robbed of my salvation to save you the trouble of spending a day at the sessions? Is that justice? Is it right? Is it fair to me?

Mazzini [*rising and leaning across the table persuasively as if it were a pulpit desk or a shop counter*]. Come, come! let me shew you how you can turn your very crimes to account. Why not set up as a locksmith? You must know more about locks than most honest men?

The Burglar. Thats true, sir. But I couldnt set up as a locksmith under twenty pounds.

Randall. Well, you can easily steal twenty pounds. You will find it in the nearest bank.

The Burglar [*horrified*]. Oh what a thing for a gentleman to put into the head of a poor criminal scrambling out of the bottomless pit as it were Oh, shame on you, sir! Oh, God forgive you! [*He throws himself into the big chair and covers his face as if in prayer.*]

Lady Utterword. Really, Randall!

Hector. It seems to me that we shall have to take up a collection for this inopportunely contrite sinner.

Lady Utterword. But twenty pounds is ridiculous.

The Burglar [*looking up quickly*]. I shall have to buy a lot of tools, lady.

Lady Utterword. Nonsense: you have your burgling kit.

The Burglar. Whats a jimmy and a centrebit and an acetylene welding plant and a bunch of skeleton keys? I shall want a forge, and a smithy, and a shop, and fittings. I cant hardly do it for twenty.

Hector. My worthy friend, we havent got twenty pounds.

The Burglar [*now master of the situation*]. You can raise it among you, cant you?

Mrs Hushabye. Give him a sovereign, Hector, and get rid of him.

Hector [*giving him a pound*]. There! Off with you.

The Burglar [*rising and taking the money very ungratefully*]. I wont promise nothing. You have more on you than a quid: all the lot of you, I mean.

Lady Utterword [*vigorously*]. Oh, let us prosecute him and have done with it. I have a conscience too, I hope; and I do not feel at all sure that we have any right to let him go, especially if he is going to be greedy and impertinent.

The Burglar [*quickly*]. All right, lady, all right. Ive no wish to be anything but agreeable. Good evening, ladies and gentlemen; and thank you kindly.

[*He is hurrying out when he is confronted in the doorway by Captain Shotover.*]

Captain Shotover [*fixing the burglar with a piercing regard*]. Whats this? Are there two of you?

The Burglar [*falling on his knees before the Captain in abject terror*]. Oh my good Lord, what have I done? Dont tell me its your house Ive broken into, Captain Shotover.

[*The captain seizes him by the collar; drags him to his feet; and leads him to the middle of the group, Hector fall-*

ing back beside his wife to make way for them.]

Captain Shotover [*turning him towards Ellie*]. Is that your daughter? [*He releases him.*]

The Burglar. Well, how do I know, Captain? You know the sort of life you and me has led. Any young lady of that age might be my daughter anywhere in the wide world, as you might say.

Captain Shotover [*to Mazzini*]. You are not Billy Dunn. This is Billy Dunn. Why have you imposed on me?

The Burglar [*indignantly to Mazzini*]. Have you been giving yourself out to be me? You, that nigh blew my head off! Shooting yourself, in a manner of speaking!

Mazzini. My dear Captain Shotover, ever since I came into this house I have done hardly anything else but assure you that I am not Mr William Dunn, but Mazzini Dunn, a very different person.

The Burglar. He dont belong to my branch, Captain. Theres two sets in the family: the thinking Dunns and the drinking Dunns, each going their own ways. I'm a drinking Dunn: he's a thinking Dunn. But that didnt give him any right to shoot me.

Captain Shotover. So youve turned burglar, have you?

The Burglar. No, Captain: I wouldnt disgrace our old sea calling by such a thing. I am no burglar.

Lady Utterword. What were you doing with my diamonds?

Guinness. What did you break into the house for if youre no burglar?

Randall. Mistook the house for your own and came in by the wrong window, eh?

The Burglar. Well, it's no use my telling you a lie: I can take in most captains, but not Captain Shotover, because he sold himself to the devil in Zanzibar, and can divine water, spot gold, explode a cartridge in your pocket with a glance of his eye, and see the truth hidden in the heart of man. But I'm no burglar.

Captain Shotover. Are you an honest man?

The Burglar. I dont set up to be better than my fellow-creatures, and never did, as you well know, Captain. But what I do is innocent and pious. I enquire about for houses where the right sort of people live. I work it on them same as I worked it here. I break into the house; put a few spoons or diamonds in my pocket; make a noise; get caught; and take up a collection. And you wouldnt believe how hard it is to get caught when youre actually trying to. I have knocked over all the chairs in a room without a soul paying any attention to me. In the end I have had to walk out and leave the job.

Randall. When that happens, do you put back the spoons and diamonds?

The Burglar. Well, I dont fly in the face of Providence, if thats what you want to know.

Captain Shotover. Guinness: you remember this man?

Guinness. I should think I do, seeing I was married to him, the blackguard!

Hesione   ⎱ [*exclaiming* ⎰ Married to him!
Lady Utterword ⎰ *together*] ⎱ Guinness!!

The Burglar. It wasnt legal. Ive been married to no end of women. No use coming that over me.

Captain Shotover. Take him to the forecastle. [*He flings him to the door with a strength beyond his years.*]

Guinness. I suppose you mean the kitchen. They wont have him there. Do you expect servants to keep company with thieves and all sorts?

Captain Shotover. Land-thieves and water-thieves are the same flesh and blood. I'll have no boatswain on my quarterdeck. Off with you both.

The Burglar. Yes, Captain. [*He goes out humbly.*]

Mazzini. Will it be safe to have him in the house like that?

Guinness. Why didnt you shoot him, sir? If I'd known who he was, I'd have shot him myself. [*She goes out.*]

Mrs Hushabye. Do sit down, everybody. [*She sits down on the sofa.*]

[*They all move except Ellie. Mazzini resumes his seat. Randall sits down in the window-seat near the starboard door, again making a pendulum of his poker, and studying it as Galileo might have done. Hector sits on his left, in the middle. Mangan, forgotten, sits in the port corner. Lady Utterword takes the big chair. Captain Shotover goes into the pantry in deep abstraction. They all look after him; and Lady Utterword coughs consciously.*]

Mrs Hushabye. So Billy Dunn was poor nurse's little romance. I knew there had been somebody.

Randall. They will fight their battles over again and enjoy themselves immensely.

Lady Utterword [*irritably*]. You are not married; and you know nothing about it, Randall. Hold your tongue.

Randall. Tyrant!

Mrs Hushabye. Well, we have had a very exciting evening. Everything will be an anticlimax after it. We'd better all go to bed.

Randall. Another burglar may turn up.

Mazzini. Oh, impossible! I hope not.

Randall. Why not? There is more than one burglar in England.

Mrs Hushabye. What do you say, Alf?

Mangan [*huffily*]. Oh, I dont matter. I'm forgotten. The burglar has put my nose out of joint. Shove me into a corner and have done with me.

Mrs Hushabye [*jumping up mischievously, and going to him*]. Would you like a walk on the heath, Alfred? With me?

Ellie. Go, Mr Mangan. It will do you good. Hesione will soothe you.

Mrs Hushabye [*slipping her arm under his and pulling him upright*]. Come, Alfred. There is a moon: it's like the night in *Tristan and Isolde*. [*She caresses his arm and draws him to the port garden door.*]

Mangan [*writhing but yielding*]. How can you have the face —the heart— [*He breaks down and is heard sobbing as she takes him out.*]

Lady Utterword. What an extraordinary way to behave! What is the matter with the man?

Ellie [*in a strangely calm voice, staring into an imaginary distance*]. His heart is breaking: that is all. [*The Captain appears at the pantry door, listening.*] It is a curious sensation: the sort of pain that goes mercifully beyond our powers of feeling. When your heart is broken, your boats are burned: nothing matters any more. It is the end of happiness and the beginning of peace.

Lady Utterword [*suddenly rising in a rage, to the astonishment of the rest*]. How dare you?

Hector. Good heavens! Whats the matter?

Randall [*in a warning whisper*]. Tch—tch—tch! Steady.

Ellie [*surprised and haughty*]. I was not addressing you particularly, Lady Utterword. And I am not accustomed to be asked how dare I.

Lady Utterword. Of course not. Anyone can see how badly you have been brought up.

Mazzini. Oh, I hope not, Lady Utterword. Really!

Lady Utterword. I know very well what you meant. The impudence!

Ellie. What on earth do you mean?

Captain Shotover [*advancing to the table*]. She means that her heart will not break. She has been longing all her life for someone to break it. At last she has become afraid she has none to break.

Lady Utterword [*flinging herself on her knees and throwing her arms round him*]. Papa: dont say you think Ive no heart.

Captain Shotover [*raising her with grim tenderness*]. If you had no heart how could you want to have it broken, child?

Hector [*rising with a bound*]. Lady Utterword: you are not to be trusted. You have made a scene. [*He runs out into the garden through the starboard door.*]

Lady Utterword. Oh! Hector, Hector! [*She runs out after him.*]

Randall. Only nerves, I assure you. [*He rises and follows her, waving the poker in his agitation.*] Ariadne! Ariadne! For God's sake be careful. You will— [*He is gone.*]

Mazzini [*rising*]. How distressing! Can I do anything, I wonder?

Captain Shotover [*promptly taking his chair and setting to work at the drawing-board*]. No. Go to bed. Goodnight.

Mazzini [*bewildered*]. Oh! Perhaps you are right.

Ellie. Goodnight, dearest. [*She kisses him.*]

Mazzini. Goodnight, love. [*He makes for the door, but turns aside to the bookshelves.*] I'll just take a book. [*He takes one.*] Goodnight. [*He goes out, leaving Ellie alone with the Captain.*]

[*The Captain is intent on his drawing. Ellie, standing sentry over his chair, contemplates him for a moment.*]

Ellie. Does nothing ever disturb you, Captain Shotover?

Captain Shotover. Ive stood on the bridge for eighteen hours in a typhoon. Life here is stormier; but I can stand it.

Ellie. Do you think I ought to marry Mr Mangan?

Captain Shotover [*never looking up*]. One rock is as good as another to be wrecked on.

Ellie. I am not in love with him.

Captain Shotover. Who said you were?

Ellie. You are not surprised?

Captain Shotover. Surprised! At my age!

Ellie. It seems to me quite fair. He wants me for one thing: I want him for another.

Captain Shotover. Money?

Ellie. Yes.

Captain Shotover. Well, one turns the cheek: the other kisses it. One provides the cash: the other spends it.

Ellie. Who will have the best of the bargain, I wonder?

Captain Shotover. You. These fellows live in an office all day. You will have to put up with him from dinner to breakfast; but you will both be asleep most of that time. All day you will be quit of him; and you will be shopping with his money. If that is too much for you, marry a seafaring man: you will be bothered with him only three weeks in the year, perhaps.

Ellie. That would be best of all, I suppose.

Captain Shotover. It's a dangerous thing to be married right up to the hilt, like my daughter's husband. The man is at home all day, like a damned soul in hell.

Ellie. I never thought of that before.

Captain Shotover. If youre marrying for business, you cant be too businesslike.

Ellie. Why do women always want other women's husbands?

Captain Shotover. Why do horse-thieves prefer a horse that is broken-in to one that is wild?

Ellie [*with a short laugh*]. I suppose so. What a vile world it is!

Captain Shotover. It doesnt concern me. I'm nearly out of it.

Ellie. And I'm only just beginning.

Captain Shotover. Yes; so look ahead.

Ellie. Well, I think I am being very prudent.

Captain Shotover. I didnt say prudent. I said look ahead.

Ellie. Whats the difference?

Captain Shotover. It's prudent to gain the whole world and lose your own soul. But dont forget that your soul sticks to you if you stick to it; but the world has a way of slipping through your fingers.

Ellie [*wearily, leaving him and beginning to wander restlessly about the room*]. I'm sorry, Captain Shotover; but it's no use talking like that to me. Old-fashioned people are no use to me. Old-fashioned people think you can have a soul without money. They think the less money you have, the more soul you have. Young people nowadays know better. A soul is a very expensive thing to keep: much more so than a motor car.

Captain Shotover. Is it? How much does your soul eat?

Ellie. Oh, a lot. It eats music and pictures and books and mountains and lakes and beautiful things to wear and nice people to be with. In this country you cant have them without lots of money: that is why our souls are so horribly starved.

Captain Shotover. Mangan's soul lives on pigs' food.

Ellie. Yes: money is thrown away on him. I suppose his soul was starved when he was young. But it will not be thrown away on me. It is just because I want to save my soul that I am marrying for money. All the women who are not fools do.

Captain Shotover. There are other ways of getting money. Why dont you steal it?

Ellie. Because I dont want to go to prison.

Captain Shotover. Is that the only reason? Are you quite sure honesty has nothing to do with it?

Ellie. Oh, you are very old-fashioned, Captain. Does any modern girl believe that the legal and illegal ways of getting money are the honest and dishonest ways? Mangan robbed my father and my father's friends. I should rob all the money back from Mangan if the police would let me. As they wont, I must get it back by marrying him.

Captain Shotover. I cant argue: I'm too old: my mind is made up and finished. All I can tell you is that, old-fashioned or new-fashioned, if you sell yourself, you deal your soul a blow that all the books and pictures and concerts and scenery in the world wont heal. [*He gets up suddenly and makes for the pantry.*]

Ellie [*running after him and seizing him by the sleeve*]. Then why did you sell yourself to the devil in Zanzibar?

Captain Shotover [*stopping, startled*]. What?

Ellie. You shall not run away before you answer. I have found out that trick of yours. If you sold yourself, why shouldnt I?

Captain Shotover. I had to deal with men so degraded that they wouldnt obey me unless I swore at them and kicked them and beat them with my fists. Foolish people took young thieves off the streets; flung them into a training ship where they were taught to fear the cane instead of fearing God; and thought theyd made men and sailors of them by private subscription. I tricked these thieves into believing I'd sold myself to the devil. It saved my soul from the kicking and swearing that was damning me by inches.

Ellie [*releasing him*]. I shall pretend to sell myself to Boss

Mangan to save my soul from the poverty that is damning me by inches.

Captain Shotover. Riches will damn you ten times deeper. Riches wont save even your body.

Ellie. Old-fashioned again. We know now that the soul is the body, and the body the soul. They tell us they are different because they want to persuade us that we can keep our souls if we let them make slaves of our bodies. I am afraid you are no use to me, Captain.

Captain Shotover. What did you expect? A Savior, eh? Are you old-fashioned enough to believe in that?

Ellie. No. But I thought you were very wise, and might help me. Now I have found you out. You pretend to be busy, and think of fine things to say, and run in and out to surprise people by saying them, and get away before they can answer you.

Captain Shotover. It confuses me to be answered. It discourages me. I cannot bear men and women. I have to run away. I must run away now. [*He tries to.*]

Ellie [*again seizing his arm*]. You shall not run away from me. I can hypnotize you. You are the only person in the house I can say what I like to. I know you are fond of me. Sit down. [*She draws him to the sofa.*]

Captain Shotover [*yielding*]. Take care: I am in my dotage. Old men are dangerous: it doesnt matter to them what is going to happen to the world.

[*They sit side by side on the sofa. She leans affectionately against him, her head on his shoulder, eyes half closed.*]

Ellie [*dreamily*]. I should have thought nothing else mattered to old men. They cant be very interested in what is going to happen to themselves.

Captain Shotover. A man's interest in the world is only the overflow from his interest in himself. When you are a child your vessel is not yet full; so you care for nothing but your own affairs. When you grow up, your vessel overflows; and you are a politician, a philosopher, or an explorer and adventurer. In old age the vessel dries up: there is no overflow: you are a child again. I can give you the memories of my ancient wisdom: mere scraps and leavings; but I no longer really care for anything but my own little wants and hobbies. I sit here working out my old ideas as a means of destroying my fellow-creatures. I see my daughters and their men living foolish lives of romance and sentiment and snobbery. I see you, the younger generation, turning from their romance and sentiment and snobbery to money and comfort and hard common sense. I was ten times happier on the bridge in the typhoon, or frozen into Arctic ice for months in darkness, than you or they have ever been. You are looking for a rich husband. At your age I looked for hardship, danger, horror, and death, that I might feel the life in me more intensely. I did not let the fear of death govern my life; and my reward was, I had my life. You are going to let the fear of poverty govern your life; and your reward will be that you will eat, but you will not live.

Ellie [*sitting up impatiently*]. But what can I do? I am not a sea captain: I cant stand on bridges in typhoons, or go slaughtering seals and whales in Greenland's icy mountains. They wont let women be captains. Do you want me to be a stewardess?

Captain Shotover. There are worse lives. The stewardesses could come ashore if they liked; but they sail and sail and sail.

Ellie. What could they do ashore but marry for money? I dont want to be a stewardess: I am too bad a sailor. Think of something else for me.

Captain Shotover. I cant think so long and continuously. I am too old. I must go in and out. [*He tries to rise.*]

Ellie [*pulling him back*]. You shall not. You are happy here, arent you?

Captain Shotover. I tell you it's dangerous to keep me. I cant keep awake and alert.

Ellie. What do you run away for? To sleep?

Captain Shotover. No. To get a glass of rum.

Ellie [*frightfully disillusioned*]. Is that it? How disgusting! Do you like being drunk?

Captain Shotover. No: I dread being drunk more than anything in the world. To be drunk means to have dreams; to go soft; to be easily pleased and deceived; to fall into the clutches of women. Drink does that for you when you are young. But when you are old: very very old, like me, the dreams come by themselves. You dont know how terrible that is: you are young: you sleep at night only, and sleep soundly. But later on you will sleep in the afternoon. Later still you will sleep even in the morning; and you will awake tired, tired of life. You will never be free from dozing and dreams: the

dreams will steal upon your work every ten minutes
unless you can awaken yourself with rum. I drink now
to keep sober; but the dreams are conquering: rum
is not what it was: I have had ten glasses since you
came; and it might be so much water. Go get me another: Guinness knows where it is. You had better see
for yourself the horror of an old man drinking.

Ellie. You shall not drink. Dream. I like you to dream. You
must never be in the real world when we talk together.

Captain Shotover. I am too weary to resist or too weak. I
am in my second childhood. I do not see you as you
really are. I cant remember what I really am. I feel
nothing but the accursed happiness I have dreaded all
my life long: the happiness that comes as life goes, the
happiness of yielding and dreaming instead of resisting
and doing, the sweetness of the fruit that is going rotten.

Ellie. You dread it almost as much as I used to dread losing
my dreams and having to fight and do things. But that
is all over for me: my dreams are dashed to pieces. I
should like to marry a very old, very rich man. I should
like to marry you. I had much rather marry you than
marry Mangan. Are you very rich?

Captain Shotover. No. Living from hand to mouth. And I
have a wife somewhere in Jamaica: a black one. My
first wife. Unless she's dead.

Ellie. What a pity! I feel so happy with you. [*She takes his
hand, almost unconsciously, and pats it.*] I thought I
should never feel happy again.

Captain Shotover. Why?

Ellie. Dont you know?

Captain Shotover. No.

Ellie. Heartbreak. I fell in love with Hector, and didnt know
he was married.

Captain Shotover. Heartbreak? Are you one of those who
are so sufficient to themselves that they are only happy
when they are stripped of everything, even of hope?

Ellie [*gripping the hand*]. It seems so; for I feel now as if
there was nothing I could not do, because I want
nothing.

Captain Shotover. Thats the only real strength. Thats genius.
Thats better than rum.

Ellie [*throwing away his hand*]. Rum! Why did you spoil it?

[*Hector and Randall come in from the garden through the
starboard door.*]

Hector. I beg your pardon. We did not know there was anyone here.

Ellie [*rising*]. That means that you want to tell Mr Randall the story about the tiger. Come, Captain: I want to talk to my father; and you had better come with me.

Captain Shotover [*rising*]. Nonsense! the man is in bed.

Ellie. Aha! Ive caught you. My real father has gone to bed; but the father you gave me is in the kitchen. You knew quite well all along. Come. [*She draws him out into the garden with her through the port door.*]

Hector. Thats an extraordinary girl. She has the Ancient Mariner on a string like a Pekinese dog.

Randall. Now that they have gone, shall we have a friendly chat?

Hector. You are in what is supposed to be my house. I am at your disposal.

[*Hector sits down in the draughtsman's chair, turning it to face Randall, who remains standing, leaning at his ease against the carpenter's bench.*]

Randall. I take it that we may be quite frank. I mean about Lady Utterword.

Hector. You may. I have nothing to be frank about. I never met her until this afternoon.

Randall [*straightening up*]. What! But you are her sister's husband.

Hector. Well, if you come to that, you are her husband's brother.

Randall. But you seem to be on intimate terms with her.

Hector. So do you.

Randall. Yes; but I am on intimate terms with her. I have known her for years.

Hector. It took her years to get to the same point with you that she got to with me in five minutes, it seems.

Randall [*vexed*]. Really, Ariadne is the limit. [*He moves away huffishly towards the windows.*]

Hector [*coolly*]. She is, as I remarked to Hesione, a very enterprising woman.

Randall [*returning, much troubled*]. You see, Hushabye, you are what women consider a good-looking man.

Hector. I cultivated that appearance in the days of my vanity; and Hesione insists on my keeping it up. She makes me wear these ridiculous things [*indicating his Arab costume*] because she thinks me absurd in evening dress.

Randall. Still, you do keep it up, old chap. Now, I assure
   you I have not an atom of jealousy in my disposition—

Hector. The question would seem to be rather whether your
   brother has any touch of that sort.

Randall. What! Hastings! Oh, dont trouble about Hastings.
   He has the gift of being able to work sixteen hours a
   day at the dullest detail, and actually likes it. That gets
   him to the top wherever he goes. As long as Ariadne
   takes care that he is fed regularly, he is only too thankful to anyone who will keep her in good humor for
   him.

Hector. And as she has all the Shotover fascination, there
   is plenty of competition for the job, eh?

Randall [*angrily*]. She encourages them. Her conduct is perfectly scandalous. I assure you, my dear fellow, I
   havent an atom of jealousy in my composition; but she
   makes herself the talk of every place she goes to by
   her thoughtlessness. It's nothing more: she doesnt
   really care for the men she keeps hanging about her;
   but how is the world to know that? It's not fair to
   Hastings. It's not fair to me.

Hector. Her theory is that her conduct is so correct—

Randall. Correct! She does nothing but make scenes from
   morning till night. You be careful, old chap. She will
   get you into trouble: that is, she would if she really
   cared for you.

Hector. Doesnt she?

Randall. Not a scrap. She may want your scalp to add to her
   collection; but her true affection has been engaged years
   ago. You had really better be careful.

Hector. Do you suffer much from this jealousy?

Randall. Jealousy! I jealous! My dear fellow, havent I told
   you that there is not an atom of—

Hector. Yes. And Lady Utterword told me she never made
   scenes. Well, dont waste your jealousy on my moustache. Never waste jealousy on a real man: it is the
   imaginary hero that supplants us all in the long run.
   Besides, jealousy does not belong to your easy man-of-
   the-world pose, which you carry so well in other respects.

Randall. Really, Hushabye, I think a man may be allowed
   to be a gentleman without being accused of posing.

Hector. It is a pose like any other. In this house we know
   all the poses: our game is to find out the man under

the pose. The man under your pose is apparently Ellie's favorite, Othello.

Randall. Some of your games in this house are damned annoying, let me tell you.

Hector. Yes: I have been their victim for many years. I used to writhe under them at first; but I became accustomed to them. At last I learned to play them.

Randall. If it's all the same to you, I had rather you didnt play them on me. You evidently dont quite understand my character, or my notions of good form.

Hector. Is it your notion of good form to give away Lady Utterword?

Randall [*a childishly plaintive note breaking into his huff*]. I have not said a word against Lady Utterword. This is just the conspiracy over again.

Hector. What conspiracy?

Randall. You know very well, sir. A conspiracy to make me out to be pettish and jealous and childish and everything I am not. Everyone knows I am just the opposite.

Hector [*rising*]. Something in the air of the house has upset you. It often does have that effect. [*He goes to the garden door and calls Lady Utterword with commanding emphasis.*] Ariadne!

Lady Utterword [*at some distance*]. Yes.

Randall. What are you calling her for? I want to speak—

Lady Utterword [*arriving breathless*]. Yes. You really are a terribly commanding person. Whats the matter?

Hector. I do not know how to manage your friend Randall. No doubt you do.

Lady Utterword. Randall: have you been making yourself ridiculous, as usual? I can see it in your face. Really, you are the most pettish creature.

Randall. You know quite well, Ariadne, that I have not an ounce of pettishness in my disposition. I have made myself perfectly pleasant here. I have remained absolutely cool and imperturbable in the face of a burglar. Imperturbability is almost too strong a point of mine. But [*putting his foot down with a stamp, and walking angrily up and down the room*] I insist on being treated with a certain consideration. I will not allow Hushabye to take liberties with me. I will not stand your encouraging people as you do.

Hector. The man has a rooted delusion that he is your husband.

Lady Utterword. I know. He is jealous. As if he had any right to be! He compromises me everywhere. He makes scenes all over the place. Randall: I will not allow it. I simply will not allow it. You had no right to discuss me with Hector. I will not be discussed by men.

Hector. Be reasonable, Ariadne. Your fatal gift of beauty forces men to discuss you.

Lady Utterword. Oh indeed! what about your fatal gift of beauty?

Hector. How can I help it?

Lady Utterword. You could cut off your moustache: I cant cut off my nose. I get my whole life messed up with people falling in love with me. And then Randall says I run after men.

Randall. I——

Lady Utterword. Yes you do: you said it just now. Why cant you think of something else than women? Napoleon was quite right when he said that women are the occupation of the idle man. Well, if ever there was an idle man on earth, his name is Randall Utterword.

Randall. Ariad——

Lady Utterword [*overwhelming him with a torrent of words*]. Oh yes you are: it's no use denying it. What have you ever done? What good are you? You are as much trouble in the house as a child of three. You couldnt live without your valet.

Randall. This is——

Lady Utterword. Laziness! You are laziness incarnate. You are selfishness itself. You are the most uninteresting man on earth. You cant even gossip about anything but yourself and your grievances and your ailments and the people who have offended you. [*Turning to Hector.*] Do you know what they call him, Hector?

> *Hector* } [*speaking* { Please dont tell me.
> *Randall* } *together*] { I'll not stand it——

Lady Utterword. Randall the Rotter: that is his name in good society.

Randall [*shouting*]. I'll not bear it, I tell you. Will you listen to me, you infernal—— [*He chokes.*]

Lady Utterword. Well: go on. What were you going to call me? An infernal what? Which unpleasant animal is it to be this time?

Randall [*foaming*]. There is no animal in the world so hateful as a woman can be. You are a maddening devil.

Hushabye: you will not believe me when I tell you that I have loved this demon all my life; but God knows I have paid for it. [*He sits down in the draughtsman's chair, weeping.*]

Lady Utterword [*standing over him with triumphant contempt*]. Cry-baby!

Hector [*gravely, coming to him*]. My friend: the Shotover sisters have two strange powers over men. They can make them love; and they can make them cry. Thank your stars that you are not married to one of them.

Lady Utterword [*haughtily*]. And pray, Hector—

Hector [*suddenly catching her round the shoulders; swinging her right round him and away from Randall; and gripping her throat with the other hand*]. Ariadne: if you attempt to start on me, I'll choke you: do you hear? The cat-and-mouse game with the other sex is a good game; but I can play your head off at it. [*He throws her, not at all gently, into the big chair, and proceeds, less fiercely but firmly.*] It is true that Napoleon said that woman is the occupation of the idle man. But he added that she is the relaxation of the warrior. Well, *I* am the warrior. So take care.

Lady Utterword [*not in the least put out, and rather pleased by his violence*]. My dear Hector: I have only done what you asked me to do.

Hector. How do you make that out, pray?

Lady Utterword. You called me in to manage Randall, didnt you? You said you couldnt manage him yourself.

Hector. Well, what if I did? I did not ask you to drive the man mad.

Lady Utterword. He isnt mad. Thats the way to manage him. If you were a mother, youd understand.

Hector. Mother! What are you up to now?

Lady Utterword. It's quite simple. When the children got nerves and were naughty, I smacked them just enough to give them a good cry and a healthy nervous shock. They went to sleep and were quite good afterwards. Well, I cant smack Randall: he is too big; so when he gets nerves and is naughty, I just rag him till he cries. He will be all right now. Look: he is half asleep already. [*Which is quite true.*]

Randall [*waking up indignantly*]. I'm not. You are most cruel, Ariadne. [*Sentimentally.*] But I suppose I must forgive you, as usual. [*He checks himself in the act of yawning.*]

Lady Utterword [*to Hector*]. Is the explanation satisfactory, dread warrior?

Hector. Some day I shall kill you, if you go too far. I thought you were a fool.

Lady Utterword [*laughing*]. Everybody does, at first. But I am not such a fool as I look. [*She rises complacently.*] Now, Randall: go to bed. You will be a good boy in the morning.

Randall [*only very faintly rebellious*]. I'll go to bed when I like. It isnt ten yet.

Lady Utterword. It is long past ten. See that he goes to bed at once, Hector. [*She goes into the garden.*]

Hector. Is there any slavery on earth viler than this slavery of men to women?

Randall [*rising resolutely*]. I'll not speak to her tomorrow. I'll not speak to her for another week. I'll give her such a lesson. I'll go straight to bed without bidding her goodnight. [*He makes for the door leading to the hall.*]

Hector. You are under a spell, man. Old Shotover sold himself to the devil in Zanzibar. The devil gave him a black witch for a wife; and these two demon daughters are their mystical progeny. I am tied to Hesione's apronstring; but I'm her husband; and if I did go stark staring mad about her, at least we became man and wife. But why should you let yourself be dragged about and beaten by Ariadne as a toy donkey is dragged about and beaten by a child? What do you get by it? Are you her lover?

Randall. You must not misunderstand me. In a higher sense —in a Platonic sense—

Hector. Psha! Platonic sense! She makes you her servant; and when pay-day comes round, she bilks you: that is what you mean.

Randall [*feebly*]. Well, if I dont mind, I dont see what business it is of yours. Besides, I tell you I am going to punish her. You shall see: *I* know how to deal with women. I'm really very sleepy. Say goodnight to Mrs Hushabye for me, will you, like a good chap. Goodnight. [*He hurries out.*]

Hector. Poor wretch! Oh women! women! women! [*He lifts his fists in invocation to heaven.*] Fall. Fall and crush. [*He goes out into the garden.*]

*In the garden, Hector, as he comes out through the glass
door of the poop, finds Lady Utterword lying voluptuously
in the hammock on the east side of the flagstaff, in the circle
of light cast by the electric arc, which is like a moon in its
opal globe. Beneath the head of the hammock, a campstool.
On the other side of the flagstaff, on the long garden seat,
Captain Shotover is asleep, with Ellie beside him, leaning
affectionately against him on his right hand. On his left is a
deck chair. Behind them in the gloom, Hesione is strolling
about with Mangan. It is a fine still night, moonless.*

Lady Utterword. What a lovely night! It seems made for us.

Hector. The night takes no interest in us. What are we to
the night? [*He sits down moodily in the deck chair.*]

Ellie [*dreamily, nestling against the Captain*]. Its beauty
soaks into my nerves. In the night there is peace for the
old and hope for the young.

Hector. Is that remark your own?

Ellie. No. Only the last thing the Captain said before he
went to sleep.

Captain Shotover. I'm not asleep.

Hector. Randall is. Also Mr Mazzini Dunn. Mangan too,
probably.

Mangan. No.

Hector. Oh, you are there. I thought Hesione would have
sent you to bed by this time.

Mrs Hushabye [*coming to the back of the garden seat, into
the light, with Mangan*]. I think I shall. He keeps telling me he has a presentiment that he is going to die.
I never met a man so greedy for sympathy.

Mangan [*plaintively*]. But I have a presentiment. I really
have. And you wouldnt listen.

Mrs Hushabye. I was listening for something else. There was
a sort of splendid drumming in the sky. Did none of

you hear it? It came from a distance and then died away.

Mangan. I tell you it was a train.

Mrs Hushabye. And *I* tell you, Alf, there is no train at this hour. The last is nine forty-five.

Mangan. But a goods train.

Mrs Hushabye. Not on our little line. They tack a truck on to the passenger train. What can it have been, Hector?

Hector. Heaven's threatening growl of disgust at us useless futile creatures. [*Fiercely.*] I tell you, one of two things must happen. Either out of that darkness some new creation will come to supplant us as we have supplanted the animals, or the heavens will fall in thunder and destroy us.

Lady Utterword [*in a cool instructive manner, wallowing comfortably in her hammock*]. We have not supplanted the animals, Hector. Why do you ask heaven to destroy this house, which could be made quite comfortable if Hesione had any notion of how to live? Dont you know what is wrong with it?

Hector. We are wrong with it. There is no sense in us. We are useless, dangerous, and ought to be abolished.

Lady Utterword. Nonsense! Hastings told me the very first day he came here, nearly twenty-four years ago, what is wrong with the house.

Captain Shotover. What! The numskull said there was something wrong with my house!

Lady Utterword. I said Hastings said it; and he is not in the least a numskull.

Captain Shotover. Whats wrong with my house?

Lady Utterword. Just what is wrong with a ship, papa. Wasnt it clever of Hastings to see that?

Captain Shotover. The man's a fool. Theres nothing wrong with a ship.

Lady Utterword. Yes there is.

Mrs Hushabye. But what is it? Dont be aggravating, Addy.

Lady Utterword. Guess.

Hector. Demons. Daughters of the witch of Zanzibar. Demons.

Lady Utterword. Not a bit. I assure you, all this house needs to make it a sensible, healthy, pleasant house, with good appetites and sound sleep in it, is horses.

Mrs Hushabye. Horses! What rubbish!

Lady Utterword. Yes: horses. Why have we never been able to let this house? Because there are no proper stables. Go anywhere in England where there are natural, wholesome, contented, and really nice English people; and what do you always find? That the stables are the real centre of the household; and that if any visitor wants to play the piano the whole room has to be upset before it can be opened, there are so many things piled on it. I never lived until I learned to ride; and I shall never ride really well because I didnt begin as a child. There are only two classes in good society in England: the equestrian classes and the neurotic classes. It isnt mere convention: everybody can see that the people who hunt are the right people and the people who dont are the wrong ones.

Captain Shotover. There is some truth in this. My ship made a man of me; and a ship is the horse of the sea.

Lady Utterword. Exactly how Hastings explained your being a gentleman.

Captain Shotover. Not bad for a numskull. Bring the man here with you next time: I must talk to him.

Lady Utterword. Why is Randall such an obvious rotter? He is well bred; he has been at a public school and a university; he has been in the Foreign Office; he knows the best people and has lived all his life among them. Why is he so unsatisfactory, so contemptible? Why cant he get a valet to stay with him longer than a few months? Just because he is too lazy and pleasure-loving to hunt and shoot. He strums the piano, and sketches, and runs after married women, and reads literary books and poems. He actually plays the flute; but I never let him bring it into my house. If he would only— [*She is interrupted by the melancholy strains of a flute coming from an open window above. She raises herself indignantly in the hammock.*] Randall: you have not gone to bed. Have you been listening? [*The flute replies pertly*]:

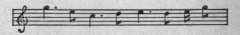

How vulgar! Go to bed instantly, Randall: how dare you? [*The window is slammed down. She subsides.*]

How can anyone care for such a creature!

Mrs Hushabye. Addy: do you think Ellie ought to marry poor Alfred merely for his money?

Mangan [*much alarmed*]. Whats that? Mrs Hushabye: are my affairs to be discussed like this before everybody?

Lady Utterword. I dont think Randall is listening now.

Mangan. Everybody is listening. It isnt right.

Mrs Hushabye. But in the dark, what does it matter? Ellie doesnt mind. Do you, Ellie?

Ellie. Not in the least. What is your opinion, Lady Utterword? You have so much good sense.

Mangan. But it isnt right. It— [*Mrs Hushabye puts her hand on his mouth.*] Oh, very well.

Lady Utterword. How much money have you, Mr Mangan?

Mangan. Really—No: I cant stand this.

Lady Utterword. Nonsense, Mr Mangan! It all turns on your income, doesnt it?

Mangan. Well, if you come to that, how much money has she?

Ellie. None.

Lady Utterword. You are answered, Mr Mangan. And now, as you have made Miss Dunn throw her cards on the table, you cannot refuse to shew your own.

Mrs Hushabye. Come, Alf! out with it! How much?

Mangan [*baited out of all prudence*]. Well, if you want to know, I have no money and never had any.

Mrs Hushabye. Alfred: you mustnt tell naughty stories.

Mangan. I'm not telling you stories. I'm telling you the raw truth.

Lady Utterword. Then what do you live on, Mr Mangan?

Mangan. Travelling expenses. And a trifle of commission.

Captain Shotover. What more have any of us but travelling expenses for our life's journey?

Mrs Hushabye. But you have factories and capital and things?

Mangan. People think I have. People think I'm an industrial Napoleon. Thats why Miss Ellie wants to marry me. But I tell you I have nothing.

Ellie. Do you mean that the factories are like Marcus's tigers? That they dont exist?

Mangan. They exist all right enough. But theyre not mine. They belong to syndicates and shareholders and all sorts of lazy good-for-nothing capitalists. I get money from such people to start the factories. I find people like Miss Dunn's father to work them, and keep a tight hand so as to make them pay. Of course I make them keep me going pretty well; but it's a dog's life; and I dont own anything.

Mrs Hushabye. Alfred, Alfred: you are making a poor mouth of it to get out of marrying Ellie.

Mangan. I'm telling the truth about my money for the first time in my life; and it's the first time my word has ever been doubted.

Lady Utterword. How sad! Why dont you go in for politics, Mr Mangan?

Mangan. Go in for politics! Where have you been living? I am in politics.

Lady Utterword. I'm sure I beg your pardon. I never heard of you.

Mangan. Let me tell you, Lady Utterword, that the Prime Minister of this country asked me to join the Government without even going through the nonsense of an election, as the dictator for a great public department.

Lady Utterword. As a Conservative or a Liberal?

Mangan. No such nonsense. As a practical business man. [*They all burst out laughing.*] What are you all laughing at?

Mrs Hushabye. Oh, Alfred, Alfred!

Ellie. You! who have to get my father to do everything for you!

Mrs Hushabye. You! who are afraid of your own workmen!

Hector. You! with whom three women have been playing cat and mouse all the evening!

Lady Utterword. You must have given an immense sum to the party funds, Mr Mangan.

Mangan. Not a penny out of my own pocket. The syndicate found the money: they knew how useful I should be to them in the Government.

Lady Utterword. This is most interesting and unexpected, Mr Mangan. And what have your administrative achievements been, so far?

Mangan. Achievements? Well, I dont know what you call achievements; but Ive jolly well put a stop to the games of the other fellows in the other departments. Every man of them thought he was going to save the country all by himself, and do me out of the credit and out of my chance of a title. I took good care that if they wouldnt let me do it they shouldnt do it themselves either. I may not know anything about my own machinery; but I know how to stick a ramrod into the other fellow's. And now they all look the biggest fools going.

Hector. And in heaven's name, what do you look like?

Mangan. I look like the fellow that was too clever for all the others, dont I? If that isnt a triumph of practical business, what is?

Hector. Is this England, or is it a madhouse?

Lady Utterword. Do you expect to save the country, Mr Mangan?

Mangan. Well, who else will? Will your Mr Randall save it?

Lady Utterword. Randall the rotter! Certainly not.

Mangan. Will your brother-in-law save it with his moustache and his fine talk?

Hector. Yes, if they will let me.

Mangan [*sneering*]. Ah! Will they let you?

Hector. No. They prefer you.

Mangan. Very well then, as youre in a world where I'm appreciated and youre not, youd best be civil to me, hadnt you? Who else is there but me?

Lady Utterword. There is Hastings. Get rid of your ridiculous sham democracy; and give Hastings the necessary powers, and a good supply of bamboo to bring the British native to his senses: he will save the country with the greatest ease.

Captain Shotover. It had better be lost. Any fool can govern with a stick in his hand. *I* could govern that way. It is not God's way. The man is a numskull.

Lady Utterword. The man is worth all of you rolled into one. What do you say, Miss Dunn?

Ellie. I think my father would do very well if people did not put upon him and cheat him and despise him because he is so good.

Mangan [*contemptuously*]. I think I see Mazzini Dunn getting into parliament or pushing his way into the Government. Weve not come to that yet, thank God! What do you say, Mrs Hushabye?

Mrs Hushabye. Oh, *I* say it matters very little which of you governs the country so long as we govern you.

Hector. We? Who is we, pray?

Mrs Hushabye. The devil's granddaughters, dear. The lovely women.

Hector [*raising his hands as before*]. Fall, I say; and deliver us from the lures of Satan!

Ellie. There seems to be nothing real in the world except my father and Shakespear. Marcus's tigers are false; Mr Mangan's millions are false; there is nothing really strong and true about Hesione but her beautiful black hair; and Lady Utterword's is too pretty to be real. The one thing that was left to me was the Captain's seventh degree of concentration; and that turns out to be—

Captain Shotover. Rum.

Lady Utterword [*placidly*]. A good deal of my hair is quite genuine. The Duchess of Dithering offered me fifty guineas for this [*touching her forehead*] under the impression that it was a transformation; but it is all natural except the color.

Mangan [*wildly*]. Look here: I'm going to take off all my clothes. [*He begins tearing off his coat.*]

Lady Utterword.	[*in consterna-tion*]	Mr Mangan!
Captain Shotover.		Whats that?
Hector.		Ha! ha! Do. Do.
Ellie.		Please dont.

Mrs Hushabye [*catching his arm and stopping him*]. Alfred! for shame! Are you mad?

Mangan. Shame! What shame is there in this house? Let's all strip stark naked. We may as well do the thing thoroughly when we're about it. Weve stripped ourselves morally naked: well, let us strip ourselves physically naked as well, and see how we like it. I tell you I cant bear this. I was brought up to be respectable. I dont mind the women dyeing their hair and the men drinking: it's human nature. But it's not human nature to tell everybody about it. Every time one of you opens your mouth I go like this [*he cowers as if to avoid a missile*] afraid of what will come next. How are we to have any self-respect if we dont keep it up that we're better than we really are?

Lady Utterword. I quite sympathize with you, Mr Mangan. I have been through it all; and I know by experience that men and women are delicate plants and must be cultivated under glass. Our family habit of throwing stones in all directions and letting the air in is not only unbearably rude, but positively dangerous. Still, there is no use catching physical colds as well as moral ones; so please keep your clothes on.

Mangan. I'll do as I like: not what you tell me. Am I a child or a grown man? I wont stand this mothering tyranny. I'll go back to the city, where I'm respected and made much of.

Mrs Hushabye. Goodbye, Alf. Think of us sometimes in the city. Think of Ellie's youth!

Ellie. Think of Hesione's eyes and hair!

Captain Shotover. Think of this garden in which you are not a dog barking to keep the truth out!

Hector. Think of Lady Utterword's beauty! her good sense! her style!

Lady Utterword. Flatterer. Think, Mr Mangan, whether you can really do any better for yourself elsewhere: that is the essential point, isnt it?

Mangan [*surrendering*]. All right: all right. I'm done. Have it your own way. Only let me alone. I dont know whether I'm on my head or my heels when you all start on me like this. I'll stay. I'll marry her. I'll do anything for a quiet life. Are you satisfied now?

Ellie. No. I never really intended to make you marry me, Mr Mangan. Never in the depths of my soul. I only wanted to feel my strength: to know that you could not escape if I chose to take you.

Mangan [*indignantly*]. What! Do you mean to say you are going to throw me over after my acting so handsome?

Lady Utterword. I should not be too hasty, Miss Dunn. You can throw Mr Mangan over at any time up to the last moment. Very few men in his position go bankrupt. You can live very comfortably on his reputation for immense wealth.

Ellie. I cannot commit bigamy, Lady Utterword.

Mrs Hushabye.		Bigamy! Whatever on earth are you talking about, Ellie?
Lady Utterword.	[*exclaiming all together*]	Bigamy! What do you mean, Miss Dunn?
Mangan.		Bigamy! Do you mean to say youre married already?
Hector.		Bigamy! This is some enigma.

Ellie. Only half an hour ago I became Captain Shotover's white wife.

Mrs Hushabye. Ellie! What nonsense! Where?

Ellie. In heaven, where all true marriages are made.

Lady Utterword. Really, Miss Dunn! Really, papa!

Mangan. He told me *I* was too old! And him a mummy!

Hector [*quoting Shelley*].

> "Their altar the grassy earth outspread,
> And their priest the muttering wind."

Ellie. Yes: I, Ellie Dunn, give my broken heart and my strong sound soul to its natural captain, my spiritual husband and second father.

[*She draws the Captain's arm through hers, and pats his hand. The Captain remains fast asleep.*]

Mrs Hushabye. Oh, thats very clever of you, pettikins. Very clever. Alfred: you could never have lived up to Ellie. You must be content with a little share of me.

Mangan [*sniffing and wiping his eyes*]. It isnt kind— [*His emotion chokes him.*]

Lady Utterword. You are well out of it, Mr Mangan. Miss Dunn is the most conceited young woman I have met since I came back to England.

Mrs Hushabye. Oh, Ellie isnt conceited. Are you, pettikins?

Ellie. I know my strength now, Hesione.

Mangan. Brazen, I call you. Brazen.

Mrs Hushabye. Tut tut, Alfred: dont be rude. Dont you feel how lovely this marriage night is, made in heaven? Arent you happy, you and Hector? Open your eyes: Addy and Ellie look beautiful enough to please the most fastidious man: we live and love and have not a care in the world. We women have managed all that for you. Why in the name of common sense do you go on as if you were two miserable wretches?

Captain Shotover. I tell you happiness is no good. You can be happy when you are only half alive. I am happier now I am half dead than ever I was in my prime. But there is no blessing on my happiness.

Ellie [*her face lighting up*]. Life with a blessing! that is what I want. Now I know the real reason why I couldnt marry Mr Mangan: there would be no blessing on our marriage. There is a blessing on my broken heart. There is a blessing on your beauty, Hesione. There is a blessing on your father's spirit. Even on the lies of Marcus there is a blessing; but on Mr Mangan's money there is none.

Mangan. I dont understand a word of that.

Ellie. Neither do I. But I know it means something.

Mangan. Dont say there was any difficulty about the blessing. I was ready to get a bishop to marry us.

Mrs Hushabye. Isnt he a fool, pettikins?

Hector [*fiercely*]. Do not scorn the man. We are all fools.

[*Mazzini, in pyjamas and a richly colored silk dressing-gown, comes from the house, on Lady Utterword's side.*]

Mrs Hushabye. Oh! here comes the only man who ever resisted me. Whats the matter, Mr Dunn? Is the house on fire?

Mazzini. Oh no: nothing's the matter: but really it's impossible to go to sleep with such an interesting conversation going on under one's window, and on such a beautiful night too. I just had to come down and join you all. What has it all been about?

Mrs Hushabye. Oh, wonderful things, soldier of freedom.

Hector. For example, Mangan, as a practical business man, has tried to undress himself and has failed ignominiously; whilst you, as an idealist, have succeeded brilliantly.

Mazzini. I hope you dont mind my being like this, Mrs Hushabye. [*He sits down on the campstool.*]

Mrs Hushabye. On the contrary, I could wish you always like that.

Lady Utterword. Your daughter's match is off, Mr Dunn. It seems that Mr Mangan, whom we all supposed to be a man of property, owns absolutely nothing.

Mazzini. Well of course I knew that, Lady Utterword. But if people believe in him and are always giving him money, whereas they dont believe in me and never give me any, how can I ask poor Ellie to depend on what I can do for her?

Mangan. Dont you run away with this idea that I have nothing. I——

Hector. Oh, dont explain. We understand. You have a couple of thousand pounds in exchequer bills, 50,000 shares worth tenpence a dozen, and half a dozen tabloids of cyanide of potassium to poison yourself with when you are found out. Thats the reality of your millions.

Mazzini. Oh no, no, no. He is quite honest: the businesses are genuine and perfectly legal.

Hector [*disgusted*]. Yah! Not even a great swindler!

Mangan. So you think. But Ive been too many for some honest men, for all that.

Lady Utterword. There is no pleasing you, Mr Mangan. You are determined to be neither rich nor poor, honest nor dishonest.

Mangan. There you go again. Ever since I came into this silly house I have been made to look like a fool, though I'm as good a man in this house as in the city.

Ellie [*musically*]. Yes: this silly house, this strangely happy house, this agonizing house, this house without foundations. I shall call it Heartbreak House.

Mrs Hushabye. Stop, Ellie; or I shall howl like an animal.

Mangan [*breaks into a low snivelling*]!!!

Mrs Hushabye. There! you have set Alfred off.

Ellie. I like him best when he is howling.

Captain Shotover. Silence! [*Mangan subsides into silence.*] I say, let the heart break in silence.

Hector. Do you accept that name for your house?

Captain Shotover. It is not my house: it is only my kennel.

Hector. We have been too long here. We do not live in this house: we haunt it.

Lady Utterword [*heart torn*]. It is dreadful to think how you have been here all these years while I have gone round the world. I escaped young; but it has drawn me back. It wants to break my heart too. But it shant. I have left you and it behind. It was silly of me to come back. I felt sentimental about papa and Hesione and the old place. I felt them calling to me.

Mazzini. But what a very natural and kindly and charming human feeling, Lady Utterword!

Lady Utterword. So I thought, Mr Dunn. But I know now that it was only the last of my influenza. I found that I was not remembered and not wanted.

Captain Shotover. You left because you did not want us. Was there no heartbreak in that for your father? You tore yourself up by the roots; and the ground healed up and brought forth fresh plants and forgot you. What right had you to come back and probe old wounds?

Mrs Hushabye. You were a complete stranger to me at first, Addy; but now I feel as if you had never been away.

Lady Utterword. Thank you, Hesione; but the influence is quite cured. The place may be Heartbreak House to you, Miss Dunn, and to this gentleman from the city who seems to have so little self-control; but to me it is only a very ill-regulated and rather untidy villa without any stables.

Hector. Inhabited by——?

Ellie. A crazy old sea captain and a young singer who adores him.

Mrs Hushabye. A sluttish female, trying to stave off a double chin and an elderly spread, vainly wooing a born soldier of freedom.

Mazzini. Oh, really, Mrs Hushabye——

Mangan. A member of His Majesty's Government that everybody sets down as a nincompoop: dont forget him, Lady Utterword.

Lady Utterword. And a very fascinating gentleman whose chief occupation is to be married to my sister.

Hector. All heartbroken imbeciles.

Mazzini. Oh no. Surely, if I may so, rather a favorable specimen of what is best in our English culture. You are very charming people, most advanced, unprejudiced, frank, humane, unconventional, democratic, free-thinking, and everything that is delightful to thoughtful people.

Mrs Hushabye. You do us proud, Mazzini.

Mazzini. I am not flattering, really. Where else could I feel perfectly at ease in my pyjamas? I sometimes dream that I am in very distinguished society, and suddenly I have nothing on but my pyjamas! Sometimes I havent even pyjamas. And I always feel overwhelmed with confusion. But here, I dont mind in the least: it seems quite natural.

Lady Utterword. An infallible sign that you are not now in really distinguished society, Mr Dunn. If you were in my house, you would feel embarrassed.

Mazzini. I shall take particular care to keep out of your house, Lady Utterword.

Lady Utterword. You will be quite wrong, Mr Dunn. I should make you very comfortable; and you would not have the trouble and anxiety of wondering whether you should wear your purple and gold or your green and crimson dressing-gown at dinner. You complicate life instead of simplifying it by doing these ridiculous things.

Ellie. Your house is not Heartbreak House: is it, Lady Utterword?

Hector. Yet she breaks hearts, easy as her house is. That poor devil upstairs with his flute howls when she twists his heart, just as Mangan howls when my wife twists his.

Lady Utterword. That is because Randall has nothing to do but have his heart broken. It is a change from having his head shampooed. Catch anyone breaking Hastings' heart!

Captain Shotover. The numskull wins, after all.

Lady Utterword. I shall go back to my numskull with the greatest satisfaction when I am tired of you all, clever as you are.

Mangan [*huffily*]. I never set up to be clever.

Lady Utterword. I forgot you, Mr Mangan.

Mangan. Well, I dont see that quite, either.

Lady Utterword. You may not be clever, Mr Mangan; but you are successful.

Mangan. But I dont want to be regarded merely as a successful man. I have an imagination like anyone else. I have a presentiment—

Mrs Hushabye. Oh, you are impossible, Alfred. Here I am devoting myself to you; and you think of nothing but your ridiculous presentiment. You bore me. Come and talk poetry to me under the stars. [*She drags him away into the darkness.*]

Mangan [*tearfully, as he disappears*]. Yes: it's all very well to make fun of me; but if you only knew—

Hector [*impatiently*]. How is all this going to end?

Mazzini. It wont end, Mr Hushabye. Life doesnt end: it goes on.

Ellie. Oh, it cant go on for ever. I'm always expecting something. I dont know what it is; but life must come to a point sometime.

Lady Utterword. The point for a young woman of your age is a baby.

Hector. Yes, but, damn it, I have the same feeling; and *I* cant have a baby.

Lady Utterword. By deputy, Hector.

Hector. But I have children. All that is over and done with for me: and yet I too feel that this cant last. We sit here talking, and leave everything to Mangan and to chance and to the devil. Think of the powers of destruction that Mangan and his mutual admiration gang wield! It's madness: it's like giving a torpedo to a badly brought up child to play at earthquakes with.

Mazzini. I know. I used often to think about that when I
was young.

Hector. Think! Whats the good of thinking about it? Why
didnt you do something?

Mazzini. But I did. I joined societies and made speeches and
wrote pamphlets. That was all I could do. But, you
know, though the people in the societies thought they
knew more than Mangan, most of them wouldnt have
joined if they had known as much. You see they had
never had any money to handle or any men to manage.
Every year I expected a revolution, or some frightful
smash-up: it seemed impossible that we could blunder
and muddle on any longer. But nothing happened, except, of course, the usual poverty and crime and drink
that we are used to. Nothing ever does happen. It's
amazing how well we get along, all things considered.

Lady Utterword. Perhaps somebody cleverer than you and
Mr Mangan was at work all the time.

Mazzini. Perhaps so. Though I was brought up not to believe in anything, I often feel that there is a great deal
to be said for the theory of an overruling Providence,
after all.

Lady Utterword. Providence! I meant Hastings.

Mazzini. Oh, I beg your pardon, Lady Utterword.

Captain Shotover. Every drunken skipper trusts to Providence. But one of the ways of Providence with drunken
skippers is to run them on the rocks.

Mazzini. Very true, no doubt, at sea. But in politics, I assure
you, they only run into jellyfish. Nothing happens.

Captain Shotover. At sea nothing happens to the sea. Nothing happens to the sky. The sun comes up from the
east and goes down to the west. The moon grows from
a sickle to an arc lamp, and comes later and later
until she is lost in the light as other things are lost in
the darkness. After the typhoon, the flying-fish glitter
in the sunshine like birds. It's amazing how they get
along, all things considered. Nothing happens, except
something not worth mentioning.

Ellie. What is that, O Captain, my captain?

Captain Shotover [*savagely*]. Nothing but the smash of the
drunken skipper's ship on the rocks, the splintering of
her rotten timbers, the tearing of her rusty plates, the
drowning of the crew like rats in a trap.

Ellie. Moral: dont take rum.

Captain Shotover [*vehemently*]. That is a lie, child. Let a man drink ten barrels of rum a day, he is not a drunken skipper until he is a drifting skipper. Whilst he can lay his course and stand on his bridge and steer it, he is no drunkard. It is the man who lies drinking in his bunk and trusts to Providence that I call the drunken skipper, though he drank nothing but the waters of the River Jordan.

Ellie. Splendid! And you havent had a drop for an hour. You see you dont need it: your own spirit is not dead.

Captain Shotover. Echoes: nothing but echoes. The last shot was fired years ago.

Hector. And this ship that we are all in? This soul's prison we call England?

Captain Shotover. The captain is in his bunk, drinking bottled ditch-water; and the crew is gambling in the forecastle. She will strike and sink and split. Do you think the laws of God will be suspended in favor of England because you were born in it?

Hector. Well, I dont mean to be drowned like a rat in a trap. I still have the will to live. What am I to do?

Captain Shotover. Do? Nothing simpler. Learn your business as an Englishman.

Hector. And what may my business as an Englishman be, pray?

Captain Shotover. Navigation. Learn it and live; or leave it and be damned.

Ellie. Quiet, quiet: youll tire yourself.

Mazzini. I thought all that once, Captain; but I assure you nothing will happen.

[*A dull distant explosion is heard.*]

Hector [*starting up*]. What was that?

Captain Shotover. Something happening. [*He blows his whistle.*] Breakers ahead!

[*The light goes out.*]

Hector [*furiously*]. Who put that light out? Who dared put that light out?

Nurse Guinness [*running in from the house to the middle of the esplanade*]. I did, sir. The police have telephoned to say we'll be summoned if we dont put that light out: it can be seen for miles.

Hector. It shall be seen for a hundred miles. [*He dashes into the house.*]

Nurse Guinness. The rectory is nothing but a heap of bricks, they say. Unless we can give the rector a bed he has nowhere to lay his head this night.

Captain Shotover. The Church is on the rocks, breaking up. I told him it would unless it headed for God's open sea.

Nurse Guinness. And you are all to go down to the cellars.

Captain Shotover. Go there yourself, you and all the crew. Batten down the hatches.

Nurse Guinness. And hide beside the coward I married! I'll go on the roof first. [*The lamp lights up again.*] There! Mr Hushabye's turned it on again.

The Burglar [*hurrying in and appealing to Nurse Guinness*]. Here: wheres the way to that gravel pit? The boot-boy says theres a cave in the gravel pit. Them cellars is no use. Wheres the gravel pit, Captain?

Nurse Guinness. Go straight on past the flagstaff until you fall into it and break your dirty neck. [*She pushes him contemptuously towards the flagstaff, and herself goes to the foot of the hammock and waits there, as it were by Ariadne's cradle.*]

[*Another and louder explosion is heard. The burglar stops and stands trembling.*]

Ellie [*rising*]. That was nearer.

Captain Shotover. The next one will get us. [*He rises.*] Stand by, all hands, for judgment.

The Burglar. Oh my Lordy God! [*He rushes away frantically past the flagstaff into the gloom.*]

Mrs Hushabye [*emerging panting from the darkness*]. Who was that running away? [*She comes to Ellie.*] Did you hear the explosions? And the sound in the sky: it's splendid: it's like an orchestra: it's like Beethoven.

Ellie. By thunder, Hesione: it is Beethoven.

[*She and Hesione throw themselves into one another's arms in wild excitement. The light increases.*]

Mazzini [*anxiously*]. The light is getting brighter.

Nurse Guinness [*looking up at the house*]. It's Mr Hushabye turning on all the lights in the house and tearing down the curtains.

Randall [*rushing in in his pyjamas, distractedly waving a flute*]. Ariadne: my soul, my precious, go down to the cellars: I beg and implore you, go down to the cellars!

Lady Utterword [*quite composed in her hammock*]. The governor's wife in the cellars with the servants! Really, Randall!

Randall. But what shall I do if you are killed?

Lady Utterword. You will probably be killed, too, Randall. Now play your flute to shew that you are not afraid; and be good. Play us Keep the home fires burning.

Nurse Guinness [*grimly*]. Theyll keep the home fires burning for us: them up there.

Randall [*having tried to play*]. My lips are trembling. I cant get a sound.

Mazzini. I hope poor Mangan is safe.

Mrs Hushabye. He is hiding in the cave in the gravel pit.

Captain Shotover. My dynamite drew him there. It is the hand of God.

Hector [*returning from the house and striding across to his former place*]. There is not half light enough. We should be blazing to the skies.

Ellie [*tense with excitement*]. Set fire to the house, Marcus.

Mrs Hushabye. My house! No.

Hector. I thought of that; but it would not be ready in time.

Captain Shotover. The judgment has come. Courage will not save you; but it will shew that your souls are still alive.

Mrs Hushabye. Sh-sh! Listen: do you hear it now? It's magnificent.

[*They all turn away from the house and look up, listening.*]

Hector [*gravely*]. Miss Dunn: you can do no good here. We of this house are only moths flying into the candle. You had better go down to the cellar.

Ellie [*scornfully*]. I dont think.

Mazzini. Ellie, dear, there is no disgrace in going to the cellar. An officer would order his soldiers to take cover. Mr Hushabye is behaving like an amateur. Mangan and the burglar are acting very sensibly; and it is they who will survive.

Ellie. Let them. I shall behave like an amateur. But why should you run any risk?

Mazzini. Think of the risk those poor fellows up there are running!

Nurse Guinness. Think of them, indeed, the murdering blackguards! What next?

[*A terrific explosion shakes the earth. They reel back into their seats, or clutch the nearest support. They hear the falling of the shattered glass from the windows.*]

Mazzini. Is anyone hurt?

Hector. Where did it fall?

Nurse Guinness [*in hideous triumph*]. Right in the gravel pit:
   I seen it. Serve un right! I seen it. [*She runs away
   towards the gravel pit, laughing harshly.*]

Hector. One husband gone.

Captain Shotover. Thirty pounds of good dynamite wasted.

Mazzini. Oh, poor Mangan!

Hector. Are you immortal that you need pity him? Our turn
   next.

[*They wait in silence and intense expectation. Hesione and
   Ellie hold each other's hand tight. A distant explosion
   is heard.*]

Mrs Hushabye [*relaxing her grip*]. Oh! they have passed us.

Lady Utterword. The danger is over, Randall. Go to bed.

Captain Shotover. Turn in, all hands. The ship is safe. [*He
   sits down and goes asleep.*]

Ellie [*disappointedly*]. Safe!

Hector [*disgustedly*]. Yes, safe. And how damnably dull the
   world has become again suddenly! [*He sits down.*]

Mazzini [*sitting down*]. I was quite wrong, after all. It is we
   who have survived; and Mangan and the burglar—

Hector. —the two burglars—

Lady Utterword. —the two practical men of business—

Mazzini. —both gone. And the poor clergyman will have
   to get a new house.

Mrs Hushabye. But what a glorious experience! I hope theyll
   come again tomorrow night.

Ellie [*radiant at the prospect*]. Oh, I hope so.

[*Randall at last succeeds in keeping the home fires burning
   on his flute.*]

John Galsworthy **Loyalties**

Some Platitudes
Concerning Drama (1909)

BY JOHN GALSWORTHY

A drama must be shaped so as to have a spire of meaning. Every grouping of life and character has its inherent moral; and the business of the dramatist is so to pose the group as to bring that moral poignantly to the light of day. Such is the moral that exhales from plays like *Lear, Hamlet,* and *Macbeth.* But such is not the moral to be found in the great bulk of contemporary Drama. The moral of the average play is now, and probably has always been, the triumph at all costs of a supposed immediate ethical good over a supposed immediate ethical evil.

The vice of drawing these distorted morals has permeated the drama to its spine; discolored its art, humanity, and significance; infected its creators, actors, audience, critics; too often turned it from a picture into a caricature. A drama which lives under the shadow of the distorted moral forgets how to be free, fair, and fine—forgets so completely that it often prides itself on having forgotten.

Now, in writing plays, there are, in this matter of the moral, three courses open to the serious dramatist. The first is: To definitely set before the public that which it wishes to have set before it, the views and codes of life by which the public lives and in which it believes. This way is the most common, successful, and popular. It makes the dramatist's position sure, and not too obviously authoritative.

The second course is: To definitely set before the public those views and codes of life by which the dramatist himself lives, those theories in which he himself believes, the more effectively if they are the opposite of what the public wishes to have placed before it, presenting them so that the audience may swallow them like powder in a spoonful of jam.

There is a third course: To set before the public no cut-and-dried codes, but the phenomena of life and character, selected and combined, *but not distorted,* by the dramatist's outlook, set down without fear, favor, or prejudice, leaving the public to draw such poor moral as nature may afford. This third method requires a certain detachment; it requires a sympathy with, a love of, and a curiosity as to, things for their own sake; it requires a far view, together with patient industry, for no immediately practical result.

It was once said of Shakespeare that he had never done any good to anyone, and never would. This, unfortunately, could not, in the sense in which the word "good" was then meant, be said of most modern dramatists. In truth, the good that Shakespeare did to humanity was of a remote, and, shall we say, eternal nature; something of the good that men get from having the sky and the sea to look at. And this partly because he was, in his greater plays at all events, free from the habit of drawing a distorted moral. Now, the playwright who supplies to the public the facts of life distorted by the moral which it expects, does so that he may do the public what he considers an immediate good, by fortifying its prejudices; and the dramatist who supplies to the public facts distorted by his own advanced morality, does so because he considers that he will at once benefit the public by substituting for its worn-out ethics, his own. In both cases the advantage the dramatist hopes to confer on the public is immediate and practical.

But matters change, and morals change; men remain —and to set men, and the facts about them, down faithfully, so that they draw for us the moral of their natural actions, may also possibly be of benefit to the community. It is, at all events, harder then to set men and facts down, as they ought, or ought not to be. This, however, is not to say that a dramatist should, or indeed can, keep himself and his temperamental philosophy out of his work. As a man lives and thinks, so will he write. But it is certain, that to the making of good drama, as to the practice of every other art, there must be brought an almost passionate love of discipline, a white heat of self-respect, a desire to make the truest, fairest, best thing in one's power; and that to these must be added an eye that does not flinch. Such qualities alone will bring to a drama the selfless character which soaks it with inevitability.

The word "pessimist" is frequently applied to the few dramatists who have been content to work in this way. It has been applied, among others, to Euripides, to Shakespeare, to Ibsen; it will be applied to many in the future.

Nothing, however, is more dubious than the way in which these two words "pessimist" and "optimist" are used; for the optimist appears to be he who cannot bear the world as it is, and is forced by his nature to picture it as it ought to be, and the pessimist one who cannot only bear the world as it is, but loves it well enough to draw it faithfully. The true lover of the human race is surely he who can put up with it in all its forms, in vice as well as in virtue, in defeat no less than in victory; the true seer he who sees not only joy but sorrow, the true painter of human life one who blinks at nothing. It may be that he is also, incidentally, its true benefactor.

In the whole range of the social fabric there are only two impartial persons, the scientist and the artist, and under the latter heading such dramatists as desire to write not only for today, but for tomorrow, must strive to come.

But dramatists being as they are made—past remedy— it is perhaps more profitable to examine the various points at which their qualities and defects are shown.

The plot! A good plot is that sure edifice which slowly rises out of the interplay of circumstance on temperament, and temperament on circumstance, within the enclosing atmosphere of an idea. A human being is the best plot there is; it may be impossible to see why he is a good plot, because the idea within which he was brought forth cannot be fully grasped; but it is plain that *he is a good plot.* He is organic. And so it must be with a good play. Reason alone produces no good plots; they come by original sin, sure conception, and instinctive after-power of selecting what benefits the germ. A bad plot, on the other hand, is simply a row of stakes, with a character impaled on each—characters who would have liked to live, but came to untimely grief; who started bravely, but fell on these stakes, placed beforehand in a row, and were transfixed one by one, while their ghosts stride on, squeaking and gibbering, through the play. Whether these stakes are made of facts or of ideas, according to the nature of the dramatist who planted them, their effect on the unfortunate characters is the same; the creatures were begotten to be staked, and staked they are! The demand for a good plot, not unfrequently heard, commonly signifies: "Tickle my sensations by stuffing the play with arbitrary adventures, so that I need not be troubled to take the characters seriously. Set the persons of the play to action, regardless of time, sequence, atmosphere, and probability!"

Now, true dramatic action is what characters do, at once contrary, as it were, to expectation, and yet because they have already done other things. No dramatist should let his audience know what is coming; but neither should he suffer his characters to act without making his audience feel that those actions are in harmony with temperament, and arise from previous known actions, together with the temperaments and previous known actions of the other characters in the play. The dramatist who hangs his characters to his plot, instead of hanging his plot to his characters, is guilty of cardinal sin.

The dialogue! Good dialogue again is character, marshaled so as continually to stimulate interest or excitement. The reason good dialogue is seldom found in plays is merely that it is hard to write, for it requires not only a knowledge of what interests or excites, but such a feeling for character as brings misery to the dramatist's heart when his creations speak as they should not speak—ashes to his mouth when they say things for the sake of saying them—disgust when they are "smart."

The art of writing true dramatic dialogue is an austere art, denying itself all license, grudging every sentence devoted to the mere machinery of the play, suppressing all jokes and epigrams severed from character, relying for fun and pathos on the fun and tears of life. From start to finish good dialogue is handmade, like good lace; clear, of fine texture, furthering with each thread the harmony and strength of a design to which all must be subordinated.

But good dialogue is also spiritual action. In so far as the dramatist divorces his dialogue from spiritual action—that is to say, from progress of events, or toward events which are significant of character—he is stultifying τὸ δράμα the thing done; he may make pleasing disquisitions, he is not making drama. And in so far as he twists character to suit his moral or his plot, he is neglecting a first principle, that truth to Nature which alone invests art with handmade quality.

The dramatist's license, in fact, ends with his design. In conception alone he is free. He may take what character or group of characters he chooses, see them with what eyes, knit them with what idea, within the limits of his temperament; but once taken, seen, and knitted, he is bound to treat them like a gentleman, with the tenderest consideration of their mainsprings. Take care of character; action and dialogue will take care of themselves! The true dramatist gives full rein to his temperament in the scope and nature of his subject; having once selected subject and characters, he is just, gentle, restrained, neither gratifying his lust for praise at the expense of his offspring, nor using them as puppets to flout his audience. Being himself the nature that brought them forth, he guides them in the course predestined at their conception. So only have they a chance of defying Time, which is always lying in wait to destroy the false, topical, or fashionable, all—in a word—that is not based on the permanent elements of human nature. The perfect dramatist rounds up his characters and facts within the ring-fence of a dominant idea which fulfills the craving of his spirit; having got them there, he suffers them to live their own lives.

Plot, action, character, dialogue! But there is yet another subject for a platitude. Flavor! An impalpable quality, less easily captured than the scent of a flower, the peculiar and most essential attribute of any work of art! It is the thin, poignant spirit which hovers up out of a play, and is as much its differentiating essence as is caffeine of coffee. Flavor, in fine, is the spirit of the dramatist projected into his work in a state of volatility, so that no one can exactly lay hands on it, here, there, or anywhere. This distinctive essence of a play, marking its brand, is the one thing at which the dramatist cannot work, for it is outside his consciousness. A man may have many moods, he has but one spirit; and this spirit he communicates in some subtle, unconscious way to all his work. It waxes and wanes with the currents of his vitality, but no more alters than a chestnut changes into an oak.

For, in truth, dramas are very like unto trees, springing from seedlings, shaping themselves inevitably in accordance with the laws fast hidden within themselves, drinking sustenance from the earth and air, and in conflict with the natural forces round them. So they slowly come to full growth, until warped, stunted, or risen to fair and gracious height, they stand open to all the winds. And the trees that spring from each dramatist are of different race; he is the spirit of his own sacred grove, into which no stray tree can by any chance enter.

One more platitude. It is not unfashionable to pit one form of drama against another—holding up the naturalistic to the disadvantage of the epic; the epic to the belittlement of the fantastic; the fantastic to the detriment of the naturalistic. Little purpose is thus served. The essential meaning, truth, beauty, and irony of things may be revealed under all these forms. Vision over life and human nature can be as keen and just, the revelation as true, inspiring, delight-giving, and thought-provoking, whatever fashion be employed—it is simply a question of doing it well enough to uncover the kernel of the nut. Whether the violet come from Russia, from Parma, or from England, matters little. Close by the Greek temples at Paestum there are violets that seem redder, and sweeter, than any ever seen—as though they have sprung up out of the footprints of some old pagan goddess; but under the April sun, in a Devonshire lane, the little blue scentless violets capture every bit as much of the spring. And so it is with drama—no matter what its form—it need only be the "real thing," need only have caught some of the precious fluids, revelation, or delight, and imprisoned them within a chalice to which we may put our lips and continually drink.

And yet, starting from this last platitude, one may perhaps be suffered to speculate as to the particular forms that our renascent drama is likely to assume. For our drama is renascent, and nothing will stop its growth. It is not renascent because this or that man is writing, but because of a new spirit. A spirit that is no doubt in part the gradual outcome of the impact on our home-grown art, of Russian, French, and Scandinavian influences, but which in the main rises from an awakened humanity in the conscience of our time.

What, then, are to be the main channels down which the renascent English drama will float in the coming years? It is more than possible that these main channels will come to be two in number and situate far apart.

The one will be the broad and clear-cut channel of naturalism, down which will course a drama poignantly shaped, and inspired with high intention, but faithful to the seething and multiple life around us, drama such as some are inclined to term photographic, deceived by a seeming simplicity into forgetfulness of the old proverb, *"Ars est celare artem,"* and oblivious of the fact that, to be vital, to grip, such drama is in every respect as dependent on imagination, construction, selection, and elimination—the main laws of artistry—as ever was the romantic or rhapsodic play. The question of naturalistic technique will bear, indeed, much more study than has yet been given to it. The aim of the dramatist employing it is obviously to create such an illusion of actual life passing on the stage as to compel the spectator to pass through an experience of his own, to think, and talk, and move with the people he sees thinking, talking, and moving in front of him. A false phrase, a single word out of tune or time, will destroy that illusion and spoil the surface as surely as a stone heaved into a still pool shatters the image seen there. But this is only the beginning of the reason why the naturalistic is the most exacting and difficult of all techniques. It is easy enough to *reproduce* the exact conversation and movements of persons in a room; it is desperately hard to *produce* the perfectly natural conversation and movements of those persons, when each natural phrase spoken and each natural movement made has not only to contribute toward the growth and perfection of a drama's soul, but also to be a revelation, phrase by phrase, movement by movement, of essential traits of character. To put it another way, naturalistic art, when alive, indeed to be alive at all, is simply the art of manipulating a procession of most delicate symbols. Its service is the swaying and focusing of men's feelings and thought in the various departments of human life. It will be like a steady lamp, held up from time to time, in whose light things will be seen for a space clearly and in due proportion, freed from the mists of prejudice and partisanship.

And the other of these two main channels will, I think, be a twisting and delicious stream, which will bear on its breast new barques of poetry, shaped, it may be, like prose, but a prose incarnating through its fantasy and symbolism all the deeper aspirations, yearning, doubts, and mysterious stirrings of the human spirit; a poetic prose drama, emotionalizing us by its diversity and purity of form and invention, and whose province will be to disclose the elemental soul of man and the forces of Nature, not perhaps as the old tragedies disclosed them, not necessarily in the epic mood, but always with beauty and in the spirit of discovery.

Such will, I think, be the two vital forms of our drama in the coming generation. And between these two forms there must be no crude unions; they are too far apart, the cross is too violent. For, where there is a seeming blend of lyricism and naturalism, it will on examination be found, I think, to exist only in plays whose subjects or settings—as in Synge's *Playboy of the Western World,* or in Mr. Masefield's *Nan*—

are so removed from our ken that we cannot really tell, and therefore do not care, whether an absolute illusion is maintained. The poetry which may and should exist in naturalistic drama, can only be that of perfect rightness of proportion, rhythm, shape—the poetry, in fact, that lies in all vital things. It is the ill-mating of forms that has killed a thousand plays. We want no more bastard drama; no more attempts to dress out the simple dignity of everyday life in the peacock's feathers of false lyricism; no more straw-stuffed heroes or heroines; no more rabbits and goldfish from the conjurer's pockets, nor any limelight. Let us have starlight, moonlight, sunlight, and the light of our own self-respects.

Act 1.

 Scene I. *Charles Winsor's* dressing-room at Meldon Court, near Newmarket, of a night in early October.

 Scene II. *De Levis's* bedroom at Meldon Court, a few minutes later.

Act 2.

 Scene I. The card room of a London Club between four and five in the afternoon, three weeks later.

 Scene II. The sitting-room of the *Dancy's* flat, the following morning.

Act 3.

 Scene I. Old *Mr. Jacob Twisden's* room at *Twisden & Graviter's* in Lincoln's Inn Fields at four in the afternoon, three months later.

 Scene II. The same, next morning at half-past ten.

 Scene III. The sitting-room of the *Dancy's* flat, an hour later.

scene ONE

*The dressing-room of Charles Winsor, owner of Meldon
Court, near Newmarket; about eleven-thirty at night. The
room has pale grey walls, unadorned; the curtains are drawn
over a window Back Left Centre. A bed lies along the wall,
Left. An open door, Right Back, leads into Lady Adela's
bedroom; a door, Right Forward, into a long corridor, on to
which abut rooms in a row, the whole length of the house's
left wing. Winsor's dressing-table, with a light over it, is
Stage Right of the curtained window. Pyjamas are laid out
on the bed, which is turned back. Slippers are handy, and
all the usual gear of a well-appointed bed-dressing-room.
Charles Winsor, a tall, fair, good-looking man about thirty-
eight, is taking off a smoking-jacket.*

Winsor. Hallo! Adela!
Voice of Lady Adela [*from her bedroom*]. Hallo!
Winsor. In bed?
Voice of Lady Adela. No.
[*She appears in the doorway in under-garment and a wrap-
per. She, too, is fair, about thirty-five, rather delicious,
and suggestive of porcelain.*]
Winsor. Win at Bridge?
Lady Adela. No fear.
Winsor. Who did?
Lady Adela. Lord St Erth and Ferdy De Levis.
Winsor. That young man has too much luck—the young
    bounder won two races today; and he's as rich as
    Croesus.
Lady Adela. Oh! Charlie, he did look so exactly as if he'd
    sold me a carpet when I was paying him.
Winsor [*changing into slippers*]. His father did sell carpets,
    wholesale, in the City.

Lady Adela. Really? And you say I haven't intuition! [*With a finger on her lips.*] Morison's in there.

Winsor [*motioning towards the door, which she shuts*]. Ronny Dancy took a tenner off him, anyway, before dinner.

Lady Adela. No! How?

Winsor. Standing jump on to a book-case four feet high. De Levis had to pay up, and sneered at him for making money by parlour tricks. That young Jew gets himself disliked.

Lady Adela. Aren't you rather prejudiced?

Winsor. Not a bit. I like Jews. That's not against him— rather the contrary these days. But he pushes himself. The General tells me he's deathly keen to get into the Jockey Club. [*Taking off his tie.*] It's amusing to see him trying to get round old St Erth.

Lady Adela. If Lord St Erth and General Canynge backed him he'd get in if he *did* sell carpets!

Winsor. He's got some pretty good horses. [*Taking off his waistcoat.*] Ronny Dancy's on his bones again, I'm afraid. He had a bad day. When a chap takes to doing parlour stunts for a bet—it's a sure sign. What made him chuck the Army?

Lady Adela. He says it's too dull, now there's no fighting.

Winsor. Well, he can't exist on backing losers.

Lady Adela. Isn't it just like him to get married now? He really is the most reckless person.

Winsor. Yes. He's a queer chap. I've always liked him, but I've never quite made him out. What do you think of his wife?

Lady Adela. Nice child; awfully gone on him.

Winsor. Is *he*?

Lady Adela. Quite indecently—both of them. [*Nodding towards the wall, Left.*] They're next door.

Winsor. Who's beyond them?

Lady Adela. De Levis; and Margaret Orme at the end. Charlie, do you realise that the bathroom out there has to wash those four?

Winsor. I know.

Lady Adela. Your grandfather was crazy when he built this wing; six rooms in a row with balconies like an hotel, and only one bath—if we hadn't put ours in.

Winsor [*looking at his watch*]. Half-past eleven. [*Yawns.*] Newmarket always makes me sleepy. You're keeping

Morison up. [*Lady Adela goes to the door, blowing a kiss. Charles goes up to his dressing-table and begins to brush his hair, sprinkling on essence. There is a knock on the corridor door.*] Come in. [*De Levis enters, clad in pyjamas and flowered dressing-gown. He is a dark, good-looking, rather Eastern young man. His face is long and disturbed.*] Hallo! De Levis! Anything I can do for you?

De Levis [*in a voice whose faint exoticism is broken by a vexed excitement*]. I say, I'm awfully sorry, Winsor, but I thought I'd better tell you at once. I've just had— er—rather a lot of money stolen.

Winsor. What! [*There is something of outrage in his tone and glance, as who should say: "In my house?"*] How do you mean *stolen*?

De Levis. I put it under my pillow and went to have a bath; when I came back it was gone.

Winsor. Good Lord! How much?

De Levis. Nearly a thousand—nine hundred and seventy, I think.

Winsor. Phew! [*Again the faint tone of outrage, that a man should have so much money about him.*]

De Levis. I sold my Rosemary filly today on the course to Kentman the bookie, and he paid me in notes.

Winsor. What? That weed Dancy gave you in the Spring?

De Levis. Yes. But I tried her pretty high the other day; and she's in the Cambridgeshire. I was only out of my room a quarter of an hour, and I locked my door.

Winsor [*again outraged*]. You *locked*—

De Levis [*not seeing the fine shade*]. Yes, and had the key here. [*He taps his pocket.*] Look here! [*He holds out a pocket-book.*] It's been stuffed with my shaving papers.

Winsor [*between feeling that such things don't happen, and a sense that he will have to clear it up*]. This is damned awkward, De Levis.

De Levis [*with steel in his voice*]. Yes, I should like it back.

Winsor. Have you got the numbers of the notes?

De Levis. No.

Winsor. What were they?

De Levis. One hundred, three fifties, and the rest tens and fives.

Winsor. What d'you want me to do?

De Levis. Unless there's anybody you think—

Winsor [*eyeing him*]. Is it likely?

De Levis. Then I think the police ought to see my room.
    It's a lot of money.

Winsor. Good Lord! We're not in Town; there'll be nobody
    nearer than Newmarket at this time of night—four
    miles.

[*The door from the bedroom is suddenly opened and Lady
    Adela appears. She has on a lace cap over her finished
    hair, and the wrapper.*]

Lady Adela [*closing the door*]. What is it? Are you ill, Mr.
    De Levis?

Winsor. Worse; he's had a lot of money stolen. Nearly a
    thousand pounds.

Lady Adela. Gracious! Where?

De Levis. From under my pillow, Lady Adela—my door
    was locked—I was in the bathroom.

Lady Adela. But how fearfully thrilling!

Winsor. Thrilling! What's to be done? He wants it back.

Lady Adela. Of course! [*With sudden realisation.*] Oh! But—
    Oh! it's quite too unpleasant!

Winsor. Yes! What am I to do? Fetch the servants out of
    their rooms? Search the grounds? It'll make the devil
    of a scandal.

De Levis. Who's next to me?

Lady Adela [*coldly*]. Oh! Mr. De Levis!

Winsor. Next to you? The Dancys on this side, and Miss
    Orme on the other. What's that to do with it?

De Levis. They may have heard something.

Winsor. Let's get them. But Dancy was downstairs when I
    came up. Get Morison, Adela! No, look here! When
    was this exactly? Let's have as many alibis as we can.

De Levis. Within the last twenty minutes, certainly.

Winsor. How long has Morison been up with you?

Lady Adela. I came up at eleven, and rang for her at once.

Winsor [*looking at his watch*]. Half an hour. Then she's all
    right. Send her for Margaret and the Dancys—there's
    nobody else in this wing. No; send her to bed. We don't
    want gossip. D'you mind going yourself, Adela?

Lady Adela. Consult General Canynge, Charlie.

Winsor. Right. Could you get him too? D'you really want the
    police, De Levis?

De Levis [*stung by the faint contempt in his tone of voice*].
    Yes, I do.

Winsor. Then, look here, dear! Slip into my study and tele-
    phone to the police at Newmarket. There'll be some-

body there; they're sure to have drunks. I'll have
   Treasure up, and speak to him. [*He rings the bell.*]

[*Lady Adela goes out into her room and closes the door.*]

Winsor. Look here, De Levis! This isn't an hotel. It's the sort
   of thing that doesn't happen in a decent house. Are you
   sure you're not mistaken, and didn't have them stolen
   on the course?

De Levis. Absolutely. I counted them just before putting
   them under my pillow; then I locked the door and had
   the key here. There's only one door, you know.

Winsor. How was your window?

De Levis. Open.

Winsor [*drawing back the curtains of his own window*].
   You've got a balcony like this. Any sign of a ladder or
   anything?

De Levis. No.

Winsor. It must have been done from the window, unless
   someone had a skeleton key. Who knew you'd got that
   money? Where did Kentman pay you?

De Levis. Just around the corner in the further paddock.

Winsor. Anybody about?

De Levis. Oh, yes!

Winsor. Suspicious?

De Levis. I didn't notice anything.

Winsor. You must have been marked down and followed
   here.

De Levis. How would they know my room?

Winsor. Might have got it somehow. [*A knock from the
   corridor.*] Come in.

[*Treisure, the Butler, appears, a silent, grave man of almost
   supernatural conformity. De Levis gives him a quick,
   hard look, noted and resented by Winsor.*]

Treisure [*to Winsor*]. Yes, sir?

Winsor. Who valets Mr. De Levis?

Treisure. Roberts, sir.

Winsor. When was he up last?

Treisure. In the ordinary course of things, about ten o'clock,
   sir.

Winsor. When did he go to bed?

Treisure. I dismissed at eleven.

Winsor. But did he go?

Treisure. To the best of my knowledge. Is there anything *I*
   can do, sir?

Winsor [*disregarding a sign from De Levis*]. Look here,

Treisure, Mr. De Levis has had a large sum of money taken from his bedroom within the last half hour.

Treisure. Indeed, sir!

Winsor. Robert's quite all right, isn't he?

Treisure. He is, sir.

De Levis. How do you know?

[*Treisure's eyes rest on De Levis.*]

Treisure. I am a pretty good judge of character, sir, if you'll excuse me.

Winsor. Look here, De Levis, eighty or ninety notes must have been pretty bulky. You didn't have them on you at dinner?

De Levis. No.

Winsor. Where did you put them?

De Levis. In a boot, and the boot in my suitcase, and locked it.

[*Treisure smiles faintly.*]

Winsor [*again slightly outraged by such precautions in his house*]. And you found it locked—and took them from there to put under your pillow?

De Levis. Yes.

Winsor. Run your mind over things, Treisure—has any stranger been about?

Treisure. No, sir.

Winsor. This seems to have happened between 11:15 and 11:30. Is that right? [*De Levis nods.*] Any noise—anything outside—anything suspicious anywhere?

Treisure [*running his mind—very still*]. No, sir.

Winsor. What time did you shut up?

Treisure. I should say about eleven-fifteen, sir. As soon as Major Colford and Captain Dancy had finished billiards. What was Mr. De Levis doing out of his room, if I may ask, sir?

Winsor. Having a bath; with his room locked and the key in his pocket.

Treisure. Thank you, sir.

De Levis [*conscious of indefinable suspicion*]. Damn it! What do you mean? I *was.*

Treisure. I beg your pardon, sir.

Winsor [*concealing a smile*]. Look here, Treisure, it's infernally awkward for everybody.

Treisure. It is, sir.

Winsor. What do you suggest?

Treisure. The proper thing, sir, I suppose, would be a cordon and a complete search—in our interests.

Winsor. I entirely refuse to suspect anybody.

Treisure. But if Mr. De Levis feels otherwise, sir?

De Levis [*stammering*]. All I know is—the money was there, and it's gone.

Winsor [*compunctious*]. Quite! It's pretty sickening for you. But so it is for anybody else. However, we must do our best to get it back for you.

[*A knock on the door.*]

Winsor. Hallo! [*Treisure opens the door, and General Canynge enters.*] Oh! It's you, General. Come in. Adela's told you? [*General Canynge nods. He is a slim man of about sixty, very well preserved, intensely neat and self-contained, and still in evening dress. His eyelids droop slightly, but his eyes are keen and his expression astute.*] Well, General, what's the first move?

Canynge [*lifting his eyebrows*]. Mr. De Levis presses the matter?

De Levis [*flicked again*]. Unless you think it's too plebeian of me, General Canynge—a thousand pounds.

Canynge [*drily*]. Just so! Then we must wait for the police, Winsor. Lady Adela has got through to them. What height are these rooms from the ground, Treisure?

Treisure. Twenty-three feet from the terrace, sir.

Canynge. Any ladders near?

Treisure. One in the stables, sir, very heavy. No others within three hundred yards.

Canynge. Just slip down, and see whether that's been moved.

Treisure. Very good, General. [*He goes out.*]

De Levis [*uneasily*]. Of course, he—I suppose you—

Winsor. We do.

Canynge. You had better leave this in our hands, De Levis.

De Levis. Certainly; only, the way he—

Winsor [*curtly*]. Treisure has been here since he was a boy. I should as soon suspect myself.

De Levis [*looking from one to the other—with sudden anger*]. You seem to think—! What was I to do? Take it lying down and let whoever it is get clear off? I suppose it's natural to want my money back?

[*Canynge looks at his nails; Winsor out of the window.*]

Winsor [*turning*]. Of course, De Levis!

De Levis [*sullenly*]. Well, I'll go to my room. When the police come, perhaps you'll let me know. [*He goes out.*]

Winsor. Phew! Did you ever see such a dressing-gown?

[*The door is opened. Lady Adela and Margaret Orme come in. The latter is a vivid young lady of about twenty-five in a vivid wrapper; she is smoking a cigarette.*]

Lady Adela. I've told the Dancys—she was in bed. And I got through to Newmarket, Charles, and Inspector Dede is coming like the wind on a motor cycle.

Margaret. Did you say "like the wind," Adela? He must have imagination. Isn't this gorgeous? Poor little Ferdy!

Winsor [*vexed*]. You might take it seriously, Margaret; it's pretty beastly for us all. What time did *you* come up?

Margaret. I came up with Adela. Am I suspected, Charles? How thrilling!

Winsor. Did you hear anything?

Margaret. Only little Ferdy splashing.

Winsor. And saw nothing?

Margaret. Not even that, alas!

Lady Adela [*with a finger held out*]. Leste! Un peu leste! Oh! Here are the Dancys. Come in, you two!

[*Mabel and Ronald Dancy enter. She is a pretty young woman with bobbed hair, fortunately, for she has just got out of bed, and is in her nightgown and a wrapper. Dancy is in his smoking-jacket. He has a pale, determined face with high cheek-bones, small, deep-set dark eyes, reddish crisp hair, and looks like a horseman.*]

Winsor. Awfully sorry to disturb you, Mrs. Dancy; but I suppose you and Ronny haven't heard anything. De Levis's room is just beyond Ronny's dressing-room, you know.

Mabel. I've been asleep nearly half an hour, and Ronny's only just come up.

Canynge. Did you happen to look out of your window, Mrs. Dancy?

Mabel. Yes. I stood there quite five minutes.

Canynge. When?

Mabel. Just about eleven, I should think. It was raining hard then.

Canynge. Yes, it's just stopped. You saw nothing?

Mabel. No.

Dancy. What time does he say the money was taken?

Winsor. Between the quarter and half past. He'd locked his door and had the key with him.

Margaret. How quaint! Just like an hotel. Does he put his
   boots out?

Lady Adela. Don't be so naughty, Meg.

Canynge. When exactly did *you* come up, Dancy?

Dancy. About ten minutes ago. I'd only just got into my
   dressing-room before Lady Adela came. I've been writing letters in the hall since Colford and I finished billiards.

Canynge. You weren't up or anything in between?

Dancy. No.

Margaret. The mystery of the grey room.

Dancy. Oughtn't the grounds to be searched for foot-marks?

Canynge. That's for the police.

Dancy. The deuce! Are they coming?

Canynge. Directly. [*A knock.*] Yes? [*Treasure enters.*] Well?

Treasure. The ladder has not been moved, General. There
   isn't a sign.

Winsor. All right. Get Robert up, but don't say anything to
   him. By the way, we're expecting the police.

Treasure. I trust they will not find a mare's nest, sir, if I may
   say so. [*He goes.*]

Winsor. De Levis has got wrong with Treasure. [*Suddenly.*]
   But, I say, what would any of us have done if *we'd* been
   in his shoes?

Margaret. A thousand pounds? I can't even conceive having
   it.

Dancy. We probably shouldn't have found it out.

Lady Adela. No—but if we had.

Dancy. Come to you—as he did.

Winsor. Yes; but there's a way of doing things.

Canynge. We shouldn't have wanted the police.

Margaret. No. That's it. The hotel touch.

Lady Adela. Poor young man; I think we're rather hard on
   him.

Winsor. He sold that weed you gave him, Dancy, to Kentman, the bookie, and these were the proceeds.

Dancy. Oh!

Winsor. He'd tried her high, he said.

Dancy [*grimly*]. He would.

Mabel. Oh! Ronny, what bad luck!

Winsor. He must have been followed here. [*At the window.*]
   After rain like that, there ought to be footmarks.

[*The splutter of a motor cycle is heard.*]

Margaret. Here's the wind!

Winsor. What's the move now, General?

Canynge. You and I had better see the Inspector in De
Levis's room, Winsor. [*To the others.*] If you'll all be
handy, in case he wants to put questions for himself.

Margaret. I hope he'll want me; it's just too thrilling.

Dancy. I hope he won't want me; I'm dog-tired. Come on,
Mabel. [*He puts his arm in his wife's.*]

Canynge. Just a minute, Charles. [*He draws close to Winsor
as the others are departing to their rooms.*]

Winsor. Yes, General?

Canynge. We must be careful with this Inspector fellow.
If he pitches hastily on somebody in the house it'll be
very disagreeable.

Winsor. By Jove! It *will*.

Canynge. We don't want to rouse any ridiculous suspicion.

Winsor. Quite. [*A knock.*] Come in!

[*Treisure enters.*]

Treisure. Inspector Dede, sir.

Winsor. Show him in.

Treisure. Robert is in readiness, sir; but I could swear he
knows nothing about it.

Winsor. All right. [*Treisure reopens the door, and says:*
"Come in, please." *The Inspector enters, blue, formal,
moustachioed, with a peaked cap in his hand.*] Good-
evening, Inspector. Sorry to have brought you out at
this time of night.

Inspector. Good evenin', sir. Mr. Winsor? You're the owner
here, I think?

Winsor. Yes. General Canynge.

Inspector. Good evenin', General. I understand, a large sum
of money?

Winsor. Yes. Shall we go straight to the room it was taken
from? One of my guests, Mr. De Levis. It's the third
room on the left.

Canynge. We've not been in there yet, Inspector; in fact,
we've done nothing, except to find out that the stable
ladder has not been moved. We haven't even searched
the grounds.

Inspector. Right, sir; I've brought a man with me.

[*They go out.*]

The curtain falls.

Interval of a minute.

The bedroom of De Levis is the same in shape as Winsor's dressing-room, except that there is only one door—to the corridor. The furniture, however, is differently arranged; a small four-poster bedstead stands against the wall, Right Back, jutting into the room. A chair, on which De Levis's clothes are thrown, stands at its foot. There is a dressing-table against the wall to the left of the open windows, where the curtains are drawn back and a stone balcony is seen. Against the wall to the right of the window is a chest of drawers, and a washstand is against the wall, Left. On a small table to the right of the bed an electric reading lamp is turned up, and there is a light over the dressing-table. The Inspector is standing plumb centre looking at the bed, and De Levis by the back of the chair at the foot of the bed. Winsor and Canynge are close to the door, Right Forward.

Inspector [*finishing a note*]. Now, sir, if this is the room as you left it for your bath, just show us exactly what you did after takin' the pocket-book from the suitcase. Where was that, by the way?
De Levis [*pointing*]. Where it is now—under the dressing-table. [*He comes forward to the front of the chair, opens the pocket-book, goes through the pretence of counting his shaving papers, closes the pocket-book, takes it to the head of the bed and slips it under the pillow. Makes the motion of taking up his pyjamas, crosses below the Inspector to the washstand, takes up a bath sponge, crosses to the door, takes out the key, opens the door.*]
Inspector [*writing*]. We now have the room as it was when the theft was committed. Reconstruct accordin' to 'uman nature, gentlemen—assumin' the thief to be in the room, what would he try first?—the clothes, the dressin' table, the suitcase, the chest of drawers and last,

---

1 The same set is used for this Scene, with the different arrangement of furniture, as specified.

the bed. [*He moves accordingly, examining the glass on the dressing-table, the surface of the suitcase, and the handles of the drawers, with a spy-glass, for finger-marks.*]

Canynge [*sotto voce to Winsor*]. The order would have been just the other way.

[*The Inspector goes on hands and knees and examines the carpet between the window and the bed.*]

De Levis. Can I come in again?

Inspector [*standing up*]. Did you open the window, sir, or was it open when you first came in?

De Levis. I opened it.

Inspector. Drawin' the curtains back first?

De Levis. Yes.

Inspector [*sharply*]. Are you sure there was nobody in the room already?

De Levis [*taken aback*]. I don't know. I never thought. I didn't look under the bed, if you mean that.

Inspector [*jotting*]. Did not look under bed. Did you look under it after the theft?

De Levis. No. I didn't.

Inspector. Ah! Now, what *did* you do after you came back from your bath? Just give us that precisely.

De Levis. Locked the door and left the key in. Put back my sponge, and took off my dressing-gown and put it there. [*He points to the footrails of the bed.*] Then I drew the curtains again.

Inspector. Shutting the window?

De Levis. No. I got into bed, felt for my watch to see the time. My hand struck the pocket-book, and somehow it felt thinner. I took it out, looked into it, and found the notes gone, and these shaving papers instead.

Inspector. Let me have a look at those, sir. [*He applies the spy-glasses.*] And then?

De Levis. I think I just sat on the bed.

Inspector. Thinkin' and cursin' a bit, I suppose. Ye'es?

De Levis. Then I put on my dressing-gown and went straight to Mr. Winsor.

Inspector. Not lockin' the door?

De Levis. No.

Inspector. Exactly. [*With a certain finality.*] Now, sir, what time did you come up?

De Levis. About eleven.

Inspector. Precise, if you can give it me.

De Levis. Well, I *know* it was eleven-fifteen when I put my watch under my pillow, before I went to the bath, and I suppose I'd been about a quarter of an hour undressing. I should say after eleven, if anything.

Inspector. Just undressin'? Didn't look over your bettin' book?

De Levis. No.

Inspector. No prayers or anything?

De Levis. No.

Inspector. Pretty slippy with your undressin' as a rule?

De Levis. Yes. Say five past eleven.

Inspector. Mr. Winsor, what time did the gentleman come to you.

Winsor. Half-past eleven.

Inspector. How do you fix that, sir?

Winsor. I'd just looked at the time, and told my wife to send her maid off.

Inspector. Then we've got it fixed between 11:15 and 11:30. [*Jots.*] Now, sir, before we go further I'd like to see your butler and the footman that valets this gentleman.

Winsor [*with distaste*]. Very well, Inspector; only—my butler has been with us from a boy.

Inspector. Quite so. This is just clearing the ground, sir.

Winsor. General, d'you mind touching that bell?

[*Canynge rings a bell by the bed.*]

Inspector. Well, gentlemen, there are four possibilities. Either the thief was here all the time, waiting under the bed, and slipped out after this gentleman had gone to Mr. Winsor. Or he came in with a key that fits the lock; and I'll want to see all the keys in the house. Or he came in with a skeleton key and out by the window, probably droppin' from the balcony. Or he came in by the window with a rope or ladder and out the same way. [*Pointing.*] There's a footmark here from a big foot which has been out of doors since it rained.

Canynge. Inspector—you er—walked up to the window when you first came into the room.

Inspector [*stiffly*]. I had not overlooked that, General.

Canynge. Of course.

[*A knock on the door relieves a certain tension.*]

Winsor. Come in.

[*The footman Robert, a fresh-faced young man, enters, followed by Treisure.*]

Inspector. You valet Mr.—Mr. De Levis, I think?

Robert. Yes, sir.

Inspector. At what time did you take his clothes and boots?

Robert. Ten o'clock, sir.

Inspector [*with a pounce*]. Did you happen to look under his bed?

Robert. No, sir.

Inspector. Did you come up again, to bring the clothes back?

Robert. No, sir; they're downstairs.

Inspector. Did you come up again for anything?

Robert. No, sir.

Inspector. What time did you go to bed?

Robert. Just after eleven, sir.

Inspector [*scrutinising him*]. Now, be careful. Did you go to bed at all?

Robert. No, sir.

Inspector. Then why did you say you did? There's been a theft here, anything you say may be used against you.

Robert. Yes, sir. I meant, I went to my room.

Inspector. Where is your room?

Robert. On the ground floor, at the other end of the right wing, sir.

Winsor. It's the extreme end of the house from this, Inspector. He's with the other two footmen.

Inspector. Were you there alone?

Robert. No, sir. Thomas and Frederick was there too.

Treasure. That's right; I've seen them.

Inspector [*holding up his hand for silence*]. Were you out of the room again after you went in?

Robert. No, sir.

Inspector. What were you doing, if you didn't go to bed?

Robert [*to Winsor*]. Beggin' your pardon, sir, we were playin' Bridge.

Inspector. Very good. You can go. I'll see *them* later on.

Robert. Yes, sir. They'll say the same as me. [*He goes out, leaving a smile on the face of all except the Inspector and De Levis.*]

Inspector [*sharply*]. Call him back.

[*Treasure calls* "Robert," *and the Footman reenters.*]

Robert. Yes, sir?

Inspector. Did you notice anything particular about Mr. De Levis's clothes?

Robert. Only that they were very good, sir.

Inspector. I mean—anything peculiar?

Robert [*after reflection*]. Yes, sir.

Inspector. Well?

Robert. A pair of his boots this evenin' was reduced to one, sir.

Inspector. What did you make of that?

Robert. I thought he might have thrown the other at a cat or something.

Inspector. Did you look for it?

Robert. No, sir; I meant to draw his attention to it in the morning.

Inspector. Very good.

Robert. Yes, sir. [*He goes again.*]

Inspector [*looking at De Levis*]. Well, sir, there's *your* story corroborated.

De Levis [*stiffly*]. I don't know why it should need corroboration, Inspector.

Inspector. In my experience, you can never have too much of that. [*To Winsor.*] I understand there's a lady in the room on this side [*pointing Left*] and a gentleman on this [*pointing Right*]. Were they in their rooms?

Winsor. Miss Orme was; Captain Dancy not.

Inspector. Do they know of the affair?

Winsor. Yes.

Inspector. Well, I'd just like the keys of their doors for a minute. My man will get them. [*He goes to the door, opens it, and speaks to a constable in the corridor. To Treisure.*] You can go with him. [*Treisure goes out.*] In the meantime I'll just examine the balcony. [*He goes out on the balcony, followed by De Levis.*]

Winsor [*to Canynge*]. Damn De Levis and his money! It's deuced invidious, all this, General.

Canynge. The Inspector's no earthly.

[*There is a simultaneous re-entry of the Inspector from the balcony and of Treisure and the Constable from the corridor.*]

Constable [*handing key*]. Room on the left, sir. [*Handing key.*] Room on the right, sir.

[*The Inspector tries the keys in the door, watched with tension by the others. The keys fail.*]

Inspector. Put them back. [*Hands keys to Constable, who goes out, followed by Treisure.*] I'll have to try every key in the house, sir.

Winsor. Inspector, do you really think it necessary to disturb the whole house and knock up all my guests? It's most disagreeable, all this, you know. The loss of the money is not such a great matter. Mr. De Levis has a very large income.

Canynge. You could get the numbers of the notes from Kentman, the bookmaker, Inspector; he'll probably have the big ones, anyway.

Inspector [*shaking his head*]. A bookie. I don't suppose he will, sir. It's come and go with them, all the time.

Winsor. We don't want a Meldon Court scandal, Inspector.

Inspector. Well, Mr. Winsor, I've formed my theory. [*As he speaks, De Levis comes in from the balcony.*] And I don't say to try the keys is necessary to it; but strictly, I ought to exhaust the possibilities.

Winsor. What do you say, De Levis? D'you want everybody in the house knocked up so that their keys can be tried?

De Levis [*whose face, since his return, expresses a curious excitement*]. No, I don't.

Inspector. Very well, gentlemen. In my opinion the thief walked in before the door was locked, probably during dinner; and was under the bed. He escaped by dropping from the balcony—the creeper at that corner [*he points stage Left*] has been violently wrenched. I'll go down now, and examine the grounds, and I'll see you again, sir. [*He makes another entry in his note-book.*] Good-night, then, gentlemen!

Canynge. Good-night!

Winsor [*with relief*]. I'll come with you, Inspector. [*He escorts him to the door, and they go out.*]

De Levis [*suddenly*]. General, I know who took them.

Canynge. The deuce you do! Are you following the Inspector's theory?

De Levis [*contemptuously*]. That ass! [*Pulling the shaving papers out of the case.*] No! The man who put those there was clever and cool enough to wrench that creeper off the balcony, as a blind. Come and look here, General. [*He goes to the window; the General follows. De Levis points stage Right.*] See the rail of my balcony, and the rail of the next? [*He holds up the cord of his dressing-gown, stretching his arms out.*] I've measured it with this. Just over seven feet, that's all! If a man can take a standing jump on to a narrow book-case four feet high and balance there, he'd make nothing of that. And, look here! [*He goes out on the balcony and returns with a bit of broken creeper in his hand,*

and holds it out into the light.] Someone's stood on that
—the stalk's crushed—the inner corner too, where he'd
naturally stand when he took his jump back.

Canynge [*after examining it—stiffly*]. That other balcony is
young Dancy's, Mr. De Levis; a soldier and a gentleman. This is an extraordinary insinuation.

De Levis. Accusation.

Canynge. What!

De Levis. I have intuitions, General; it's in my blood. I see
the whole thing. Dancy came up, watched me into the
bathroom, tried my door, slipped back into his dressing-
room, saw my window was open, took that jump,
sneaked the notes, filled the case up with these,
wrenched the creeper there [*he points stage Left*] for
a blind, jumped back, and slipped downstairs again.
It didn't take him four minutes altogether.

Canynge [*very gravely*]. This is outrageous, De Levis. Dancy
says he was downstairs all the time. You must either
withdraw unreservedly, or I must confront you with
him.

De Levis. If he'll return the notes and apologise, I'll do
nothing—except cut him in future. He gave me that
filly, you know, as a hopeless weed, and he's been
pretty sick ever since, that he was such a flat as not to
see how good she was. Besides, he's hard up, I know.

Canynge [*after a vexed turn up and down the room*]. It's
mad, sir, to jump to conclusions like this.

De Levis. Not so mad as the conclusion Dancy jumped to
when he lighted on my balcony.

Canynge. Nobody could have taken this money who did not
know you had it.

De Levis. How do you know that he didn't?

Canynge. Do you know that he did?

De Levis. I haven't the least doubt of it.

Canynge. Without any proof. This is very ugly, De Levis.
I must tell Winsor.

De Levis [*angrily*]. Tell the whole blooming lot. You think
I've no feelers, but I've felt the atmosphere here, I can
tell you, General. If I were in Dancy's shoes and he in
mine, your tone to me would be very different.

Canynge [*suavely frigid*]. I'm not aware of using any tone,
as you call it. But this is a private house, Mr. De Levis,
and something is due to our host and to the *esprit de
corps* that exists among gentlemen.

De Levis. Since when is a thief a gentleman? Thick as thieves—a good motto, isn't it?

Canynge. That's enough! [*He goes to the door, but stops before opening it.*] Now, look here! I have some knowledge of the world. Once an accusation like this passes beyond these walls no one can foresee the consequences. Captain Dancy is a gallant fellow, with a fine record as a soldier; and only just married. If he's as innocent as—Christ—mud will stick to him, unless the real thief is found. In the old days of swords, either you or he would not have gone out of this room alive. If you persist in this absurd accusation, you will *both* of you go out of this room dead in the eyes of Society: you for bringing it, he for being the object of it.

De Levis. Society! Do you think I don't know that I'm only tolerated for my money? Society can't add injury to insult and have my money as well, that's all. If the notes are restored I'll keep my mouth shut; if they're not, I shan't. I'm certain I'm right. I ask nothing better than to be confronted with Dancy; but, if you prefer it, deal with him in your own way—for the sake of your *esprit de corps.*

Canynge. 'Pon my soul, Mr. Levis, you go too far.

De Levis. Not so far as I shall go, General Canynge, if those notes aren't given back.

[*Winsor comes in.*]

Winsor. Well, De Levis, I'm afraid that's all we can do for the present. So very sorry this should have happened in my house.

Canynge [*after a silence*]. There's a development, Winsor. Mr. De Levis accuses one of your guests.

Winsor. What?

Canynge. Of jumping from his balcony to this, taking the notes, and jumping back. I've done my best to dissuade him from indulging the fancy—without success. Dancy must be told.

De Levis. You can deal with Dancy in your own way. All I want is the money back.

Canynge [*drily*]. Mr. De Levis feels that he is only valued for his money, so that it is essential for him to have it back.

Winsor. Damn it! This is monstrous, De Levis. I've known Ronald Dancy since he was a boy.

Canynge. You talk about adding injury to insult, De Levis.
What do you call such treatment of a man who gave
you the mare out of which you made this thousand
pounds?

De Levis. I didn't want the mare; I took her as a favour.

Canynge. With an eye to possibilities, I venture to think—
the principle guides a good many transactions.

De Levis [*as if flicked on a raw spot*]. In my race, do you
mean?

Canynge [*coldly*]. I said nothing of the sort.

De Levis. No; you don't *say* these things, any of you.

Canynge. Nor did I think it.

De Levis. Dancy does.

Winsor. Really; De Levis, if this is the way you repay hospitality——

De Levis. Hospitality that skins my feelings and costs me a
thousand pounds!

Canynge. Go and get Dancy, Winsor; but don't say anything to him.

[*Winsor goes out.*]

Canynge. Perhaps you will kindly control yourself, and
leave this to me.

[*De Levis turns to the window and lights a cigarette. Winsor
comes back, followed by Dancy.*]

Canynge. For Winsor's sake, Dancy, we don't want any
scandal or fuss about this affair. We've tried to make
the police understand that. To my mind the whole thing
turns on our finding who knew that De Levis had this
money. It's about that we want to consult you.

Winsor. Kentman paid De Levis round the corner in the
further paddock, he says.

[*De Levis turns round from the window, so that he and
Dancy are staring at each other.*]

Canynge. Did you hear anything that throws light, Dancy?
As it was your filly originally, we thought perhaps you
might.

Dancy. I? No.

Canynge. Didn't hear of the sale on the course at all?

Dancy. No.

Canynge. Then you can't suggest anyone who could have
known? Nothing else was taken, you see.

Dancy. De Levis is known to be rolling, as I am known to
be stony.

Canynge. There are a good many people still rolling, besides
  Mr. De Levis, but not many people with so large a sum
  in their pocket-books.

Dancy. He won two races.

De Levis. Do you suggest that I bet in ready money?

Dancy. I don't know how you bet, and I don't care.

Canynge. You can't help us, then?

Dancy. No, I can't. Anything else? [*He looks fixedly at De
  Levis.*]

Canynge [*putting his hand on Dancy's arm*]. Nothing else,
  thank you, Dancy.

[*Dancy goes. Canynge puts his hand up to his face. A moment's silence.*]

Winsor. You see, De Levis? He didn't even know you'd got
  the money.

De Levis. Very conclusive.

Winsor. Well! You *are*——!

[*There is a knock on the door, and the Inspector enters.*]

Inspector. I'm just going, gentlemen. The grounds, I'm sorry
  to say, have yielded nothing. It's a bit of a puzzle.

Canynge. You've searched thoroughly?

Inspector. We have, General. I can pick up nothing near the
  terrace.

Winsor [*after a look at De Levis, whose face expresses too
  much*]. H'm! You'll take it up from the other end, then,
  Inspector?

Inspector. Well, we'll see what we can do with the bookmakers about the numbers, sir. Before I go, gentlemen
  —you've had time to think it over—there's no one you
  suspect in the house, I suppose?

[*De Levis's face is alive and uncertain. Canynge is staring
  at him very fixedly.*]

Winsor [*emphatically*]. No.

[*De Levis turns and goes out on to the balcony.*]

Inspector. If you're coming in to the racing tomorrow, sir,
  you might give us a call. I'll have seen Kentman by
  then.

Winsor. Right you are, Inspector. Good-night, and many
  thanks.

Inspector. You're welcome, sir. [*He goes out.*]

Winsor. Gosh! I thought that chap [*with a nod towards the
  balcony*] was going to——! Look here, General, we *must*
  stop his tongue. Imagine it going the rounds. They may

never find the real thief, you know. It's the very devil for Dancy.

Canynge. Winsor! Dancy's sleeve was damp.

Winsor. How d'you mean?

Canynge. Quite damp. It's been raining.

[*The two look at each other.*]

Winsor. I—I don't follow—[*His voice is hesitative and lower, showing that he does.*]

Canynge. It was coming down hard; a minute out in it would have been enough—[*He motions with his chin towards the balcony.*]

Winsor [*hastily*]. He must have been out on his balcony since.

Canynge. It stopped before I came up, half an hour ago.

Winsor. He's been leaning on the wet stone, then.

Canynge. With the outside of the *upper* part of the arm?

Winsor. Against the wall, perhaps. There may be a dozen explanations. [*Very low and with great concentration.*] I entirely and absolutely refuse to believe anything of the sort against Ronald Dancy—in my house. Dash it, General, we must do as we'd be done by. It hits us all —it hits us all. The thing's intolerable.

Canynge. I agree. Intolerable. [*Raising his voice.*] Mr. De Levis.

[*De Levis returns into view, in the centre of the open window.*]

Canynge [*with cold decision*]. Young Dancy was an officer and is a gentleman; this insinuation is pure supposition, and you must not make it. Do you understand me?

De Levis. My tongue is still mine, General, if my money isn't!

Canynge [*unmoved*]. Must not. You're a member of three Clubs, you want to be a member of a fourth. No one who makes such an insinuation against a fellow-guest in a country house, except on absolute proof, can do so without complete ostracism. Have we your word to say nothing?

De Levis. Social blackmail? H'm!

Canynge. Not at all—simply warning. If you consider it necessary in your interests to start this scandal—no matter how, we shall consider it necessary in ours to dissociate ourselves completely from one who so recklessly disregards the unwritten code.

De Levis. Do you think your code applies to me? Do you, General?

Canynge. To anyone who aspires to be a gentleman, sir.

De Levis. Ah! But you haven't known *me* since I was a boy.

Canynge. Make up your mind.

[*A pause.*]

De Levis. I'm not a fool, General. I know perfectly well that you can get me ousted.

Canynge [*icily*]. Well?

De Levis [*sullenly*]. I'll say nothing about it, unless I get more proof.

Canynge. Good. We have implicit faith in Dancy.

[*There is a moment's encounter of eyes; the General's steady, shrewd, impassive; Winsor's angry and defiant; De Levis's mocking, a little triumphant, malicious. Then Canynge and Winsor go to the door, and pass out.*]

De Levis [*to himself*]. Rats!

                                              The curtain falls.

scene ONE

Afternoon, three weeks later, in the card room of a London Club. A fire is burning, Left. A door, Right, leads to the billiard-room. Rather Left of Centre, at a card table, Lord St Erth, an old John Bull, sits facing the audience; to his right is General Canynge, to his left Augustus Borring, an essential Clubman, about thirty-five years old, with a very slight and rather becoming stammer or click in his speech. The fourth Bridge player, Charles Winsor, stands with his back to the fire.

Borring. And the r-rub.

Winsor. By George! You do hold cards, Borring.

St Erth [*who has lost*]. Not a patch on the old whist—this game. Don't know why I play it—never did.

Canynge. St Erth, shall we raise the flag for whist again?

Winsor. No go, General. You can't go back on pace. No getting a man to walk when he knows he can fly. The young men won't look at it.

Borring. Better develop it so that t-two can sit out, General.

St Erth. We ought to have stuck to the old game. Wish I'd gone to Newmarket, Canynge, in spite of the weather.

Canynge [*looking at his watch*]. Let's hear what's won the Cambridgeshire. Ring, won't you, Winsor?

[*Winsor rings.*]

St Erth. By the way, Canynge, young De Levis was black-balled.

Canynge. What!

St Erth. I looked in on my way down.

[*Canynge sits very still and Winsor utters a disturbed sound.*]

Borring. But of c-course he was, General. What did you expect?

[*A Footman enters.*]

Footman. Yes, my lord?

St Erth. What won the Cambridgeshire?

Footman. Rosemary, my lord. Sherbet second; Barbizon third. Nine to one the winner.

Winsor. Thank you. That's all.

[*Footman goes.*]

Borring. Rosemary! And De Levis sold her! But he got a good p-price, I suppose.

[*The other three look at him.*]

St Erth. Many a slip between price and pocket, young man.

Canynge. Cut! [*They cut.*]

Borring. I say, is that the yarn that's going round about his having a lot of m-money stolen in a country house? By Jove! He'll be pretty s-sick.

Winsor. You and I, Borring. [*He sits down in Canynge's chair, and the General takes his place by the fire.*]

Borring. Phew! Won't Dancy be mad! He gave that filly away to save her keep. He was rather pleased to find somebody who'd take her. Kentman must have won a p-pot. She was at thirty-threes a fortnight ago.

St Erth. All the money goes to fellows who don't know a horse from a haystack.

Canynge [*profoundly*]. And care less. Yes! We want men racing to whom a horse means something.

Borring. I thought the horse m-meant the same to everyone, General—chance to get the b-better of one's neighbour.

Canynge [*with feeling*]. The horse is a noble animal, sir, as you'd know if you'd owed your life to them as often as I have.

Borring. They always try to *take* mine, General. I shall never belong to the noble f-fellowship of the horse.

St Erth [*drily*]. Evidently. Deal!

[*As Borring begins to deal the door is opened and Major Colford appears—a lean and moustached cavalryman.*]

Borring. Hallo, C-Colford.

Colford. General! [*Something in the tone of his voice brings them all to a standstill.*]

Colford. I want your advice. Young De Levis in there [*he points to the billiard-room from which he has just come*] has started a blasphemous story—

Canynge. One moment. Mr. Borring, d'you mind—

Colford. It makes no odds, General. Four of us in there

heard him. He's saying it was Ronald Dancy robbed
him down at Winsor's. The fellow's mad over losing
the price of that filly now she's won the Cambridgeshire.

Borring [*all ears*]. Dancy! Great S-Scott!

Colford. Dancy's in the Club. If he hadn't been I'd have
taken it on myself to wring the bounder's neck.

[*Windsor and Borring have risen. St Erth alone remains
seated.*]

Canynge [*after consulting St Erth with a look*]. Ask De
Levis to be good enough to come in here. Borring, you
might see that Dancy doesn't leave the Club. We shall
want him. Don't say anything to him, and use your tact
to keep people off.

[*Borring goes out, followed by Colford.*]

Winsor. Result of hearing he was blackballed—pretty slippy.

Canynge. St Erth, I told you there was good reason when
I asked you to back young De Levis. Winsor and I
knew of this insinuation; I wanted to keep his tongue
quiet. It's just wild assertion; to have it bandied about
was unfair to Dancy. The duel used to keep people's
tongues in order.

St Erth. H'm! It never settled anything, except who could
shoot straightest.

Colford [*reappearing*]. De Levis says he's nothing to add to
what he said to you before, on the subject.

Canynge. Kindly tell him that if he wishes to remain a member of this Club he must account to the Committee for
such a charge against a fellow-member. Four of us are
here, and form a quorum.

[*Colford goes out again.*]

St Erth. Did Kentman ever give the police the numbers of
those notes, Winsor?

Winsor. He only had the numbers of two—the hundred, and
one of the fifties.

St Erth. And they haven't traced 'em?

Winsor. Not yet.

[*As he speaks, De Levis comes in. He is in a highly-coloured,
not to say excited state. Colford follows him.*]

De Levis. Well, General Canynge! It's a little too strong all
this—a little too strong. [*Under emotion his voice is
slightly more exotic.*]

Canynge [*calmly*]. It is obvious, Mr. De Levis, that you and

Captain Dancy can't both remain members of this Club. We ask you for an explanation before requesting one resignation or the other.

De Levis. You've let me down.

Canynge. What!

De Levis. Well, I shall tell people that you and Lord St Erth backed me up for one Club, and asked me to resign from another.

Canynge. It's a matter of indifference to me, sir, what you tell people.

St Erth [*drily*]. You seem a venomous young man.

De Levis. I'll tell you what seems to me venomous, my lord —chasing a man like a pack of hounds because he isn't your breed.

Canynge. You appear to have your breed on the brain, sir. Nobody else does, so far as I know.

De Levis. Suppose I had robbed Dancy, would you chase him out for complaining of it?

Colford. My God! If you repeat that—

Canynge. Steady, Colford!

Winsor. You make this accusation that Dancy stole your money in my house on no proof—no proof; and you expect Dancy's friends to treat you as if you were a gentleman! That's too strong, if you like!

De Levis. No proof? Kentman told me at Newmarket yesterday that Dancy *did* know of the sale. He told Goole, and Goole says that he himself spoke of it to Dancy.

Winsor. Well—if he did?

De Levis. Dancy told you he *didn't* know of it in General Canynge's presence, and mine. [*To Canynge.*] You can't deny that, if you want to.

Canynge. Choose your expressions more nicely, please!

De Levis. Proof! Did they find any footmarks in the grounds below that torn creeper? Not a sign! You saw how he can jump; he won ten pounds from me that same evening betting on what he knew was a certainty. That's your Dancy—a common sharper!

Canynge [*nodding towards the billiard-room*]. Are those fellows still in there, Colford?

Colford. Yes.

Canynge. Then bring Dancy up, will you? But don't say anything to him.

Colford [*to De Levis*]. You may think yourself damned lucky if he doesn't break your neck. [*He goes out. The three who are left with De Levis avert their eyes from him.*]

De Levis [*smouldering*]. I have a memory, and a sting too. Yes, my lord—since you are good enough to call me venomous. [*To Canynge.*] I quite understand—I'm marked for Coventry now, whatever happens. Well, I'll take Dancy with me.

St Erth [*to himself*]. This Club has always had a decent, quiet name.

Winsor. Are you going to retract, and apologise in front of Dancy and the members who heard you?

De Levis. No fear!

St Erth. You must be a very rich man, sir. A jury is likely to take the view that money can hardly compensate for an accusation of that sort.

[*De Levis stands silent.*]

Canynge. Courts of law require proof.

St Erth. He can make it a criminal action.

Winsor. Unless you stop this at once, you may find yourself in prison. *If* you can stop it, that is.

St Erth. If I were young Dancy, nothing should induce me.

De Levis. But you didn't steal my money, Lord St Erth.

St Erth. You're deuced positive, sir. So far as I could understand it, there were a dozen ways you could have been robbed. It seems to me you value other men's reputations very lightly.

De Levis. Confront me with Dancy and give me fair play.

Winsor [*aside to Canynge*]. Is it fair to Dancy not to let him know?

Canynge. Our duty is to the Club now, Winsor. We must have this cleared up.

[*Colford comes in, followed by Borring and Dancy.*]

St Erth. Captain Dancy, a serious accusation has been made against you by this gentleman in the presence of several members of the Club.

Dancy. What is it?

St Erth. That you robbed him of that money at Winsor's.

Dancy [*hard and tense*]. Indeed! On what grounds is he good enough to say that?

De Levis [*tense too*]. You gave me that filly to save yourself her keep, and you've been mad about it ever since; you knew from Goole that I had sold her to Kentman and been paid in cash, yet I heard you myself deny that you knew it. You had the next room to me, and you can jump like a cat, as we saw that evening; I found some creepers crushed by a weight on my balcony on that side. When I went to the bath your door was open, and when I came back it was shut.

Canynge. That's the first we have heard about the door.

De Levis. I remembered it afterwards.

St Erth. Well, Dancy?

Dancy [*with intense deliberation*]. I'll settle this matter with any weapons, when and where he likes.

St Erth [*drily*]. It can't be settled that way—you know very well. You must take it to the Courts, unless he retracts.

Dancy. Will you retract?

De Levis. Why did you tell General Canynge you didn't know Kentman had paid me in cash?

Dancy. Because I didn't.

De Levis. Then Kentman and Goole lied—for no reason?

Dancy. That's nothing to do with me.

De Levis. If you were downstairs all the time, as you say, why was your door first open and then shut?

Dancy. Being downstairs, how should I know? The wind, probably.

De Levis. I should like to hear what your wife says about it.

Dancy. Leave my wife alone, you damned Jew!

St Erth. Captain Dancy!

De Levis [*white with rage*]. Thief!

Dancy. Will you fight?

De Levis. You're very smart—dead men tell no tales. No! Bring your action, and we shall see.

[*Dancy takes a step towards him, but Canynge and Winsor interpose.*]

St. Erth. That'll do, Mr. De Levis; we won't keep you. [*He looks round.*] Kindly consider your membership suspended till this matter has been threshed out.

De Levis [*tremulous with anger*]. Don't trouble yourselves about my membership. I resign it. [*To Dancy.*] You called me a damned Jew. My race was old when you were all savages. I am proud to be a Jew. *Au revoir,* in the Courts. [*He goes out, and silence follows his departure.*]

St Erth. Well, Captain Dancy?

Dancy. If the brute won't fight, what am I to do, sir?

St Erth. We've told you—take action, to clear your name.

Dancy. Colford, you saw me in the hall writing letters after our game.

Colford. Certainly I did; you were there when I went to the smoking-room.

Canynge. How long after you left the billiard-room?

Colford. About five minutes.

Dancy. It's impossible for me to prove that I was there all the time.

Canynge. It's for De Levis to prove what he asserts. You heard what he said about Goole?

Dancy. If he told me, I didn't take it in.

St Erth. This concerns the honour of the Club. Are you going to take action?

Dancy [*slowly*]. That is a very expensive business, Lord St Erth, and I'm hard up. I must think it over. [*He looks round from face to face.*] Am I to take it that there is a doubt in your minds, gentlemen?

Colford [*emphatically*]. No.

Canynge. That's not the question, Dancy. This accusation was overheard by various members, and we represent the Club. If you don't take action, judgment will naturally go by default.

Dancy. I might prefer to look on the whole thing as beneath contempt. [*He turns and goes out. When he is gone there is an even longer silence than after De Levis's departure.*]

St Erth [*abruptly*]. I don't like it.

Winsor. I've known him all his life.

Colford. You may have my head if he did it, Lord St Erth. He and I have been in too many hotels together. By Gad! My toe itches for that fellow's butt end.

Borring. I'm sorry; but has he t-taken it in quite the right way? I should have thought—hearing it s-suddenly—

Colford. Bosh!

Winsor. It's perfectly damnable for him.

St Erth. More damnable if he did it, Winsor.

Borring. The Courts are b-beastly distrustful, don't you know.

Colford. His word's good enough for me.

Canynge. We're as anxious to believe Dancy as you, Colford, for the honour of the Army and the Club.

Winsor. Of course, he'll bring a case, when he's thought it over.

St Erth. What are we to do in the meantime?

Colford. If Dancy's asked to resign, you may take my resignation too.

Borring. I thought his wanting to f-fight him a bit screeny.

Colford. Wouldn't you have wanted a shot at the brute? A law court? Pah!

Winsor. Yes. What'll be his position even if he wins?

Borring. Damages, and a stain on his c-character.

Winsor. Quite so, unless they find the real thief. People always believe the worst.

Colford [*glaring at Borring*]. They do.

Canynge. There *is* no decent way out of a thing of this sort.

St. Erth. No. [*Rising.*] It leaves a bad taste. I'm sorry for young Mrs. Dancy—poor woman!

Borring. Are you going to play any more?

St Erth [*abruptly*]. No, sir. Good night to you. Canynge, can I give you a lift? [*He goes out, followed by Canynge.*]

Borring [*after a slight pause*]. Well, I shall go and take the t-temperature of the Club. [*He goes out.*]

Colford. Damn that effeminate stammering chap. What can we do for Dancy, Winsor?

Winsor. Colford! [*A slight pause.*] The General felt his coat sleeve that night, and it was wet.

Colford. Well! What proof's that? No, by George! An old school-fellow, a brother officer, and a pal.

Winsor. If he did it—

Colford. He didn't. But if he did, I'd stick to him, and see him through it, if I could. [*Winsor walks over to the fire, stares into it, turns round and stares at Colford, who is standing motionless.*] Yes, by God!

The curtain falls.

scene TWO [2]

Morning of the following day. The Dancys' flat. In the sitting-room of this small abode Mabel Dancy and Margaret Orme are sitting full face to the audience, on a couch in the centre of the room, in front of the imaginary window. There is a fireplace, Left, with fire burning; a door below it, Left, and a door on the Right, facing the audience, leads to a

---

[2] This should be a small set capable of being set quickly within that of the previous scene.

*corridor and the outer door of the flat, which is visible. Their
voices are heard in rapid exchange; then as the curtain rises,
so does Mabel.*

Mabel. But it's monstrous!

Margaret. Of course! [*She lights a cigarette and hands the
case to Mabel, who, however, sees nothing but her
own thoughts.*] De Levis might just as well have pitched
on me, except that I can't jump more than six inches
in these skirts.

Mabel. It's wicked! Yesterday afternoon at the Club, did
you say? Ronny hasn't said a word to me. Why?

Margaret [*with a long puff of smoke*]. Doesn't want you
bothered.

Mabel. But—Good heavens!—Me!

Margaret. Haven't you found out, Mabel, that he isn't exactly communicative? No desperate character is.

Mabel. Ronny?

Margaret. Gracious! Wives *are* at a disadvantage, especially
early on. You've never hunted with him, my dear. I
have. He takes more sudden decisions than any man
I ever knew. He's taking one now, I'll bet.

Mabel. That beast, De Levis! I was in our room next door
all the time.

Margaret. Was the door into Ronny's dressing-room open?

Mabel. I don't know; I—I think it was.

Margaret. Well, you can say so in Court anyway. Not that
it matters. Wives are liars by law.

Mabel [*staring down at her*]. What do you mean—Court?

Margaret. My dear, he'll have to bring an action for defama-
tion of character, or whatever they call it.

Mabel. Were they talking of this last night at the Winsors'?

Margaret. Well, you know a dinner-table, Mabel—Scandal
is heaven-sent at this time of year.

Mabel. It's terrible, such a thing—terrible!

Margaret [*gloomily*]. If only Ronny weren't known to be
so broke.

Mabel [*with her hands to her forehead*]. I can't realise—I
simply can't. If there's a case would it be all right
afterwards?

Margaret. Do you remember St Offert—cards? No, you
wouldn't—you were in high frocks. Well, St Offert got
damages, but he also got the hoof, underneath. He

lives in Ireland. There isn't the slightest connection, so far as I can see, Mabel, between innocence and reputation. Look at me.

Mabel. We'll fight it tooth and nail!

Margaret. Mabel, you're pure wool, right through; everybody's sorry for you.

Mabel. It's for *him* they ought—

Margaret [*again handing the cigarette-case*]. Do smoke, old thing. [*Mabel takes a cigarette this time, but does not light it.*] It isn't altogether simple. General Canynge was there last night. You don't mind my being beastly frank, do you?

Mabel. No. I want it.

Margaret. Well, he's all for *esprit de corps* and that. But he was awfully silent.

Mabel. I hate half-hearted friends. Loyalty comes before everything.

Margaret. Ye-es; but loyalties cut up against each other sometimes, you know.

Mabel. I *must* see Ronny. D'you mind if I go and try to get him on the telephone?

Margaret. Rather not. [*Mabel goes out by the door, Left.*] Poor kid! [*She curls herself into a corner of the sofa, as if trying to get away from life. The bell rings. Margaret stirs, gets up, and goes out into the corridor, where she opens the door to Lady Adela Winsor, whom she precedes into the sitting-room.*] Enter the second murderer! D'you know that child knew nothing?

Lady Adela. Where is she?

Margaret. Telephoning. Adela, if there's going to be an action, we shall be witnesses. I shall wear black georgette with an écru hat. Have you ever given evidence?

Lady Adela. Never.

Margaret. It must be too frightfully thrilling.

Lady Adela. Oh! Why did I ever ask that wretch De Levis? I used to think him pathetic. Meg—did you know— Ronald Dancy's coat was wet? The General happened to feel it.

Margaret. So that's why he was so silent.

Lady Adela. Yes; and after the scene in the Club yesterday he went to see those bookmakers, and Goole—what a name!—is sure he told Dancy about the sale.

Margaret [*suddenly*]. I don't care. He's my third cousin. Don't you feel you *couldn't*, Adela?

Lady Adela. Couldn't—what?

Margaret. Stand for De Levis against one of ourselves?

Lady Adela. That's very narrow, Meg.

Margaret. Oh! I know lots of splendid Jews, and I rather liked Ferdy; but when it comes to the point——! *They* all stick together; why shouldn't we? It's in the blood. Open your jugular, and see if you haven't got it.

Lady Adela. My dear, my great grandmother was a Jewess. I'm very proud of her.

Margaret. Inoculated. [*Stretching herself.*] Prejudices, Adela —or are they loyalties—I don't know—criss-cross— we all cut each other's throats from the best of motives.

Lady Adela. Oh! I shall remember that. Delightful! [*Holding up a finger.*] You got it from Bergson, Meg. Isn't he wonderful?

Margaret. Yes; have you ever read him?

Lady Adela. Well—No. [*Looking at the bedroom door.*] That poor child! I quite agree. I shall tell everybody it's ridiculous. You don't really think Ronald Dancy—?

Margaret. I don't know, Adela. There are people who simply can't live without danger. I'm rather like that myself. They're all right when they're getting the D.S.O. or shooting man-eaters; but if there's no excitement going, they'll make it—out of sheer craving. I've seen Ronny Dancy do the maddest things for no mortal reason except the risk. He's had a past, you know.

Lady Adela. Oh! Do tell!

Margaret. He did splendidly in the war, of course, because it suited him; but—just before—don't you remember— a very queer bit of riding?

Lady Adela. No.

Margaret. Most dare-devil thing—but not quite. You must remember—it was awfully talked about. And then, of course, right up to his marriage—[*She lights a cigarette.*]

Lady Adela. Meg, you're very tantalising!

Margaret. A foreign-looking girl—most plummy. Oh! Ronny's got charm—this Mabel child doesn't know in the least what she's got hold of!

Lady Adela. But they're so fond of each other!

Margaret. That's the mistake. The General isn't mentioning the coat, is he?

Lady Adela. Oh, no! It was only to Charles.

[*Mabel returns.*]

Margaret. Did you get him?

Mabel. No; he's not at Tattersall's, nor at the Club.

[*Lady Adela rises and greets her with an air which suggests bereavement.*]

Lady Adela. Nobody's going to believe this, my dear.

Mabel [*looking straight at her*]. Nobody who does need come here, or trouble to speak to *us* again.

Lady Adela. That's what I was afraid of; you're going to be defiant. Now don't! Just be perfectly natural.

Mabel. So easy, isn't it? I could kill anybody who believes such a thing.

Margaret. You'll want a solicitor, Mabel. Go to old Mr. Jacob Twisden.

Lady Adela. Yes; he's so comforting.

Margaret. He got my pearls back once—without loss of life. A frightfully good fireside manner. Do get him here, Mabel, and have a heart-to-heart talk, all three of you!

Mabel [*suddenly*]. Listen! There's Ronny!

[*Dancy comes in.*]

Dancy [*with a smile*]. Very good of you to have come.

Margaret. Yes. We're just going. Oh! Ronny, this is quite too— [*But his face dries her up; and sidling past, she goes.*]

Lady Adela. Charles sent his —love— [*Her voice dwindles on the word, and she, too, goes.*]

Dancy [*crossing to his wife*]. What have they been saying?

Mabel. Ronny! Why didn't you tell me?

Dancy. I wanted to see De Levis again first.

Mabel. That wretch! How dare he? Darling! [*She suddenly clasps and kisses him. He does not return the kiss, but remains rigid in her arms, so that she draws away and looks at him.*] It's hurt you awfully, I know.

Dancy. Look here, Mabel! Apart from that muck—this is a ghastly tame-cat sort of life. Let's cut it and get out to Nairobi. I can scare up the money for that.

Mabel [*aghast*]. But how can we? Everybody would say—

Dancy. Let them! We shan't be here.

Mabel. I couldn't bear people to think—

Dancy. I don't care a damn what people think—monkeys and cats. I never could stand their rotten menagerie. Besides, what does it matter how I act; if I bring an action and get damages—if I pound him to a jelly—it's all no good! I can't *prove* it. There'll be plenty of people unconvinced.

Mabel. But they'll find the real thief.

Dancy [*with a queer little smile*]. Will staying here help them to do that?

Mabel [*in a sort of agony*]. Oh! I couldn't—it looks like running away. We *must* stay and fight it!

Dancy. Suppose I didn't get a verdict—you never can tell.

Mabel. But you must—I was there all the time, with the door open.

Dancy. Was it?

Mabel. I'm almost sure.

Dancy. Yes. But you're my wife.

Mabel [*bewildered*]. Ronny, I don't understand—suppose I'd been accused of stealing pearls!

Dancy [*wincing*]. I can't.

Mabel. But I might—just as easily. What would you think of me if I ran away from it?

Dancy. I see. [*A pause.*] All right! You shall have a run for your money. I'll go and see old Twisden.

Mabel. Let me come! [*Dancy shakes his head.*] Why not? I can't be happy a moment unless I'm fighting this.

[*Dancy puts out his hand suddenly and grips hers.*]

Dancy. You are a little brick!

Mabel. [*Pressing his hand to her breast and looking into his face.*] Do you know what Margaret called you?

Ronny. No.

Mabel. A desperate character.

Dancy. Ha! I'm not a tame cat, any more than she.

[*The bell rings. Mabel goes out to the door and her voice is heard saying coldly:*]

Mabel. Will you wait a minute, please? [*Returning.*] It's De Levis—to see you. [*In a low voice.*] Let me see him alone first. Just for a minute! Do!

Dancy [*after a moment's silence*]. Go ahead! [*He goes out into the bedroom.*]

Mabel [*going to the door, Right*]. Come in. [*De Levis comes in, and stands embarrassed.*] Yes?

De Levis [*with a slight bow*]. Your husband, Mrs. Dancy?

Mabel. He is in. Why do you want to see him?

De Levis. He came round to my rooms just now, when I was out. He threatened me yesterday. I don't choose him to suppose I'm afraid of him.

Mabel [*with a great and manifest effort at self-control*]. Mr. De Levis, you are robbing my husband of his good name.

De Levis [*sincerely*]. I admire your trustfulness, Mrs. Dancy.

Mabel [*staring at him*]. How can you do it? What do you want? What's your motive? You can't possibly believe that my husband is a *thief!*

De Levis. Unfortunately.

Mabel. How dare you? How dare you? Don't you know that I was in our bedroom all the time with the door open? Do you accuse me too?

De Levis. No, Mrs. Dancy.

Mabel. But you do. I must have seen, I must have heard.

De Levis. A wife's memory is not very good when her husband is in danger.

Mabel. In other words, I'm lying.

De Levis. No. Your wish is mother to your thought, that's all.

Mabel [*after staring again with a sort of horror, turns to get control of herself. Then turning back to him.*] Mr. De Levis, I appeal to you as a gentleman to behave to us as you would we should behave to you. Withdraw this wicked charge, and write an apology that Ronald can show.

De Levis. Mrs. Dancy, I am not a gentleman, I am only a —damned Jew. Yesterday I might possibly have withdrawn to spare you. But when my race is insulted I have nothing to say to your husband, but as he wishes to see me, I've come. Please let him know.

Mabel [*regarding him again with that look of horror—slowly*]. I think what you are doing is too horrible for words.

[*De Levis gives her a slight bow, and as he does so Dancy comes quickly in, Left. The two men stand with the length of the sofa between them. Mabel, behind the sofa, turns her eyes on her husband, who has a paper in his right hand.*]

De Levis. You came to see me.

Dancy. Yes. I want you to sign this.

De Levis. I will sign nothing.

Dancy. Let me read it: "I apologise to Captain Dancy for the reckless and monstrous charge I made against him, and I retract every word of it."

De Levis. Not much!

Dancy. You will sign.

De Levis. I tell you this is useless. I will sign nothing. The charge is true; you wouldn't be playing this game if it weren't. I'm going. You'll hardly try violence in the presence of your wife; and if you try it anywhere else —look out for yourself.

Dancy. Mabel, I want to speak to him alone.

Mabel. No, no!

De Levis. Quite right, Mrs. Dancy. Black and tan swash-buckling will only make things worse for him.

Dancy. So you shelter behind a woman, do you, you skulking cur!

[*De Levis takes a step, with fists clenched and eyes blazing. Dancy, too, stands ready to spring—the moment is cut short by Mabel going quickly to her husband.*]

Mabel. Don't, Ronny. It's undignified! He isn't worth it.

[*Dancy suddenly tears the paper in two, and flings it into the fire.*]

Dancy. Get out of here, you swine!

[*De Levis stands a moment irresolute, then, turning to the door, he opens it, stands again for a moment with a smile on his face, then goes. Mabel crosses swiftly to the door, and shuts it as the outer door closes. Then she stands quite still, looking at her husband—her face expressing a sort of startled suspense.*]

Dancy [*turning and looking at her*]. Well! Do you agree with him?

Mabel. What do you mean?

Dancy. That I wouldn't be playing this game unless—

Mabel. Don't! You hurt me!

Dancy. Yes. You don't know much of me, Mabel.

Mabel. Ronny!

Dancy. What did you say to that swine?

Mabel [*her face averted*]. That he was robbing *us.* [*Turning to him suddenly.*] Ronny—you—didn't? I'd rather know.

Dancy. Ha! I thought that was coming.

Mabel [*covering her face*]. Oh! How horrible of me—how horrible!

Dancy. Not at all. The thing looks bad.

Mabel [*dropping her hands*]. If *I* can't believe in you, who can? [*Going to him, throwing her arms round him, and looking up into his face.*] Ronny! If all the world—*I'd* believe in you. You know I would.

Dancy. That's all right, Mabs! That's all right! [*His face, above her head, is contorted for a moment, then hardens into a mask.*] Well, what shall we do?

Mabel. Oh! Let's go to that lawyer—let's go at once!

Dancy. All right. Get your hat on.

[*Mabel passes him, and goes into the bedroom, Left. Dancy, left alone, stands quite still, staring before him. With a sudden shrug of his shoulders he moves quickly to his hat and takes it up just as Mabel returns, ready to go out. He opens the door; and crossing him, she stops in the doorway, looking up with a clear and trustful gaze as*

The curtain falls.

scene ONE

Three months later. Old Mr. Jacob Twisden's Room, at the offices of Twisden & Graviter, is Lincoln's Inn Fields, is spacious, with two large windows at back, a fine old fireplace. Right, a door below it, and two doors, Left. Between the windows is a large table sideways to the window wall, with a chair in the middle on the right-hand side, a chair against the wall, and a client's chair on the left-hand side.

Graviter, Twisden's much younger partner, is standing in front of the right-hand window, looking out on to the Fields, where the lamps are being lighted, and a taxi's engine is running down below. He turns his sanguine, shrewd face from the window towards a grandfather clock, between the doors, Left, which is striking "four." The door, Left Forward, is opened.

Young Clerk [*entering*]. A Mr. Gilman, sir, to see Mr. Twisden.
Graviter. By appointment?
Young Clerk. No, sir. But important, he says.
Graviter. I'll see him.
[*The Clerk goes. Graviter sits right of table. The Clerk returns, ushering in an oldish man, who looks what he is, the proprietor of a large modern grocery store. He wears a dark overcoat and carries a pot hat. His gingery-grey moustache and mutton-chop whiskers give him the expression of a cat.*]
Graviter [*sizing up his social standing*]. Mr. Gilman? Yes.
Gilman [*doubtfully*]. Mr. Jacob Twisden?
Graviter [*smiling*]. His partner. Graviter my name is.
Gilman. Mr. Twisden's not in, then?
Graviter. No. He's at the Courts. They're just up; he should be in directly. But he'll be busy.
Gilman. Old Mr. Jacob Twisden—I've heard of him.
Graviter. Most people have.
[*A pause.*]

Gilman. It's this Dancy-De Levis case that's keepin' him at the Courts, I suppose? [*Graviter nods.*] Won't be finished for a day or two? [*Graviter shakes his head.*] No. Astonishin' the interest taken in it.

Graviter. As you say.

Gilman. The Smart Set, eh? This Captain Dancy got the D.S.O., didn't he? [*Graviter nods.*] Sad to have a thing like that said about you. I thought he gave his evidence well; and his wife too. Looks as if this De Levis had got some private spite. *Searchy la femme,* I said to Mrs. Gilman only this morning, before I—

Graviter. By the way, sir, what is your business?

Gilman. Well, my business here—No, if you'll excuse me, I'd rather wait and see old Mr. Jacob Twisden. It's delicate, and I'd like his experience.

Graviter [*with a shrug*]. Very well; then, perhaps you'll go in there. [*He moves towards the door, Left Back.*]

Gilman. Thank you. [*Following.*] You see, I've never been mixed up with the law—

Graviter [*opening the door*]. No?

Gilman. And I don't want to begin. When you do, you don't know where you'll stop, do you? You see, I've only come from a sense of duty; and—other reasons.

Graviter. Not uncommon.

Gilman [*producing card*]. This is my card. Gilman's—several branches, but this is the 'ead.

Graviter [*scrutinising card*]. Exactly.

Gilman. Grocery—I daresay you know me; or your wife does. They say old Mr. Jacob Twisden refused a knighthood. If it's not a rude question, why was that?

Graviter. Ask him, sir; ask him.

Gilman. I said to my wife at the time, "He's holdin' out for a baronetcy."

[*Graviter closes the door with an exasperated smile.*]

Young Clerk [*opening the door, Left Forward*]. Mr. Winsor, sir, and Miss Orme.

[*They enter, and the Clerk withdraws.*]

Graviter. How d'you do, Miss Orme? How do you do, Winsor?

Winsor. Twisden not back, Graviter?

Graviter. Not yet.

Winsor. Well, they've got through De Levis's witnesses. Sir Frederic was at the very top of his form. It's looking quite well. But I hear they've just subpoenaed Canynge after all. His evidence is to be taken tomorrow.

Graviter. Oho!

Winsor. I said Dancy ought to have called him.

Graviter. We considered it. Sir Frederic decided that he could use him better in cross-examination.

Winsor. Well! I don't know that. Can I go and see him before he gives evidence tomorow?

Graviter. I should like to hear Mr. Jacob on that, Winsor. He'll be in directly.

Winsor. They had Kentman, and Goole, the Inspector, the other bobby, my footman, Dancy's banker, and his tailor.

Graviter. Did we shake Kentman or Goole?

Winsor. Very little. Oh! by the way, the numbers of those two notes were given, and I see they're published in the evening papers. I suppose the police wanted that. I tell you what I find, Graviter—a general feeling that there's something behind it all that doesn't come out.

Graviter. The public wants its money's worth—always does in these Society cases; they brew so long beforehand, you see.

Winsor. They're looking for something lurid.

Margaret. When I was in the box, I thought they were looking for me. [*Taking out her cigarette-case.*] I suppose I mustn't smoke, Mr. Graviter?

Graviter. Do!

Margaret. Won't Mr. Jacob have a fit?

Graviter. Yes, but not till you've gone.

Margaret. Just a whiff. [*She lights a cigarette.*]

Winsor [*suddenly*]. It's becoming a sort of Dreyfus case—people taking sides quite outside the evidence.

Margaret. There are more of the chosen in Court every day. Mr. Graviter, have you noticed the two on the jury?

Graviter [*with a smile*]. No; I can't say—

Margaret. Oh! but quite distinctly. Don't you think they ought to have been challenged?

Graviter. De Levis might have challenged the other ten, Miss Orme.

Margaret. Dear me, now! I never thought of that.

[*As she speaks, the door Left Forward is opened and old Mr. Jacob Twisden comes in. He is tallish and narrow, sixty-eight years old, grey, with narrow little whiskers curling round his narrow ears, and a narrow bow ribbon curling round his collar. He wears a long, narrow-tailed*

*coat, and strapped trousers on his narrow legs. His
nose and face are narrow, shrewd, and kindly. He has a
way of narrowing his shrewd and kindly eyes. His nose
is seen to twitch and sniff.*]

Twisden. Ah! How are you, Charles? How do you do, my
dear?

Margaret. Dear Mr. Jacob, I'm smoking. Isn't it disgusting?
But they don't allow it in Court, you know. Such a pity!
The Judge might have a hookah. Oh! wouldn't he look
sweet—the darling!

Twisden [*with a little, old-fashioned bow*]. It does not become everybody as it becomes you, Margaret.

Margaret. Mr. Jacob, how charming! [*With a slight grimace
she puts out her cigarette.*]

Graviter. Man called Gilman waiting in there to see you
specially.

Twisden. Directly. Turn up the light, would you, Graviter?

Graviter [*turning up the light*]. Excuse me. [*He goes.*]

Winsor. Look here, Mr. Twisden—

Twisden. Sit down; sit down, my dear. [*And he himself sits
behind the table, as a cup of tea is brought in to him by
the Young Clerk, with two Marie biscuits in the saucer.*]
Will you have some, Margaret?

Margaret. No, dear Mr. Jacob.

Twisden. Charles?

Winsor. No, thanks.

[*The door is closed.*]

Twisden [*dipping a biscuit in the tea*]. Now, then?

Winsor. The General knows something which on the face of
it looks rather queer. Now that he's going to be called,
oughtn't Dancy to be told of it, so that he may be ready
with his explanation, in case it comes out?

Twisden [*pouring some tea into the saucer*]. Without knowing, I can't tell you.

[*Winsor and Margaret exchange looks, and Twisden drinks
from the saucer.*]

Margaret. Tell him, Charles.

Winsor. Well! It rained that evening at Meldon. The General happened to put his hand on Dancy's shoulder,
and it was damp.

[*Twisden puts the saucer down and replaces the cup in it.
They both look intently at him.*]

Twisden. I take it that General Canynge won't say anything
he's not compelled to say.

Margaret. No, of course; but, Mr. Jacob, they might ask; they know it rained. And he is such a George Washington.

Twisden [*toying with a pair of tortoise-shell glasses*]. They didn't ask either of *you*. Still—no harm in your telling Dancy.

Winsor. I'd rather *you* did it, Margaret.

Margaret. I daresay. [*She mechanically takes out her cigarette-case, catches the lift of Twisden's eyebrows, and puts it back.*]

Winsor. Well, we'll go together. I don't want Mrs. Dancy to hear.

Margaret. Do tell me, Mr. Jacob; is he going to win?

Twisden. I think so, Margaret; I think so.

Margaret. It'll be too frightful if he doesn't get a verdict, after all this. But I don't know what we shall do when it's over. I've been sitting in that Court all these three days, watching, and it's made me feel there's nothing we like better than seeing people skinned. Well, bye-bye, bless you!

[*Twisden rises and pats her hand.*]

Winsor. Half a second, Margaret. Wait for me. [*She nods and goes out.*] Mr. Twisden, what do you really think?

Twisden. I am Dancy's lawyer, my dear Charles, as well as yours.

Winsor. Well, can I go and see Canynge?

Twisden. Better not.

Winsor. If they get that out of him, and recall me, am I to say he told me of it at the time?

Twisden. You didn't feel the coat yourself? And Dancy wasn't present? Then what Canynge told you is not evidence. *We'll* stop your being asked.

Winsor. Thank goodness. Good-bye! [*Winsor goes out.*]

[*Twisden, behind his table, motionless, taps his teeth with the eyeglasses in his narrow, well-kept hand. After a long shake of his head and a shrug of his rather high shoulders he sniffs, goes to the window and opens it. Then crossing to the door, Left Back, he throws it open and says:*]

Twisden. At your service, sir. [*Gilman comes forth, nursing his pot hat.*] Be seated. [*Twisden closes the window behind him, and takes his seat.*]

Gilman [*taking the client's chair, to the left of the table*]. Mr. Twisden, I believe? My name's Gilman, head of

Gilman's Department Stores. You have my card.

Twisden [*looking at the card*]. Yes. What can we do for you?

Gilman. Well, I've come to you from a sense of duty, sir, and also a feelin' of embarrassment. [*He takes from his breast pocket an evening paper.*] You see, I've been followin' this Dancy case—it's a good deal talked of in Putney—and I read this at half-past two this afternoon. To be precise, at 2:25. [*He rises and hands the paper to Twisden, and with a thick gloved forefinger indicates a passage.*] When I read these numbers, I 'appened to remember givin' change for a fifty-pound note—don't often 'ave one in, you know—so I went to the cash-box out of curiosity, to see that I 'adn't got it. Well, I 'ad; and here it is. [*He draws out from his breast pocket and lays before Twisden a fifty-pound banknote.*] It was brought in to change by a customer of mine three days ago, and he got value for it. Now, that's a stolen note, it seems, and you'd like to know what I did. Mind you, that customer of mine I've known 'im—well—eight or nine years; an Italian he is— wine salesman, and so far's I know, a respectable man—foreign-lookin', but nothin' more. Now, this was at 'alf-past two, and I was at my head branch at Putney, where I live. I want you to mark the time, so as you'll see I 'aven't wasted a minute. I took a cab and I drove straight to my customer's private residence in Putney, where he lives with his daughter—Ricardos his name is, Paolio Ricardos. They tell me there that he's at his business shop in the City. So off I go in the cab again, and there I find him. Well, sir, I showed this paper to him and I produced the note. "Here," I said, "you brought this to me and you got value for it." Well, that man was taken aback. If I'm a judge, Mr. Twisden, he was taken aback, not to speak in a guilty way, but he was, as you might say, flummoxed. "Now," I said to him, "where did you get it— that's the point?" He took his time to answer, and then he said: "Well, Mr. Gilman," he said, "you know me; I am an honourable man. I can't tell you offhand, but I am above the board." He's foreign, you know, in his expressions. "Yes," I said, "that's all very well," I said, "but here I've got a stolen note and you've got the value for it. Now I tell you," I said, "what I'm going to do; I'm going straight with this note to Mr. Jacob Twisden, who's got this Dancy-DeLevis case in 'and. He's a well-

known Society lawyer," I said, "of great experience."
"Oh!" he said, "that is what you do?"—funny the way
he speaks! "Then I come with you!"—And I've got him
in the cab below. I want to tell you everything before
he comes up. On the way I tried to get something out
of him, but I couldn't—I could *not*. "This is very awkward," I said at last. "It is, Mr. Gilman," was the reply;
and he began to talk about his Sicilian claret—a very
good wine, mind you; but under the circumstances it
seemed to me uncalled for. Have I made it clear to you?

Twisden [*who has listened with extreme attention*]. Perfectly, Mr. Gilman. I'll send down for him. [*He touches
a hand-bell. The Young Clerk appears at the door, Left
Forward.*] A gentleman in a taxi—waiting. Ask him to
be so good as to step up. Oh! and send Mr. Graviter
here again.

[*The Young Clerk goes out.*]

Gilman. As I told you, sir, I've been followin' this case. It's
what you might call piquant. And I should be very glad
if it came about that this helped Captain Dancy. I
take an interest, because, to tell you the truth [*confidentially*] I don't like—well, not to put too fine a point upon
it—'Ebrews. They work harder; they're more sober;
they're honest; and they're everywhere. I've nothing
against them, but the fact is—they get *on* so.

Twisden [*cocking an eye*]. A thorn in the flesh, Mr. Gilman.

Gilman. Well, I prefer my own countrymen, and that's the
truth of it. [*As he speaks, Graviter comes in by the door,
Left Forward.*]

Twisden [*pointing to the newspaper and the note*]. Mr. Gilman has brought this, of which he is holder for value.
His customer, who changed it three days ago, is coming
up.

Graviter. The fifty-pounder. I see. [*His face is long and re-
flective.*]

Young Clerk [*entering*]. Mr. Ricardos, sir. [*He goes out.*]

[*Ricardos is a personable, Italian-looking man in a frock
coat, with a dark moustachioed face and dark hair a
little grizzled. He looks anxious, and bows.*]

Twisden. Mr. Ricardos? My name is Jacob Twisden. My
partner. [*Holding up a finger, as Ricardos would speak.*]
Mr. Gilman has told us about this note. You took it to
him, he says, three days ago; that is, on Monday, and
received cash for it?

Ricardos. Yes, sare.

Twisden. You were *not* aware that it was stolen?

Ricardos [*with his hand to his breast*]. Oh! no, sare.

Twisden. You received it from——?

Ricardos. A minute, sare; I would weesh to explain—[*with an expressive shrug*] in private.

Twisden [*nodding*]. Mr. Gilman, your conduct has been most prompt. You may safely leave the matter in our hands, now. Kindly let us retain this note; and ask for my cashier as you go out and give him [*he writes*] this. He will reimburse you. We will take any necessary steps ourselves.

Gilman [*in slight surprise, with modest pride*]. Well, sir, I'm in your 'ands. I must be guided by you, with your experience. I'm glad you think I acted rightly.

Twisden. Very rightly, Mr. Gilman—very rightly. [*Rising.*] Good-afternoon!

Gilman. Good-afternoon, sir. Good-afternoon, gentlemen! [*To Twisden.*] I'm sure I'm very 'appy to have made your acquaintance, sir. It's a well-known name.

Twisden. Thank you.

[*Gilman retreats, glances at Ricardos, and turns again.*]

Gilman. I suppose there's nothing else I ought to do, in the interests of the law? I'm a careful man.

Twisden. If there is, Mr. Gilman, we will let you know. We have your address. You may make your mind easy; but don't speak of this. It might interfere with Justice.

Gilman. Oh! I shouldn't dream of it. I've no wish to be mixed up in anything conspicuous. That's not my principle at all. Good-day, gentlemen. [*He goes.*]

Twisden [*seating himself*]. Now, sir, will you sit down. [*But Ricardos does not sit; he stands looking uneasily across the table at Graviter.*] You may speak out.

Ricardos. Well, Mr. Tweesden and sare, this matter is very serious for me, and very delicate—it concairns my honour. I am in a great difficulty.

Twisden. When in difficulty—complete frankness, sir.

Ricardos. It is a family matter, sare, I——

Twisden. Let me be frank with you. [*Telling his points off on his fingers.*] We have your admission that you changed this stopped note for value. It will be our duty to inform the Bank of England that it has been traced to you. You will have to account to them for your possession of it. I suggest to you that it will be far better to account frankly to us.

Ricardos [*taking out a handkerchief and quite openly wiping his hands and forehead*]. I received this note, sare, with others, from a gentleman, sare, in settlement of a debt of honour, and I know nothing of where he got them.

Twisden. H'm! that is very vague. If that is all you can tell us, I'm afraid—

Ricardos. Gentlemen, this is very painful for me. It is my daughter's good name— [*He again wipes his brow.*]

Twisden. Come, sir, speak out!

Ricardos [*desperately*]. The notes were a settlement to her from this gentleman, of whom she was a great friend.

Twisden [*suddenly*]. I am afraid we must press you for the name of the gentleman.

Ricardos. Sare, if I give it to you, and it does 'im 'arm, what will my daughter say? This is a bad matter for me. He behaved well to her; and she is attached to him still; sometimes she is crying yet because she lost him. And now we betray him, perhaps, who knows? This is very unpleasant for me. [*Taking up the paper.*] Here it gives the number of another note—a 'undred-pound note. I 'ave that too. [*He takes a note from his breast pocket.*]

Graviter. How much did he give you in all?

Ricardos. For my daughter's settlement one thousand pounds. I understand he did not wish to give a cheque because of his marriage. So I did not think anything about it being in notes, you see.

Twisden. When did he give you this money?

Ricardos. The middle of Octobare last.

Twisden [*suddenly looking up*]. Mr. Ricardos, was it. Captain Dancy?

Ricardos [*again wiping his forehead*]. Gentlemen, I am so fond of my daughter. I have only the one, and no wife.

Twisden [*with an effort*]. Yes, yes; but I must know.

Ricardos. Sare, if I tell you, will you give me your good word that my daughter shall not hear of it?

Twisden. So far as we are able to prevent it—certainly.

Ricardos. Sare, I trust you. It was Captain Dancy.

[*A long pause.*]

Graviter [*suddenly*]. Were you blackmailing him?

Twisden [*holding up his hand*]. My partner means, did you press him for this settlement?

Ricardos. I did think it my duty to my daughter to ask that he make compensation to her.

Twisden. With threats that you would tell his wife?

Ricardos [*with a shrug*]. Captain Dancy was a man of honour. He said: "Of course I will do this." I trusted him. And a month later I did remind him, and he gave me this money for her. I do not know where he got it—I do not know. Gentlemen, I have invested it all on her—every penny—except this note, for which I had the purpose to buy her a necklace. That is the swearéd truth.

Twisden. I must keep this note. [*He touches the hundred-pound note.*] You will not speak of this to anyone. *I* may recognise that you were a holder for value received—others might take a different view. Good-day, sir. Graviter, see Mr. Ricardos out, and take his address.

Ricardos [*pressing his hands over the breast of his frock coat—with a sigh*]. Gentlemen, I beg you—remember what I said. [*With a roll of his eyes.*] My daughter—I am not happee. Good-day. [*He turns and goes out slowly, Left Forward, followed by Graviter.*]

Twisden [*to himself*]. Young Dancy! [*He pins the two notes together and places them in an envelope, then stands motionless except for his eyes and hands, which restlessly express the disturbance within him. Graviter returns, carefully shuts the door, and going up to him, hands him Ricardos' card. Looking at the card.*] Villa Benvenuto. This will have to be verified, but I'm afraid it's true. That man was not acting.

Graviter. What's to be done about Dancy?

Twisden. Can you understand a gentleman—?

Graviter. I don't know, sir. The war loosened "form" all over the place. I saw plenty of that myself. And some men have no moral sense. From the first I've had doubts.

Twisden. We can't go on with the case.

Graviter. Phew! . . . [*A moment's silence.*] Gosh! It's an awful thing for his wife.

Twisden. Yes.

Graviter [*touching the envelope*]. Chance brought this here, sir. That man won't talk. He's too scared.

Twisden. Gilman.

Graviter. Too respectable. If De Levis got those notes back, and the rest of the money, anonymously?

Twisden. But the case, Graviter; the case.

Graviter. I don't believe this alters what I've been thinking.

Twisden. Thought is one thing—knowledge another. There's

duty to our profession. Ours is a fine calling. On the good faith of solicitors a very great deal hangs. [*He crosses to the hearth as if warmth would help him.*]

Graviter. It'll let him in for a prosecution. He came to us in confidence.

Twisden. Not as against the law.

Graviter. No. I suppose not. [*A pause.*] By Jove, I don't like losing this case. I don't like the admission we backed such a wrong 'un.

Twisden. Impossible to go on. Apart from ourselves, there's Sir Frederic. We must disclose to him—can't let him go on in the dark. Complete confidence between solicitor and counsel is the essence of professional honour.

Graviter. What are you going to do then, sir?

Twisden. See Dancy at once. Get him on the 'phone.

Graviter [*taking up the telephone*]. Get me Captain Dancy's flat. . . . What? . . . [*To Twisden.*] Mrs. Dancy is here. That's *à propos* with a vengeance. Are you going to see her, sir?

Twisden [*after a moment's painful hesitation*]. I must.

Graviter [*telephoning*]. Bring Mrs. Dancy up. [*He turns to the window. Mabel Dancy is shown in, looking very pale. Twisden advances from the fire, and takes her hand.*]

Mabel. Major Colford's taken Ronny off in his car for the night. I thought it would go him good. I said I'd come round in case there was anything you wanted to say before tomorrow.

Twisden [*taken aback*]. Where have they gone?

Mabel. I don't know, but he'll be home before ten o'clock tomorrow. Is there anything?

Twisden. Well, I'd like to see him before the Court sits. Send him on here as soon as he comes.

Mabel [*with her hand to her forehead*]. Oh! Mr. Twisden, when will it be over? My head's getting awful sitting in that Court.

Twisden. My dear Mrs. Dancy; there's no need at all for you to come down tomorrow; take a rest and nurse your head.

Mabel. Really and truly?

Twisden. Yes; it's the very best thing you can do.

[*Graviter turns his head, and looks at them unobserved.*]

Mabel. How do you think it's going?

Twisden. It went very well today; very well indeed.

Mabel. You must be awfully fed up with us.

Twisden. My dear young lady, that's our business. [*He takes her hand. Mabel's face suddenly quivers. She draws her hand away, and covers her lips with it.*] There, there! You want a day off badly.

Mabel. I'm tired of—! Thank you so much for all you're doing. Good-night! Good-night, Mr. Graviter!

Graviter. Good-night, Mrs. Dancy. [*Mabel goes.*] D'you know, I believe she knows.

Twisden. No, no! She believes in him implicitly. A staunch little woman. Poor thing!

Graviter. Hasn't that shaken you, sir? It has me.

Twisden. No, no! I—I can't go on with the case. It's breaking faith. Get Sir Frederic's chambers.

Graviter [*telephoning, and getting a reply, looks round at Twisden*]. Yes?

Twisden. Ask if I can come round and see him.

Graviter [*telephoning*]. Can Sir Frederic spare Mr. Twisden a few minutes now if he comes round? [*Receiving reply.*] He's gone down to Brighton for the night.

Twisden. H'm! What hotel?

Graviter [*telephoning*]. What's his address? What . . . ? [*To Twisden.*] The Bedford.

Twisden. I'll go down.

Graviter [*telephoning*]. Thank you. All right. [*He rings off.*]

Twisden. Just look out the trains down and up early tomorrow. [*Graviter takes up an A B C, and Twisden takes up the Ricardos card.*] Send to this address in Putney, verify the fact that Ricardos has a daughter, and give me a trunk call to Brighton. Better go yourself, Graviter. If you see her, don't say anything, of course—invent some excuse. [*Graviter nods.*] I'll be up in time to see Dancy.

Graviter. By George! I feel bad about this.

Twisden. Yes. But professional honour comes first. What time is that train? [*He bends over the A B C.*]

                                        The curtain falls.

scene TWO

The same room on the following morning at ten-twenty-five, by the Grandfather clock. The Young Clerk is ushering in

Dancy, whose face is perceptibly harder than it was three months ago, like that of a man who has lived under great restraint.

Dancy. He wanted to see me before the Court sat.

Young Clerk. Yes, sir. Mr. Twisden will see you in one minute. He had to go out of town last night. [*He prepares to open the waiting-room door.*]

Dancy. Were *you* in the war?

Young Clerk. Yes.

Dancy. How can you stick this?

Young Clerk [*with a smile*]. My trouble was to stick that, sir.

Dancy. But you get no excitement from year's end to year's end. It'd drive me mad.

Young Clerk [*shyly*]. A case like this is pretty exciting. I'd give a lot to see us win it.

Dancy [*staring at him*]. Why? What is it to you?

Young Clerk. I don't know, sir. It's—it's like football—you want your side to win. [*He opens the waiting-room door. Expanding.*] You see some rum starts, too, in a lawyer's office in a quiet way.

[*Dancy enters the waiting-room, and the Young Clerk, shutting the door, meets Twisden as he comes in, Left Forward, and takes from him overcoat, top hat, and a small bag.*]

Young Clerk. Captain Dancy's waiting, sir. [*He indicates the waiting-room.*]

Twisden [*narrowing his lips*]. Very well. Mr. Graviter gone to the Courts?

Young Clerk. Yes, sir.

Twisden. Did he leave anything for me?

Young Clerk. On the table, sir.

Twisden [*taking up an envelope*]. Thank you. [*The Clerk goes. Opening the envelope and reading.*] "All corroborates." H'm! [*He puts it in his pocket and takes out of an envelope the two notes, lays them on the table, and covers them with a sheet of blotting-paper; stands a moment preparing himself, then goes to the door of the waiting-room, opens it, and says:*] Now, Captain Dancy. Sorry to have kept you waiting.

Dancy [*entering*]. Winsor came to me yesterday about General Canynge's evidence Is that what you wanted to speak to me about?

Twisden. No. It isn't that.

Dancy [*looking at his wristwatch*]. By me it's just on the half-hour, sir.

Twisden. Yes. I don't want you to go to the Court.

Dancy. Not?

Twisden. I have very serious news for you.

Dancy [*wincing and collecting himself*]. Oh!

Twisden. These two notes. [*He uncovers the notes.*] After the Court rose yesterday we had a man called Ricardos here. [*A pause.*] Is there any need for me to say more?

Dancy [*unflinching*]. No. What now?

Twisden. Our duty was plain; we could not go on with the case. I have consulted Sir Frederic. He felt—he felt that he must throw up his brief, and he will do that the moment the Court sits. Now I want to talk to you about what you're going to do.

Dancy. That's very good of you, considering.

Twisden. I don't pretend to understand, but I imagine you may have done this in a moment of reckless bravado, feeling, perhaps, that as you gave the mare to De Levis, the money was by rights as much yours as his. [*Stopping Dancy, who is about to speak, with a gesture.*] To satisfy a debt of honour to this—lady; and, no doubt, to save your wife from hearing of it from the man Ricardos. Is that so?

Dancy. To the life.

Twisden. It was mad, Captain Dancy, mad!—But the question now is: What do you owe to your wife? She doesn't dream—I suppose?

Dancy [*with a twitching face*]. No.

Twisden. We can't tell what the result of this collapse will be. The police have the theft in hand. They may issue a warrant. The money could be refunded, and the costs paid—somehow that can all be managed. But it may not help. In any case, what end is served by your staying in the country. You can't save your honour—that's gone. You can't save your wife's peace of mind. If she sticks to you—do you think she will?

Dancy. Not if she's wise.

Twisden. Better go! There's a war in Morocco.

Dancy [*with a bitter smile*]. Good old Morocco!

Twisden. Will you go, then, at once, and leave me to break it to your wife?

Dancy. I don't know yet.

Twisden. You must decide quickly, to catch a boat train.

Many a man has made good. You're a fine soldier.

Dancy. There are alternatives.

Twisden. Now, go straight from this office. You've a passport, I suppose; you won't need a visa for France, and
from there you can find means to slip over. Have you
got money on you? [*Dancy nods.*] We will see what we
can do to stop or delay proceedings.

Dancy. It's all damned kind of you. [*With difficulty.*] But I
must think of my wife. Give me a few minutes.

Twisden. Yes, yes; go in there and think it out. [*He goes to
the door, Right, and opens it. Dancy passes him and
goes out. Twisden rings a bell and stands waiting.*]

Clerk [*entering*]. Yes, sir?

Twisden. Tell them to call a taxi.

Clerk [*who has a startled look*]. Yes, sir. Mr. Graviter has
come in, sir, with General Canynge. Are you disen-
gaged?

Twisden. Yes. [*The Clerk goes out, and almost immediately
Graviter and Canynge enter.*] Good-morning, General.
[*To Graviter.*] Well?

Graviter. Sir Frederic got up at once and said that since the
publication of the numbers of those notes, information
had reached him which forced him to withdraw from
the case. Great sensation, of course. I left Bromley in
charge. There'll be a formal verdict for the defendant,
with costs. Have you told Dancy?

Twisden. Yes. He's in there deciding what he'll do.

Canynge [*grave and vexed*]. This is a dreadful thing, Twisden. I've been afraid of it all along. A soldier! A gallant
fellow, too. What on earth got into him?

Twisden. There's no end to human nature, General.

Graviter. You can see queerer things in the papers, any day.

Canynge. That poor young wife of his! Winsor gave me a
message for you, Twisden. If money's wanted quickly
to save proceedings, draw on him. Is there anything *I*
can do?

Twisden. I've advised him to go straight off to Morocco.

Canynge. I don't know that an asylum isn't the place for
him. He must be off his head at moments. That jump
—crazy! He'd have got a verdict on that alone—if
they'd seen those balconies. I was looking at them when
I was down there last Sunday. Daring thing, Twisden.
Very few men, on a dark night—He risked his life
twice. That's a shrewd fellow—young De Levis. He

spotted Dancy's nature.

[*The Young Clerk enters.*]

Clerk. The taxi's here, sir. Will you see Major Colford and Miss Orme?

Twisden. Graviter—No; show them in.

[*The Young Clerk goes.*]

Canynge. Colford's badly cut up.

[*Margaret Orme and Colford enter.*]

Colford [*striding forward*]. There must be some mistake about this, Mr. Twisden.

Twisden. Hssh! Dancy's in there. He's admitted it.

[*Voices are subdued at once.*]

Colford. What? [*With emotion.*] If it were my own brother, I couldn't feel it more. But—damn it! What right had that fellow to chuck up the case—without letting him know, too. I came down with Dancy this morning, and he knew nothing about it.

Twisden [*coldly*]. That was unfortunately unavoidable.

Colford. Guilty or not, you ought to have stuck to him—it's not playing the game, Mr. Twisden.

Twisden. You must allow me to judge where my duty lay, in a very hard case.

Colford. I thought a man was safe with his solicitor.

Canynge. Colford, you don't understand professional etiquette.

Colford. No, thank God!

Twisden. When you have been as long in your profession as I have been in mine, Major Colford, you will know that duty to your calling outweighs duty to friend or client.

Colford. But I serve the Country.

Twisden. And I serve the Law, sir.

Canynge. Graviter, give me a sheet of paper. I'll write a letter for him.

Margaret [*going up to Twisden*]. Dear Mr. Jacob—pay De Levis. You know my pearls—put them up the spout again. Don't let Ronny be—

Twisden. Money isn't the point, Margaret.

Margaret. It's ghastly! It really is.

Colford. I'm going in to shake hands with him. [*He starts to cross the room.*]

Twisden. Wait! We want him to go straight off to Morocco. Don't upset him. [*To Colford and Margaret.*] I think you had better go. If, a little later, Margaret, you could go round to Mrs. Dancy—

Colford. Poor little Mabel Dancy! It's perfect hell for her.

[*They have not seen that Dancy has opened the door behind them.*]

Dancy. It is!

[*They all turn round in consternation.*]

Colford [*with a convulsive movement*]. Old boy!

Dancy. No good, Colford. [*Gazing round at them.*] Oh! clear out. I can't stand commiseration—and let me have some air.

[*Twisden motions to Colford and Margaret to go; and as he turns to Dancy, they go out. Graviter also moves towards the door. The General sits motionless. Graviter goes out.*]

Twisden. Well?

Dancy. I'm going home, to clear up things with my wife. General Canynge, I don't quite know why I did the damned thing. But I did, and there's an end of it.

Canynge. Dancy, for the honour of the Army, avoid further scandal if you can. I've written a letter to a friend of mine in the Spanish War Office. It will get you a job in their war. [*Canynge closes the envelope.*]

Dancy. Very good of you. I don't know if I can make use of it.

[*Canynge stretches out the letter, which Twisden hands to Dancy, who takes it. Graviter reopens the door.*]

Twisden. What is it?

Graviter. De Levis is here.

Twisden. De Levis? Can't see him.

Dancy. Let him in!

[*After a moment's hesitation Twisden nods, and Graviter goes out. The three wait in silence with their eyes fixed on the door, the General sitting at the table, Twisden by his chair, Dancy between him and the door Right. De Levis comes in and shuts the door. He is advancing towards Twisden when his eyes fall on Dancy, and he stops.*]

Twisden. You wanted to see me?

De Levis [*moistening his lips*]. Yes. I came to say that—that I overheard—I am afraid a warrant is to be issued. I wanted you to realise—it's not *my* doing. I'll give it no support. I'm content. I don't want my money. I don't even want costs. Dancy, do you understand?

[*Dancy does not answer, but looks at him with nothing alive in his face but his eyes.*]

Twisden. We are obliged to you, sir. It was good of you to
    come.

De Levis [*with a sort of darting pride*]. Don't mistake me.
    I didn't come because I feel Christian. I am a Jew.
    I will take no money—not even that which was stolen.
    Give it to a charity. I'm proved right. And now I'm
    done with the damned thing. Good-morning! [*He makes
    a little bow to Canynge and Twisden, and turns to face
    Dancy, who has never moved. The two stand motion-
    less, looking at each other, then De Levis shrugs his
    shoulders and walks out. When he is gone there is a
    silence.*]

Canynge [*suddenly*]. You heard what he said, Dancy. You
    have no time to lose.

[*But Dancy does not stir.*]

Twisden. Captain Dancy?

[*Slowly, without turning his head, rather like a man in a
    dream, Dancy walks across the room, and goes out.*]

                                            The curtain falls.

scene THREE

*The Dancys' sitting-room, a few minutes later. Mabel Dancy
is sitting alone on the sofa with a newspaper on her lap; she
is only just-up, and has a bottle of smelling-salts in her hand.
Two or three other newspapers are dumped on the arm of
the sofa. She topples the one off her lap and takes up another
as if she couldn't keep away from them; drops it in turn, and
sits staring before her, sniffing at the salts. The door, Right,
is opened and Dancy comes in.*

Mabel [*utterly surprised*]. Ronny! Do they want me in Court?
Dancy. No.
Mabel. What is it, then? Why are you back?
Dancy. Spun.
Mabel [*blank*]. Spun? What do you mean? What's spun?
Dancy. The case. They've found out through those notes.
Mabel. Oh! [*Staring at his face.*] Who?
Dancy. Me!
Mabel [*after a moment of horrified stillness*]. Don't Ronny!
    Oh! No! Don't! [*She buries her face in the pillows of
    the sofa. Dancy stands looking down at her.*]

Dancy. Pity you wouldn't come to Africa three months ago.

Mabel. Why didn't you tell me then? I would have gone.

Dancy. You wanted this case. Well, it's fallen down.

Mabel. Oh! Why didn't I face it? But I couldn't—I *had* to believe.

Dancy. And now you can't. It's the end, Mabel.

Mabel [*looking up at him*]. No.

[*Dancy goes suddenly on his knees and seizes her hand.*]

Dancy. Forgive me!

Mabel [*putting her hand on his head*]. Yes; oh, yes! I think I've known a long time, really. Only—why? What made you?

Dancy [*getting up and speaking in jerks*]. It was a crazy thing to do; but, damn it, I was only looting a looter. The money was as much mine as his. A decent chap would have offered me half. You didn't see the brute look at me that night at dinner as much as to say: "You blasted fool!" It made me mad. That wasn't a bad jump —twice over. Nothing in the war took quite such nerve. [*Grimly.*] I rather enjoyed that evening.

Mabel. But—money! To keep it!

Dancy [*sullenly*]. Yes, but I had a debt to pay.

Mabel. To a woman?

Dancy. A debt of honour—it wouldn't wait.

Mabel. It was—it was to a woman. Ronny, don't lie any more.

Dancy [*grimly*]. Well! I wanted to save your knowing. I'd promised a thousand. I had a letter from her father that morning, threatening to tell you. All the same, if that tyke hadn't jeered at me for parlour tricks!—But what's the good of all this now? [*Sullenly.*] Well—it may cure you of loving me. Get over that, Mab; I never was worth it—and I'm done for!

Mabel. The woman—have you—since—?

Dancy [*energetically*]. No! You supplanted her. But if you'd known I was leaving a woman for you, you'd never have married me. [*He walks over to the hearth. Mabel too gets up. She presses her hands to her forehead, then walks blindly round to behind the sofa and stands looking straight in front of her.*]

Mabel [*coldly*]. What has happened, exactly?

Dancy. Sir Frederic chucked up the case. I've seen Twisden; they want me to run for it to Morocco.

Mabel. To the war there?

Dancy. Yes. There's to be a warrant out.

Mabel. A prosecution? Prison? Oh, go! Don't wait a minute! Go!

Dancy. Blast them!

Mabel. Oh, Ronny! Please! Please! Think what you'll want. I'll pack. Quick! No! Don't wait to take things. Have you got money?

Dancy [*nodding*]. This'll be good-bye, then!

Mabel [*after a moment's struggle*]. Oh! No! No, no! I'll follow——I'll come out to you there.

Dancy. D'you mean you'll stick to me?

Mabel. Of course I'll stick to you.

[*Dancy seizes her hand and puts it to his lips. The bell rings.*]

Mabel [*in terror*]. Who's that? [*The bell rings again. Dancy moves towards the door.*] No! Let *me*! [*She passes him and steals out to the outer door of the flat, where she stands listening. The bell rings again. She looks through the slit of the letter-box. While she is gone Dancy stands quite still, till she comes back.*]

Mabel. Through the letter-box—I can see—It's—it's police. Oh! God . . . Ronny! I can't bear it.

Dancy. Heads up, Mab! Don't show the brutes!

Mabel. Whatever happens, I'll go on loving you. If it's prison —*I'll wait*. Do you understand? I don't care what you did— I don't *care!* I'm just the same. I will be just the same when you come back to me.

Dancy [*slowly*]. That's not in human nature.

Mabel. It is. It's in *me*.

Dancy. I've crocked up your life.

Mabel. No, no! Kiss me!

[*A long kiss, till the bell again startles them apart, and there is a loud knock.*]

Dancy. They'll break the door in. It's no good—we must open. Hold them in check a little. I want a minute or two.

Mabel [*clasping him*]. Ronny! Oh, Ronny! It won't be for long—I'll be waiting! I'll be waiting—I swear it.

Dancy. Steady, Mab! [*Putting her back from him.*] Now! [*He opens the bedroom door, Left, and stands waiting for her to go. Summoning up her courage, she goes to open the outer door. A sudden change comes over Dancy's face; from being stony it grows almost maniacal. Under his breath.*] No! No! By God! No! [*He goes out into the bedroom, closing the door behind him.*

Mabel has now opened the outer door, and disclosed Inspector Dede and the Young Constable who were summoned to Meldon Court on the night of the theft, and have been witnesses in the case. Their voices are heard.]

Mabel. Yes?

Inspector. Captain Dancy in, madam?

Mabel. I am not quite sure—I don't think so.

Inspector. I wish to speak to him a minute. Stay here, Grover. Now, madam!

Mabel. Will you come in while I see?

[*She comes in, followed by the Inspector.*]

Inspector. I should think you must be sure, madam. This is not a big place.

Mabel. He was changing his clothes to go out. I think he has gone.

Inspector. What's that door?

Mabel. To our bedroom.

Inspector [*moving towards it*]. He'll be in there, then.

Mabel. What do you want, Inspector?

Inspector [*melting*]. Well, madam, it's no use disguising it. I'm exceedingly sorry, but I've a warrant for his arrest.

Mabel. Inspector!

Inspector. I'm sure I've every sympathy for you, madam; but I must carry out my instructions.

Mabel. And break my heart?

Inspector. Well, madam, we're—we're not allowed to take that into consideration. The Law's the Law.

Mabel. Are you married?

Inspector. I am.

Mabel. If you—your wife—[*The Inspector raises his hand, deprecating. Speaking low.*] Just half an hour! Couldn't you! It's two lives—two whole lives! We've only been married four months. Come back in half an hour. It's such a little thing—nobody will know. Nobody. Won't you?

Inspector. Now, madam—you must know my duty.

Mabel. Inspector, I beseech you—just half an hour.

Inspector. No, no—don't you try to undermine me—I'm sorry for you; but don't you try it! [*He tries the handle, then knocks at the door.*]

Dancy's Voice. One minute!

Inspector. It's locked. [*Sharply.*] Is there another door to that room? Come, now! [*The bell rings. Moving to-*

wards the door, Left; to the Constable.] Who's that out
there?

Constable. A lady and gentleman, sir.

Inspector. What lady and—Stand by, Grover!

Dancy's Voice. All right! You can come in *now.*

[*There is the noise of a lock being turned. And almost immediately the sound of a pistol shot in the bedroom.
Mabel rushes to the door, tears it open, and disappears
within, followed by the Inspector, just as Margaret
Orme and Colford come in from the passage, pursued
by the Constable. They, too, all hurry to the bedroom
door and disappear for a moment; then Colford and
Margaret reappear, supporting Mabel, who faints as
they lay her on the sofa. Colford takes from her hand
an envelope, and tears it open.*]

Colford. It's addressed to me. [*He reads it aloud to Margaret
in a low voice.*] "Dear Colford,—This is the only decent
thing I can do. It's too damned unfair to her. It's only
another jump. A pistol keeps faith. Look after her.
Colford—my love to her, and you."

[*Margaret gives a sort of choking sob, then, seeing the smell-
ing bottle, she snatches it up, and turns to revive Mabel.*]

Colford. Leave her! The longer she's unconscious, the better.

Inspector [*reentering*]. This is a very serious business, sir.

Colford [*sternly*]. Yes, Inspector; you've done for my best
friend.

Inspector. I, sir? He shot himself.

Colford. Hari-kari.

Inspector. Beg pardon?

Colford [*he points with the letter to Mabel*]. For her sake,
and his own.

Inspector [*putting out his hand*]. I'll want that, sir.

Colford [*grimly*]. You shall have it read at the inquest. Till
then—it's addressed to me, and I stick to it.

Inspector. Very well, sir. Do you want to have a look at him?

[*Colford passes quickly into the bedroom, followed by the
Inspector. Margaret remains kneeling beside Mabel.*]
*Colford comes quickly back. Margaret looks up at him.
He stands very still.*]

Colford. Neatly—through the heart.

Margaret [*wildly*]. Keeps faith! We've all done that. It's not
enough.

Colford [*looking down at Mabel*]. All right, old boy!

                                              The Curtain Falls.

Noël Coward **Private Lives**

AN INTIMATE COMEDY IN THREE ACTS

For Jeffery from Noël

Shanghai 1930

Noël Coward: An Appreciation
of his Work in the Theatre

BY TERENCE RATTIGAN

All playwrights of experience suffer, in varying degree, from persecution mania, coupled with amnesia, on the subject of their past treatment at the hands of dramatic critics. Noël Coward is no exception. I have heard him state, with apparently firm conviction, that his greatest successes had always had uniformly bad notices, and though the occasion for this remark was the characteristically generous urge to minister comfort after a first night to a sorely wounded colleague, nevertheless one has only to read the prefaces to his collected plays to realize that it would have needed no great degree of duplicity on his part to have induced him to utter so barefaced a mis-statement.

For mis-statement it certainly is. Let him confound himself by re-reading, for instance, St. John Ervine's panegyric on *This Year of Grace!*—I suppose the best notice ever written anywhere by anyone about anything—or Agate's pæan about *Bitter-Sweet*—it's not bad to be compared to Wagner—or Parsons' rhapsody about *Cavalcade,* with its closing words—which could not surely have been entirely displeasing at the time: "Drury Lane has come into its own again—our national theatre has a theme worthy of itself."

It is in fact very pleasant to read now these tributes to Coward from major and responsible critics—and there are many others beside those I have cited—not merely because, in removing a libel it does belated justice to the Press—and who wants to do justice to the Press?—but mainly because it relieves my conscience of a certain burden of guilt regarding a past misdeed and opens the way to a frank confession. Probably the most irritating, unimaginative, pompous, patronizing and misguided notice Coward could ever have received was written by myself.

Received, fortunately, does not mean read, or our friendship would certainly have perished before it was begun. The article, all traces of which have happily now disappeared, was published in 1931 in an Oxford undergraduate magazine for which I acted as dramatic critic, and which on this occasion had commissioned me to write a notice of *Caval-cade*. My fee was a matinée upper circle seat at Drury Lane and my third-class return fare to London—I did not consider myself underpaid—and before going I received a fairly strong hint from my editor that I was not expected to be over-effusive. It appeared that the rival undergraduate magazine had published, the week before, an article entitled "Noël Coward: Genius and Prophet." My own notice, therefore, when composed, bore the heading: "No, no, Noël." Our journalistic standards were racier than our rivals'.

The notice, on the other hand, was not racy at all. With immense portentousness it asked itself the question: Whither Noël Coward? and more in sorrow than in anger answered itself: "No whither at all." His early plays had led serious students of the drama to believe that a young, revolutionary dramatist of immense promise had emerged. Alas, he had succumbed to the lures of mere commercial success, and sold his soul to the devils of Shaftesbury Avenue. *Cavalcade* was only an ephemeral triumph, made possible by the political climate of 1931. At the first change in that climate, which must come in a few years, it would be forgotten, while its author's reputation would hardly outlast the 'thirties. If only he had continued in the path set by *The Vortex* (which I had not been allowed to see, my parents not considering it suitable but which I knew to be serious) or *Post-Mortem* (which I had at least read) then his fame would have been secure. Alas, he had chosen the easy road, the road that can only lead to oblivion. Ah well. *Requiescat Noël Coward in pace.* He was quite good while he lasted.

I am emboldened to remind myself of this act of juvenile delinquency by the interesting discovery, of a judgment delivered, a whole year earlier than mine, by a brilliant and world-famous critic who, having the excuse neither of extreme youth nor of editorial instruction, should now be blushing far more rosily than I. Mr. Ivor Brown, writing of *Private Lives* in October 1930, asked himself the question: ". . . what the younger critics of 1950 will say of Mr. Noël Coward . . ." and answered himself thus: "Within a few years the student of drama will be sitting in complete bewilderment before the text of *Private Lives,* wondering what on earth those fellows of 1930 saw in so flimsy a trifle."

I am sure that Mr. Ivor Brown, the best and most generous of critics, would hasten to agree with me that the above-quoted judgment is not just a floater but a real old-fashioned clangeroo; while he would certainly and categorically answer his question about "the younger critics of 1950" did I not now have the happy chance of expiating my own offence by answering it for him.

The younger critics of 1950 say of Noël Coward exactly what they have always said of him, that he is a brilliant man of the theatre, a fine craftsman and a superb entertainer. They admit, as ever, his wit, and doubt, as ever, his wisdom. They grant, as ever, his skill, and deplore, as ever, its shallowness. They worry, as they have worried for the last thirty years or more, about his future, and are gravely perturbed about his apparent inability to develop as a dramatist. In the meantime they admit that the play—whatever Coward play of the 'fifties they happen to be writing about—*Relative Values*, say, or *South Sea Bubble*—they admit freely that it is brilliantly and hilariously entertaining and a good deal better than other plays of its kind to be seen in London at the same moment.

They may, on occasions, say worse things, and on others, perhaps, better, but I believe that the foregoing is a fair résumé of modern critical opinion regarding Coward, which has varied by hardly an iota from that current in the early 'twenties.

If that is so, a curious fact emerges. A playwright who, from his earliest days, has been assured that his vogue cannot possibly last, founded as it is upon a superficial method, a highly personal idiom and a complete lack of characterization, that he is no more than a brilliant flash in the pan, fated, because of his inability to develop, to fade quickly into limbo—this same playwright, after thirty-five years of not particularly arduous toil, finds himself with his vogue not only undiminished but surely more firmly established than ever. Are his first nights less brilliant now than in the 'twenties? Is his name less widely known? Are his sayings and doings less widely reported in the Press? Is it so easy to get a table at the Café de Paris when he is performing there? Incidentally, and in parenthesis, what an incredible thing it is that Coward, who when still in his twenties had already seemed to have done everything that a man could do in the field of entertainment, should, in his fifties, have found yet one more world to conquer, and have conquered it, as he has conquered all others, with such masterful Alexandrine ease.

In 1956, then, the star of Noël Coward, that has never at any period burnt very dim, is blazing over our heads more dazzlingly than ever before. In the history of the theatre no other fashionable playwright has held sway for quite so long. Maugham's reign was shorter, though admittedly its end was self-determined. Pinero and Henry Arthur Jones both saw their popularity wane in the early nineteen-hundreds. Shaw hardly counts as a "fashionable" playwright and both Barrie's and Galsworthy's decline was spectacular.

How, then, do we explain Coward's longevity? Not, plainly, by mere luck. Luck certainly plays a large part in the theatre, but no man's luck lasts for thirty-five years.

Logic seems to provide us with a choice between two answers. The secret of Coward's continuing popularity lies either in the fact that he writes the sort of play that is as entertaining to an audience of the 'fifties as to one of the 'twenties—i.e., the sort of play that does not "date"—or the critics are wrong and he *has* in fact developed as a playwright.

I believe the truth to be a combination of the two. His plays, in general, do not "date." Admittedly the idiom is personal and he often writes much as, in real life, he speaks; but that is merely to say that he writes with wit; and wit is a quality that does not date. The things that do date, in the theatre, are attitudes of mind inspired by purely contemporary factors—political opinions, for instance, or moral judgments, or messages on How To Save The World. All such paraphernalia are happily mainly absent from Coward's work. He is interested only in humanity, its quirks and foibles, its vanities and idiocies, its prejudices and pomposities, and these things, as Congreve and Sheridan have taught us, are changeless. What is more, he expresses that interest with a verbal dexterity unmatched in our time. It is not a difficult idiom to imitate—and many have done so—but it is impossible to reproduce. In fact, it is the imitators who now sound dated, not Coward.

I will return later to this question of Coward's use of the spoken word, an all-important factor in any assessment of his work, but for the moment I must attempt to make good my other claim—that he *has,* contrary to most critics' opinion, developed as a dramatist since the 'twenties.

Now the word "develop" is probably the most fearsome weapon in the whole critical armory. It is continually being brandished over our heads, making us all morbidly self-conscious—the worst failing any creative writer can have—miserably sure that we are all pathological cases of acute arrested development, and inducing us all to try to write the sort of plays of which we are not only incapable at the moment, but will probably never be capable, even if we live to the age of Bernard Shaw.

Now Coward, very wisely, has never fallen for this trap. He knows, as we all know in our hearts but possibly recognize with less clarity than he, that "development" in the critics' sense is pure bunk. A playwright writes the best play of which he is capable at any given time, and he writes it in the style and the method which best fit his own particular talent. To do anything else is not only self-betrayal, but arrant folly. If, for instance, Christopher Fry were to allow himself to be goaded by those critics who are continually begging him to find a good plot into writing a whodunit on the lines of *Dial M for Murder,* I hardly feel I am guilty of libel when I say with absolute conviction that, however hard he tried, I am sure he would do it very, very badly. Equally fatal would it surely be if Noel Coward tried to write like Strindberg; although it might, I suppose, be claimed that he once did. But I suspect that *Point Valaine* was composed far more because he wanted to give the Lunts two whoppingly effective parts than because of the critics' urgings that he should write a play of serious moment. The truth still remains. Throughout his career Noël Coward has most wisely continued to write like Noël Coward, and like nobody else.

How then has he developed? I would say, in the way we all develop—not only all creative writers, but indeed all members of the human race, whatever their craft or occupation—by the simple process of growing older and gathering experience. Is it said that Coward still writes as if he were a boy? If it is it can only be because the critic has confused exuberance with vitality. Exuberance Coward put aside after the very early plays. Vitality he has never lost, and, let us hope, never will. Take three comedies of the later period, *Present Laughter, Blithe Spirit* and *Relative Values,* and compare them to *The Young Idea, Fallen Angels* and *Hay Fever*. Which are the more carefully constructed, gracefully composed and stylishly expressed? I'll leave it to you—to name, incidentally, another comedy of the exuberant era. To me the answer is obvious.

I suppose that the kernel of the critics' argument regarding Coward's development is that he has not developed from a writer of comedy to a writer of serious drama. Pinero is cited as an example. The progression from *Dandy Dick* to *The Second Mrs. Tanqueray* is a "development" spectacularly apparent to all, and which critics lustily applaud. But surely the point about such a "development"—I leave on one side the question whether *Dandy Dick* was all that inferior a work to *Mrs. Tanqueray*—is that no man becomes a serious dramatist who has not the firm ambition of becoming so. I hardly believe that Coward has. True, he has written serious plays, and some of them, notably *Still Life* and *The Astonished Heart*, are among the best things he has given us. But it is difficult, one feels, for him to sustain a serious mood for long—the two plays cited above are one-acters—unless gripped by some such violent passion as the anger that must have inspired *Peace in Our Time* and *Post-Mortem*, and the patriotic fervor that must have inspired *This Happy Breed* and *Cavalcade*. The more turbulent emotions are not always conducive to the best work. Despite the recent prevalence of "angry" plays by "angry" young men, I have always held the, perhaps, prejudiced view that it is really the gentler emotions—pity, compassion, nostalgia, love, regret—that are likely to inspire the most worthwhile and durable drama. Anger rarely breeds understanding, and without understanding a play becomes too subjective to make good drama. Exciting, perhaps, at its immediate impact; but forgotten soon afterwards.

This view, I repeat, is a personal one, as indeed is my firm belief that the four plays mentioned above will not last in the memory of posterity a tenth as long as *Private Lives, Present Laughter* and *Hands Across the Sea*.

It is with a brief study of these three masterpieces that I would like to end this foreword. I have said masterpieces and I will not lightly retract, for these three happen to be my favorite "Coward" comedies, and that fact, in itself, is sufficient justification to me for my choice of word.

Authors usually write shockingly badly about their own work, and the author of *Private Lives* is no exception. In his preface to the play he has the barefaced effrontery to dismiss it as ". . . a reasonably well-constructed duologue for two experienced performers, with a couple of extra puppets thrown in to assist the plot and to provide contrast . . . as a complete play it leaves a lot to be desired. . . ."

Exactly what, I would like to know, does it leave to be desired? Does its poor, bemused creator not realize that *Private Lives* deals with a theme of timeless and universal significance—the equation of love and hatred—and that it deals with it not only with grace and wisdom and hilarity, but with an objective truth that endows it with that touching quality that is so often the concomitant of great comedy? What if it *is* just "a duologue for two experienced performers"? So, if I may express myself thus cursorily, what? The duologue reveals two characters alive and fresh and glowing, and, withal, high-spirited enough to make their duel over the three acts an evening of intoxicating delight. What, then, I repeat, are we left desiring? One day I really must have this out with him in person.

Present Laughter deals with no theme of more universal significance than that most theatre people are mad, and that those about them usually have a pretty hectic time looking after them. But for sheer virtuosity it probably beats anything else that Coward has done. It also firmly nails the lie that Coward cannot create minor characters. Roland Maule is a superb creation, and so, in their lesser ways, are Monica Reed, Miss Erikson and Fred.

It is in this play, that would have been burdened in lesser hands by a trite plot and a conventional theme, that Coward's verbal dexterity, to which I have already alluded, seems to me to reach its fullest fruition. I cite as example a speech of the actor, Garry Essendine, in the third act. It is a long speech, as speeches go these days, but it bears the virtue, as do all good pieces of prose writing, of being quite "uncuttable." And so I quote it in full:

> *Garry*. I'm sick to death of being stuffed with everybody's confidences. I'm bulging with them. You all of you come to me over and over again and pour your damned tears and emotions and sentiment over me until I'm wet through. You're all just as badly behaved as I am really, in many ways a great deal worse. You believe in your lachrymose, amorous hangovers, whereas I at least have the grace to take mine lightly. You wallow and I laugh because I believe now and I

always have believed that there's far too much nonsense talked about sex. You, Morris, happen to like
taking your paltry attachments seriously. You like suffering and plunging into orgies of jealousy and torturing
yourself and everyone else. That's your way of enjoying yourself. Henry's technique is a little different; he
plumps for the domestic blend. That's why he got tired
of Joanna so quickly. Anyhow, he's beautifully suited
with poor Elvira. She's been knee-deep in pasture ever
since she left Roedean. Joanna's different again. She
devotes a great deal of time to sex, but not for any
of the intrinsic pleasures of it, merely as a means to an
end. She's a collector, a go-getter, an attractive, un-
scrupulous pirate. I personally am none of these things.
To me the whole business is vastly overrated. I enjoy
it for what it's worth and fully intend to go on doing
so for as long as anybody's interested, and when the
time comes that they're not I shall be perfectly content
to settle down with an apple and a good book!

The aspiring playwright would do well to read this speech
to himself aloud and to use his reaction to it as a touchstone
of his own sense of theatre. If at the end of it he feels no
more than that it is a reasonably well-phrased prose passage,
and is blind to its *theatrical* brilliance, its use of words as
stage music—"lachrymose, amorous hangovers"—the exact
spacing and the timing of the laughs, and the superbly skil-
ful comic climax of "apple and a good book," if he be blind
to all this, then let him throw away his pen for ever, or
just become a novelist.

Hands Across the Sea is, I think, just about the best short
comedy ever written. In form it is little more than an elon-
gated revue sketch, embracing a single situation, and a not
particularly promising one at that, but to it Coward brought
to bear his full armory of comic invention. Unencumbered
by the exigencies of plot or characterization, the author's
flight of fancy transports us into a world of hilarious lunacy
in which, by some magic, he persuades us that the only
unreal elements are the sad, dreadfully sane couple from
Malaya, crouching timidly in a corner, and watching the
goings-on with wide, wondering eyes. Them we instantly
reject, as "things from another world." Everything else—
the duck that quacks "Land of Hope and Glory" when its
behind is pinched, the Maharajah who may or may not have

a religious objection to Douglas Byng, the son of a lunatic mother who did something unspeakable in Hong Kong because, apparently, of the climate—all this we accept as substantial, tangible, true and of this world.

It is an intensely funny play both in performance—and who that was lucky enough to see her will ever forget Gertrude Lawrence in the part—and in reading. But I think it is a good deal more than just an intensely funny play. The Aldwych farces were intensely funny. *Hands Across the Sea* has qualities of imagination—albeit an outrageous imagination—that raise it to the level of a work of art.

There are many other Coward plays I could and indeed would like to write about. I have chosen these three because they are my favorites, and my space is running short. I could have written about his music, although I am not qualified to do so, save to say that I have found it almost invariably delightful. I could also, I suppose, have touched on his lyrics, which would have brought me to the inevitable judgment that they are the best of their kind since W. S. Gilbert. I could have praised his skill as an actor, and as director, I could have mentioned his talent as a film-maker, and I could have noted that he has written at least two short stories that deserve posterity's attention. Let us face the fact frankly that the man's talent is too extraordinary and too diffuse to be covered in a few brief pages. He is simply a phenomenon, and one that is unlikely to occur ever again in theatre history. Let us at least be grateful that it is our own epoch that the phenomenon has so signally adorned.

CHARACTERS

Amanda Prynne
Victor Prynne, her husband
Louise, a maid
Sibyl Chase
Elyot Chase, her husband

act 1

The Scene is the terrace of a hotel in France. There are two French windows at the back opening on to two separate suites. The terrace space is divided by a line of small trees in tubs, and, down-stage, running parallel with the footlights, there is a low stone balustrade. Upon each side of the line of tree tubs is a set of suitable terrace furniture, a swinging seat, two or three chairs, and a table. There are orange and white awnings shading the windows, as it is summer.

When the curtain rises it is about eight o'clock in the evening. There is an orchestra playing not very far off. Sibyl Chase opens the windows on the Right, and steps out on to the terrace. She is very pretty and blonde, and smartly dressed in travelling clothes. She comes down stage, stretches her arms wide with a little sigh of satisfaction, and regards the view with an ecstatic expression.

Sibyl [*calling*]. Elli, Elli dear, do come out. It's so lovely.
Elyot [*inside*]. Just a minute.
[*After a pause Elyot comes out. He is about thirty, quite slim and pleasant looking, and also in travelling clothes. He walks right down to the balustrade and looks thoughtfully at the view. Sibyl stands beside him, and slips her arm through his.*]
Elyot. Not so bad.
Sibyl. It's heavenly. Look at the lights of that yacht reflected in the water. Oh dear, I'm so happy.
Elyot [*smiling*]. Are you?
Sibyl. Aren't you?
Elyot. Of course I am. Tremendously happy.
Sibyl. Just to think, here we are, you and I, married!
Elyot. Yes, things have come to a pretty pass.

Sibyl. Don't laugh at me, you mustn't be *blasé* about honey-
    moons just because this is your second.

Elyot [*frowning*]. That's silly.

Sibyl. Have I annoyed you by saying that?

Elyot. Just a little.

Sibyl. Oh, darling, I'm so sorry. [*She holds her face up to
    his.*] Kiss me.

Elyot [*doing so*]. There.

Sibyl. Ummm, not so very enthusiastic.

Elyot [*kissing her again*]. That better?

Sibyl. Three times, please, I'm superstitious.

Elyot [*kissing her*]. You really are very sweet.

Sibyl. Are you glad you married me?

Elyot. Of course I am.

Sibyl. How glad?

Elyot. Incredibly, magnificently glad.

Sibyl. How lovely.

Elyot. We ought to go in and dress.

Sibyl. Gladder than before?

Elyot. Why do you keep harping on that?

Sibyl. It's in my mind, and yours too, I expect.

Elyot. It isn't anything of the sort.

Sibyl. She was pretty, wasn't she? Amanda?

Elyot. Very pretty.

Sibyl. Prettier than I am?

Elyot. Much.

Sibyl. Elyot!

Elyot. She was pretty and sleek, and her hands were long
    and slim, and her legs were long and slim, and she
    danced like an angel. You dance very poorly, by the
    way.

Sibyl. Could she play the piano as well as I can?

Elyot. She couldn't play the piano at all.

Sibyl [*triumphantly*]. Aha! Had she my talent for organisa-
    tion?

Elyot. No, but she hadn't your mother either.

Sibyl. I don't believe you like mother.

Elyot. Like her! I can't bear her.

Sibyl. Elyot! She's a darling, underneath.

Elyot. I never got underneath.

Sibyl. It makes me unhappy to think you don't like mother.

Elyot. Nonsense. I believe the only reason you married me
    was to get away from her.

Sibyl. I married you because I loved you.

Elyot. Oh dear, oh dear, oh dear, oh dear!

Sibyl. I love you far more than Amanda loved you. I'd never make you miserable like she did.

Elyot. We made each other miserable.

Sibyl. It was all her fault, you know it was.

Elyot [*with vehemence*]. Yes, it was. Entirely her fault.

Sibyl. She was a fool to lose you.

Elyot. We lost each other.

Sibyl. She lost you, with her violent tempers and carryings on.

Elyot. Will you stop talking about Amanda?

Sibyl. But I'm very glad, because if she hadn't been uncontrolled, and wicked, and unfaithful, we shouldn't be here now.

Elyot. She wasn't unfaithful.

Sibyl. How do you know? I bet she was. I bet she was unfaithful every five minutes.

Elyot. It would take a far more concentrated woman than Amanda to be unfaithful every five minutes.

Sibyl [*anxiously*]. You do hate her, don't you?

Elyot. No, I don't hate her. I think I despise her.

Sibyl [*with satisfaction*]. That's much worse.

Elyot. And yet I'm sorry for her.

Sibyl. Why?

Elyot. Because she's marked for tragedy; she's bound to make a mess of everything.

Sibyl. If it's all her fault, I don't see that it matters much.

Elyot. She has some very good qualities.

Sibyl. Considering what a hell she made of your life, I think you are very nice about her. Most men would be vindictive.

Elyot. What's the use of that? It's all over now, such a long time ago.

Sibyl. Five years isn't very long.

Elyot [*seriously*]. Yes it is.

Sibyl. Do you think you could ever love her again?

Elyot. Now then, Sibyl.

Sibyl. But could you?

Elyot. Of course not, I love you.

Sibyl. Yes, but you love me differently; I know that.

Elyot. More wisely perhaps.

Sibyl. I'm glad. I'd rather have that sort of love.

Elyot. You're right. Love is no use unless it's wise, and kind, and undramatic. Something steady and sweet, to smooth

out your nerves when you're tired. Something tremen-
dously cosy; and unflurried by scenes and jealousies.
That's what I want, what I've always wanted really.
Oh my dear, I do hope it's not going to be dull for you.

Sibyl. Sweetheart, as tho' you could ever be dull.

Elyot. I'm much older than you.

Sibyl. Not so very much.

Elyot. Seven years.

Sibyl [*snuggling up to him*]. The music has stopped now and
you can hear the sea.

Elyot. We'll bathe tomorrow morning.

Sibyl. I mustn't get sunburnt.

Elyot. Why not?

Sibyl. I hate it on women.

Elyot. Very well, you shan't then. I hope you don't hate it
on men.

Sibyl. Of course I don't. It's suitable to men.

Elyot. You're a completely feminine little creature, aren't
you?

Sibyl. Why do you say that?

Elyot. Everything in its place.

Sibyl. What do you mean?

Elyot. If you feel you'd like me to smoke a pipe, I'll try and
master it.

Sibyl. I like a man to be a man, if that's what you mean.

Elyot. Are you going to understand me, and manage me?

Sibyl. I'm going to try to understand you.

Elyot. Run me without my knowing it?

Sibyl [*withdrawing slightly*]. I think you're being a little
unkind.

Elyot. No, I don't mean to be. I was only wondering.

Sibyl. Well?

Elyot. I was wondering what was going on inside your mind,
what your plans are really?

Sibyl. Plans; oh, Elli!

Elyot. Apart from loving me and all that, you must have
plans.

Sibyl. I haven't the faintest idea what you're talking about.

Elyot. Perhaps it's subconscious then, age-old instincts working away deep down, mincing up little bits of experience for future use, watching me carefully like a
little sharp-eyed, blonde kitten.

Sibyl. How can you be so horrid.

Elyot. I said Kitten, not Cat.

Sibyl. Kittens grow into cats.

Elyot. Let that be a warning to you.

Sibyl [*slipping her arm through his again*]. What's the matter, darling; are you hungry?

Elyot. Not a bit.

Sibyl. You're very strange all of a sudden, and rather cruel. Just because I'm feminine. It doesn't mean that I'm crafty and calculating.

Elyot. I didn't say you were either of those things.

Sibyl. I hate these half masculine women who go banging about.

Elyot. I hate anybody who goes banging about.

Sibyl. I should think you needed a little quiet womanliness after Amanda.

Elyot. Why will you keep on talking about her?

Sibyl. It's natural enough, isn't it?

Elyot. What do you want to find out?

Sibyl. Why did you really let her divorce you?

Elyot. She divorced me for cruelty, and flagrant infidelity. I spent a whole week-end at Brighton with a lady called Vera Williams. She had the nastiest looking hair brush I have ever seen.

Sibyl. Misplaced chivalry, I call it. Why didn't you divorce her?

Elyot. It would not have been the action of a gentleman, whatever that may mean.

Sibyl. I think she got off very lightly.

Elyot. Once and for all will you stop talking about her.

Sibyl. Yes, Elli dear.

Elyot. I don't wish to see her again or hear her name mentioned.

Sibyl. Very well, darling.

Elyot. Is that understood?

Sibyl. Yes, darling. Where did you spend your honeymoon?

Elyot. St. Moritz. Be quiet.

Sibyl. I hate St. Moritz.

Elyot. So do I, bitterly.

Sibyl. Was she good on skis?

Elyot. Do you want to dine downstairs here, or at the Casino?

Sibyl. I love you, I love you, I love you.

Elyot. Good, let's go in and dress.

Sibyl. Kiss me first.

Elyot [*kissing her*]. Casino?

Sibyl. Yes. Are you a gambler? You never told me.

Elyot. Every now and then.

Sibyl. I shall come and sit just behind your chair and bring you luck.

Elyot. That will be fatal.

[*They go off into their suite. There is a slight pause and then Victor Prynne enters from the Left suite. He is quite nice looking, about thirty or thirty-five. He is dressed in a light travelling suit. He sniffs the air, looks at the view, and then turns back to the window.*]

Victor [*calling*]. Mandy.

Amanda [*inside*]. What?

Victor. Come outside, the view is wonderful.

Amanda. I'm still damp from the bath. Wait a minute— [*Victor lights a cigarette. Presently Amanda comes out on to the terrace. She is quite exquisite with a gay face and a perfect figure. At the moment she is wearing a negligee.*] I shall catch pneumonia, that's what I shall catch.

Victor [*looking at her*]. God!

Amanda. I beg your pardon?

Victor. You look wonderful.

Amanda. Thank you, darling.

Victor. Like a beautiful advertisement for something.

Amanda. Nothing peculiar, I hope.

Victor. I can hardly believe it's true. You and I, here alone together, married!

Amanda [*rubbing her face on his shoulder*]. That stuff's very rough.

Victor. Don't you like it?

Amanda. A bit hearty, isn't it?

Victor. Do you love me?

Amanda. Of course, that's why I'm here.

Victor. More than—

Amanda. Now then, none of that.

Victor. No, but do you love me more than you loved Elyot?

Amanda. I don't remember, it's such a long time ago.

Victor. Not so very long.

Amanda [*flinging out her arms*]. All my life ago.

Victor. I'd like to break his damned neck.

Amanda [*laughing*]. Why?

Victor. For making you unhappy.

Amanda. It was mutual.

Victor. Rubbish! It was all his fault, you know it was.

Amanda. Yes, it was, now I come to think about it.

Victor. Swine!

Amanda. Don't be so vehement, darling.

Victor. I'll never treat you like that.

Amanda. That's right.

Victor. I love you too much.

Amanda. So did he.

Victor. Fine sort of love that is. He struck you once, didn't he?

Amanda. More than once.

Victor. Where?

Amanda. Several places.

Victor. What a cad.

Amanda. I struck him too. Once I broke four gramophone records over his head. It was very satisfying.

Victor. You must have been driven to distraction.

Amanda. Yes, I was, but don't let's talk about it, please. After all, it's a dreary subject for our honeymoon night.

Victor. He didn't know when he was well off.

Amanda. Look at the lights of that yacht reflected in the water. I wonder whose it is.

Victor. We must bathe tomorrow.

Amanda. Yes. I want to get a nice sunburn.

Victor [*reproachfully*]. Mandy!

Amanda. Why, what's the matter?

Victor. I hate sunburnt women.

Amanda. Why?

Victor. It's somehow, well, unsuitable.

Amanda. It's awfully suitable to me, darling.

Victor. Of course if you really want to.

Amanda. I'm absolutely determined. I've got masses of lovely oil to rub all over myself.

Victor. Your skin is so beautiful as it is.

Amanda. Wait and see. When I'm done a nice crisp brown, you'll fall in love with me all over again.

Victor. I couldn't love you more than I do now.

Amanda. Oh, dear. I did so hope our honeymoon was going to be progressive.

Victor. Where did you spend the last one?

Amanda [*warningly*]. Victor.

Victor. I want to know.

Amanda. St. Moritz. It was very attractive.

Victor. I hate St. Moritz.

Amanda. So do I.

Victor. Did he start quarrelling with you right away?

Amanda. Within the first few days. I put it down to the high altitudes.

Victor. And you loved him?

Amanda. Yes, Victor.

Victor. You poor child.

Amanda. You must try not to be pompous, dear. [*She turns away.*]

Victor [*hurt*]. Mandy!

Amanda. I don't believe I'm a bit like what you think I am.

Victor. How do you mean?

Amanda. I was never a poor child.

Victor. Figure of speech, dear, that's all.

Amanda. I suffered a good deal, and had my heart broken. But it wasn't an innocent girlish heart. It was jagged with sophistication. I've always been sophisticated, far too knowing. That caused many of my rows with Elyot. I irritated him because he knew I could see through him.

Victor. I don't mind how much you see through me.

Amanda. Sweet. [*She kisses him.*]

Victor. I'm going to make you happy.

Amanda. Are you?

Victor. Just by looking after you, and seeing that you're all right, you know.

Amanda [*a trifle wistfully*]. No, I don't know.

Victor. I think you love me quite differently from the way you loved Elyot.

Amanda. Do stop harping on Elyot.

Victor. It's true, though, isn't it?

Amanda. I love you much more calmly, if that's what you mean.

Victor. More lastingly?

Amanda. I expect so.

Victor. Do you remember when I first met you?

Amanda. Yes. Distinctly.

Victor. At Marion Vale's party.

Amanda. Yes.

Victor. Wasn't it wonderful?

Amanda. Not really, dear. It was only redeemed from the completely commonplace by the fact of my having hiccoughs.

Victor. I never noticed them.

Amanda. Love at first sight.

Victor. Where did you first meet Elyot?

Amanda. To hell with Elyot.

Victor. Mandy!

Amanda. I forbid you to mention his name again. I'm sick
of the sound of it. You must be raving mad. Here we
are on the first night of our honeymoon, with the moon
coming up, and the music playing, and all you can do
is to talk about my first husband. It's downright sacri-
legious.

Victor. Don't be angry.

Amanda. Well, it's very annoying.

Victor. Will you forgive me?

Amanda. Yes; only don't do it again.

Victor. I promise.

Amanda. You'd better go and dress now, you haven't bathed
yet.

Victor. Where shall we dine, downstairs here, or at the
Casino?

Amanda. The Casino is more fun, I think.

Victor. We can play Boule afterwards.

Amanda. No, we can't, dear.

Victor. Don't you like dear old Boule?

Amanda. No, I hate dear old Boule. We'll play a nice game
of Chemin de fer.

Victor [*apprehensively*]. Not at the big table?

Amanda. Maybe at the biggest table.

Victor. You're not a terrible gambler, are you?

Amanda. Inveterate. Chance rules my life.

Victor. What nonsense.

Amanda. How can you say it's nonsense? It was chance
meeting you. It was chancing falling in love; it's chance
that we're here, particularly after your driving. Everything that happens is chance.

Victor. You know I feel rather scared of you at close quar-
ters.

Amanda. That promises to be very embarrassing.

Victor. You're somehow different now, wilder than I thought
you were, more strained.

Amanda. Wilder! Oh Victor, I've never felt less wild in my
life. A little strained, I grant you, but that's the newly
married atmosphere; you can't expect anything else.
Honeymooning is a very overrated amusement.

Victor. You say that because you had a ghastly experience
before.

Amanda. There you go again.

Victor. It couldn't fail to embitter you a little.

Amanda. The honeymoon wasn't such a ghastly experience really; it was afterwards that was so awful.

Victor. I intend to make you forget it all entirely.

Amanda. You won't succeed by making constant references to it.

Victor. I wish I knew you better.

Amanda. It's just as well you don't. The "woman"—in italics —should always retain a certain amount of alluring feminine mystery for the "man"—also in italics.

Victor. What about the man? Isn't he allowed to have any mystery?

Amanda. Absolutely none. Transparent as glass.

Victor. Oh, I see.

Amanda. Never mind, darling; it doesn't necessarily work out like that; it's only supposed to.

Victor. I'm glad I'm normal.

Amanda. What an odd thing to be glad about. Why?

Victor. Well, aren't you?

Amanda. I'm not so sure I'm normal.

Victor. Oh, Mandy, of course you are, sweetly, divinely normal.

Amanda. I haven't any peculiar cravings for Chinamen or old boots, if that's what you mean.

Victor [*scandalised*]. Mandy!

Amanda. I think very few people are completely normal really, deep down in their private lives. It all depends on a combination of circumstances. If all the various cosmic thingummys fuse at the same moment, and the right spark is struck, there's no knowing what one mightn't do. That was the trouble with Elyot and me, we were like two violent acids bubbling about in a nasty little matrimonial bottle.

Victor. I don't believe you're nearly as complex as you think you are.

Amanda. I don't think I'm particularly complex, but I know I'm unreliable.

Victor. You're frightening me horribly. In what way unreliable?

Amanda. I'm so apt to see things the wrong way round.

Victor. What sort of things?

Amanda. Morals. What one should do and what one shouldn't.

Victor [*fondly*]. Darling, you're so sweet.

Amanda. Thank you, Victor, that's most encouraging. You really must have your bath now. Come along.

Victor. Kiss me.

Amanda [*doing so*]. There, dear, hurry now; I've only got to slip my dress on and then I shall be ready.

Victor. Give me ten minutes.

Amanda. I'll bring the cocktails out here when they come.

Victor. All right.

Amanda. Go along now, hurry.

[*They both disappear into their suite. After a moment's pause Elyot steps carefully on to the terrace carrying a tray upon which are two champagne cocktails. He puts the tray down on the table.*]

Elyot [*calling*]. Sibyl.

Sibyl [*inside*]. Yes.

Elyot. I've brought the cocktails out here, hurry up.

Sibyl. I can't find my lipstick.

Elyot. Never mind, send down to the kitchen for some cochineal.

Sibyl. Don't be so silly.

Elyot. Hurry.

[*Elyot saunters down to the balustrade. He looks casually over on to the next terrace, and then out at the view. He looks up at the moon and sighs, then he sits down in a chair with his back towards the line of tubs, and lights a cigarette. Amanda steps gingerly on to her terrace carrying a tray with two champagne cocktails on it. She is wearing a charmingly simple evening gown, her cloak is flung over her right shoulder. She places the tray carefully on the table, puts her cloak over the back of a chair, and sits down with her back towards Elyot. She takes a small mirror from her handbag, and scrutinizes her face in it. The orchestra downstairs strikes up a new melody. Both Elyot and Amanda give a little start. After a moment, Elyot pensively begins to hum the tune the band is playing. It is a sentimental, romantic little tune. Amanda hears him, and clutches at her throat suddenly as though she were suffocating. Then she jumps up noiselessly, and peers over the line of tubs. Elyot, with his back to her, continues to sing obliviously. She sits down again, relaxing with a gesture almost of despair. Then she looks anxiously over her shoulder at the window in case Victor should be listen-*]

*ing, and then, with a little smile, she takes up the
melody herself, clearly. Elyot stops dead and gives a
gasp, then he jumps up, and stands looking at her. She
continues to sing, pretending not to know that he is
there. At the end of the song, she turns slowly, and
faces him.*]

Amanda. Thoughtful of them to play that, wasn't it?

Elyot [*in a stifled voice*]. What are you doing here?

Amanda. I'm on honeymoon.

Elyot. How interesting, so am I.

Amanda. I hope you're enjoying it.

Elyot. It hasn't started yet.

Amanda. Neither has mine.

Elyot. Oh, my God!

Amanda. I can't help feeling that this is a little unfortunate.

Elyot. Are you happy?

Amanda. Perfectly.

Elyot. Good. That's all right, then, isn't it?

Amanda. Are you?

Elyot. Ecstatically.

Amanda. I'm delighted to hear it. We shall probably meet
again sometime. Au revoir! [*She turns.*]

Elyot [*firmly*]. Good-bye.

[*She goes indoors without looking back. He stands gazing
after her with an expression of horror on his face. Sibyl
comes brightly on to the terrace in a very pretty evening
frock.*]

Sibyl. Cocktail, please. [*Elyot doesn't answer.*] Elli, what's
the matter?

Elyot. I feel very odd.

Sibyl. Odd, what do you mean, ill?

Elyot. Yes, ill.

Sibyl [*alarmed*]. What sort of ill?

Elyot. We must leave at once.

Sibyl. Leave!

Elyot. Yes, dear. Leave immediately.

Sibyl. Elli!

Elyot. I have a strange foreboding.

Sibyl. You must be mad.

Elyot. Listen, darling. I want you to be very sweet, and
patient, and understanding, and not be upset, or ask
any questions, or anything. I have an absolute conviction that our whole future happiness depends upon our
leaving here instantly.

Sibyl. Why?

Elyot. I can't tell you why.

Sibyl. But we've only just come.

Elyot. I know that, but it can't be helped.

Sibyl. What's happened, what has happened?

Elyot. Nothing has happened.

Sibyl. You've gone out of your mind.

Elyot. I haven't gone out of my mind, but I shall if we stay here another hour.

Sibyl. You're not drunk, are you?

Elyot. Of course I'm not drunk. What time have I had to get drunk?

Sibyl. Come down and have some dinner, darling, and then you'll feel ever so much better.

Elyot. It's no use trying to humour me. I'm serious.

Sibyl. But darling, please be reasonable. We've only just arrived; everything's unpacked. It's our first night together. We can't go away now.

Elyot. We can have our first night together in Paris.

Sibyl. We shouldn't get there until the small hours.

Elyot [*with a great effort at calmness*]. Now please, Sibyl, I know it sounds crazy to you, and utterly lacking in reason and sense, but I've got second sight over certain things. I'm almost psychic. I've got the most extraordinary sensation of impending disaster. If we stay here something appalling will happen. I know it.

Sibyl [*firmly*]. Hysterical nonsense.

Elyot. It isn't hysterical nonsense. Presentiments are far from being nonsense. Look at the woman who cancelled her passage on the *Titanic*. All because of a presentiment.

Sibyl. I don't see what that has to do with it.

Elyot. It has everything to do with it. She obeyed her instincts, that's what she did, and saved her life. All I ask is to be allowed to obey my instincts.

Sibyl. Do you mean that there's going to be an earthquake or something?

Elyot. Very possibly, very possibly indeed, or perhaps a violent explosion.

Sibyl. They don't have earthquakes in France.

Elyot. On the contrary, only the other day they felt a distinct shock at Toulon.

Sibyl. Yes, but that's in the South where it's hot.

Elyot. Don't quibble, Sibyl.

Sibyl. And as for explosions, there's nothing here that can explode.

Elyot. Oho, isn't there.

Sibyl. Yes, but Elli—

Elyot. Darling, be sweet. Bear with me. I beseech you to bear with me.

Sibyl. I don't understand. It's horrid of you to do this.

Elyot. I'm not doing anything. I'm only asking you, imploring you to come away from this place.

Sibyl. But I love it here.

Elyot. There are thousands of other places far nicer.

Sibyl. It's a pity we didn't go to one of them.

Elyot. Now, listen, Sibyl—

Sibyl. Yes, but why are you behaving like this, why, why, why?

Elyot. Don't ask why. Just give in to me. I swear I'll never ask you to give into me over anything again.

Sibyl [*with complete decision*]. I won't think of going tonight. It's utterly ridiculous. I've done quite enough travelling for one day, and I'm tired.

Elyot. You're as obstinate as a mule.

Sibyl. I like that, I must say.

Elyot [*hotly*]. You've got your nasty little feet dug into the ground, and you don't intend to budge an inch, do you?

Sibyl [*with spirit*]. No, I do not.

Elyot. If there's one thing in the world that infuriates me, it's sheer wanton stubbornness. I should like to cut off your head with a meat axe.

Sybil. How dare you talk to me like that, on our honeymoon night.

Elyot. Damn our honeymoon night. Damn it, damn it, damn it!

Sibyl [*bursting into tears*]. Oh, Elli, Elli—

Elyot. Stop crying. Will you or will you not come away with me to Paris?

Sibyl. I've never been so miserable in my life. You're hateful and beastly. Mother was perfectly right. She said you had shifty eyes.

Elyot. Well, she can't talk. Hers are so close together, you couldn't put a needle between them.

Sibyl. You don't love me a little bit. I wish I were dead.

Elyot. Will you or will you not come to Paris?

Sibyl. No, no I won't.

Elyot. Oh, my God! [*He stamps indoors.*]

Sibyl [*following him, wailing*]. Oh, Elli, Elli, Elli—
[*Victor comes stamping out of the French windows on the left, followed by Amanda.*]

Victor. You were certainly right when you said you weren't normal. You're behaving like a lunatic.

Amanda. Not at all. All I have done is to ask you a little favour.

Victor. Little favour indeed.

Amanda. If we left now we could be in Paris in a few hours.

Victor. If we crossed Siberia by train we could be in China in a fortnight, but I don't see any reason to do it.

Amanda. Oh, Victor darling—please, please—be sensible, just for my sake.

Victor. Sensible!

Amanda. Yes, sensible. I shall be absolutely miserable if we stay here. You don't want me to be absolutely miserable all through my honeymoon, do you?

Victor. But why on earth didn't you think of your sister's tragedy before?

Amanda. I forgot.

Victor. You couldn't forget a thing like that.

Amanda. I got the places muddled. Then when I saw the Casino there in the moonlight, it all came back to me.

Victor. When did all this happen?

Amanda. Years ago, but it might just as well have been yesterday. I can see her now lying dead, with that dreadful expression on her face. Then all that awful business of taking the body home to England. It was perfectly horrible.

Victor. I never knew you had a sister.

Amanda. I haven't any more.

Victor. There's something behind all this.

Amanda. Don't be silly. What could there be behind it?

Victor. Well, for one thing, I know you're lying.

Amanda. Victor!

Victor. Be honest. Aren't you?

Amanda. I can't think how you can be so mean and suspicious.

Victor [*patiently*]. You're lying, Amanda. Aren't you?

Amanda. Yes, Victor.

Victor. You never had a sister, dead or alive?

Amanda. I believe there was a stillborn one in 1902.

Victor. What is your reason for all this?

Amanda. I told you I was unreliable.

Victor. Why do you want to leave so badly?

Amanda. You'll be angry if I tell you the truth.

Victor. What is it?

Amanda. I warn you.

Victor. Tell me. Please tell me.

Amanda. Elyot's here.

Victor. What!

Amanda. I saw him.

Victor. When?

Amanda. Just now, when you were in the bath.

Victor. Where was he?

Amanda [*hesitatingly*]. Down there, in a white suit. [*She points over the balustrade.*]

Victor [*sceptically*]. White suit?

Amanda. Why not? It's summer, isn't it?

Victor. You're lying again.

Amanda. I'm not. He's here. I swear he is.

Victor. Well, what of it?

Amanda. I can't enjoy a honeymoon with you, with Elyot liable to bounce in at any moment.

Victor. Really, Mandy.

Amanda. Can't you see how awful it is? It's the most embarrassing thing that ever happened to me in my whole life.

Victor. Did he see you?

Amanda. No, he was running.

Victor. What was he running for?

Amanda. How on earth do I know? Don't be so annoying.

Victor. Well, as long as he didn't see you it's all right, isn't it?

Amanda. It isn't all right at all. We must leave immediately.

Victor. But why?

Amanda. How can you be so appallingly obstinate?

Victor. I'm not afraid of him.

Amanda. Neither am I. It isn't a question of being afraid. It's just a horrible awkward situation.

Victor. I'm damned if I can see why our whole honeymoon should be upset by Elyot.

Amanda. My last one was.

Victor. I don't believe he's here at all.

Amanda. He is I tell you. I saw him.

Victor. It was probably an optical illusion. This half light is very deceptive.

Amanda. It was no such thing.

Victor. I absolutely refuse to change all our plans at the last

moment, just because you think you've seen Elyot. It's
unreasonable and ridiculous of you to demand it. Even
if he is here I can't see that it matters. He'll probably
feel much more embarrassed than you, and a damned
good job too; and if he annoys you in any way I'll knock
him down.

Amanda. That would be charming.

Victor. Now don't let's talk about it any more.

Amanda. Do you mean to stand there seriously and imagine
that the whole thing can be glossed over as easily as
that?

Victor. I'm not going to leave, Mandy. If I start giving into
you as early as this, our lives will be unbearable.

Amanda [*outraged*]. Victor!

Victor [*calmly*]. You've worked yourself up into a state over
a situation which really only exists in your mind.

Amanda [*controlling herself with an effort*]. Please, Victor,
please, for this last time I implore you. Let's go to Paris
now, tonight. I mean it with all my heart—please—

Victor [*with gentle firmness*]. No, Mandy!

Amanda. I see quite clearly that I have been foolish enough
to marry a fat old gentleman in a club armchair.

Victor. It's no use being cross.

Amanda. You're a pompous ass.

Victor [*horrified*]. Mandy!

Amanda [*enraged*]. Pompous ass, that's what I said, and
that's what I meant. Blown out with your own importance.

Victor. Mandy, control yourself.

Amanda. Get away from me. I can't bear to think I'm married to such rugged grandeur.

Victor [*with great dignity*]. I shall be in the bar. When you
are ready to come down and dine, let me know.

Amanda [*flinging herself into a chair*]. Go away, go away.

[*Victor stalks off, at the same moment that Elyot stamps on,
on the other side, followed by Sibyl in tears.*]

Elyot. If you don't stop screaming, I'll murder you.

Sibyl. I wish to heaven I'd never seen you in my life, let
alone married you. I don't wonder Amanda left you, if
you behaved to her as you've behaved to me. I'm going
down to have dinner by myself and you can just do
what you like about it.

Elyot. Do, and I hope it chokes you.

Sibyl. Oh Elli, Elli—

[*She goes wailing indoors. Elyot stamps down to the balustrade and lights a cigarette, obviously trying to control his nerves. Amanda sees him, and comes down too.*]

Amanda. Give me one for God's sake.

Elyot [*hands her his case laconically*]. Here.

Amanda [*taking a cigarette*]. I'm in such a rage.

Elyot [*lighting up*]. So am I.

Amanda. What are we to do?

Elyot. I don't know.

Amanda. Whose yacht is that?

Elyot. The Duke of Westminster's I expect. It always is.

Amanda. I wish I were on it.

Elyot. I wish you were too.

Amanda. There's no need to be nasty.

Elyot. Yes there is, every need. I've never in my life felt a greater urge to be nasty.

Amanda. And you've had some urges in your time, haven't you?

Elyot. If you start bickering with me, Amanda, I swear I'll throw you over the edge.

Amanda. Try it, that's all, just try it.

Elyot. You've upset everything, as usual.

Amanda. I've upset everything! What about you?

Elyot. Ever since the first moment I was unlucky enough to set eyes on you, my life has been insupportable.

Amanda. Oh do shut up, there's no sense in going on like that.

Elyot. Nothing's any use. There's no escape, ever.

Amanda. Don't be melodramatic.

Elyot. Do you want a cocktail? There are two here.

Amanda. There are two over here as well.

Elyot. We'll have my two first. [*Amanda crosses over into Elyot's part of the terrace. He gives her one, and keeps one himself.*]

Amanda. Shall we get roaring screaming drunk?

Elyot. I don't think that would help. We did it once before and it was a dismal failure.

Amanda. It was lovely at the beginning.

Elyot. You have an immoral memory Amanda. Here's to you. [*They raise their glasses solemnly and drink.*]

Amanda. I tried to get away the moment after I'd seen you, but he wouldn't budge.

Elyot. What's his name.

Amanda. Victor, Victor Prynne.

Elyot [*toasting*]. Mr. and Mrs. Victor Prynne. [*He drinks*.] Mine wouldn't budge either.

Amanda. What's her name?

Elyot. Sibyl.

Amanda [*toasting*]. Mr. and Mrs. Elyot Chase. [*She drinks*.] God pity the poor girl.

Elyot. Are you in love with him?

Amanda. Of course.

Elyot. How funny.

Amanda. I don't see anything particularly funny about it; you're in love with yours aren't you?

Elyot. Certainly.

Amanda. There you are then.

Elyot. There we both are then.

Amanda. What's she like?

Elyot. Fair, very pretty, plays the piano beautifully.

Amanda. Very comforting.

Elyot. How's yours?

Amanda. I don't want to discuss him.

Elyot. Well, it doesn't matter, he'll probably come popping out in a minute and I shall see for myself. Does he know I'm here?

Amanda. Yes, I told him.

Elyot [*with sarcasm*]. That's going to make things a whole lot easier.

Amanda. You needn't be frightened, he won't hurt you.

Elyot. If he comes near me I'll scream the place down.

Amanda. Does Sibyl know I'm here?

Elyot. No, I pretended I'd had a presentiment. I tried terribly hard to persuade her to leave for Paris.

Amanda. I tried too, it's lucky we didn't both succeed, isn't it? Otherwise we should probably all have joined up in Rouen or somewhere.

Elyot [*laughing*]. In some frowsy little hotel.

Amanda [*laughing too*]. Oh dear, it would have been much, much worse.

Elyot. I can see us all sailing down in the morning for an early start.

Amanda [*weakly*]. Lovely, oh lovely.

Elyot. Glorious! [*They both laugh helplessly*.]

Amanda. What's happened to yours?

Elyot. Didn't you hear her screaming? She's downstairs in the dining-room I think.

Amanda. Mine is being grand, in the bar.

Elyot. It really is awfully difficult.

Amanda. Have you known her long?

Elyot. About four months. We met in a house party in Norfolk.

Amanda. Very flat, Norfolk.

Elyot. How old is dear Victor?

Amanda. Thirty-four, or five; and Sibyl?

Elyot. I blush to tell you, only twenty-three.

Amanda. You've gone a mucker alright.

Elyot. I shall reserve my opinion of your choice until I've met dear Victor.

Amanda. I wish you wouldn't go on calling him "Dear Victor." It's extremely irritating.

Elyot. That's how I see him. Dumpy, and fair, and very considerate, with glasses. Dear Victor.

Amanda. As I said before I would rather not discuss him. At least I have good taste enough to refrain from making cheap gibes at Sibyl.

Elyot. You said Norfolk was flat.

Amanda. That was no reflection on her, unless she made it flatter.

Elyot. Your voice takes on an acid quality whenever you mention her name.

Amanda. I'll never mention it again.

Elyot. Good, and I'll keep off Victor.

Amanda [*with dignity*]. Thank you.

[*There is silence for a moment. The orchestra starts playing the same tune that they were singing previously.*]

Elyot. That orchestra has a remarkable small repertoire.

Amanda. They don't seem to know anything but this, do they? [*She sits down on the balustrade, and sings it, softly. Her eyes are looking out to sea, and her mind is far away. Elyot watches her while she sings. When she turns to him at the end, there are tears in her eyes. He looks away awkwardly and lights another cigarette.*]

Elyot. You always had a sweet voice, Amanda.

Amanda [*a little huskily*]. Thank you.

Elyot. I'm awfully sorry about all this, really I am. I wouldn't have had it happen for the world.

Amanda. I know. I'm sorry too. It's just rotten luck.

Elyot. I'll go away tomorrow whatever happens, so don't you worry.

Amanda. That's nice of you.

Elyot. I hope everything turns out splendidly for you, and that you'll be very happy.

Amanda. I hope the same for you, too.

[*The music, which has been playing continually through this little scene, returns persistently to the refrain. They both look at one another and laugh.*]

Elyot. Nasty insistent little tune.

Amanda. Extraordinary how potent cheap music is.

Elyot. What exactly were you remembering at that moment?

Amanda. The Palace Hotel Skating Rink in the morning, bright strong sunlight, and everybody whirling round in vivid colours, and you kneeling down to put on my skates for me.

Elyot. You'd fallen on your fanny a few moments before.

Amanda. It was beastly of you to laugh like that, I felt so humiliated.

Elyot. Poor darling.

Amanda. Do you remember waking up in the morning, and standing on the balcony, looking out across the valley?

Elyot. Blue shadows on white snow, cleanness beyond belief, high above everything in the world. How beautiful it was.

Amanda. It's nice to think we had a few marvellous moments.

Elyot. A few. We had heaps really, only they slip away into the background, and one only remembers the bad ones.

Amanda. Yes. What fools we were to ruin it all. What utter, utter fools.

Elyot. You feel like that too, do you?

Amanda [*wearily*]. Of course.

Elyot. Why did we?

Amanda. The whole business was too much for us.

Elyot. We were so ridiculously over in love.

Amanda. Funny wasn't it?

Elyot [*sadly*]. Horribly funny.

Amanda. Selfishness, cruelty, hatred, possessiveness, petty jealousy. All those qualities came out in us just because we loved each other.

Elyot. Perhaps they were there anyhow.

Amanda. No, it's love that does it. To hell with love.

Elyot. To hell with love.

Amanda. And yet here we are starting afresh with two quite different people. In love all over again, aren't we? [*Elyot doesn't answer.*] Aren't we?

Elyot. No.

Amanda. Elyot.

Elyot. We're not in love all over again, and you know it.
    Good night, Amanda. [*He turns abruptly, and goes
    towards the French windows.*]

Amanda. Elyot—don't be silly—come back.

Elyot. I must go and find Sibyl.

Amanda. I must go and find Victor.

Elyot [*savagely*]. Well, why don't you?

Amanda. I don't want to.

Elyot. It's shameful, shameful of us.

Amanda. Don't: I feel terrible. Don't leave me for a minute,
    I shall go mad if you do. We won't talk about ourselves
    any more, we'll talk about outside things, anything you
    like, only just don't leave me until I've pulled myself
    together.

Elyot. Very well. [*There is a dead silence.*]

Amanda. What have you been doing lately? During these last
    years?

Elyot. Travelling about. I went round the world you know
    after—

Amanda [*hurriedly*]. Yes, yes, I know. How was it?

Elyot. The world?

Amanda. Yes.

Elyot. Oh, highly enjoyable.

Amanda. China must be very interesting.

Elyot. Very big, China.

Amanda. And Japan—

Elyot. Very small.

Amanda. Did you eat sharks' fins, and take your shoes off,
    and use chopsticks and everything?

Elyot. Practically everything.

Amanda. And India, the burning Ghars, or Ghats, or what-
    ever they are, and the Taj Mahal. How was the Taj
    Mahal?

Elyot [*looking at her*]. Unbelievable, a sort of dream.

Amanda. That was the moonlight I expect, you must have
    seen it in the moonlight.

Elyot [*never taking his eyes off her face*]. Yes, moonlight is
    cruelly deceptive.

Amanda. And it didn't look like a biscuit box did it? I've
    always felt that it might.

Elyot [*quietly*]. Darling, darling, I love you so.

Amanda. And I do hope you met a sacred Elephant. They're lint white I believe, and very, very sweet.

Elyot. I've never loved anyone else for an instant.

Amanda [*raising her hand feebly in protest*]. No, no, you mustn't—Elyot—stop.

Elyot. You love me, too, don't you? There's no doubt about it anywhere, is there?

Amanda. No, no doubt anywhere.

Elyot. You're looking very lovely you know, in this damned moonlight. Your skin is clear and cool, and your eyes are shining, and you're growing lovelier and lovelier every second as I look at you. You don't hold any mystery for me, darling, do you mind? There isn't a particle of you that I don't know, remember, and want.

Amanda [*softly*]. I'm glad, my sweet.

Elyot. More than any desire anywhere, deep down in my deepest heart I want you back again—please—

Amanda [*putting her hand over his mouth*]. Don't say any more, you're making me cry so dreadfully.

[*He pulls her gently into his arms and they stand silently, completely oblivious to everything but the moment, and each other. When finally, they separate, they sit down, rather breathlessly, on the balustrade.*]

Amanda. What now? Oh darling, what now?

Elyot. I don't know, I'm lost, utterly.

Amanda. We must think quickly, oh quickly—

Elyot. Escape?

Amanda. Together?

Elyot. Yes, of course, now, now.

Amanda. We can't, we can't, you know we can't.

Elyot. We must.

Amanda. It would break Victor's heart.

Elyot. And Sibyl's too probably, but they're bound to suffer anyhow. Think of the hell we'd lead them into if we stayed. Infinitely worse than any cruelty in the world, pretending to love them, and loving each other, so desperately.

Amanda. We must tell them.

Elyot. What?

Amanda. Call them, and tell them.

Elyot. Oh no, no, that's impossible.

Amanda. It's honest.

Elyot. I can't help how honest it is, it's too horrible to think of. How should we start? What should we say?

Amanda. We should have to trust to the inspiration of the moment.

Elyot. It would be a moment completely devoid of inspiration. The most appalling moment imaginable. No, no, we can't, you must see that, we simply can't.

Amanda. What do you propose to do then? As it is they might appear at any moment.

Elyot. We've got to decide instantly one way or another. Go away together now, or stay with them, and never see one another again, ever.

Amanda. Don't be silly, what choice is there?

Elyot. No choice at all, come— [*He takes her hand.*]

Amanda. No, wait. This is sheer raving madness, something's happened to us, we're not sane.

Elyot. We never were.

Amanda. Where can we go?

Elyot. Paris first, my car's in the garage, all ready.

Amanda. They'll follow us.

Elyot. That doesn't matter, once the thing's done.

Amanda. I've got a flat in Paris.

Elyot. Good.

Amanda. It's in the Avenue Montaigne. I let it to Freda Lawson, but she's in Biarritz, so it's empty.

Elyot. Does Victor know?

Amanda. No, he knows I have one but he hasn't the faintest idea where.

Elyot. Better and better.

Amanda. We're being so bad, so terribly bad, we'll suffer for this, I know we shall.

Elyot. Can't be helped.

Amanda. Starting all those awful rows all over again.

Elyot. No, no, we're older and wiser now.

Amanda. What difference does that make? The first moment either of us gets a bit nervy, off we'll go again.

Elyot. Stop shilly-shallying, Amanda.

Amanda. I'm trying to be sensible.

Elyot. You're only succeeding in being completely idiotic.

Amanda. Idiotic indeed! What about you?

Elyot. Now look here Amanda—

Amanda [*stricken*]. Oh my God!

Elyot [*rushing to her and kissing her*]. Darling, darling, I didn't mean it—

Amanda. I won't move from here unless we have a compact, a sacred, sacred compact never to quarrel again.

Elyot. Easy to make but difficult to keep.

Amanda. No, no, it's the bickering that always starts it. The moment we notice we're bickering, either of us, we must promise on our honour to stop dead. We'll invent some phrase or catchword, which when either of us says it, automatically cuts off all conversation for at least five minutes.

Elyot. Two minutes dear, with an option of renewal.

Amanda. Very well, what shall it be?

Elyot [*hurriedly*]. Solomon Isaacs.

Amanda. All right, that'll do.

Elyot. Come on, come on.

Amanda. What shall we do if we meet either of them on the way downstairs?

Elyot. Run like stags.

Amanda. What about clothes?

Elyot. I've got a couple of bags I haven't unpacked yet.

Amanda. I've got a small trunk.

Elyot. Send the porter up for it.

Amanda. Oh this is terrible—terrible—

Elyot. Come on, come on, don't waste time.

Amanda. Oughtn't we to leave notes or something?

Elyot. No, no, no, we'll telegraph from somewhere on the road.

Amanda. Darling, I daren't, it's too wicked of us, I simply daren't;

Elyot [*seizing her in his arms and kissing her violently*]. Now will you behave?

Amanda. Yes, but Elyot darling—

Elyot. Solomon Isaacs!

[*They rush off together through Elyot's suite. After a moment or so, Victor steps out on to the terrace and looks round anxiously. Then he goes back indoors again, and can be heard calling "Mandy." Finally he again comes out on to the terrace and comes despondently down to the balustrade. He hears Sibyl's voice calling "Elli" and looks round as she comes out of the French windows. She jumps slightly upon seeing him.*]

Victor. Good evening.

Sibyl [*rather flustered*]. Good-evening—I was—er—looking for my husband.

Victor. Really, that's funny. I was looking for my wife.

Sibyl. Quite a coincidence. [*She laughs nervously.*]

Victor [*after a pause*]. It's very nice here isn't it?

Sibyl. Lovely.

Victor. Have you been here long?

Sibyl. No, we only arrived today.

Victor. Another coincidence. So did we.

Sibyl. How awfully funny.

Victor. Would you care for a cocktail?

Sibyl. Oh no thank you—really—

Victor. There are two here on the table.

[*Sibyl glances at the two empty glasses on the balustrade, and tosses her head defiantly.*]

Sibyl. Thanks very much, I'd love one.

Victor. Good, here you are. [*Sibyl comes over to Victor's side of the terrace. He hands her one and takes one himself.*]

Sibyl. Thank you.

Victor [*with rather forced gaiety*]. To absent friends. [*He raises his glass.*]

Sibyl [*raising hers*]. To absent friends. [*They both laugh rather mirthlessly and then sit down on the balustrade, pensively sipping their cocktails and looking at the view.*] It's awfully pretty isn't it? The moonlight, and the lights of that yacht reflected in the water—

Victor. I wonder who it belongs to.

The Curtain Slowly Falls

The Scene is Amanda's flat in Paris. A few days have elapsed since Act 1. The flat is charmingly furnished, its principal features being a Steinway Grand on the Left, facing slightly up stage. Down stage centre, a very large comfortable sofa, behind which is a small table. There is also another sofa somewhere about, and one or two small tables, and a gramophone. The rest can be left to the discretion and taste of the decorator.

When the Curtain Rises it is about ten o'clock in the evening. The windows are wide open, and the various street sounds of Paris can be heard but not very loudly as the apartment is high up.

Amanda and Elyot are seated opposite one another at the table. They have finished dinner and are dallying over coffee and liqueurs. Amanda is wearing pajamas, and Elyot a comfortable dressing-gown.

Amanda. I'm glad we let Louise go. I am afraid she is going to have a cold.

Elyot. Going to have a cold; she's been grunting and snorting all the evening like a whole herd of bison.

Amanda [*thoughtfully*]. Bison never sounds right to me somehow. I have a feeling it ought to be bisons, a flock of bisons.

Elyot. You might say a covey of bisons, or even a school of bisons.

Amanda. Yes, lovely. The Royal London School of Bisons. Do you think Louise is happy at home?

Elyot. No, profoundly miserable.

Amanda. Family beastly to her?

Elyot [*with conviction*]. Absolutely vile. Knock her about dreadfully I expect, make her eat the most disgusting food, and pull her fringe.

Amanda [*laughing*]. Oh, poor Louise.

Elyot. Well, you know what the French are.

Amanda. Oh yes, indeed. I know what the Hungarians are too.

Elyot. What are they?

Amanda. Very wistful. It's all those Pretzles I shouldn't wonder.

Elyot. And the Poostza; I always felt the Poostza was far too big, Danube or no Danube.

Amanda. Have you ever crossed the Sahara on a camel?

Elyot. Frequently. When I was a boy we used to do it all the time. My grandmother had a lovely seat on a camel.

Amanda. There's no doubt about it, foreign travel's the thing.

Elyot. Would you like some brandy?

Amanda. Just a little. [*He pours some into her glass and some into his own.*]

Elyot. I'm glad we didn't go out tonight.

Amanda. Or last night.

Elyot. Or the night before.

Amanda. There's no reason to, really, when we're cosy here.

Elyot. Exactly.

Amanda. It's nice, isn't it?

Elyot. Strangely peaceful. It's an awfully bad reflection on our characters. We ought to be absolutely tortured with conscience.

Amanda. We are, every now and then.

Elyot. Not nearly enough.

Amanda. We sent Victor and Sibyl a nice note from wherever it was; what more can they want?

Elyot. You're even more ruthless than I am.

Amanda. I don't believe in crying over my bridge before I've eaten it.

Elyot. Very sensible.

Amanda. Personally I feel grateful for a miraculous escape. I know now that I should never have been happy with Victor. I was a fool ever to consider it.

Elyot. You did a little more than consider it.

Amanda. Well, you can't talk.

Elyot. I wonder whether they met each other, or whether they've been suffering alone.

Amanda. Oh dear, don't let's go on about it, it really does make one feel rather awful.

Elyot. I suppose one or other or both of them will turn up here eventually.

Amanda. Bound to; it won't be very nice, will it?

Elyot [*cheerfully*]. Perfectly horrible.

Amanda. Do you realise that we're living in sin?

Elyot. Not according to the Catholics, Catholics don't recognise divorce. We're married as much as ever we were.

Amanda. Yes, dear, but we're not Catholics.

Elyot. Never mind, it's nice to think they'd sort of back us up. We were married in the eyes of heaven, and we still are.

Amanda. We may be alright in the eyes of Heaven, but we look like being in the hell of a mess socially.

Elyot. Who cares?

Amanda. Are we going to marry again, after Victor and Sibyl divorce us?

Elyot. I suppose so. What do you think?

Amanda. I feel rather scared of marriage really.

Elyot. It is a frowsy business.

Amanda. I believe it was just the fact of our being married, and clamped together publicly, that wrecked us before.

Elyot. That, and not knowing how to manage each other.

Amanda. Do you think we know how to manage each other now?

Elyot. This week's been very successful. We've hardly used Solomon Isaacs at all.

Amanda. Solomon Isaacs is so long, let's shorten it to sollocks.

Elyot. All right.

Amanda. Darling, you do look awfully sweet in your little dressing-gown.

Elyot. Yes, it's pretty ravishing, isn't it?

Amanda. Do you mind if I come round and kiss you?

Elyot. A pleasure, Lady Agatha.

[*Amanda comes round the table, kisses him, picks up the coffee pot, and returns to her chair.*]

Amanda. What fools we were to subject ourselves to five years' unnecessary suffering.

Elyot. Perhaps it wasn't unnecessary, perhaps it mellowed and perfected us like beautiful ripe fruit.

Amanda. When we were together, did you really think I was unfaithful to you?

Elyot. Yes, practically every day.

Amanda. I thought you were too; often I used to torture myself with visions of your bouncing about on divans with awful widows.

Elyot. Why widows?

Amanda. I was thinking of Claire Lavenham really.

Elyot. Oh Claire.

Amanda [*sharply*]. What did you say "Oh Claire" like that for? It sounded far too careless to me.

Elyot [*wistfully*]. What a lovely creature she was.

Amanda. Lovely, lovely, lovely!

Elyot [*blowing her a kiss*]. Darling!

Amanda. Did you ever have an affair with her? Afterwards I mean?

Elyot. Why do you want to know?

Amanda. Curiosity, I suppose.

Elyot. Dangerous.

Amanda. Oh not now, not dangerous now. I wouldn't expect you to have been celibate during those five years, any more than I was.

Elyot [*jumping*]. What?

Amanda. After all, Claire was undeniably attractive. A trifle over vivacious I always thought, but that was probably because she was fundamentally stupid.

Elyot. What do you mean about not being celibate during those five years?

Amanda. What do you think I mean?

Elyot. Oh God! [*He looks down miserably.*]

Amanda. What's the matter?

Elyot. You know perfectly well what's the matter.

Amanda [*gently*]. You mustn't be unreasonable, I was only trying to stamp out the memory of you. I expect your affairs well outnumbered mine anyhow.

Elyot. That is a little different. I'm a man.

Amanda. Excuse me a moment while I get a caraway biscuit and change my crinoline.

Elyot. It doesn't suit women to be promiscuous.

Amanda. It doesn't suit men for women to be promiscuous.

Elyot [*with sarcasm*]. Very modern dear; really your advanced views quite startle me.

Amanda. Don't be cross, Elyot, I haven't been so dreadfully loose actually. Five years is a long time, and even if I did nip off with someone every now and again, they were none of them very serious.

Elyot [*rising from the table and walking away*]. Oh, do stop it please—

Amanda. Well, what about you?

Elyot. Do you want me to tell you?

Amanda. No, no, I don't—I take everything back—I don't.

Elyot [*viciously*]. I was madly in love with a woman in South Africa.

Amanda. Did she have a ring through her nose?

Elyot. Don't be revolting.

Amanda. We're tormenting one another. Sit down, sweet, I'm scared.

Elyot [*slowly*]. Very well. [*He sits down thoughtfully.*]

Amanda. We should have said Sollocks ages ago.

Elyot. We're in love alright.

Amanda. Don't say it so bitterly. Let's try to get the best out of it this time, instead of the worst.

Elyot [*stretching his hand across the table*]. Hand please.

Amanda [*clasping it*]. Here.

Elyot. More comfortable?

Amanda. Much more.

Elyot [*after a slight pause*]. Are you engaged for this dance?

Amanda. Funnily enough I was, but my partner was suddenly taken ill.

Elyot [*rising and going to the gramophone*]. It's this damned smallpox epidemic.

Amanda. No, as a matter of fact it was kidney trouble.

Elyot. You'll dance it with me I hope?

Amanda [*rising*]. I shall be charmed.

Elyot [*as they dance*]. Quite a good floor, isn't it?

Amanda. Yes, I think it needs a little Borax.

Elyot. I love Borax.

Amanda. Is that the Grand Duchess Olga lying under the piano?

Elyot. Yes, her husband died a few weeks ago, you know, on his way back from Pulborough. So sad.

Amanda. What on earth was he doing in Pulborough?

Elyot. Nobody knows exactly, but there have been the usual stories.

Amanda. I see.

Elyot. Delightful parties Lady Bundle always gives, doesn't she?

Amanda. Entrancing. Such a dear old lady.

Elyot. And so gay. Did you notice her at supper blowing all those shrimps through her ear trumpet?

[*The tune comes to an end. Amanda sits on the edge of the sofa, pensively.*]

Elyot. What are you thinking about?

Amanda. Nothing in particular.

Elyot. Come on, I know that face.

Amanda. Poor Sibyl.

Elyot. Sibyl?

Amanda. Yes, I suppose she loves you terribly.

Elyot. Not as much as all that, she didn't have a chance to get really under way.

Amanda. I expect she's dreadfully unhappy.

Elyot. Oh, do shut up, Amanda, we've had all that out before.

Amanda. We've certainly been pretty busy trying to justify ourselves.

Elyot. It isn't a question of justifying ourselves; it's the true values of the situation that are really important. The moment we saw one another again we knew it was no use going on. We knew it instantly really, although we tried to pretend to ourselves that we didn't. What we've got to be thankful for is that we made the break straight away, and not later.

Amanda. You think we should have done it anyhow?

Elyot. Of course, and things would have been in a worse mess than they are now.

Amanda. And what if we'd never happened to meet again. Would you have been quite happy with Sibyl?

Elyot. I expect so.

Amanda. Oh, Elyot!

Elyot. You needn't look so stricken. It would have been the same with you and Victor. Life would have been smooth, and amicable, and quite charming, wouldn't it?

Amanda. Poor dear Victor. He certainly did love me.

Elyot. Splendid.

Amanda. When I met him I was so lonely and depressed, I felt that I was getting old, and crumbling away unwanted.

Elyot. It certainly is horrid when one begins to crumble.

Amanda [*wistfully*]. He used to look at me hopelessly like a lovely spaniel, and I sort of melted like snow in the sunlight.

Elyot. That must have been an edifying spectacle.

Amanda. Victor really had a great charm.

Elyot. You must tell me all about it.

Amanda. He had a positive mania for looking after me, and protecting me.

Elyot. That would have died down in time, dear.

Amanda. You mustn't be rude, there's no necessity to be rude.

Elyot. I wasn't in the least rude; I merely made a perfectly rational statement.

Amanda. Your voice was decidedly bitter.

Elyot. Victor had glorious legs, hadn't he? And fascinating ears.

Amanda. Don't be silly.

Elyot. He probably looked radiant in the morning, all flushed and tumbled on the pillow.

Amanda. I never saw him on the pillow.

Elyot. I'm surprised to hear it.

Amanda [*angrily*]. Elyot!

Elyot. There's no need to be cross.

Amanda. What did you mean by that?

Elyot. I'm sick of listening to you yap, yap, yap, yap, yap, yapping about Victor.

Amanda. Now listen Elyot, once and for all—

Elyot. Oh my dear, Sollocks! Sollocks!—two minutes—Sollocks.

Amanda. But—

Elyot [*firmly*]. Sollocks! [*They sit in dead silence, looking at each other. Amanda makes a sign that she wants a cigarette. Elyot gets up, hands her the box, and lights one for her and himself. Amanda rises and walks over to the window, and stands there, looking out for a moment. Presently Elyot joins her. She slips her arm through his, and they kiss lightly. They draw the curtains and then come down and sit side by side on the sofa. Elyot looks at his watch. Amanda raises her eyebrows at him and he nods, then they both sigh, audibly.*] That was a near thing.

Amanda. It was my fault. I'm terribly sorry, darling.

Elyot. I was very irritating, I know I was. I'm sure Victor was awfully nice, and you're perfectly right to be sweet about him.

Amanda. That's downright handsome of you. Sweetheart! [*She kisses him.*]

Elyot [*leaning back with her on the sofa*]. I think I love you more than ever before. Isn't it ridiculous? Put your feet up.

[*She puts her legs across his, and they snuggle back together in the corner of the sofa, his head resting on her shoulder.*]

Amanda. Comfortable?

Elyot. Almost, wait a minute. [*He struggles a bit and then settles down with a sigh.*]

Amanda. How long, Oh Lord, how long?

Elyot [*drowsily*]. What do you mean, "how long, Oh Lord, how long?"

Amanda. This is far too perfect to last.

Elyot. You have no faith, that's what's wrong with you.

Amanda. Absolutely none.

Elyot. Don't you believe in—? [*He nods upwards.*]

Amanda. No, do you?

Elyot [*shaking his head*]. No. What about—? [*He points downwards.*]

Amanda. Oh dear no.

Elyot. Don't you believe in anything?

Amanda. Oh yes, I believe in being kind to everyone, and giving money to old beggar women, and being as gay as possible.

Elyot. What about after we're dead?

Amanda. I think a rather gloomy merging into everything, don't you?

Elyot. I hope not, I'm a bad merger.

Amanda. You won't know a thing about it.

Elyot. I hope for a glorious oblivion, like being under gas.

Amanda. I always dream the most peculiar things under gas.

Elyot. Would you be young always? If you could choose?

Amanda. No, I don't think so, not if it meant having awful bull's glands popped into me.

Elyot. Cows for you dear. Bulls for me.

Amanda. We certainly live in a marvellous age.

Elyot. Too marvellous. It's alright if you happen to be a specialist at something, then you're too concentrated to pay attention to all the other things going on. But, for the ordinary observer, it's too much.

Amanda [*snuggling closer*]. Far, far too much.

Elyot. Take the radio for instance.

Amanda. Oh darling, don't let's take the radio.

Elyot. Well, aeroplanes then, and Cosmic Atoms, and Television, and those gland injections we were talking about just now.

Amanda. It must be so nasty for the poor animals, being experimented on.

Elyot. Not when the experiments are successful. Why in

Vienna I believe you can see whole lines of decrepit old rats carrying on like Tiller Girls.

Amanda [*laughing*]. Oh, how very, very sweet.

Elyot [*burying his face in her shoulder*]. I do love you so.

Amanda. Don't blow, dear heart, it gives me the shivers.

Elyot [*trying to kiss her*]. Swivel your face round a bit more.

Amanda [*obliging*]. That better?

Elyot [*kissing her lingeringly*]. Very nice, thank you kindly.

Amanda [*twining her arms around his neck*]. Darling, you're so terribly, terribly dear, and sweet, and attractive. [*She pulls his head down to her again and they kiss lovingly.*]

Elyot [*softly*]. We were raving mad, ever to part, even for an instant.

Amanda. Utter imbeciles.

Elyot. I realised it almost immediately, didn't you?

Amanda. Long before we got our decree.

Elyot. My heart broke on that damned trip round the world. I saw such beautiful things, darling. Moonlight shining on old temples, strange barbaric dances in jungle villages, scarlet flamingoes flying over deep, deep blue water. Breathlessly lovely, and completely unexciting because you weren't there to see them with me.

Amanda [*kissing him again*]. Take me please, take me at once, let's make up for lost time.

Elyot. Next week?

Amanda. Tomorrow.

Elyot. Done.

Amanda. I must see those dear flamingoes. [*There is a pause.*] Eight years all told, we've loved each other. Three married and five divorced.

Elyot. Angel. Angel. Angel. [*He kisses her passionately.*]

Amanda [*struggling slightly*]. No, Elyot, stop now, stop—

Elyot. Why should I stop? You know you adore being made love to.

Amanda [*through his kisses*]. It's so soon after dinner.

Elyot [*jumping up rather angrily*]. You really do say most awful things.

Amanda [*tidying her hair*]. I don't see anything particularly awful about that.

Elyot. No sense of glamour, no sense of glamour at all.

Amanda. It's difficult to feel really glamorous with a crick in the neck.

Elyot. Why didn't you say you had a crick in your neck?

Amanda [*sweetly*]. It's gone now.

Elyot. How convenient. [*He lights a cigarette.*]

Amanda [*holding out her hand*]. I want one please.

Elyot [*throwing her one*]. Here.

Amanda. Match?

Elyot [*impatiently*]. Wait a minute, can't you?

Amanda. Chivalrous little love.

Elyot [*throwing the matches at her*]. Here.

Amanda [*coldly*]. Thank you very much indeed. [*There is a silence for a moment.*]

Elyot. You really can be more irritating than anyone in the world.

Amanda. I fail to see what I've done that's so terribly irritating.

Elyot. You have no tact.

Amanda. Tact. You have no consideration.

Elyot [*walking up and down*]. Too soon after dinner indeed.

Amanda. Yes, much too soon.

Elyot. That sort of remark shows rather a common sort of mind I'm afraid.

Amanda. Oh it does, does it?

Elyot. Very unpleasant, makes me shudder.

Amanda. Making all this fuss just because your silly vanity is a little upset.

Elyot. Vanity. What do you mean, vanity?

Amanda. You can't bear the thought that there are certain moments when our chemical, what d'you call 'ems, don't fuse properly.

Elyot [*derisively*]. Chemical what d'you call 'ems. Please try to be more explicit.

Amanda. You know perfectly well what I mean, and don't you try to patronise me.

Elyot [*loudly*]. Now look here, Amanda—

Amanda [*suddenly*]. Darling Sollocks! Oh, for God's sake, Sollocks!

Elyot. But listen—

Amanda. Sollocks, Sollocks, Oh dear—triple Sollocks!

[*They stand looking at one another in silence for a moment, then Amanda flings herself down on the sofa and buries her face in the cushions. Elyot looks at her, then goes over to the piano. He sits down and begins to play idly. Amanda raises her head, screws herself round on the sofa, and lies there listening. Elyot blows a kiss to her and goes on playing. He starts to sing softly to her,*

*never taking his eyes off her. When he has finished the
little refrain, whatever it was, he still continues to play it
looking at her.*]

Amanda. Big romantic stuff, darling.

Elyot [*smiling*]. Yes, big romantic stuff.

[*He wanders off into another tune. Amanda sits up crossed
legged on the sofa, and begins to sing it, then, still
singing, she comes over and perches on the piano. They
sing several old refrains from dead and gone musical
comedies finishing with the song that brought them
together again in the first Act. Finally Amanda comes
down and sits next to him on the piano stool, they both
therefore have their backs half turned to the audience.
She rests her head on his shoulder, until finally his
fingers drop off the keys, and they melt into one another's arms.*]

Elyot [*after a moment*]. You're the most thrilling, exciting
woman that was ever born.

Amanda [*standing up, and brushing her hand lightly over
his mouth*]. Dearest, dearest heart—

[*He catches at her hand and kisses it, and then her arm,
until he is standing up, embracing her ardently. She
struggles a little, half laughing, and breaks away, but he
catches her, and they finish up on the sofa again,
clasped in each other's arms, both completely given up
to the passion of the moment, until the telephone bell
rings violently, and they both spring apart.*]

Elyot. Good God!

Amanda. Do you think it's them?

Elyot. I wonder.

Amanda. Nobody knows we're here except Freda, and she
wouldn't ring up.

Elyot. It must be them then.

Amanda. What are we to do?

Elyot [*suddenly*]. We're alright darling, aren't we—whatever
happens?

Amanda. Now and always, Sweet.

Elyot. I don't care then. [*He gets up and goes defiantly over
to the telephone, which has been ringing incessantly
during the little preceding scene.*]

Amanda. It was bound to come sooner or later.

Elyot [*at telephone*]. Hallo—hallo—what—comment? Madame, qui? 'allo—'allo—oui c'est ça. Oh, Madame Duvallon—Oui, oui, oui. [*He puts his hand over the*

mouthpiece.] It's only somebody wanting to talk to the dear Madame Duvallon.

Amanda. Who's she?

Elyot. I haven't the faintest idea. [*At telephone.*] Je regrette beaucoup Monsieur, mais Madame Duvallon viens de partir—cette après midi, pour Madagascar. [*He hangs up the telephone.*] Whew; that gave me a fright.

Amanda. It sent shivers up my spine.

Elyot. What shall we do if they suddenly walk in on us?

Amanda. Behave exquisitely.

Elyot. With the most perfect poise?

Amanda. Certainly, I shall probably do a Court Curtsey.

Elyot [*sitting on the edge of the sofa*]. Things that ought to matter dreadfully, don't matter at all when one's happy, do they?

Amanda. What is so horrible is that one can't stay happy.

Elyot. Darling, don't say that.

Amanda. It's true. The whole business is a very poor joke.

Elyot. Meaning that sacred and beautiful thing, Love?

Amanda. Yes, meaning just that.

Elyot [*striding up and down the room dramatically*]. What does it all mean, that's what I ask myself in my ceaseless quest for ultimate truth. Dear God, what does it all mean?

Amanda. Don't laugh at me, I'm serious.

Elyot [*seriously*]. You mustn't be serious, my dear one, it's just what they want.

Amanda. Who's they?

Elyot. All the futile moralists who try to make life unbearable. Laugh at them. Be flippant. Laugh at everything, all their sacred shibboleths. Flippancy brings out the acid in their damned sweetness and light.

Amanda. If I laugh at everything, I must laugh at us too.

Elyot. Certainly you must. We're figures of fun alright.

Amanda. How long will it last, this ludicrous, overbearing love of ours?

Elyot. Who knows?

Amanda. Shall we always want to bicker and fight?

Elyot. No, that desire will fade, along with our passion.

Amanda. Oh dear, shall we like that?

Elyot. It all depends on how well we've played.

Amanda. What happens if one of us dies? Does the one that's left still laugh?

Elyot. Yes, yes, with all his might.

Amanda [*wistfully clutching his hand*]. That's serious enough, isn't it?

Elyot. No, no, it isn't. Death's very laughable, such a cunning little mystery. All done with mirrors.

Amanda. Darling, I believe you're talking nonsense.

Elyot. So is everyone else in the long run. Let's be superficial and pity the poor Philosophers. Let's blow trumpets and squeakers, and enjoy the party as much as we can, like very small, quite idiotic school-children. Let's savour the delight of the moment. Come and kiss me darling, before your body rots, and worms pop in and out of your eye sockets.

Amanda. Elyot, worms don't pop.

Elyot [*kissing her*]. I don't mind what you do see? You can paint yourself bright green all over, and dance naked in the Place Vendome, and rush off madly with all the men in the world, and I shan't say a word, as long as you love me best.

Amanda. Thank you, dear. The same applies to you, except that if I catch you so much as looking at another woman, I'll kill you.

Elyot. Do you remember that awful scene we had in Venice?

Amanda. Which particular one?

Elyot. The one when you bought that little painted wooden snake on the Piazza, and put it on my bed.

Amanda. Oh Charles. That was his name, Charles. He did wriggle so beautifully.

Elyot. Horrible thing, I hated it.

Amanda. Yes, I know you did. You threw it out of the window into the Grand Canal. I don't think I'll ever forgive you for that.

Elyot. How long did the row last?

Amanda. It went on intermittently for days.

Elyot. The worst one was in Cannes when your curling irons burnt a hole in my new dressing-gown. [*He laughs.*]

Amanda. It burnt my comb too, and all the towels in the bathroom.

Elyot. That was a rouser, wasn't it?

Amanda. That was the first time you ever hit me.

Elyot. I didn't hit you very hard.

Amanda. The manager came in and found us rolling on the floor, biting and scratching like panthers. Oh dear, oh dear— [*She laughs helplessly.*]

Elyot. I shall never forget his face. [*They both collapse with laughter.*]

Amanda. How ridiculous, how utterly, utterly ridiculous.

Elyot. We were very much younger then.

Amanda. And very much sillier.

Elyot. As a matter of fact the real cause of that row was Peter Burden.

Amanda. You knew there was nothing in that.

Elyot. I didn't know anything of the sort, you took presents from him.

Amanda. Presents: only a trivial little brooch.

Elyot. I remember it well, bristling with diamonds. In the worst possible taste.

Amanda. Not at all, it was very pretty. I still have it, and I wear it often.

Elyot. You went out of your way to torture me over Peter Burden.

Amanda. No, I didn't, you worked the whole thing up in your jealous imagination.

Elyot. You must admit that he was in love with you, wasn't he?

Amanda. Just a little perhaps. Nothing serious.

Elyot. You let him kiss you. You said you did.

Amanda. Well, what of it?

Elyot. What of it!

Amanda. It gave him a lot of pleasure, and it didn't hurt me.

Elyot. What about me?

Amanda. If you hadn't been so suspicious and nosey you'd never have known a thing about it.

Elyot. That's a nice point of view I must say.

Amanda. Oh dear, I'm bored with this conversation.

Elyot. So am I, bored stiff. [*He goes over to the table.*] Want some brandy?

Amanda. No thanks.

Elyot. I'll have a little, I think.

Amanda. I don't see why you want it, you've already had two glasses.

Elyot. No particular reason, anyhow they were very small ones.

Amanda. It seems so silly to go on, and on, and on with a thing.

Elyot [*pouring himself out a glassful*]. You can hardly call three liqueur glasses in a whole evening going on, and on, and on.

Amanda. It's become a habit with you.

Elyot. You needn't be so grand, just because you don't happen to want any yourself at the moment.

Amanda. Don't be so stupid.

Elyot [*irritably*]. Really Amanda—

Amanda. What?

Elyot. Nothing. [*Amanda sits down on the sofa, and, taking a small mirror from her bag, gazes at her face critically, and then uses some lipstick and powder. A trifle nastily.*] Going out somewhere dear?

Amanda. No, just making myself fascinating for you.

Elyot. That reply has broken my heart.

Amanda. The woman's job is to allure the man. Watch me a minute will you?

Elyot. As a matter of fact that's perfectly true.

Amanda. Oh, no, it isn't.

Elyot. Yes it is.

Amanda [*snappily*]. Oh be quiet.

Elyot. It's a pity you didn't have any more brandy; it might have made you a little less disagreeable.

Amanda. It doesn't seem to have worked such wonders with you.

Elyot. Snap, snap, snap; like a little adder.

Amanda. Adders don't snap, they sting.

Elyot. Nonsense, they have a little bag of venom behind their fangs and they snap.

Amanda. They sting.

Elyot. They snap.

Amanda [*with exasperation*]. I don't care, do you understand? I don't care. I don't mind if they bark, and roll about like hoops.

Elyot [*after a slight pause*]. Did you see much of Peter Burden after our divorce?

Amanda. Yes, I did, quite a lot.

Elyot. I suppose you let him kiss you a good deal more then.

Amanda. Mind your own business.

Elyot. You must have had a riotous time. [*Amanda doesn't answer, so he stalks about the room.*] No restraint at all—very enjoyable—you never had much anyhow.

Amanda. You're quite insufferable; I expect it's because you're drunk.

Elyot. I'm not in the least drunk.

Amanda. You always had a weak head.

Elyot. I think I mentioned once before that I only had three minute liqueur glasses of brandy the whole evening long. A child of two couldn't get drunk on that.

Amanda. On the contrary, a child of two could get violently drunk on only one glass of brandy.

Elyot. Very interesting. How about a child of four, and a child of six, and a child of nine?

Amanda [*turning her head away*]. Oh do shut up.

Elyot [*witheringly*]. We might get up a splendid little debate about that, you know, Intemperate Tots.

Amanda. Not very funny, dear; you'd better have some more brandy.

Elyot. Very good idea, I will. [*He pours out another glass and gulps it down defiantly.*]

Amanda. Ridiculous ass.

Elyot. I beg your pardon?

Amanda. I said ridiculous ass!

Elyot [*with great dignity*]. Thank you. [*There is a silence. Amanda gets up, and turns the gramophone on.*] You'd better turn that off, I think.

Amanda [*coldly*]. Why?

Elyot. It's very late and it will annoy the people upstairs.

Amanda. There aren't any people upstairs. It's a photographer's studio.

Elyot. There are people downstairs, I suppose?

Amanda. They're away in Tunis.

Elyot. This is no time of the year for Tunis. [*He turns the gramophone off.*]

Amanda [*icily*]. Turn it on again, please.

Elyot. I'll do no such thing.

Amanda. Very well, if you insist on being boorish and idiotic. [*She gets up and turns it on again.*]

Elyot. Turn it off. It's driving me mad.

Amanda. You're far too temperamental. Try to control yourself.

Elyot. Turn it off.

Amanda. I wont. [*Elyot rushes at the gramophone. Amanda tries to ward him off. They struggle silently for a moment then the needle screeches across the record.*] There now, you've ruined the record. [*She takes it off and scrutinises it.*]

Elyot. Good job, too.

Amanda. Disagreeable pig.

Elyot [*suddenly stricken with remorse*]. Amanda darling—
Sollocks.

Amanda [*furiously*]. Sollocks yourself. [*She breaks the record over his head.*]

Elyot [*staggering*]. You spiteful little beast. [*He slaps her face. She screams loudly and hurls herself sobbing with rage on to the sofa, with her face buried in the cushions.*]

Amanda [*wailing*]. Oh, oh, oh—

Elyot. I'm sorry, I didn't mean it—I'm sorry, darling, I swear I didn't mean it.

Amanda. Go away, go away, I hate you. [*Elyot kneels on the sofa and tries to pull her round to look at him.*]

Elyot. Amanda—listen—listen—

Amanda [*turning suddenly, and fetching him a welt across the face*]. Listen indeed; I'm sick and tired of listening to you, you damned sadistic bully.

Elyot [*with great grandeur*]. Thank you. [*He stalks towards the door, in stately silence. Amanda throws a cushion at him, which misses him and knocks down a lamp and a vase on the side table. Elyot laughs falsely.*] A pretty display I must say.

Amanda [*wildly*]. Stop laughing like that.

Elyot [*continuing*]. Very amusing indeed.

Amanda [*losing control*]. Stop—stop—stop— [*She rushes at him, he grabs her hands and they sway about the room, until he manages to twist her round by the arms so that she faces him, closely, quivering with fury*]—I hate you—do you hear? You're conceited, and overbearing, and utterly impossible!

Elyot [*shouting her down*]. You're a vile tempered loose-living wicked little beast, and I never want to see you again so long as I live. [*He flings her away from him, she staggers, and falls against a chair. They stand gasping at one another in silence for a moment.*]

Amanda [*very quietly*]. This is the end, do you understand? The end, finally and forever. [*She goes to the door, which opens on to the landing, and wrenches it open. He rushes after her and clutches her wrist.*]

Elyot. You're not going like this.

Amanda. Oh yes I am.

Elyot. You're not.

Amanda. I am; let go of me— [*He pulls her away from*

the door, and once more they struggle. This time a standard lamp crashes to the ground. Amanda, breathlessly, as they fight.] You're a cruel fiend, and I hate and loathe you; thank God I've realised in time what you're really like; marry you again, never, never, never. . . . I'd rather die in torment—

Elyot [*at the same time*]. Shut up; shut up. I wouldn't marry you again if you came crawling to me on your bended knees, you're a mean, evil minded, little vampire—I hope to God I never set eyes on you again as long as I live—

[*At this point in the proceedings they trip over a piece of carpet, and fall on to the floor, rolling over and over in paroxysms of rage. Victor and Sibyl enter quietly, through the open door, and stand staring at them in horror. Finally Amanda breaks free and half gets up, Elyot grabs her leg, and she falls against a table, knocking it completely over.*]

Amanda [*screaming*]. Beast; brute; swine; cad; beast; beast; brute; devil— [*She rushes back at Elyot who is just rising to his feet, and gives him a stinging blow, which knocks him over again. She rushes blindly off Left, and slams the door, at the same moment that he jumps up and rushes off Right, also slamming the door. Victor and Sibyl advance apprehensively into the room, and sink on to the sofa—*

The Curtain Falls

The Scene is the same as Act 2. Is is the next morning. The time is about eight-thirty. Victor and Sibyl have drawn the two sofas across the doors Right, and Left, and are stretched on them, asleep. Victor is in front of Amanda's door, and Sibyl in front of Elyot's.

The room is in chaos, as it was left the night before.

As the curtain rises, there is the rattling of a key in the lock of the front door, and Louise enters. She is rather a frowsy looking girl, and carries a string bag with various bundles of eatables crammed into it, notably a long roll of bread, and a lettuce. She closes the door after her, and in the half light trips over the standard lamp lying on the floor. She puts her string bag down, and gropes her way over to the window. She draws the curtains, letting sunlight stream into the room. When she looks round, she gives a little cry of horror. Then she sees Victor and Sibyl sleeping peacefully, and comes over and scrutinises each of them with care, then she shakes Sibyl by the shoulder.

Sibyl [*waking*]. Oh dear.

Louise. Bon jour, Madame.

Sibyl [*bewildered*]. What?—Oh—bon jour.

Louise. Qu'est-ce que vous faites ici, madame?

Sibyl. What—what?—Wait a moment, attendez un instant —oh dear—

Victor [*sleepily*]. What's happening? [*Jumping up.*] Of course, I remember now. [*He sees Louise.*] Oh!

Louise [*firmly*]. Bon jour, Monsieur.

Victor. Er—bon jour—What time is it?

Louise [*rather dully*]. Eh, Monsieur?

Sibyl [*sitting up on the sofa*]. Quelle heure est-il s'il vous plaît?

Louise. C'est neuf heures moins dix, madame.

Victor. What did she say?

Sibyl. I think she said nearly ten o'clock.

Victor [*taking situation in hand*]. Er—voulez—er—wake—reveillez Monsieur et Madame—er—toute suite?

Louise [*shaking her head*]. Non, Monsieur. Il m'est absolument defendu de les appeler jusqu'à ce qu'ils sonnent. [*She takes her bag and goes off into the kitchen. Victor and Sibyl look at each other helplessly.*]

Sibyl. What are we to do?

Victor [*with determination*]. Wake them ourselves. [*He goes towards Amanda's door.*]

Sibyl. No, no, wait a minute.

Victor. What's the matter?

Sibyl [*plaintively*]. I couldn't face them yet, really, I couldn't; I feel dreadful.

Victor. So do I. [*He wanders gloomily over to the window.*] It's a lovely morning.

Sibyl. Lovely. [*She bursts into tears.*]

Victor [*coming to her*]. I say, don't cry.

Sibyl. I can't help it.

Victor. Please don't, please—

Sibyl. It's all so squalid, I wish we hadn't stayed; what's the use?

Victor. We've got to see them before we go back to England, we must get things straightened out.

Sibyl [*sinking down on to the sofa*]. Oh dear, oh dear, oh dear, I wish I were dead.

Victor. Hush, now, hush. Remember your promise. We've got to see this through together and get it settled one way or another.

Sibyl [*sniffling*]. I'll try to control myself, only I'm so . . . so tired, I haven't slept properly for ages.

Victor. Neither have I.

Sibyl. If we hadn't arrived when we did, they'd have killed one another.

Victor. They must have been drunk.

Sibyl. She hit him.

Victor. He'd probably hit her, too, earlier on.

Sibyl. I'd no idea anyone ever behaved like that; it's so disgusting, so degrading, Elli of all people—oh dear— [*She almost breaks down again, but controls herself.*]

Victor. What an escape you've had.

Sibyl. What an escape we've both had.

[*Amanda opens her door and looks out. She is wearing travelling clothes, and is carrying a small suit-case. She jumps, upon seeing Sibyl and Victor.*]

Amanda. Oh!—good morning.

Victor [*with infinite reproach in his voice*]. Oh, Amanda.

Amanda. Will you please move this sofa, I can't get out.

[*Victor moves the sofa, and she advances into the room and goes towards the door.*]

Victor. Where are you going?

Amanda. Away.

Victor. You can't.

Amanda. Why not?

Victor. I want to talk to you.

Amanda [*wearily*]. What on earth is the use of that?

Victor. I must talk to you.

Amanda. Well, all I can say is, it's very inconsiderate. [*She plumps the bag down by the door and comes down to Victor.*]

Victor. Mandy, I—

Amanda [*gracefully determined to rise above the situation*]. I suppose you're Sibyl; how do you do? [*Sibyl turns her back on her.*] Well, if you're going to take up that attitude, I fail to see the point of your coming here at all.

Sibyl. I came to see Elyot.

Amanda. I've no wish to prevent you, he's in there, probably wallowing in an alcoholic stupor.

Victor. This is all very unpleasant, Amanda.

Amanda. I quite agree, that's why I want to go away.

Victor. That would be shirking; this must be discussed at length.

Amanda. Very well, if you insist, but not just now, I don't feel up to it. Has Louise come yet?

Victor. If Louise is the maid, she's in the kitchen.

Amanda. Thank you. You'd probably like some coffee, excuse me a moment. [*She goes off into the kitchen.*]

Sibyl. Well! How dare she?

Victor [*irritably*]. How dare she what?

Sibyl. Behave so calmly, as though nothing had happened.

Victor. I don't see what else she could have done.

Sibyl. Insufferable I call it.

[*Elyot opens his door and looks out.*]

Elyot [*seeing them*]. Oh God. [*He shuts the door again quickly.*]

Sibyl. Elyot—Elyot— [*She rushes over to the door and bangs on it.*] Elyot—Elyot—Elyot—

Elyot [*inside*]. Go away.

Sibyl [*falling on to the sofa*]. Oh, oh, oh. [*She bursts into tears again.*]

Victor. Do pull yourself together for heaven's sake.

Sibyl. I can't, I can't—oh, oh, oh—

[*Amanda reenters.*]

Amanda. I've ordered some coffee and rolls, they'll be here soon. I must apologise for the room being so untidy. [*She picks up a cushion, and pats it into place on the sofa. There is a silence except for Sibyl's sobs. Amanda looks at her, and then at Victor; then she goes off into her room again, and shuts the door.*]

Victor. It's no use crying like that, it doesn't do any good.

[*After a moment, during which Sibyl makes renewed efforts to control her tears, Elyot opens the door immediately behind her, pushes the sofa, with her on it, out of the way, and walks towards the front door. He is in travelling clothes, and carrying a small suitcase.*]

Sibyl [*rushing after him*]. Elyot, where are you going?

Elyot. Canada.

Sibyl. You can't go like this, you can't.

Elyot. I see no point in staying.

Victor. You owe it to Sibyl to stay.

Elyot. How do you do, I don't think we've met before.

Sibyl. You must stay, you've got to stay.

Elyot. Very well, if you insist. [*He plumps his bag down.*] I'm afraid the room is in rather a mess. Have you seen the maid Louise?

Victor. She's in the kitchen.

Elyot. Good. I'll order some coffee. [*He makes a movement towards the kitchen.*]

Victor [*stopping him*]. No, your—er—my—er—Amanda has already ordered it.

Elyot. Oh, I'm glad the old girl's up and about.

Victor. We've got to get things straightened out, you know.

Elyot [*looking around the room*]. Yes, it's pretty awful. We'll get the concierge up from downstairs.

Victor. You're being purposely flippant, but it's no good.

Elyot. Sorry. [*He lapses into silence.*]

Victor [*after a pause*]. What's to be done?

Elyot. I don't know.

Sibyl [*with spirit*]. It's all perfectly horrible. I feel smirched and unclean as though slimy things had been crawling all over me.

Elyot. Maybe they have, that's a very old sofa.

Victor. If you don't stop your damned flippancy, I'll knock your head off.

Elyot [*raising his eyebrows*]. Has it ever struck you that flippancy might cover a very real embarrassment?

Victor. In a situation such as this, it's in extremely bad taste.

Elyot. No worse than bluster, and invective. As a matter of fact, as far as I know, this situation is entirely without precedent. We have no prescribed etiquette to fall back upon. I shall continue to be flippant.

Sibyl. Oh Elyot, how can you—how can you.

Elyot. I'm awfully sorry, Sibyl.

Victor. It's easy enough to be sorry.

Elyot. On the contrary. I find it exceedingly difficult. I seldom regret anything. This is a very rare and notable exception, a sort of red-letter day. We must all make the most of it.

Sibyl. I'll never forgive you, never. I wouldn't have believed anyone could be so callous and cruel.

Elyot. I absolutely see your point, and as I said before, I'm sorry.

[*There is silence for a moment. Then Amanda comes in again. She has obviously decided to carry everything off in a high-handed manner.*]

Amanda [*in social tones*]. What! Breakfast not ready yet? Really, these French servants are too slow for words. [*She smiles gaily.*] What a glorious morning. [*She goes to the window.*] I do love Paris, it's so genuinely gay. Those lovely trees in the Champs Elysées, and the little roundabouts for the children to play on, and those shiny red taxis. You can see Sacre Coeur quite clearly today, sometimes it's a bit misty, particularly in August, all the heat rising up from the pavements you know.

Elyot [*drily*]. Yes, dear, we know.

Amanda [*ignoring him*]. And it's heavenly being so high up. I found this flat three years ago, quite by merest chance. I happened to be staying at the Plaza Athenée, just down the road—

Elyot [*enthusiastically*]. Such a nice hotel, with the most enchanting courtyard with a fountain that goes plop-plopplopplopplopplopplopplopplop—

Victor. This is ridiculous, Amanda.

Elyot [*continuing*]. Plop plop plop plop plop plop plop plop plop plop—

Amanda [*overriding him*]. Now, Victor, I refuse to discuss anything in the least important until after breakfast. I couldn't concentrate now, I know I couldn't.

Elyot [*sarcastically*]. What manner. What poise. How I envy it. To be able to carry off the most embarrassing situation with such tact, and delicacy, and above all—such subtlety. Go on Amanda, you're making everything so much easier. We shall all be playing Hunt the Slipper in a minute.

Amanda. Please don't address me, I don't wish to speak to you.

Elyot. Splendid.

Amanda. And what's more, I never shall again as long as I live.

Elyot. I shall endeavour to rise above it.

Amanda. I've been brought up to believe that it's beyond the pale, for a man to strike a woman.

Elyot. A very poor tradition. Certain women should be struck regularly, like gongs.

Amanda. You're an unmitigated cad, and a bully.

Elyot. And you're an ill mannered, bad tempered slattern.

Amanda [*loudly*]. Slattern indeed.

Elyot. Yes, slattern, slattern, slattern, and fishwife.

Victor. Keep your mouth shut, you swine.

Elyot. Mind your damned business.

[*They are about to fight, when Sibyl rushes between them.*]

Sibyl. Stop, stop, it's no use going on like this. Stop, please. [*To Amanda.*] Help me, do, do, do, help me—

Amanda. I'm not going to interfere. Let them fight if they want to, it will probably clear the air anyhow.

Sibyl. Yes but—

Amanda. Come into my room, perhaps you'd like to wash or something.

Sibyl. No, but—

Amanda [*firmly*]. Come along.

Sibyl. Very well. [*She tosses her head at Elyot, and Amanda drags her off.*]

Victor [*belligerently*]. Now then!

Elyot. Now then what?

Victor. Are you going to take back those things you said to Amanda?

Elyot. Certainly, I'll take back anything, if only you'll stop
　　bellowing at me.

Victor [*contemptuously*]. You're a coward too.

Elyot. They want us to fight, don't you see?

Victor. No, I don't, why should they?

Elyot. Primitive feminine instincts—warring males—very
　　enjoyable.

Victor. You think you're very clever, don't you?

Elyot. I think I'm a bit cleverer than you, but apparently
　　that's not saying much.

Victor [*violently*]. What?

Elyot. Oh, do sit down.

Victor. I will not.

Elyot. Well, if you'll excuse me, I will, I'm extremely tired.
　　[*He sits down.*]

Victor. Oh, for God's sake, behave like a man.

Elyot [*patiently*]. Listen a minute, all this belligerency is very
　　right and proper and highly traditional, but if only you'll
　　think for a moment, you'll see that it won't get us very
　　far.

Victor. To hell with all that.

Elyot. I should like to explain that if you hit me, I shall cer-
　　tainly hit you, probably equally hard, if not harder. I'm
　　just as strong as you I should imagine. Then you'd hit
　　me again, and I'd hit you again, and we'd go on until
　　one or other was knocked out. Now if you'll explain
　　to me satisfactorily how all that can possibly improve
　　the situation, I'll tear off my coat, and we'll go at one
　　another hammer and tongs, immediately.

Victor. It would ease my mind.

Elyot. Only if you won.

Victor. I should win alright.

Elyot. Want to try?

Victor. Yes.

Elyot [*jumping up*]. Here goes then—[*He tears off his coat.*]

Victor. Just a moment.

Elyot. Well?

Victor. What did you mean about them wanting us to fight?

Elyot. It would be balm to their vanity.

Victor. Do you love Amanda?

Elyot. Is this a battle or a discussion? If it's the latter I shall
　　put on my coat again, I don't want to catch a chill.

Victor. Answer my question, please.

Elyot. Have a cigarette?

Victor [*stormily*]. Answer my question.

Elyot. If you analyse it, it's rather a silly question.

Victor. Do you love Amanda?

Elyot [*confidentially*]. Not very much this morning, to be perfectly frank, I'd like to wring her neck. Do you love her?

Victor. That's beside the point.

Elyot. On the contrary, it's the crux of the whole affair. If you do love her still, you can forgive her, and live with her in peace and harmony until you're ninety-eight.

Victor. You're apparently even more of a cad than I thought you were.

Elyot. You are completely in the right over the whole business, don't imagine I'm not perfectly conscious of that.

Victor. I'm glad.

Elyot. It's all very unfortunate.

Victor. Unfortunate. My God!

Elyot. It might have been worse.

Victor. I'm glad you think so.

Elyot. I do wish you'd stop about being so glad about everything.

Victor. What do you intend to do? That's what I want to know. What do you intend to do?

Elyot [*suddenly serious*]. I don't know, I don't care.

Victor. I suppose you realise that you've broken that poor little woman's heart?

Elyot. Which poor little woman?

Victor. Sibyl, of course.

Elyot. Oh, come now, not as bad as that. She'll get over it, and forget all about me.

Victor. I sincerely hope so . . . for her sake.

Elyot. Amanda will forget all about me too. Everybody will forget all about me. I might just as well lie down and die in fearful pain and suffering, nobody would care.

Victor. Don't talk such rot.

Elyot. You must forgive me for taking rather a gloomy view of everything but the fact is, I suddenly feel slightly depressed.

Victor. I intend to divorce Amanda, naming you as co-respondent.

Elyot. Very well.

Victor. And Sibyl will divorce you for Amanda. It would be foolish of either of you to attempt any defence.

Elyot. Quite.

Victor. And the sooner you marry Amanda again, the better.

Elyot. I'm not going to marry Amanda.

Victor. What?

Elyot. She's a vile tempered wicked woman.

Victor. You should have thought of that before.

Elyot. I did think of it before.

Victor [*firmly*]. You've got to marry her.

Elyot. I'd rather marry a ravening Leopard.

Victor [*angrily*]. Now look here. I'm sick of all this shilly-shallying. You're getting off a good deal more lightly than you deserve; you can consider yourself damned lucky I didn't shoot you.

Elyot [*with sudden vehemence*]. Well, if you'd had a spark of manliness in you, you would have shot me. You're all fuss and fume, one of these cotton-wool Englishmen. I despise you.

Victor [*through clenched teeth*]. You despise me?

Elyot. Yes, utterly. You're nothing but a rampaging gas bag! [*He goes off into his room and slams the door, leaving Victor speechless with fury, Amanda and Sibyl re-enter.*]

Amanda [*brightly*]. Well, what's happened?

Victor [*sullenly*]. Nothing's happened.

Amanda. You ought to be ashamed to admit it.

Sibyl. Where's Elyot?

Victor. In there.

Amanda. What's he doing?

Victor [*turning angrily away*]. How do I know what he's doing?

Amanda. If you were half the man I thought you were, he'd be bandaging himself.

Sibyl [*with defiance*]. Elyot's just as strong as Victor.

Amanda [*savagely*]. I should like it proved.

Sibyl. There's no need to be so vindictive.

Amanda. You were abusing Elyot like a pickpocket to me a little while ago, now you are standing up for him.

Sibyl. I'm beginning to suspect that he wasn't quite so much to blame as I thought.

Amanda. Oh really?

Sibyl. You certainly have a very unpleasant temper.

Amanda. It's a little difficult to keep up with your rapid changes of front, but you're young and inexperienced, so I forgive you freely.

Sibyl [*heatedly*]. Seeing the depths of degradation to which age and experience have brought you, I'm glad I'm as I am!

Amanda [*with great grandeur*]. That was exceedingly rude. I think you'd better go away somewhere. [*She waves her hand vaguely.*]

Sibyl. After all, Elyot is my husband.

Amanda. Take him with you, by all means.

Sibyl. If you're not very careful, I will! [*She goes over to Elyot's door and bangs on it.*] Elyot—Elyot—

Elyot [*inside*]. What is it?

Sibyl. Let me in. Please, please let me in; I want to speak to you!

Amanda. Heaven preserve me from nice women!

Sibyl. Your own reputation ought to do that.

Amanda [*irritably*]. Oh, go to hell!

[*Elyot open the door, and Sibyl disappears inside, Amanda looks at Victor, who is standing with his back turned, staring out of the window, then she wanders about the room, making rather inadequate little attempts to tidy up. She glances at Victor again.*]

Amanda. Victor.

Victor [*without turning*]. What?

Amanda [*sadly*]. Nothing. [*She begins to wrestle with one of the sofas in an effort to get it in place. Victor turns, sees her, and comes down and helps her, in silence.*]

Victor. Where does it go?

Amanda. Over there. [*After they have placed it, Amanda sits on the edge of it and gasps a little.*] Thank you, Victor.

Victor. Don't mention it.

Amanda [*after a pause*]. What did you say to Elyot?

Victor. I told him he was beneath contempt.

Amanda. Good.

Victor. I think you must be mad, Amanda.

Amanda. I've often thought that myself.

Victor. I feel completely lost, completely bewildered.

Amanda. I don't blame you. I don't feel any too cosy.

Victor. Had you been drinking last night?

Amanda. Certainly not!

Victor. Had Elyot been drinking?

Amanda. Yes—gallons.

Victor. Used he to drink before? When you were married to him?

Amanda. Yes, terribly. Night after night he'd come home roaring and hiccoughing.

Victor. Disgusting!

Amanda. Yes, wasn't it?

Victor. Did he really strike you last night?

Amanda. Repeatedly. I'm bruised beyond recognition.

Victor [*suspecting slight exaggeration*]. Amanda!

Amanda [*putting her hand on his arm*]. Oh, Victor, I'm most awfully sorry to have given you so much trouble, really I am! I've behaved badly, I know, but something strange happened to me. I can't explain it, there's no excuse, but I am ashamed of having made you unhappy.

Victor. I can't understand it at all. I've tried to, but I can't. It all seems so unlike you.

Amanda. It isn't really unlike me, that's the trouble. I ought never to have married you; I'm a bad lot.

Victor. Amanda!

Amanda. Don't contradict me. I know I'm a bad lot.

Victor. I wasn't going to contradict you.

Amanda. Victor!

Victor. You appal me—absolutely!

Amanda. Go on, go on, I deserve it.

Victor. I didn't come here to accuse you; there's no sense in that!

Amanda. Why did you come?

Victor. To find out what you want me to do.

Amanda. Divorce me, I suppose, as soon as possible. I won't make any difficulties. I'll go away, far away, Morocco, or Tunis, or somewhere. I shall probably catch some dreadful disease, and die out there, all alone—oh dear!

Victor. It's no use pitying yourself.

Amanda. I seem to be the only one who does. I might just as well enjoy it. [*She sniffs.*] I'm thoroughly unprincipled; Sibyl was right!

Victor [*irritably*]. Sibyl's an ass.

Amanda [*brightening slightly*]. Yes, she is rather, isn't she? I can't think why Elyot ever married her.

Victor. Do you love him?

Amanda. She seems so insipid, somehow—

Victor. Do you love him?

Amanda. Of course she's very pretty, I suppose, in rather a shallow way, but still—

Victor. Amanda!

Amanda. Yes, Victor?

Victor. You haven't answered my question.

Amanda. I've forgotten what it was.

Victor [*turning away*]. You're hopeless—hopeless.

Amanda. Don't be angry, it's all much too serious to be angry about.

Victor. You're talking utter nonsense!

Amanda. No, I'm not, I mean it. It's ridiculous for us all to stand round arguing with one another. You'd much better go back to England and let your lawyers deal with the whole thing.

Victor. But what about you?

Amanda. I'll be all right.

Victor. I only want to know one thing, and you won't tell me.

Amanda. What is it?

Victor. Do you love Elyot?

Amanda. No, I hate him. When I saw him again suddenly at Deauville, it was an odd sort of shock. It swept me away completely. He attracted me; he always has attracted me, but only the worst part of me. I see that now.

Victor. I can't understand why? He's so terribly trivial and superficial.

Amanda. That sort of attraction can't be explained, it's a sort of a chemical what d'you call 'em.

Victor. Yes; it must be!

Amanda. I don't expect you to understand, and I'm not going to try to excuse myself in any way. Elyot was the first love affair of my life, and in spite of all the suffering he caused me before, there must have been a little spark left smouldering, which burst into flame when I came face to face with him again. I completely lost grip of myself and behaved like a fool, for which I shall pay all right, you needn't worry about that. But perhaps one day, when all this is dead and done with, you and I might meet and be friends. That's something to hope for, anyhow. Good-bye, Victor dear. [*She holds out her hand.*]

Victor [*shaking her hand mechanically*]. Do you want to marry him?

Amanda. I'd rather marry a boa constrictor.

Victor. I can't go away and leave you with a man who drinks, and knocks you about.

Amanda. You needn't worry about leaving me, as though I were a sort of parcel. I can look after myself.

Victor. You said just now you were going away to Tunis, to die.

Amanda. I've changed my mind, it's the wrong time of the year for Tunis. I shall go somewhere quite different. I believe Brioni is very nice in the summer.

Victor. Why won't you be serious for just one moment?

Amanda. I've told you, it's no use.

Victor. If it will make things any easier for you, I won't divorce you.

Amanda. Victor!

Victor. We can live apart until Sibyl has got her decree against Elyot, then, some time after that, I'll let you divorce me.

Amanda [*turning away*]. I see you're determined to make me serious, whether I like it or not.

Victor. I married you because I loved you.

Amanda. Stop it, Victor! Stop it! I won't listen!

Victor. I expect I love you still; one doesn't change all in a minute. You never loved me. I see that now, of course, so perhaps everything has turned out for the best really.

Amanda. I thought I loved you, honestly I did.

Victor. Yes, I know, that's all right.

Amanda. What an escape you've had.

Victor. I've said that to myself often during the last few days.

Amanda. There's no need to rub it in.

Victor. Do you agree about the divorce business?

Amanda. Yes. It's very, very generous of you.

Victor. It will save you some of the mud-slinging. We might persuade Sibyl not to name you.

Amanda [*ruefully*]. Yes, we might.

Victor. Perhaps she'll change her mind about divorcing him.

Amanda. Perhaps. She certainly went into the bedroom with a predatory look in her eye.

Victor. Would you be pleased if that happened?

Amanda. Delighted. [*She laughs suddenly. Victor looks at her, curiously. Sibyl and Elyot come out of the bedroom. There is an awkward silence for a moment.*]

Sibyl [*looking at Amanda triumphantly*]. Elyot and I have come to a decision.

Amanda. How very nice!

Victor. What is it?

Amanda. Don't be silly, Victor. Look at their faces.

Elyot. Feminine intuition, very difficult.

Amanda [*looking at Sibyl*]. Feminine determination, very praiseworthy.

Sibyl. I am not going to divorce Elyot for a year.

Amanda. I congratulate you.

Elyot [*defiantly*]. Sibyl has behaved like an angel.

Amanda. Well, it was certainly her big moment.

[*Louise comes staggering in with a large tray of coffee and rolls, etc., she stands peering over the edge of it, not knowing where to put it.*]

Elyot. Il faut le mettre sur la petite table là-bas.

Louise. Oui, monsieur.

[*Elyot and Victor hurriedly clear the things off the side table, and Louise puts the tray down, and goes back into the kitchen. Amanda and Sibyl eye one another.*]

Amanda. It all seems very amicable.

Sibyl. It is, thank you.

Amanda. I don't wish to depress you, but Victor isn't going to divorce me either.

Elyot [*looking up sharply*]. What!

Amanda. I believe I asked you once before this morning, never to speak to me again.

Elyot. I only said "What." It was a general exclamation denoting extreme satisfaction.

Amanda [*politely to Sibyl*]. Do sit down, won't you?

Sibyl. I'm afraid I must be going now. I'm catching the Golden Arrow; it leaves at twelve.

Elyot [*coaxingly*]. You have time for a little coffee surely?

Sibyl. No, I really must go!

Elyot. I shan't be seeing you again for such a long time.

Amanda [*brightly*]. Living apart? How wise!

Elyot [*ignoring her*]. Please, Sibyl, do stay!

Sibyl [*looking at Amanda with a glint in her eye*]. Very well, just for a little.

Amanda. Sit down, Victor, darling.

[*They all sit down in silence. Amanda smiles sweetly at Sibyl and holds up the coffee pot and milk jug.*] Half and half?

Sibyl. Yes, please.

Amanda [*sociably*]. What would one do without one's morning coffee? That's what I often ask myself.

Elyot. Is it?

Amanda [*withering him with a look*]. Victor, sugar for Sibyl. [*To Sibyl.*] It would be absurd for me to call you anything but Sibyl, wouldn't it?

Sibyl [*not to be outdone*]. Of course, I shall call you Mandy.
    [*Amanda represses a shudder.*]

Elyot. Oh God! We're off again. What weather! [*Amanda
    hands Sibyl her coffee.*]

Sibyl. Thank you.

Victor. What's the time?

Elyot. If the clock's still going after last night, it's ten-fifteen.

Amanda [*handing Victor cup of coffee*]. Here, Victor dear.

Victor. Thanks.

Amanda. Sibyl, sugar for Victor.

Elyot. I should like some coffee, please.

[*Amanda pours some out for him, and hands it to him in
    silence.*]

Amanda [*to Victor*]. Brioche?

Victor [*jumping*]. What?

Amanda. Would you like a brioche?

Victor. No, thank you.

Elyot. I would. And some butter, and some jam. [*He helps
    himself.*]

Amanda [*to Sibyl*]. Have you ever been to Brioni?

Sibyl. No. It's in the Adriatic, isn't it?

Victor. The Baltic, I think.

Sibyl. I made sure it was the Adriatic.

Amanda. I had an aunt who went there once.

Elyot [*with his mouth full*]. I once had an aunt who went to
    Tasmania.

[*Amanda looks at him stonily. He winks at her, and she looks
    away hurriedly.*]

Victor. Funny how the South of France has become so
    fashionable in the summer, isn't it?

Sibyl. Yes, awfully funny.

Elyot. I've been laughing about it for months.

Amanda. Personally, I think it's a bit too hot, although of
    course one can lie in the water all day.

Sibyl. Yes, the bathing is really divine!

Victor. A friend of mine has a house right on the edge of
    Cape Ferrat.

Sibyl. Really?

Victor. Yes, right on the edge.

Amanda. That must be marvellous!

Victor. Yes, he seems to like it very much.

[*The conversation languishes slightly.*]

Amanda [*with great vivacity*]. Do you know, I really think
    I love travelling more than anything else in the world!

It always gives me such a tremendous feeling of adventure. First of all, the excitement of packing, and getting your passport visa'd and everything, then the thrill of actually starting, and trundling along on trains and ships, and then the most thrilling thing of all, arriving at strange places, and seeing strange people, and eating strange foods—

Elyot. And making strange noises afterwards.

[*Amanda chokes violently. Victor jumps up and tries to offer assistance, but she waves him away, and continues to choke.*]

Victor [*to Elyot*]. That was a damned fool thing to do.

Elyot. How did I know she was going to choke?

Victor [*to Amanda*]. Here, drink some coffee.

Amanda [*breathlessly gasping*]. Leave me alone. I'll be all right in a minute.

Victor [*to Elyot*]. You waste too much time trying to be funny.

Sibyl [*up in arms*]. It's no use talking to Elyot like that; it wasn't his fault.

Victor. Of course it was his fault entirely, making rotten stupid jokes—

Sibyl. I thought what Elyot said was funny.

Victor. Well, all I can say is, you must have a very warped sense of humour.

Sibyl. That's better than having none at all.

Victor. I fail to see what humour there is in incessant trivial flippancy.

Sibyl. You couldn't be flippant if you tried until you were blue in the face.

Victor. I shouldn't dream of trying.

Sibyl. It must be very sad not to be able to see any fun in anything.

[*Amanda stops choking, and looks at Elyot. He winks at her again, and she smiles.*]

Victor. Fun! I should like you to tell me what fun there is in—

Sibyl. I pity you, I really do. I've been pitying you ever since we left Deauville.

Victor. I'm sure it's very nice of you, but quite unnecessary.

Sibyl. And I pity you more than ever now.

Victor. *Why* now particularly?

Sibyl. If you don't see why, I'm certainly not going to tell you.

Victor. I see no reason for you to try to pick a quarrel with me. I've tried my best to be pleasant to you, and comfort you.

Sibyl. You weren't very comforting when I lost my trunk.

Victor. I have little patience with people who go about losing luggage.

Sibyl. I don't go about losing luggage. It's the first time I've lost anything in my life.

Victor. I find that hard to believe.

Sibyl. Anyhow, if you'd tipped the porter enough, everything would have been all right. Small economies never pay; it's absolutely no use—

Victor. Oh, for God's sake be quiet!

[*Amanda lifts her hand as though she were going to interfere, but Elyot grabs her wrist. They look at each other for a moment, she lets her hand rest in his.*]

Sibyl [*rising from the table*]. How dare you speak to me like that!

Victor [*also rising*]. Because you've been irritating me for days.

Sibyl [*outraged*]. Oh!

Victor [*coming down to her*]. You're one of the most completely idiotic women I've ever met.

Sibyl. And you're certainly the rudest man I've ever met!

Victor. Well then, we're quits, aren't we?

Sibyl [*shrilly*]. One thing, you'll get your deserts all right.

Victor. What do you mean by that?

Sibyl. You know perfectly well what I mean. And it'll serve you right for being weak-minded enough to allow that woman to get round you so easily.

Victor. What about you? Letting that unprincipled roué persuade you to take him back again!

[*Amanda and Elyot are laughing silently. Elyot blows her a lingering kiss across the table.*]

Sibyl. He's nothing of the sort, he's just been victimized, as you were victimized.

Victor. Victimized! What damned nonsense!

Sibyl [*furiously*]. It isn't damned nonsense! You're very fond of swearing and blustering and threatening, but when it comes to the point you're as weak as water. Why, a blind cat could see what you've let yourself in for.

Victor [*equally furious*]. Stop making those insinuations.

Sibyl. I'm not insinuating anything. When I think of all the things you said about her, it makes me laugh, it does really; to see how completely she's got you again.

Victor. You can obviously speak with great authority; having had the intelligence to marry a drunkard.

Sibyl. So that's what she's been telling you. I might have known it! I suppose she said he struck her too!

Victor. Yes, she did, and I'm quite sure it's perfectly true.

Sibyl. I expect she omitted to tell you that she drank fourteen glasses of brandy last night straight off; and that the reason their first marriage was broken up was that she used to come home at all hours of the night, screaming and hiccoughing.

Victor. If he told you that, he's a filthy liar.

Sibyl. He isn't—he isn't!

Victor. And if you believe it, you're a silly scatter-brained little fool.

Sibyl [*screaming*]. How dare you speak to me like that! How dare you! I've never been so insulted in my life! How dare you!

[*Amanda and Elyot rise quietly, and go, hand in hand, towards the front door.*]

Victor [*completely giving way*]. It's a tremendous relief to me to have an excuse to insult you. I've had to listen to your weeping and wailings for days. You've clacked at me, and snivelled at me until you've nearly driven me insane, and I controlled my nerves and continued to try to help you and look after you, because I was sorry for you. I always thought you were stupid from the first, but I must say I never realised that you were a malicious little vixen as well!

Sibyl [*shrieking*]. Stop it! Stop it! You insufferable great brute. [*She slaps his face hard, and he takes her by the shoulders and shakes her like a rat, as Amanda and Elyot go smilingly out of the door, with their suitcases, and—*

The Curtain Falls.

Enid Bagnold **The Chalk Garden**

The Madrigal
in the Garden

BY GERALD WEALES

Small ironies are the particular delight of those newspaper
columns that deal in news and gossip about Broadway and its
theatrical ventures; so it was natural that the most piquant
tidbit of the 1955–56 season should have been the fact that
Enid Bagnold's *The Chalk Garden,* a play which managed at
least the success of a five-month run in New York, had been
turned down by every major London management before Irene Mayer Selznick decided to produce it here. The
real surprise, however, was that Miss Bagnold's lovely play
should have been a success at all, even in a season unusual
enough to list Giraudoux and Anouilh among its hit playwrights. *The Chalk Garden* is too many things that a Broadway hit is not. It is, first of all, primarily verbal, using
language with a delight and a delicacy that is foreign to even
our most serious playwrights. It introduces and sustains the
metaphor of the chalk garden so graciously that the attentive
playgoer cannot miss the fact that it is both a symbol and a
real garden, never one or the other. It is a non-realistic play
whose concern for reality goes far beyond the conventional
care about the aptly reported speech and the carefully observed detail of dress or drink. It is a comedy that is funny
without making laughter its sole concern (or, under the influence of Miss Bagnold, its soul concern) and a serious play
that is never pretentious. It is a play which has something to
say, but says it with such richness that six people could (did,
in fact) come away from the theater, each moved, but each
moved with a different idea of the play's truth; there is no
message that can be spelled out with the leaden, lapel-grasp-
ing insistence that sometimes informs our more messianic
playwrights.

The reactions of the daily reviewers to *The Chalk Garden*
indicate why the play should never have run for five months.
For the most part their attention was drawn only to the surface of the play; they commented favorably on the author's

wit, admired the performances, clucked appreciatively over Cecil Beaton's set. Only Walter F. Kerr in the *Herald-Tribune* seemed aware of the quality of the play and even in his praise of it he defined it as fare for special palates. Aside from Kerr, only John Chapman in the *Daily News* and Richard Watts Jr. in the *Post* recognized the importance of Mrs. St. Maugham's garden of chalk, and Watts, at least, was incensed that symbolism should spoil a good comedy. In all of the reviews there was an uneasiness, a suspicion of the play's seriousness, but an inability or a refusal to deal with it. The reviews, even though technically they were favorable, were the kind that could draw only the curious, and it must certainly have been the word-of-mouth advertising that kept the play open. Eric Bently in his column in *New Republic* admitted that he walked out in irritation after the first act of the play, but he returned to see it again and to call it the best new play of the season.

Actually, *The Chalk Garden* is the best new play of quite a few seasons. That this fact should not have been immediately apparent to the daily reviewers lies certainly in Miss Bagnold's use of language. Reviewers are not accustomed to listening carefully to plays for the same reason that instructors in freshman composition are unused to reading themes closely; they expect nothing unusual or demanding so they do not look for it. Unless T. S. Eliot's name is on the program, a play set in an English country house should make no unconventional demands on its listeners, but Miss Bagnold's does. Mrs. St. Maugham says of her granddaughter Laurel, "Words leap and change color in her mouth like fishes!", but the phrase is as descriptive of the speech of all the characters as it is of Laurel. In a way, the dialogue suggests Chekhov. The characters speak first of all to themselves and out of themselves; if occasionally they communicate, if their speeches sometimes land on listening ears, the effect is a lucky accident. In one of the conversations between Miss Madrigal and Laurel, where the subject is ostensibly the girl, as it always is so far as she is concerned, Laurel suddenly says, "Are you talking of *you?* Or of *me?*" Miss Madrigal answers, "When one feels strongly—it is always of *me!*" The ambiguity that the pronouns allow does not mask the clarity of Miss Madrigal's answer; she is defining the use of language in the play, and out of it. The interview in the first act in which Mrs. St. Maugham considers Miss Madrigal for the position of governess suggests nothing so much as the scene in *The Cherry Orchard* immediately after Madame Ranevsky returns, when Lopahin and Gaev, touched into memory speak suddenly and significantly at cross purposes:

> *Lopahin.* Yes, time flies.
> *Gaev.* What do you say?
> *Lopahin.* Time, I say, flies.
> *Gaev.* What a smell of patchouli!

That the questions and answers that pass between Mrs. St. Maugham and Miss Madrigal have the same lack of connection, that they are at once amusing and important and a little painful, does not imply that Miss Bagnold is a Chekhovian in any significant sense of follow-the-leader. It is simply that her characters, like his, talk in a way that is appropriate to them and to the intention of the play, for their speeches, which sometimes become epigrams, amusing or sententious, are not only revelatory of their characters, but they are comments on the theme or themes with which the play is concerned. And Miss Bagnold's intention is quite plainly not that of Chekhov.

Simply stated, Miss Bagnold's subject is affirmation. At a time when Norman Vincent Peale is the most successful dispenser of uplift, when Madison Avenue and the television networks and the Luce publications are pushing the upbeat, when hope is often a thing with peculiar political and economic feathers, to define Miss Bagnold's subject so badly is to damn her in some circles. But Miss Bagnold and her Miss Madrigal are not afraid of damnation, not of that kind anyway. *The Chalk Garden* is not simple or simpleminded in its treatment of affirmation, but it is quite definite. Miss Bagnold chooses life over death, health over decay, truth over fantasy, hope over despair, substance over form, salvation over damnation. She recognizes pain and suffering and futility and even, in a warm and peculiar way, gathers them in with an embrace which would—if it could—smother them.

The plot is not a complicated one. Mrs. St. Maugham, once a glittering figure in a society that is now dead or dying, has retired to the country and to eccentricity, where she devotes herself to her garden which will not grow and her granddaughter, whom she is fashioning after her own image. "She is my parchment sheet on which I write! I hope she will remember my life and times!" Laurel, at sixteen, lives completely in unreality; she is an incipient pyromaniac, for whom bonfires are laid in the garden, and a pathological liar ("She has a need for fantasy."). The child, who ran away on the night that her mother remarried, has been allowed to feed on an imagined criminal assault that supposedly befell her on that occasion. The grandmother, who resents that her own daughter did not turn out as she had planned ("She was always crying out after to be simple."), has not only kept the child but has kept the child from knowing that her mother wants her back. Into this house, which is ruled by Pinkbell, the dying butler, from his sickroom upstairs, comes the mysterious Miss Madrigal to apply for the position of governess. She is drawn by the garden and the child and stays to free the child of the house and then to try to help the grandmother grow something, anything in her garden of chalk. It is the revelation that Miss Madrigal has just come from fifteen years in prison, a reduction from an original death sentence, that finally is the lever that forces Laurel into the arms of her mother. Miss Madrigal was Laurel at another time—"A girl who lied! And lied! And when she told the truth it didn't save her!" In the words of Maitland, the peculiar manservant, once a prisoner himself, "The only hold we have on this world is the truth." In the end, Laurel accepts the truth, gives up her fantasy and returns to the world. Measured by the standards of realistic drama, the plot is impossible. The Laurel who can say, "My mother married again. She married for *love*. It has given me an adolescent repugnance to her," is plainly unlikely to make the transition from grandmother to mother, is already too sophisticated, too much a product of her grandmother's training. The play is, however, not realistic; the plot is the frame on which the philosophic drama hangs; Laurel will flourish with her mother because she is no longer planted on chalk.

It is finally the central metaphor, the chalk garden, that reaches from action to idea, that carries the play. Miss Bagnold keeps her garden neatly in its place; it is just as certainly a real, if unflourishing garden as it is the symbol that so upset Richard Watts. The endless preoccupation with which flowers might grow, kinds of fertilizer, ways of nurturing plants allows the garden to grow in its own right; the kind of portentousness that renders a cocktail party more than a cocktail party and a confidential clerk more than a confidential clerk never operates as Miss Bagnold's garden becomes more than a garden, simply because she balances her metaphor on a fine sense of comedy. When in the first act, the cold and distant Miss Madrigal is maneuvered into visiting the garden, where she sees the sick plants and Laurel dancing around a bonfire, she returns white with anger to tick off the terrible state of the garden. The prim and passionless little governess is suddenly filled with fire and excitement and the transition is comic, but just as the comedy begins to take hold, to provoke laughter, the voice of Miss Madrigal takes on a new dimension, ". . . the lilies have rust . . . there is a black spot on the roses . . . and the child is screaming in the garden." The comedy has become sober, though the laughter need not stop, and the chalk garden has been lifted off the ground and lodged in the heart of the play. From then on the garden, like Madame Ranevsky's cherry orchard, moves easily and comfortably between the natural and the symbolic.

Actually the connection between Laurel and the garden is set up before Miss Madrigal's scene, but the plants that are dropped early are not allowed to bloom until the end of the act. Earlier Laurel has said of her grandmother, "She's a great gardener, but nothing grows for her." Earlier, too, as Mrs. St. Maugham and Miss Madrigal discuss Laurel, the governess answers the grandmother's "The child's a flower. She grows in liberty," with "Weeds grow as easily." The point is not labored; it is simply there. The grandmother's attempt to raise Laurel is like her attempt to grow flowers on chalk; the girl, like the rhododendrons, is dying. When Olivia, the mother, leaves at the end of act one, she says to Miss Madrigal, "Don't go! The wind blows from the sea here and growing things need protection!" The struggle for the child is placed very definitely in terms of the garden. "You have not a green thumb, Mrs. St. Maugham, with a plant or a girl." At the end of the play, the victory won, the child released to life, the governess and the grandmother are left alone onstage, talking over a seed catalogue. Miss Madrigal is triumphant, yet suffering with the grandmother; Mrs. St. Maugham is defeated, yet still almost pathetically hopeful. By this time the lines about the garden and the lines about the grandmother's life come so closely together that there is no doubt that the subject is one. There is really no difference between Miss Madrigal's "But you have been living all this while without affection! Haven't you noticed it?" and her "When will you learn you live on chalk?" At the end of the play, when Miss Madrigal finally lays her hand on Mrs. St.

Maugham's shoulder, just as she has laid her hands on the flowers in the garden, she speaks in hope and in pain in answer to an unasked question about the Wand Flower, "It won't grow on chalk. But if *I* stay with you—and we work together—with potash—and a little granular peat . . . We can *make* it do so." There may be pathos (must that be a dirty word?) in this ending, but it is more genuinely moving than the close of many a play which attempts to achieve its identification in purely emotional terms, by the discarding of the intellectual.

Miss Madrigal, as her name implies, is more than the governess that Mrs. St. Maugham engaged. At the end of a quarrel between the two of them, Mrs. St. Maugham asks herself limply, *"What* have I let in here out of an advertisement!" and Miss Madrigal, who has exited in anger, looks on long enough to say, "The East Wind!" before she shuts the door sharply behind her. The retort is in character, but it is also definitional. In a conversation with the Judge who sentenced her, whose accidental presence as a luncheon guest serves as the release of her secret, Miss Madrigal answers his, "Of course you had to take a name," with "It's more than a name to me." The condemned murderess who learned the meaning of life through fifteen years shut away from it has become Miss Madrigal, a song of love and life, and the name that seems so wrong for her appearance is amazingly right for her function in the play.

Elevating Miss Madrigal from a character into a force involves the necessity of finding a force against which she may struggle. Mrs. St. Maugham is not that force; she is simply its instrument, really its victim. The opposition to Miss Madrigal, the dead hand on the house, is Pinkbell the butler, for Pinkbell not only oversees the house, he commands the gardening from his bedroom window. The lines are drawn explicitly at the end of act one, when, after her outburst, Miss Madrigal decides to stay, "If you will accept me . . . I will take this situation, Mrs. St. Maugham. You have been very badly advised—I think—by Mr. Pinkbell." Everyone in the house is afraid of Pinkbell; only Miss Madrigal has the courage to tell him that he is wrong. Pinkbell, as butler, functions solely in the world of form, is the arbiter of the correct thing. It was Pinkbell who, in Mrs. St. Maugham's youth, passed on the suitability not only of dress and table settings, but of the young men who came to call; it is Pinkbell who most disapproves of Olivia's second marriage, to a colonel in the army. Mrs. St. Maugham's "All butlers dream of gardening," is more than a chance remark. The dealers in hollow and meaningless form (in the second act there is much discussion of the use of two glasses for one wine, a point of decorum that only Pinkbell understands) in reaching for the substance of life, and not its decorations, are capable only of destroying. This point is made clear in the second-act quarrel:

> *Mrs. St. Maugham.* But for forty years Pinkbell has never been corrected! He is the butler who was the standard of all London!
> *Madrigal.* Let him take his standard from the garden!

Miss Madrigal's victory in the last act naturally necessitates the destruction of Pinkbell; shortly before Laurel leaves with her mother, the Nurse brings down the news that Pinkbell is dead.

Pinkbell's position as butler, Mrs. St. Maugham's concern that her life should be remembered and carried on, the reminiscence with the Judge, all these seem to suggest that, in some sense, the play is a social comedy, a chronicle of the death of one society and the birth of another, the glitter of Mrs. St. Maugham giving way to the simplicity of her daughter. It would be unwise to limit the play that sharply, but the social element is certainly there. In her novel *The Loved and Envied,* which like her earlier plays does not approach the quality of *The Chalk Garden,* Miss Bagnold deals with just the kind of society in which Pinkbell could have flourished. This novel is largely about dying; most of the characters in the book, the friends of Lady Ruby Maclean, are very old and she has to watch many of them die. Ruby, like Mrs. St. Maugham, chooses life instead of death at the end, even though she has little time in which to experiment; she has lived in the old society; she will just begin to understand the new. If the play's social context is considered in relation to the novel, the old life, the life that has now become form without meaning, must be considered to have once embodied substance. The old order is destructive only because it stands in the way of the new. Yet, in the play, the opposition between life and death is so carefully drawn that there is a suspicion that the society of Pinkbell must never have had more than a foundation in chalk.

The societal side of the play, the concern with the ritual

of life, takes a special, an almost bitter turn so far as the figure of the Judge is concerned. During the lunch, to please Laurel and Maitland, who are inquisitive about all things having to do with crime and the courts, the Judge describes his preparation for appearance in court. The description is full of pageantry and display, masquelike in its attention to the exterior, empty of inner meaning. "Learned and crumpled like a rose leaf of knowledge I snuffle and mumble. I sham deaf. I move into court with the red glory of a dried saint carried in festival. . . . *Then*—garbed and toffed with medieval meanings, obscured by ritual, carrying the gloves of justice and the cap of death—on a hollow knock—I go *in*." The butler's sense of the correct is carried from the table to the bench, justice becomes as hollow as the knock, as self-deceiving and subject to error as the etiquette of table service. The Judge underlines the connection: *"His* severity, his corklike dryness—later on, when I had to rebuke the public eye, I remembered Pinkbell! My demeanor on the bench is Pinkbell's." This is the Judge who sentenced Miss Madrigal, who as the man not the Judge admits that the sentence was "Ill-advised, ill-advised," who cannot forget the words of the convicted woman: "What I have been listening to in court is not my life. It is the shape and shadow of my life. With the accidents of truth taken out of it." At whatever point one approaches this play, and it allows for so many possibilities, one finds oneself back in the chalk garden where only the appearance of life exists, and where the necessity of escape is so insistent.

The contrast, the conflict is repeated in the character of Maitland, the comically inept serving man. He has served five years in prison as a conscientious objector and has brought away a fascination for the mechanics of prisons and courts; as Laurel says, "How you dote on justice!" It is for Maitland, as much as for Laurel, that the Judge describes his entrance into court; in contrast to Miss Madrigal, it is the trappings of justice and not the truth that attracts Maitland. Just as he is drawn to the Judge, so is he dominated by Pinkbell. He is Pinkbell's replacement, gauche, inept, awkward, but his incapacity hints at more than the comic servant. Although he is serving Mrs. St. Maugham ("But I am loyal to Madame."), being ordered about by Pinkbell, helping in the garden of chalk, his accidents, his lapses of memory, his mild rebellions, his continual resignations are all indications, some conscious, some not, that he is really on the other side. In the last act he makes his declaration, "I was born to worship the stars! But I've never known *which* stars . . ."; now he wants to follow Miss Madrigal. The governess is hardly aware of his ecstatic decision; she knows that Maitland, like Mrs. St. Maugham, like herself, is not able to make Laurel's escape. Each in his way has been shut off from life, in real or social prisons, and must piece out the little green he can on the narrow space available.

There is a further dimension to *The Chalk Garden* which must be approached with hesitation. There are indications, little more than hints, throughout the play that the play is specifically religious, although not in any doctrinaire sense. I do not mean simply that the Judge likens himself to the relic of a saint or that the preparations for lunch are discussed in ritual terms ("Even the table is laid with fragments of forgotten ritual."). If those lines were all, the play would suggest a rejection of formalized religion along with the rest of the empty forms of Pinkbell. The division of forces between Miss Madrigal and Pinkbell is, of course, a struggle between good and evil, whether the good and evil be considered in a theological, a philosophical or a social sense; but there are lines that appear to give a particular religious significance to the two characters. At the end of act one, Mrs. St. Maugham says, "The *roses!* What would you have done for them! Pinkbell ordered . . . and I *sprayed* them!" Miss Madrigal answers, "With what, I wonder! You had better have prayed for them!" The substitution of *prayed* for *sprayed* is verbally dexterous, a good line, a funny one, in character for Miss Madrigal; it might be no more than that, but it has companions. To the Judge in the last act, Miss Madrigal explains why she does not want to leave her job, "Do you believe in God? I thought God had given it to me!" At another point, Miss Madrigal seems to be defining the quality of the truth she is placing against the Judge's "shape and shadow." To the Judge's "Well, a judge does not always get to the bottom of a case," she adds, "No. It takes the pity of God to get to the bottom of things." Near the end of the play, there is this exchange:

> *Mrs. St. Maugham.* You, who have an impertinent answer to everything—is there an afterlife?
> *Madrigal.* Certainly.

Mrs. St. Maugham [*surprised*]. You say—"certainly"?
Madrigal. One does not sit alone for fifteen years with-
     out coming to conclusions.

Mrs. St. Maugham's sudden preoccupation with the afterlife
(she earlier asked the Judge the same question; he refused to
answer) may have place here simply because she is reaching
the end of her life with a sense of somehow having failed it.
Miss Madrigal's certainty may be no more than the result of
fifteen years alone, but there is a suggestion in the exchange
that it comes from a knowledge more thorough than society-
imposed contemplation. If Miss Madrigal is going to take on
a special spiritual dress, the madrigal become a psalm, it is
necessary that Pinkbell, too, take on a new significance.
There are lines, casual enough in themselves, that can take
care of that as well. Laurel quotes Miss Madrigal about
Pinkbell, "She says he's the devil in charge." At another
point, when Laurel is quoting Pinkbell about her mother,
Maitland says, "I'll have none of it! Out with the devil in
you!"

     Perhaps I am imposing a religious significance upon *The
Chalk Garden* by pushing a few lines too far, by over-inter-
pretation of speeches which intend to underline the division
of forces in the play by conventional use of religious metaphor. After all, Clifford Odets speaks easily of God in *The
Flowering Peach* without claiming a theological interpretation for his play. Still, the imposition in *The Chalk Garden*
seems to come from within the play itself and not, at least so
far as I am concerned, from a desire that the play should
speak in those terms. These lines lend themselves to interpretation because all of Miss Bagnold's lines demand attention. The danger in such a play as *The Chalk Garden* is that
one begins to look for allegorical equivalents, begins to try
to invest each character, each speech, each gesture with a
significance that finally can reduce the play itself to a shell
in which the intellectually inquisitive can pour whatever he
wants. The search for meaning becomes a game and the
meaning itself unimportant. This kind of interpretive hide-
and-seek can become as silly as it did in the days when *The
Cocktail Party* first burst on Broadway, when one clever
observer suggested—kidding, I hope—that the dinner that
Alex prepared for Edward in a kitchen supposedly empty of
supplies was really the miracle of the loaves and fishes. The
richness of *The Chalk Garden* is such that there is room for

anyone to maneuver within its frame and plant his own ideas, but the interpreter who becomes preoccupied with his own planting may find that his ideas are growing in chalk. Miss Bagnold's real triumph in *The Chalk Garden* is that she makes one care not only for the subtlety and wit of her lines, for the aptness of her metaphor, for the manipulation of her ideas, but for her characters, for Mrs. St. Maugham, for Miss Madrigal, for Maitland, for those who must stay on in the garden even more than for those who get to leave. The latter can take care of themselves. The play is a religious one, just as it is a philosophical one and a social one, just as it is a very funny comedy and a very sad one. It is a play about which one talks because it is evocative, but perhaps the most just reaction to *The Chalk Garden,* the one that Miss Bagnold most hopes for, is that one come away from the theater or the book saying, with Miss Madrigal, "I shall continue to explore—the astonishment of living!"

First Applicant [*Miss Madrigal*]

Maitland

Second Applicant

Laurel

Third Applicant

Mrs. St. Maugham

Nurse

Olivia

The Judge

Time: The present

Place: A room in a manor house, Sussex, England.

Interior: It is a sitting room, but is used also for luncheon. [*The main dining room is probably under dust sheets.*]

The room has a look of the country—and also of vigor and culture—and is much lived in. Backstage is a long refectory table under which lie in disorder baskets, garden trugs, a saw, grasscutters, a log basket with raffia. On the top are strewn scissors, strings, gardening books, flower catalogues, gardening gloves, a small watering can, trowel, etc. This table is the working-pivot of the room.

Behind it are French windows and through them a bosky, be-lilied garden runs slightly uphill.

From one high window, upstage, people standing up on the stage can see the life that goes on on the Village Green.

Act 1. A day in June

Act 2. Two months later

Act 3. Twenty minutes later

At rise, there are chairs placed as though for a meeting or an interview. On one of them sits Miss Madrigal. Maitland ushers the Little Lady, the Second Applicant, in from the hall door.

Second Applicant. Lovely, blowy weather . . .

Laurel [*entering from Maitland's door*]. Are you too here for the interview?

Second Applicant. I am applying for the post.

Laurel. My grandmother had a hundred and seven answers. [*Silence.*] I mean to her advertisement.

Second Applicant [*rising, propitiatory*]. You are the young lady—who requires a companion? [*Her hand steals out.*]

Laurel. I never shake hands. It's so animal. [*Little Lady sinks back.*] So one of you has come to look after me? We were expecting four applicants—the ones my grandmother selected from the letters. And now there are only two to choose from. [*To Little Lady.*] What are your qualifications?

Second Applicant [*anxious, leaning forward*]. Froebel trained. Long ago. But Froebel trained. And *patience*.

Laurel. Would you have patience with me?

Second Applicant. I am so fond of young people.

Laurel. I set fire to things. I am not allowed alone, except in the garden.

Second Applicant [*flustered*]. Such lovely weather for the garden. [*Carrying on bravely*.] The advertisement said "with handicraft." I am clever with my fingers. I am fond of making pretty things. [*Coy.*] Now—can *you* make a lampshade?

Laurel. All the lampshades here are made already.

Second Applicant. Will you tell me, dear, of what does the family consist?

Laurel. Of my grandmother. Of me. And Maitland. And the
   terrible old man upstairs. And his hospital nurse.

Second Applicant [*horrified*]. Your grandfather?

Laurel. Mr. Pinkbell was always the butler. Now he has a
   stroke.

Second Applicant. Who was that then?

Laurel. That was Maitland. He wears a grocer's coat. Mr.
   Pinkbell, of course, used to wear a black one and have
   a footman.

Second Applicant. But is there no one else?

Laurel. Oh, we are rich! If we have only one servant, it is
   part of my grandmother's newest theory about life. She
   says true devotion is only to be got when a man is
   worked to death and has no rival.

Second Applicant. But have you no mother?

Laurel. My mother married again. She married for *love*. It
   has given me an adolescent repugnance to her. My case
   is practically in Freud. My grandmother will explain
   it to you.

Second Applicant. And where is your father?

Laurel. My father shot himself when I was twelve. I was
   in the room. [*Turning immediately to Madrigal.*] And
   what are your qualifications?

Madrigal [*turning a frosty eye on her*]. I prefer to wait for
   your grandmother.

Laurel [*interested in this answer*]. Are you Scotch?

Madrigal. I was born in Barbados.

Laurel. Where do you live?

Madrigal. In my room.

Laurel. I am fond of painting. Can you paint?

Madrigal. What I cannot do is wait much longer.

Laurel. Oh, she'll come! Grandloo will come! She is working in the garden. She's a great gardener, but nothing
   grows for her.

[*Enter Maitland.*]

Maitland. And what are you doing wearing Madame's necklaces! Off with them. [*While removing necklaces and
   putting them in his pocket.*] You've been upstairs and
   I thought I left you happy in the garden. Out you go!
   I've got a bonfire laid at the top there. You shall light
   it when I get a minute. [*Maitland goes off with her into
   the garden.*]

Second Applicant. Do you think it's all true?

Madrigal. I should think it unlikely.

[*The Third Applicant, the Grand Lady, sails in from the hall as Maitland comes back from the garden.*]

Maitland. Who let you in?

Third Applicant. The front door stood wide open—so humane.

Maitland. Have you a letter?

Third Applicant. I wouldn't have come, dear, if I hadn't a letter. [*Waves it at him.*] Are you the butler?

Maitland. I am the manservant.

Third Applicant. A world of difference! In my days it was thought common to wear a white coat. A relic of our occupation in India.

Maitland [*following her as she wanders round the room*]. Will you sit down, please?

Third Applicant. In those days, in the Hill Stations, I was thought to have extraordinary charm. [*To applicants.*] Good morning. How do you do. [*To Maitland.*] Is this a house where there are gentlemen?

Maitland [*stiffly*]. I am not to give information.

Third Applicant. But you have only to nod. [*At the table.*] Gardening gloves . . . nicotine for wood lice . . . is your lady going up in the world or coming down? One has to be so careful.

Maitland [*outraged*]. Mrs. St. Maugham has a house in Belgrave Square!

Third Applicant. But you are left in the country, I suppose, when she goes up for the season?

Maitland. Madame is past the seasons. Take a chair, please.

Third Applicant. Not that I am applying for the post, you know . . . not really . . .

Second Applicant. Not applying?

Third Applicant. I came to have a peep . . . So nostalgic . . .

Maitland. But you're not going!

Third Applicant. I could not think of staying in a house where there is not even a nephew! [*She exits. Maitland follows her out.*]

Second Applicant [*as Maitland enters from the hall. To him*]. For the interview . . . when the interview . . . ought we to be together?

Maitland. One of you ladies can wait in the drawing room. It's dust-sheeted, but there's a chair.

Second Applicant [*rising and going toward the door with*

some speed]. One must be fair! Let it be me. This lady
was before me. [*To Madrigal.*] When you're ready, you
just call, dear! [*Exit.*]

Madrigal. She's a little light-fingered.

Maitland. That one?

Madrigal. No more than a box of matches or the *Tatler*.

Maitland. Do you know her?

Madrigal. No. But I've met those hands before. Many times.

Maitland. Met those hands? [*Looks through window.*] There
she goes!

Madrigal [*as to herself*]. They were none of them solid
applicants.

Maitland. But they wrote to Madame!

Madrigal. It's how they spend their days. They answer ad-
vertisements.

Maitland. Not meaning to take the job!

Madrigal. They are always in two minds. It makes a change
for them. . . . [*At her own words she goes a bit off the
track.*] . . . and then too she has a garden.

Maitland. It's you who have two minds, it seems! [*Eyeing
her anxiously.*] Don't *you* be flitting! If there's nobody
here—after all the advertising—who do you think's
going to get the brunt! [*Exits with chairs.*]

Madrigal [*as to herself*]. I cannot hope to be acceptable—at
the first undertaking.

Maitland [*returning*]. *You* don't need to worry! Madame's
up a tree! Today's the deadline. She's got her daughter
coming. A shy lady. A nice one. Oh, there's wheels
within wheels. If you ask me . . . Madame's afraid
she'll take the child.

Madrigal. The child's outlandish!

Maitland. Only what Madame makes her. *I* can explain her!
Nurse and Nanny I bin to her!

Madrigal. In a house like this—would I be suitable?

Maitland. She'll take you! Madame loves the unusual! [*Madrigal reacts.*] It's a middle-class failing—she says—to
run away from the unusual!

Voice [*from the garden*]. Maitland! [*Coming nearer.*] Maitland! Maitland!

Maitland. Madame!

Voice [*just outside the French window, in the garden*]. Are
my teeth on the table? [*Maitland goes to the table.*]
My bottom teeth . . .

Maitland [*searching*]. There's nothing.

[*Enter Mrs. St. Maugham pulling wheelbasket with her back to the audience.*]

Mrs. St. Maugham. Then I must have left them in the greenhouse.

Maitland. Here! Wait, Madame . . . here they are—wrapped in a handkerchief! [*Crosses and gives them to her.*]

Mrs. St. Maugham [*turns*]. Good morning.

Maitland [*crosses downstage, says over his shoulder*]. There's a dentist taken the empty house by the church. *He* might make you comfortable!

Mrs. St. Maugham [*coming downstage*]. I've tried all the dentists. You can't fit false teeth to a woman of character. As one gets older and older, the appearance becomes such a bore. [*Displeased—to Maitland.*] But I expected *five* applicants!

Maitland. Four came. Three have gone.

Mrs. St. Maugham. And one wrote me such a good letter! Gone!

Maitland. But I've kept this one.

Mrs. St. Maugham [*crossing the room toward Miss Madrigal, who rises and respectfully stands. She picks up a bunch of letters from her writing table on the way. To Madrigal.*] Shall we sit? [*Over her shoulder.*] You can go, Maitland. [*Maitland exits. With a sudden and alarming change of manner—putting on the old charm as she sits down.*] Now what questions do total strangers put to one another?

Madrigal [*re-seated. Colorlessly*]. The name is Madrigal. [*Mrs. St. Maugham selects the "Madrigal" letter from the bunch she holds. Keeps it out and puts the others down.*] I am the daughter of the late Ronald Bentham Madrigal, Rajpootnah Hussars, Indian Army. He was the son of General Bentham Madrigal—the Honorable East India Company.

Mrs. St. Maugham [*gaily*]. No, no! *That* you can't be! The Honorable East India Company was dissolved in 1860! I'm an expert! My great-grandfather was Tarr Bethune, Governor of Madras, tried for corruption in 1859, and found guilty!

Madrigal [*calmly*]. My grandfather had my father at the age of seventy-five.

Mrs. St. Maugham [*admitting the point*]. *That* might make it possible. What experience have you?

Madrigal. I have small private means. I have not taken such a post before.

Mrs. St. Maugham. Why do you apply to me?

Madrigal. The advertisement attracts me. I have been somewhat alone.

Mrs. St. Maugham. You will be able, I suppose, to give me references?

Madrigal [*coldly*]. That will be difficult.

Mrs. St. Maugham. What?

Madrigal. In fact, impossible.

[*The door stands open, and a hospital Nurse, in full uniform, stands in the doorway.*]

Nurse [*stiff, reproachful*]. We've been ringing, Mrs. St. Maugham.

Mrs. St. Maugham. I heard nothing!

Nurse. Our breakfast tray was late again.

Mrs. St. Maugham. One can't have everything!

Nurse. Mr. Pinkbell says one should have a great deal more. [*She exits, flouncing.*]

Mrs. St. Maugham. One of his cross mornings . . . Ask *me* questions, Miss Madrigal.

Madrigal. Does one have a room to oneself?

Mrs. St. Maugham [*eyes still closed*]. Life without a room to oneself is a barbarity. Luncheon here with me and my granddaughter. Your evening meal served in your room on a tray . . .

Maitland [*who, a few words before, has made an appearance in the garden to wheel away the wheelbasket, now stands at the open window*]. That can't be done!

Mrs. St. Maugham [*opening her eyes; speaking automatically, without turning*]. Ma'am.

Maitland [*as automatically*]. Ma'am.

Mrs. St. Maugham [*now turning*]. And *why* can't it?

Maitland. Because I shall be busy serving at Madame's table.

[*Phone rings offstage.*]

Mrs. St. Maugham. I hear the telephone [*Maitland exits*]. Now—now—Miss Madrigal! We are so continuously interrupted . . .

Madrigal [*whose mind is only on the telephone*]. I should tell you—in case you should ask me to—I don't answer the telephone.

Mrs. St. Maugham [*immediately interested*]. For what reason?

Madrigal. I prefer not to. [*As though realizing by Mrs. St.*

Maugham's attitude that more explanation is needed.]
It disturbs me to join two worlds.

Mrs. St. Maugham. Which . . . ?

Madrigal [*with a small wave of her hand*]. The outside . . . and the inside one.

[*Re-enter Maitland.*]

Maitland. They want you to open the village Summer Festival.

Mrs. St. Maugham. Are they holding on?

Maitland. They are.

Mrs. St. Maugham. Ask them what attendance they can insure? Last time I opened something there was nobody there.

Maitland [*deadpan*]. Madame is so unpopular.

Mrs. St. Maugham. How do *you* know?

Maitland [*as before*]. I hear it on all sides.

Mrs. St. Maugham. They tell you that when I send you down for the post. Give me my engagement book. [*Pointing to book on the secretary.*]

Maitland. That's last year's.

Mrs. St. Maugham. It does just as well. Give it to me all the same. The dates are not so different. [*As he goes for it, turning to Miss Madrigal.*] Have you lived in a village, Miss Madrigal?

[*Maitland passes the book to her.*]

Madrigal [*mumbling*]. No, Mrs. St. Maugham . . .

Mrs. St. Maugham. All the graces of life here go unvalued. In a village one is down to the bones of things. When I was at my height—though I lived here—I never knew them! They were waiting for my old age like wolves, it seems! Tell them I *won't* open it. [*Exit Maitland.*] Ah . . . where were we? My advertisement asks for handicraft. What handicraft do you suggest?

Madrigal. I have ornamented a chapel.

Mrs. St. Maugham. With your needle?

Madrigal. With my brush. I have painted a twining plant on the altar candles.

Mrs. St. Maugham [*immediately interested*]. But as the candles burnt down the painting must have melted away!

Madrigal. That was the beauty of it. Is this a quiet house?

Mrs. St. Maugham. Absolutely.

[*Wild screams are heard far up the garden. Maitland bursts through door, rushes through room and out of the French window.*]

Maitland. That child again . . . [*Disappears up garden.*]

Mrs. St. Maugham [*turning her head to glance up the garden, which she can see as she sits*]. It's my daughter's child. My granddaughter. She's so fond of screaming.

Madrigal. While I was waiting, a young girl passed through the room.

Mrs. St. Maugham. That was she! She lives with me. Did she say anything?

Madrigal [*colorless*]. Nothing of consequence.

Mrs. St. Maugham. Not the suicide of her father?

Madrigal. I think she mentioned it!

Mrs. St. Maugham [*delighted*]. Oh, Laurel—to make a drama . . . ! He died—poor man—of his liver! Oh, I *knew* there would be *something*. She has a need for fantasy.

Madrigal [*as though it were a foible*]. She does not care for the truth?

Mrs. St. Maugham. No. But I encourage her. She loves a small limelight! One must be tender with her. Alas, he *died* when she was three. Rich and a fine estate. Four Van Dykes and unique Sheraton furniture. [*Bitterly.*] Her mother's one success . . . But why speak of it! She married again.

Madrigal. And where *is* her mother?

Mrs. St. Maugham. She follows the drum—as they say— in Arabia. Stationed abroad is the term, but I dislike military language. She is coming by ship . . . I am expecting her.

Madrigal [*half rising*]. Would you sooner postpone . . .

Mrs. St. Maugham. But she does not come *here! I* should be your employer.

Madrigal [*cautiously*]. She *is* coming?

Mrs. St. Maugham [*quickly*]. In front of the child—we don't mention it. She *is* coming. One does not know why, though I shrewdly suspect it! That is the trouble here. I have an unworldly daughter! She was always crying out after to be simple. Privilege and power make selfish people—but gay ones. It seems such a waste, with all the chances of life, to want to be simple . . . [*Breaks off.*] Forgive me, Miss Madrigal, for being personal . . . But irritation is like a rash on the heart!

Madrigal [*to change the subject*]. The child—is she fond of her stepfather?

Mrs. St. Maugham [*indifferent after the outburst*]. I never asked. His rank is Colonel. My granddaughter has developed an interesting mother-hatred, which is clearly explained in Freud. You have had experience? You feel competent to deal with such things?

Madrigal [*dreamily*]. For the worse . . . or the better . . .

Mrs. St. Maugham [*sharply*]. You seem absent in mind!

Madrigal [*pulling herself together again*]. Not in mind . . . But in manner. [*Pursily.*] Your granddaughter is naturally alienated—that a sex life has broken out again in her mother.

Mrs. St. Maugham. You put it well. Exactly. The child was frenzied. [*Ring.*] When nothing would stop the wedding—she ran from the hotel into the dark . . .

Madrigal. There seems to be a bell ringing.

Mrs. St. Maugham [*getting up and talking as she crosses to house telephone*]. . . . and by some extraordinary carelessness she was violated in Hyde Park at the age of twelve. It has upset her nerves. We are waiting, as it were, for calmer weather. [*Picking up house telephone.*] You want me, Pinkbell? One moment . . . [*Hands over phone.*] Of course we put it less strongly to her mother. Apart from certain fixations connected with fire, she is a charming, intelligent girl. [*Aware now of indignation—disturbance in phone in her hand. Into phone.*] What's that! [*Listens.*] I did. I ordered it. The Extract of Humus—for the seed boxes. [*Listening.*] It should have come. I'll ring. I'll ring and ask him. [*Is about to put the receiver from her but is recalled by the voice. In despair.*] I *know*! I know! But one can't get perfection, Pinkbell! [*Replaces receiver on stand. Rings a silver bell. To herself.*] Oh . . . Isn't *jealousy* terrible!

Madrigal [*with surprising force*]. YES.

Mrs. St. Maugham. You made me jump! He's my butler. Forty years my butler. Now he's had a stroke but he keeps his finger on things.

Madrigal. He carries on at death's door.

Mrs. St. Maugham. His standards rule this house.

Madrigal [*absently*]. You must be fond of him.

Mrs. St. Maugham. Alas, no. He trains Maitland—but now Maitland won't go near him. But I shall overcome it. He's so good with the garden.

Madrigal. Maitland?

Mrs. St. Maugham. Pinkbell. He directs mine from his window. All butlers dream of gardening. We spoke of references? Who will speak for you?

Madrigal. No one will speak for me—[*In her singsong voice, staring above Mrs. St. Maugham's head.*] Extract of Humus is too rich for summer biennials.

[*Enter Maitland.*]

Mrs. St. Maugham. Has a bag of Humus been delivered at the back door?

Maitland. There's a sack there.

Mrs. St. Maugham. When did it come?

Maitland. Days ago.

Mrs. St. Maugham. And you walk by it and ignore it! How do you know someone hasn't sent me a brace of pheasants! Mr. Pinkbell says you must always report at once what comes to the back door.

Maitland. I won't take orders from the old bastard!

Mrs. St. Maugham. Am I to have trouble with you, Maitland?

Maitland. Oh, if I could please and be sure of myself.

Mrs. St. Maugham [*quiet, menacing*]. Maitland!

Maitland. Oh, if things would go smoothly.

Mrs. St. Maugham [*with deliberation and distinctness*]. Maitland, bring me the crème de menthe and two glasses. [*Maitland's chest fills with emotion. He seems about to burst. He obeys and exits. Lying back in her chair and fanning her face with her handkerchief.*] Touch and go! How frail is authority. What were you saying?

Madrigal. When?

Mrs. St. Maugham. About Humus and summer biennials.

Madrigal [*tonelessly, sleepwalkingly, eyes up again*]. Don't pep up the soil before birth. It leads them on to expect . . .

Mrs. St. Maugham [*leaning forward*]. Speak louder!

Madrigal [*with awkward and unstable loudness*]. What life won't give them.

Mrs. St. Maugham [*suddenly reminded*]. *What* was that plant you painted on the candles?

Madrigal [*eyes still fixed*]. Lapagaria. Subtropical. With waxy umbels.

Mrs. St. Maugham. Lady Dorchester had it in her wedding bouquet after the Battle of the Marne! I had forgotten it! Could I grow it in my greenhouse?

Madrigal [*by rote*]. It needs the early actinic rays. Exclude the sun again at mid-day. Counteract the high lime content in your soil with potash.

Mrs. St. Maugham. Where did you learn about such things?

Madrigal. I was put in charge of . . .

Mrs. St. Maugham. What?

Madrigal. . . . a garden.

[*Enter Maitland, carrying everything most correctly—liquor bottle, two small glasses, silver tray, and even a clean napkin over his arm. He places the tray on the table by Mrs. St. Maugham.*]

Maitland [*straightening himself*]. I wish to give my notice.

Mrs. St. Maugham [*eyes like steel*]. If I take it you will not get it back again.

Maitland. I am prepared for that.

Mrs. St. Maugham [*terrible*]. *Are* you?

Maitland [*immediately broken*]. You know I can't stand criticism! Every time a word's said against me a month's work is undone!

Mrs. St. Maugham. We all make mistakes.

Maitland [*passionately*]. But nothing should be said about them! Praise is the only thing that brings to life again a man that's been destroyed! [*Pacing up and down.*] But, oh, if I leave . . . what will you do without me! [*Another scream is heard far up the garden. Rushing to the window*] . . . and what will the child do! [*Exits running up the path.*]

Mrs. St. Maugham [*smiling in triumph. To Miss Madrigal*]. Do you know the secret of authority, Miss Madrigal? Changes of mood. The inexplicable. The thunder, the lightning, and the sudden sun. *He* won't leave me! Will you have a crème de menthe?

Madrigal [*stiffly*]. I never touch alcohol.

Mrs. St. Maugham [*drinking hers*]. Certainly he makes scenes. But I like them. He has been a prisoner.

Madrigal. A prisoner!

Mrs. St. Maugham. Five years.

Madrigal. Had you no objection?

Mrs. St. Maugham. Now that there are no subject races, one must be served by the sick, the mad and those who can't take their places in the outside world. . . [*Laurel slips silently in and stands looking out of the window.*] And served I must be. [*Turning her head.*] Laurel!

Laurel [*not turning*]. One moment, Grandloo. One moment, darling . . . I'm watching the bonfire . . . I must see it die . . . [*Turning her head round.*] I put salt on it to turn the flame blue. Blocks of it.

Mrs. St. Maugham. Who told you to put salt on it?

Laurel. The old bastard, Mr. Pinkbell.

Mrs. St. Maugham. Not now, my darling. Superlatives only between ourselves!

Laurel [*turning round and walking toward them*]. Where are the others?

Mrs. St. Maugham. This is Miss Madrigal!

Laurel. [*She walks over to Miss Madrigal, pretending to come to.*] Have you settled everything? Do you understand all about me?

Madrigal. Not yet.

Laurel. Oh, can't we have the interview together? Shall I go and fetch the book that explains me?

Mrs. St. Maugham. Not so fast. *Externalize! Externalize! my darling!* [*Maitland crosses from the garden to kitchen.*] She has quaint self-delusions. You mustn't mind them . . .

Laurel. . . . but you mustn't cross them!

Madrigal. Are you an only child?

Laurel. I am Delilah's daughter!

Mrs. St. Maugham. Words leap and change color in her mouth like fishes! Laurel is a novel one reads out loud! I too at her age . . .

Laurel. Wit often skips a generation!

Mrs. St. Maugham. She is my parchment sheet on which I write! I hope she will remember my life and times! There seems no one else to do it . . .

Laurel. I am your little immortality!

Mrs. St. Maugham. You will note—how light my finger lies upon her! The child's a flower. She grows in liberty!

Madrigal. Weeds grow as easily.

Mrs. St. Maugham. As I was saying . . .

Laurel. . . . before the interruption.

Mrs. St. Maugham. Freedom is Captain here! Calm is its Lieutenant!

[*Enter Nurse hurriedly.*]

Nurse. The madonna lilies have blown over!

Mrs. St. Maugham [*at once in a passion. Rising*]. Oh—great heavens! Maitland! He was to order the bamboos and he forgot them! Are they all down?

Nurse [*with triumph*]. *All.* And not for want of warnings! [*Exits.*]

Mrs. St. Maugham. Oh my lilies! My lilies! One waits a year for them! . . . [*Exiting fast into the garden. Enter Maitland.*]

Maitland. What was that I heard?

Laurel. The calm of Grandloo.

Maitland. But what's happened?

Madrigal. There's been an accident in the garden.

Maitland [*to Laurel, denouncingly*]. Fire!

Laurel. Wind. You didn't stake the lilies!

Maitland [*frantic, rushing to the window to look out*]. Oh, are they down! The nurse told me and I forgot! How the old bastard will be crowing!

Madrigal [*primly*]. Stake in May.

Maitland [*turning on her fiercely*]. They weren't full grown in May!

Madrigal. They should have been.

Maitland [*more fiercely*]. Is that a criticism?

Madrigal [*quietly*]. So you are the gardener here as well?

Maitland [*excited, pacing about*]. I'm everything! I'm the kingpin and the pivot and the manservant and the maid-servant and the go-between [*Turning on Laurel*] *and the fire-extinguisher!*

Laurel. Prisoner Six Five Seven Four!

Maitland [*jumping to attention*]. Sir!

Laurel. Carry your bed-area and about turn! Through the corridor second door on the left and into your cell! *March!*

Maitland. I'm all to pieces. I can't play it.

Laurel [*to Madrigal, in tragic tones*]. He was five long years in prison, Miss Madrigal.

Madrigal [*politely*]. Was it your first conviction?

Maitland [*sententious*]. Conviction! It was for my ideals! I was a Conscientious Objector.

Madrigal [*prim*]. And didn't you find it trying?

Maitland. "Trying!" Five years! Five long years! Given one chance to live and five years taken from it! An ant among a thousand ants—and taking orders from ants!

Madrigal. If it upsets you better not recall it.

Maitland. Not recall it! It's stamped on my skin and at the back of my eyes! It's in my legs when I walk up and down! In my heart that sticks with fright when *she* gets angry!

Madrigal [*sententious*]. But since you felt you had Right on your side!

Maitland. Right on my side! That didn't uphold me! I went
   in there because I wouldn't take a life, but before I
   came out I would have killed a warder!

Madrigal [*platitudinously*]. All acts became possible.

Maitland. What can *you* know of life?

Madrigal. True, it's been sheltered.

Laurel [*picking up the remaining full glass of crème de
   menthe*]. All our lives are sheltered.

Maitland. Don't do that! She'll be furious!

Laurel [*tossing it down her throat*]. Not with me. I'm not
   responsible.

Maitland [*to Madrigal*]. You'll be witness, Miss, I didn't
   touch it! I have to be on the ready for injustice in life.

Laurel. From *me*? From your little Laurel? How touchy
   you are!

Maitland. I have soft ground and hard ground to my feelings. You should mind where you step!

Laurel. I am a victim and you ought to love me.

Maitland [*angrily*]. I *do* love you—like the poor mother
   who ought by rights and reasons to take a stick to you.

Laurel. What do you expect of me! A child that's been for-
   saken by its mother!

Maitland. That's as may be! That's as those think it to be!
   I was found in a field but I don't make a fuss about it!
   [*Exits sharply.*]

Laurel [*soapily*]. Poor Maitland likes the Right even when
   the Right is wrong.

Madrigal [*platitudinously*]. He has your interests at heart.

Laurel [*with interest*]. Are you a hospital nurse?

Madrigal. Why do you ask?

Laurel. You have that unmeaning way of saying things.

Madrigal [*after a second's pause and with a little formal
   manner of adapting herself*]. Now that we are alone
   together am I to call you Laurel?

Laurel. It's my name.

Madrigal. And what are you interested in—Laurel? I mean
   —apart from yourself?

Laurel. What I *don't* like—is to be questioned.

Madrigal. I agree with you.

Laurel. But I don't like to be agreed with just in case I might
   argue! And I don't like to be read aloud to unless I
   suggest it! But if read aloud to—*I don't like emphasis!*
   And every morning I don't like "Good morning" said!
   I can see for myself what sort of a day it is!

Madrigal. You sound as if you had lady-companions before. How did you get rid of them?

Laurel. I tell Pinkbell.

Madrigal. He tells your grandmother. My mind goes more slowly than yours.

Laurel. But it was going that way. You see she *loves* to advertise! She loves what comes of it. It's like dredging in the sea, she says—so much comes up in the net!

Madrigal. I—for instance.

Laurel. Why not?

Madrigal. Doesn't she take a chance—that way?

Laurel. No, she says you get more out of life by *hap*-hazard. By the way, if you want to get on with my grandmother —you must notice her eccentricity.

Madrigal. She is fond of that?

Laurel. She adores it! The tales I let her tell me when I am in the mood!

Madrigal. Does she love you?

Laurel. She would *like* to! [*Confidentially.*] She *thinks* she does! . . . But I am only her remorse.

Madrigal. You try your foot upon the ice, don't you?

Laurel. I find you wonderfully odd. Why do you come here?

Madrigal. I have to do something with my life . . .

Laurel. What life have you been used to?

Madrigal [*softly*]. Regularity. Punctuality. Early rising . . .

Laurel. It sounds like a prison!

Madrigal. . . . and what are *you* used to?

Laurel. Doing what I like. Have you been told why I am peculiar?

Madrigal. Something was said about it.

Laurel. If you come here we'll talk for hours and hours about it! And why I hate my mother!

Madrigal. I too hated my mother. I should say it was my stepmother.

Laurel. Oh, that's just an ordinary hatred! Mine is more special.

Madrigal. The dangerous thing about hate is that it seems so reasonable.

Laurel [*unnoticing*]. Maitland won't let me say so but my mother is Jezebel! She is so overloaded with sex that it sparkles! She is golden and striped—like something in the jungle!

Madrigal. You sound proud of her. Does she never come here?

Laurel. To see me? Never! She's too busy with love! Just
   now she's in Arabia with her paramour!

Madrigal. With her . . . ?

Laurel. If you pin me down he is my stepfather! Have you
   read *Hamlet*? It tipped my mind and turned me against
   my mother.

Madrigal. Does she know you feel discarded?

Laurel. I don't. I left her! [*Pause.*] The night before she
   married—she forgot to say good night to me . . . Do
   you think that sounds a little thing?

Madrigal [*passionately*]. Oh, no! It lights up everything.

Laurel [*looking at her*]. Are you talking of *you*? Or of *me*?

Madrigal [*her hand on her breast*]. When one feels strongly
   —it is always of *me!*

Laurel [*pause*]. If you are not a spy sent by my mother, I
   shall enjoy you! Do you know about crime? Maitland
   and I share a crime library. Bit by bit we are collecting
   the Notable Crime Series.

Madrigal [*looking at her—low*]. Don't you like detective
   stories better?

Laurel. No, we like real murder! The *trials*. We act the
   parts!

Madrigal [*picking up her gloves*]. Which . . . trials have you
   got?

Laurel. So far—only Mrs. Maybrick, Lizzie Borden, Dr.
   Crippen. But Maitland likes the murder*esses* better.
   He's half in love with them. Oh—if you come here . . .

Madrigal. Here! . . .

Laurel. —couldn't we act them together? [*Gets no answer.*]
   Maitland is so slow I make him read the prisoner. Why
   does the prisoner have so little to say? [*Waits*] . . . do
   you think? [*Pause—no answer.*] What a habit you have
   —haven't you—of not answering.

Madrigal [*whose eyes have been fastened high up in the air,
   now lets them travel down to look at Laurel. Low, with
   difficulty*]. I made an answer.

Laurel. Only to yourself, I think.

Mrs. St. Maugham [*seen outside waving the armful of broken
   lilies at Pinkbell's window—shouting up to him*]. All
   gone! . . . ALL! . . . [*As she appears.*] Oh—when things
   are killed in my garden it upsets me—[*A little breathless, coming into the room*]—as when I read in the
   newspapers that my friends die!

Laurel. I should have thought as one got older one found death more natural.

Mrs. St. Maugham [*beginning to sort out the lilies on the table*]. Natural! It's as though the gods went rook-shooting when one was walking confident in the park of the world! and there are pangs and shots, and one may be for me! *Natural!*

Madrigal [*involuntarily*]. That is why a garden is a good lesson. . . .

Mrs. St. Maugham. What?

Madrigal [*looking through window at garden. Low*]. . . . so much dies in it. And so often.

Mrs. St. Maugham. It's not a lesson I look for! Take Miss Madrigal into the garden, Laurel.

Madrigal. No, I think I must be going.

Mrs. St. Maugham. I want you to see the garden.

Madrigal [*nervous*]. I'll write . . . I'll let you know . . .

Mrs. St. Maugham. There is nothing to know yet!

Madrigal. I'd better not waste your time.

Mrs. St. Maugham [*pressing her toward the garden*]. And that great bag . . . [*Takes the bag forcibly from her, puts it on a table near window.*] No one will touch it here.

Madrigal. But I'd like to see the garden.

[*Laurel and Madrigal exit, but Laurel darts back. Mrs. St. Maugham tries two lilies in vase for height.*]

Laurel [*conspiratorially, alone on garden window threshold*]. Grandloo . . . psst! . . . what do you *think?*

Mrs. St. Maugham. I never allow myself to think. I have another method. [*Carries empty vase toward Maitland's door.*]

Laurel. But . . .

Mrs. St. Maugham. While you are in the garden, listen to her. She knows her subject.

Laurel. But shall you *take* her?

Mrs. St. Maugham. Certainly not! But before she goes I want her opinion on the garden. [*Takes vase and vanishes through Maitland's door. Laurel exits. Olivia enters through main doorway. One is just aware that she is pregnant. She wears light traveling clothes, as from the East.*]

Maitland [*just offstage*]. . . . didn't you telephone?

Olivia. I thought it better just to come. [*Turning.*] How *is* my mother?

Maitland. She has health of . . . [*Grasping for the unexplain-
    able in Madame's health!*] . . . something in Nature!

Olivia. And my daughter?

Maitland. They're as thick as thieves, Madame.

Olivia. Could you look for my mother—

Maitland. Madame *was* here . . . [*He exits, and Madrigal
    enters from the garden and gets her bag from the chair.*]

Olivia. Who are you?

Madrigal. It makes no difference. [*Walking toward door,
    stopping, turning back.*] Perhaps I should tell you . . .
    the field is free for you . . .

Olivia. To see the child?

Madrigal. You have to see the grandmother first!

Olivia. Yes.

Madrigal. Looking at you I wouldn't come here if there is
    other post open to you.

Olivia. Why?

Madrigal. Because the child will make hay of you!

Olivia. She *has* made hay of me!

Madrigal. Are you the mother?

Olivia. Yes . . . Is she out there?

Madrigal. Yes.

Olivia. Please . . . go out—keep her there!

Madrigal. But I am a stranger.

Olivia. I know but sometimes one speaks the truth to a
    stranger. I'm not supposed to see her. First I must see
    my mother. Please, go out—please!

[*Madrigal exits.*]

Mrs. St. Maugham [*offstage*]. Olivia! [*Enters, carrying case,
    which she quickly puts down. To Maitland who has
    followed her into the room.*] Maitland . . . light a bon-
    fire! [*He rushes off into the garden.*] Olivia! So soon!
    But you're safe—that's all that matters!

Olivia. Mother!

Mrs. St. Maugham. Oh—let me look at you. How brown
    you are! You look like an Arab. How is the desert,
    darling? I can almost *see* the sand in your hair.

Olivia. Mother—how's the child?

Mrs. St. Maugham. Ask for me—ask for *me*, Olivia!

Olivia. I do, I would, but you ran in like a girl, and not a
    day older!

Mrs. St. Maugham. Oh, let me tell you before we talk—

Olivia. —before we quarrel!

Mrs. St. Maugham. No—not this time. I was going to say

—that I've missed you. If I'd known you were coming
I'd have driven up to see you. Whatever—and in your
condition—made you rush down here without a word!

Olivia. I flew. I got here this morning.

Mrs. St. Maugham. Like one of those crickets that leap
from a distance and fall at one's feet! How did you
do it?

Olivia. By breakfasting in Baghdad and dining in Kuffra
and taking a taxi in England. We're on a Course. I
wrote. Two months at Aldershot.

Mrs. St. Maugham [*with great distaste*]. Aldershot! Oh—
who would have thought you would have taken on that
look—so quickly—of the Colonel's Lady! What was
it they called it—Reveille! [*Sarcastic.*] How are the
bugles at dawn, Olivia?

Olivia. We don't live in a camp.

Mrs. St. Maugham. I feel sure you said you did!

Olivia. Never mind the camp. I want to talk to you.

Mrs. St. Maugham. But why down here the very second you
arrive—and without warning!

Olivia. I've come about Laurel . . .

Mrs. St. Maugham. Did you wear that scarf—on purpose
to annoy me! What you wear is a *language* to me!

Olivia [*indignant*]. Oh—that's an old battle—and an old
method!

Mrs. St. Maugham. When I've *told* you—in letter after letter.

Olivia. It's time I saw for myself, Mother!

Mrs. St. Maugham. . . . and risk the mending of her? Oh
—do you think only of *yourself*, Olivia!

Olivia. Not of myself.

Mrs. St. Maugham. That is how it has always been. To ask
is to be refused! I have asked you *not* to come—but
you *come!* I have asked you to warn me—but you
ignore it! [*Turning on her.*] How can you wear beige
with your skin that color!

Olivia. Does it never become possible to talk as one grown
woman to another!

Mrs. St. Maugham. The gap's lessening! After fifty I haven't
grown much wiser! [*Warming to the indignity*] . . . but
at *least* I know what the world has to have. Though
one cannot pass anything on! When I count my ambi-
tions and what you have made of them!

Olivia. I did what you wanted!

Mrs. St. Maugham. But how you resisted me! I was burning

for you to cut ice in the world—yet you had to be
driven out to gaiety! I had to beat you into beauty!
You had to be lit—as one lights a lantern! Decked—
like a may tree!

Olivia. Can't we be three minutes together . . .

Mrs. St. Maugham. Even your wedding dress you wore like
wrapping paper! Plain, shy, obstinate, silent. But I did
what a mother should do. I married you . . .

Olivia. But you won't meet the man *I* married—the man
I love!

Mrs. St. Maugham. Love can be had any day! Success is
far harder.

Olivia. You say that off the top of your head—where you
wore your tiara!

Mrs. St. Maugham [*turning in surprise*]. So you have found
a tongue to speak with!

Olivia. I have found many things—and learned others.
Things come late to me. I have been warmed and
praised and made to speak . . . But you won't give up
the image of me! Coltish—inept, dropping the china—
picking up the pieces . . .

Mrs. St. Maugham. It was I who picked up the pieces,
Olivia.

Olivia. I *know. But I'm without her.*

Mrs. St. Maugham. You are going to have another child!

Olivia. This child's the Unknown! Laurel's my daughter!

Mrs. St. Maugham. . . . who came to me! Who ran to me
—as an asylum from her mother!

Olivia. Oh—you find such words to change things! You talk
as if I were a light woman.

Mrs. St. Maugham. No, you are *not* light! You have never
been a light woman! You are a dark, a mute woman.
If there was lightness in you it was I who lent it to you!

Olivia. Mother! Of a thousand thousand rows between you
and me—and this not, I know, the last one—*be* on my
side! Oh—for once *be* on my side! Help me . . .

Mrs. St. Maugham. To what?

Olivia. Help me to *find* her! Help me to take her back!

Mrs. St. Maugham. Take her back! What, now? Just now!
When I have such a companion for her! A woman too
of the highest character! Of vast experience! I have
put myself out endlessly to find her!

Olivia. She can help you to prepare her. When I come back
for her . . .

Mrs. St. Maugham. You mean before the baby's born? That will be an odd moment—won't it—to come for her!

Olivia [*passionately*]. No! *It's why I want her!* Before I love the baby! I can't sleep! I can't rest. I seem to myself to have abandoned her!

Mrs. St. Maugham. To her own grandmother! I am not a baby-farmer or a headmistress or the matron of an orphanage . . .

Olivia. But she'll be a *woman!* And I'll *never have known her!*

Mrs. St. Maugham. It suited you when you first married that I should have her. Laurel came to me of her own free will and I have turned my old age into a nursery for her.

Olivia. And God has given you a second chance to be a mother!

Mrs. St. Maugham. Olivia! . . . There's no one who puts me in a passion like you do!

Olivia. And no one who knows you so well. [*Turning away.*] And knows today is hopeless.

[*Madrigal enters. Through her first two speeches she is moving across the room toward the door and her whole intention is obviously to leave.*]

Madrigal [*menacing—accusing—pulling on a glove*]. Mrs. St. Maugham—*there must be some mistake! This* is a chalk garden! Who has tried to grow rhododendrons in a *chalk* garden?

Mrs. St. Maugham. Rhododendrons? We put them in last autumn. But they're unhappy!

Madrigal. They are *dying.* They are in pure lime. Not so much as a little leaf-mold! There is no evidence of palliation.

Mrs. St. Maugham. Wait . . . wait . . . Where are you going?

Madrigal. They could have had compost! But the compost-heap is stone-cold! *Nothing in the world has been done for them!*

[*A teensy scream is heard from the garden.*]

Olivia [*to Madrigal*]. Is that Laurel? She's screaming. What's the *matter!*

Madrigal. There is nothing the matter. She is dancing round the bonfire with the manservant. [*Pulling on her last glove.*]

Mrs. St. Maugham [*quickly to Olivia*]. I should have told you—this is Miss Madrigal. [*As Madrigal moves off.*]

Not so fast! I want to ask you . . . the bergamot . . . and the gunnera . . .

Madrigal [*looking at door*]. . . . won't thrive on chalk.

Mrs. St. Maugham. There's an east slope I can grow nothing on.

Madrigal. . . . the soil can't give what it has not got. [*Turning at door as Mrs. St. Maugham still pores over the catalogue.*]

Olivia [*to Miss Madrigal*]. Don't go! The wind blows from the sea here and growing things need protection!

Madrigal [*low*]. . . . and the lilies have rust . . . there is a black spot on the roses . . . and the child is screaming in the garden.

Mrs. St. Maugham. The *roses!* What would you have done for them! Pinkbell ordered . . . and I *sprayed* them!

Madrigal [*turning, magnificent, contemptuous*]. With what, I wonder! You had better have prayed for them! [*Takes off gloves. They measure each other for a moment. Then very quiet and meaningful.*] If you will accept me . . . I will take this situation, Mrs. St. Maugham. [*Olivia quietly exits.*] You have been very badly advised—I think—by Mr. Pinkbell.

Curtain

A month or two later (to fit in with the flowers suitable to the garden—as mentioned in the text).

About mid-morning.

On the right, under the window which looks out on the Village Green, is a table which will be laid (at first) for four people. At another, center, table sits Laurel in a fresh clean frock, suitable for a girl of sixteen. She is painting a flower which is stuck in a vase in front of her, and is using an old mahogany paint box with the lid propped open. There is a saucer to mix paints in, a tumbler of water, brushes, blotting paper, etc. She seems absorbed in her work, looks from the flower to her painting, occasionally licks a brush (they are water colors).

Enter Maitland carrying a tray. On it are silver spoons and forks and a few wine glasses with stems, a rag, and a bottle of turpentine. As he talks he sets down the tray on a chair near the table he is going to lay, and uses the rag and the turpentine to rub a spot on the polished wood of the table's surface.

Maitland. All alone? Whose idea is that?

Laurel [*who does not look up*]. The Boss's.

Maitland. Not even burning the curtains?

Laurel [*with dignity*]. I am painting a flower.

Maitland [*rubbing the table*]. Occupational therapy?

Laurel. What was yours? Picking oakum?

Maitland [*pausing and looking at her a moment*]. Who would think you were weak in the head? You've given up screaming.

Laurel. My madness is older. It's too old for screaming.

Maitland. Why do you sham mad—dearest?

Laurel [*in surprise*]. "Dearest"?

Maitland. Only in a sad sort of way—I have no dearest.

Laurel. You shouldn't be sorry for yourself. It unmans you.

Maitland. It's better than being vain and in love with the glory of one's misfortune! But I'll say this for you! The Boss is fixing you!

Laurel. I'm her business and her vocation.

Maitland. Oh—who could imagine that a maiden lady could know so much about life.

Laurel. She's no maiden lady! She might be anyone! Might she be a love child?

Maitland. That's enough now!

Laurel. How prudish you are! Look how she came to us —with nothing! A lady from a shipwreck! Her brush is new and her dresses. No photographs! No belongings! Oh—she's cut off her golden past like a fish's tail! *She's had a life of passion!*

Maitland. What words you use!

Laurel. Does she get any letters? Do you spy on her?

Maitland. Who?

Laurel. Our Duke's daughter, our hired companion!

Maitland. If you are talking of Miss Madrigal she never gets a letter.

Laurel. Don't you get a hint or a sound or a sigh out of her?

Maitland. No. Do you?

Laurel. With me she's on guard. I can't surprise or ambush her. She watches me.

Maitland. Whatever she does you're the better for it.

Laurel. Mr. Pinkbell doesn't think so.

Maitland. Poison he is—but influential.

Laurel. If you ask me rows are coming!

Maitland. I don't ask you. You're too set up with yourself and pleased as a peacock to be the bone of contention.

Laurel. She says he's the devil in charge. He's ordered rhododendrons. It took a lorry to deliver them.

Maitland. What's that got to do with it?

Laurel. The Boss reversed the labels. She sent them back again.

Maitland. Whew . . . I'm for Miss Madrigal! I've no mercy on him!

Laurel. Poor Mr. Pinkbell!

Maitland. A man's no better when he's dying.

Laurel. What's in the bottle?

Maitland. Turps. Turpentine.

Laurel. Give it to me.

Maitland. How did she take our having a visitor to lunch?

Laurel. I was to wear this clean frock. Otherwise nothing.

[*Looking at it disdainfully*.] Straight as an envelope. It looks so adolescent . . . and with a judge coming!

Maitland. How do I call him?

Laurel. A judge is called m'lord.

Maitland. Oh—I wish I could see it!

Laurel. What?

Maitland. Him in his robes and his great wig and all that happens!

Laurel. How you dote on justice!

Maitland. It's the machinery and the magnificence! It's the grandness!

[*Mrs. St. Maugham enters.*]

Mrs. St. Maugham. Heavens, Maitland! Is this a morning for daydreams! . . . [*Glancing round in fever of preparation.*] The green-handled ivory knives . . . !

Maitland. Locked away.

Mrs. St. Maugham. And the key of the safe! It's years since I've seen it! We used to have celery with the Stilton . . . and the Bristol finger bowls . . . and those glasses for the brandy.

Maitland. They broke.

Mrs. St. Maugham. There was a gold cigar box that played a tune—that King Edward gave me . . .

Laurel. Is it *gold*? I used to keep a mouse in it!

Mrs. St. Maugham [*frantic*]. Go and get it!

Laurel. I can't remember where I put it . . . But isn't the man coming—old?

Mrs. St. Maugham. Puppy?

Laurel. The *Judge*?

Mrs. St. Maugham. That's what I called him! [*Hears noise of bat and ball and rushes to window.*] Oh! Are they playing out there with the hard ball again? Can you identify them?

Maitland. The one with the bat is the fishmonger's son.

Mrs. St. Maugham. You'll see! Before long! Every summer the boys with their cricket! Every summer a broken window! [*Crosses back into room.*] We shall want sherry before luncheon. Bring the sweet as well as the dry. [*Looking down at the table he has now laid.*] Shouldn't there be two wine glasses to each person!

Maitland. But there's only one wine!

Mrs. St. Maugham. Put two. I forget the reason. Oh—and the spoons outside the knives, Maitland!

Maitland [*desperately*]. You said the opposite the last time!

Mrs. St. Maugham. Never! [*A doubt enters her mind.*] Someone must know! I shall ask Pinkbell.

Laurel. Pinkbell is sulking.

Mrs. St. Maugham. Why?

Laurel. He is full of jealous rage about his Enemy.

Mrs. St. Maugham. What again! And where is she now?

Laurel. She is urging on the agapanthus lilies.

Mrs. St. Maugham. She is *what?*

Laurel. She is using diluted cow urine. One in seven.

Mrs. St. Maugham [*eager*]. Oh I must go and see at once and watch how that is done. [*Exits.*]

Laurel. Keep behind the escallonia hedge . . . the nurse is watching! [*To Maitland.*] *Prisoner six five seven four!*

Maitland. Sir!

Laurel. Do you know whose paint box this is?

Maitland. Yours.

Laurel. No. Come here and look at it. [*He moves to her.*] *She* lent it to me. The Boss. [*Pointing inside the propped-open lid, where she has been rubbing.*] Can you see where the letters are that are burnt in the wood there? Look—under the black mark. Under the smear of paint. It is C. D. . . .

Maitland. And W. It is C. D. W.

Laurel. Take the turpentine! I don't want her to see it.

[*Madrigal enters from the garden. They straighten up.*]

Laurel. Oh! Grandloo has just this minute gone to look for you!

Madrigal. I caught sight of her but I thought it best that we should not be seen together.

Laurel. She's head over heels with excitement about our guest. Does one still mind—when one is old—what men think?

Madrigal. One never knows when one is old for certain.

Laurel. She calls him Puppy. I think she was once his mistress.

Madrigal. Do you know that?

Laurel [*casual*]. No.

Madrigal. Then why do you say it?

Laurel. Why does one say things? It's more fun!

Madrigal. If you pretend—and it's believed—where are you?

Laurel [*smiling*]. Where am I?

Maitland. Floating away. The only hold we have on this world is the truth. Oh, to think I'm to feed him. A man who's got so much power!

Laurel. We can talk to him of murder. We've never had a judge here before.

Madrigal. A judge? Is the visitor that's coming a judge?

Maitland. He's here for the Courts. He's on circuit.

Madrigal. What's his name?

Maitland. It's in the newspapers. But the old bastard's got them. They are carried up to him. But I have read them on the doorstep.

Madrigal. Laurel and I will sit at a separate table for luncheon.

Maitland. Not two tables! Not with a guest! Oh—that can't be managed!

Madrigal [*swiftly changing her manner to one of treacherous interest*]. You can manage anything! Tell us what surprise you've arranged for us. What are we going to eat?

Maitland [*instantly taken in*]. Fortnum's have sent the cold cooked chickens. I have carved them. I have ornamented them with mint leaves. There is a salad and salad dressing.

Madrigal. Out of a bottle?

Maitland. Mrs. St. Maugham doesn't believe so.

Madrigal. The bottled is *so* much better—but one must never say so!

Maitland. Oh, when I have something to do, something to create, everything is clear again.

Madrigal. You look ten years younger.

Maitland [*at the door about to go*]. Oh—if we had guests oftener! The sense of rising to something! [*Exits.*]

Laurel. How you twist him round your finger! [*With a certain suspicious hostility.*] Why do we sit separately from the guest, you and I?

Madrigal. It used to be done at luncheon—in the best houses.

Laurel. Had you a life in them? [*No answer.*] *Had* you? [*Sharp.*] Who is C. D. W.?

Madrigal [*taken aback, silent. Then*]. My married sister.

Laurel. I thought you had been born unrelated.

Madrigal. Did you?

Laurel. And now you have a sister.

Madrigal. Yes.

Laurel. Suppose you were to drop down dead. To whom should we write?

Madrigal. I shall not drop down dead. [*House telephone rings.*]

Laurel [*picks it up*]. Pinkbell! In a rage! [*Listening a second,*

*then holding phone at arm's length as though it had
bitten her. Rubs her ear.*] He has asked for you! He has
practically stung me! Aren't you afraid to speak to him?
[*Offering phone to Miss Madrigal.*]

Madrigal [*accepting receiver*]. Mr. Pinkbell? [*Listens.*] Yes.
It is I, Miss Madrigal. [*Listens. Maitland enters.*] Ah—
but on that I disagree. [*Waits.*] The rhododendrons—*I*
sent them back again. [*Listens.*] I reversed the labels!
And if I could I would reverse everything! And I may
yet—we shall see! No, I'm afraid on that you are wrong,
Mr. Pinkbell. Your facts are wrong—also your deduc-
tions! Yes, and alas it is the wrong time of year to plant
them. And the wrong soil. [*Listens.*] Not at all. Don't
blame yourself. Amateur gardeners very often make
that mistake. [*Hangs up.*]

Maitland. Blame himself!

Madrigal. He made use of sarcasm.

Maitland [*breathless*]. My God, you shall have two tables!
You shall have three if you like! And the breast off both
the chickens!

Laurel. Now there'll be ructions! [*Nurse enters and crosses
to garden as others watch in silence.*]

Maitland. And with the Judge coming! In the newspapers
they say it'll be a long trial. Why, *Miss!* Haven't you
read it?

Madrigal [*to Maitland*]. Are all the glasses polished? [*Holding up a glass to the light.*]

Maitland [*eager, unheeding*]. D'you think—in Lewes
prison . . .

Madrigal [*gently*]. There's a cloud on this one. Time is
getting on!

Maitland [*taking glass from her and holding it*]. . . . this
murderer, that's lying in his cell . . .

Madrigal [*change of voice*]. No man is a murderer until he
is tried!

Maitland . . . when he first sees the Judge . . .

Madrigal. Why do you think only of the Judge? It's the jury
they work on.

Maitland. But it seems when you read about such trials, that
it must be the Judge.

Madrigal [*fiercely*]. *Read* more and you'll see it's neither.
But fate.

Maitland. How can that be?

Madrigal. Because, when it starts, there's no free will any more.

Maitland [*earnestly*]. But they work, don't they, to get at the truth?

Madrigal. Truth doesn't ring true in a court of law.

Maitland. What rings true then?

Madrigal [*to herself, trancelike*]. The likelihood. The probability. They work to make things hang together. [*Moving.*] What the prisoner listens to there is not his life. It is the shape and shadow of it. With the accidents of truth taken out of it.

[*Maitland exits.*]

Laurel. So you've been to a trial?

Madrigal [*unmoving, dead voice*]. I did not say I hadn't.

Laurel [*same tone*]. Why did you not say—when you know what store we lay by it!

Madrigal [*same tone*]. It may be I think you lay too much store by it.

Laurel [*relaxing her tone and asking as though an ordinary light question*]. How did you get in!

Madrigal [*turning, airy, disguising*]. It's surprisingly easy.

Laurel. Was it a trial for murder?

Madrigal. It would have to be to satisfy you.

Laurel. *Was* it a trial for murder?

Madrigal. Have you finished that flower?

Laurel [*Laurel doodles on a scrap of paper and continues till she breaks off to describe her home*]. As much as I can. I get tired of it.

Madrigal. Shall we read?

Laurel. I don't want to read. In my house—at home—there were so many things to do!

Madrigal. What was it like?

Laurel. My home?

Madrigal. Yes.

Laurel [*lost in thought a moment. Suddenly tipping it out hard*]. There was a stream—and a Chinese bridge—and yew trees cut like horses—and a bell on the weathervane, and a—[*sudden small break of pain*] little wood . . . called mine . . .

Madrigal. Who called it that?

Laurel. She did. My mother. And when it was raining we made an army of her cream pots and a battlefield of her dressing table . . . I used to thread her rings on safety pins . . .

Madrigal. Why do you sign your name a thousand times?

Laurel. I'm looking for which is me.

Madrigal. Tomorrow I will light that candle in the green glass candlestick and you can try to paint that.

Laurel. Paint the flame?

Madrigal. Yes.

Laurel. I am tired of fire too, Boss.

Madrigal. Let's have a game!

Laurel [*jumping up—eyes gay*]. All right. A *guessing* game!

Madrigal [*steadily*]. Very well. Do you know one?

Laurel [*fast*]. Maitland and I play one called . . . *The Sky's the Limit!*

Madrigal. How do you begin?

Laurel [*sitting down opposite her*]. We ask three questions each but if you don't answer one, I get a fourth.

Madrigal. What do we guess about?

Laurel. Let's guess about each other. [*Full stop.*] We are both mysterious.

Madrigal [*sententious*]. The human heart is mysterious. Has it got to be the truth?

Laurel. One can lie. But I get better and better at spotting lies. It's so dull playing with Maitland. He's so innocent. [*Miss Madrigal folds her hands on the table and waits.*] Now! First question . . . Are you a *maiden* lady?

Madrigal [*after a moment's reflection*]. I can't answer that.

Laurel. Why?

Madrigal. Because you throw the emphasis so oddly.

Laurel. Right. You don't answer! So now I have an extra question. Are you living under an assumed name?

Madrigal. No.

Laurel. Careful! I'm getting my lie-detector working. Do you take things here at their face value?

Madrigal. No.

Laurel. Splendid! You're getting the idea!

Madrigal [*warningly*]. This is to be your fourth question.

Laurel. Yes. Yes indeed. I must think. . . . I must be careful. [*Leaning across the table and shooting her question hard at Miss Madrigal.*] What is the full name of your married sister?

Madrigal [*staring a brief second at her*]. Clarissa Dalrymple Westerham.

Laurel [*still leaning forward*]. Is Dalrymple Westerham a double name?

Madrigal [*leaning back*]. You've *had* your questions.

Laurel [*also sitting back again*]. Yes, I have. Now yours. You've only three—unless I pass one.

Madrigal. Was your famous affair in Hyde Park on the night of your mother's marriage?

Laurel [*steadily*]. About that time.

Madrigal. What was the charge by the police?

Laurel [*wary*]. The police didn't come into it.

Madrigal [*airily*]. Did someone follow you? And try to kiss you?

Laurel [*off her guard*]. *Kiss* me! It was a case of criminal assault!

Madrigal [*following that up*]. How do you know that—if there wasn't a charge by the police?

Laurel [*pausing a second. On a different tone*]. That's one too many questions! *Now* for the deduction!

Madrigal. You didn't tell me there was a deduction.

Laurel. I forgot. It's the whole point. Mine's ready.

Madrigal. What do you deduce?

Laurel [*taking a breath—then fast, as though she might be stopped*]. . . . That you've changed so much you must have been something quite different. When you came here you were like a rusty hinge that wanted oiling. You spoke to yourself out loud without knowing it. You had been *alone.* You may have been a missionary in Central Africa. You may have escaped from a private asylum. But as a maiden lady you are an imposter. You have had a sex life of fire and brimstone. [*Changing her tone slightly—slower and more penetrating.*] About your assumed name I am not so sure . . . But you have no married sister.

Madrigal [*lightly*]. You take my breath away.

Laurel [*as lightly*]. Good at it, aren't I?

Madrigal. Yes, for a mind under a cloud.

Laurel. Now for your deduction!

Madrigal [*rising*]. Mine must keep.

Laurel. But it's the *game!* Where are you going?

Madrigal [*pleasantly*]. To my room. To be sure I have left no clues unlocked.

Laurel. To your past life?

Madrigal [*exiting, smiling*]. Yes. You have given me so much warning.

[*Laurel stands a moment looking after her. Looks around room. Then, as she looks through the crack of the opened door, she takes the silver handbell and rings it rather gently—as she would not want her grandmother to hear.*]

Maitland [*opening door, carrying a small tray with a clean glass and some salt cellars*]. Was it *you!* You're not supposed to ring it. [*Is about to go again.*]

Laurel. Maitland!

Maitland. I'm busy now! . . . [*Going, but unable to go.*] . . . *Now* what is it?

Laurel [*conspiratorial—across to him*]. The *Boss! We played the game!*

Maitland [*immediately caught*]. You didn't *dare!* You never! What did you ask her?

Laurel. Nothing. And everything. No game would uncover her! But Maitland—she knows about life!

Maitland. What sort of knowledge?

Laurel. Something—intense. Something too dreadful. Something cut in stone over her mind—to warn you when you walk in.

Maitland [*wistful*]. I too had something dreadful happen to me.

Laurel. But hers is more dreadful! That's why she has no weakness. Her eyes see through me! I'm a mouse to her.

Maitland [*tenderly*]. Are you afraid—poor dearest? Let Maitland speak to her.

Laurel [*lighting up*]. *You!* Oh *you* tell her—How they brought me . . .

Maitland. Don't talk of it!

Laurel. So small, such a little thing. How I cried . . . [*Same acting tone.*] They should have called a doctor.

Maitland. It's what I *said* they should! I argued it! Madame's got *her* ways! I've got mine! Oh—*she* would have got the moon for you! But she wasn't the one who put up with you—who fetched and carried—who read to you —You had the right to the *best* in the world! A *lady's* child! . . .

Laurel. "The Colonel's lady."

Maitland [*instantly furious*]. Not that again. I forbid you!

Laurel. Mr. Pinkbell says "Judy O'Grady."

Maitland. I'll have none of it! Out with the devil in you! For shame! And just when I was talking nicely to you!

Laurel. But I've told you . . .

Maitland. Not me you won't tell. That's got no mother! If your mother's black as soot you don't say so to *me*, girl!

Laurel. I shall scream.

Maitland. Scream away! Now we've got the Boss to get after you! Oh, the relief of it! [*He marches off in a dudgeon to door left.*]

Laurel [*pleading, following him*]. No! No—*be* nice to me! How tough you get—suddenly!

Maitland [*turning at door*]. It comes over me. The Right comes up in me. Like when they tried to make a soldier of me. All of a sudden I *see* how things should be!

[*Enter Mrs. St. Maugham from garden carrying a great sheaf of Michaelmas daisies.*]

Mrs. St. Maugham. Maitland, cut the stems three inches shorter. Put them in the blue Italian vase and three aspirin at the bottom . . . [*The door right opens and Miss Madrigal appears. Maitland remains standing with the flowers in his arms.*] Oh. Oh, indeed! [*With a rapid gesture, patting both ears and shaking them as though she had sea water in them—crossing to Miss Madrigal.*] My ears are filled with poison! What has the nurse been telling me! The poor old man upstairs is crying with rage!

Madrigal [*calmly*]. I corrected him. [*She comes into the room and closes the door after her.*]

Mr. St. Maugham. But for forty years Pinkbell has never been corrected! He is the butler who was the standard of all London!

Madrigal. Let him take his standard from the garden! I corrected his ignorance of details, dates, fundamentals, application of manure. I spoke—not of his spoons and forks—but of his shallow knowledge of the laws of growth. You can leave the room, Maitland.

Mrs. St. Maugham. That should have been said by me! But —go, Maitland! [*Maitland exits hurriedly. Mrs. St. Maugham is severe, majestic.*] Now—*now*, Miss Madrigal—this is a crisis!

Madrigal [*equally severe, majestic*]. Yes. Now you have to make your decision.

Mrs. St. Maugham [*taken aback*]. I! I have!

Madrigal. Now you have to choose between us. [*A moment's silence. Then, taking a step toward Mrs. St. Maugham —with low ferocious accusation.*] Is Mr. Pinkbell to let the moment pass when one should layer the clematis? When the gladioli should be lifted? [*Advancing another step, menacingly.*] Has anyone planted the winter aconites? And the pelargoniums? *Who* has taken cut-

ting? [*Pause. With mounting indignation.*] And the red
tobacco seed and the zinnias and the seeds of the white
cosmos for next year? Do you wish—like an amateur
—to *buy* them!

Mrs. St. Maugham [*recoiling a step—in a faltering voice*].
I—always have—bought them.

Madrigal [*at the height of her passion*]. If *that* is how you
wish to live I am no party to it! It is not possible for me
to hold communication with minds brought up on bed-
ding plants—*bought at the greengrocer's*—dying in
shallow boxes! [*A large gesture at the garden.*] Out there
every corner is crying aloud! [*Turning to door right.
Over her shoulder.*] Must I be dumb when you and I
approach together the time of year when all next summer must stand or fall by us! [*Opening door.*] Have you
time—before death—to throw away season after season? [*Exits on a sweep: door does not quite close.*]

Mrs. St. Maugham [*sinking onto nearest chair*]. *What* have I
let in here out of an advertisement!

Madrigal [*the door opens again*]. The East Wind! [*Exits.
Door now fully closed.*]

Laurel [*aghast*]. Oh—we shall lose her, Grandloo! *Don't sit
there!* Go after her! Oh *think* what she knows about the
garden!

Mrs. St. Maugham. I *am* thinking!

Laurel. Oh—she will go if she says she will! [*Leaning suddenly over her grandmother.*] You don't *want* to lose
her?

Mrs. St. Maugham [*sitting upright, galvanized at the
thought*]. For nothing on earth! I'd sooner strangle
Pinkbell! But how is it to be done?

Laurel. With a cord.

Mrs. St. Maugham. How is the *reconciliation* to be done?
And with a guest at luncheon! [*Rises and stands in
thought.*]

Laurel. Weave her in—as you say you used to do. Go after
her! Promise her the earth . . . *Promise her the garden!*

Mrs. St. Maugham. The garden . . . ? [*Going to the door,
pausing with her hand on the handle, a quick glance
upward to the ceiling.*] But . . . what shall I say to *him?*

Laurel [*also a glance upward*]. You are not *afraid* of him!

Mrs. St. Maugham [*low*]. I have always . . . *always* been
afraid of Pinkbell. [*Exits. Maitland enters.*]

Laurel. If we are to keep the Boss we must fight for her!

Maitland. Fight for her! Have you upset her?

Laurel. I haven't. Not I! She and I understand each other. [*Doorbell is heard.*] There's the bell.

Maitland. The Judge! [*Exits leaving door open. In a few moments the Judge enters, in a light overcoat, followed by Maitland.*]

Laurel [*radiantly*]. Oh—the Judge! Oh—we're all expecting you!

Judge [*smiling*]. All?

Laurel. I am. And Maitland.

Maitland [*nervous*]. Psssht!

Laurel. Take his coat. [*Maitland jumps to it.*] And my companion. Miss Madrigal. And my grandmother.

Judge. So you're the grandchild?

Laurel. Maitland, bring the sherry! [*He exits, she calls after him.*] The dry and the sweet—remember!

[*Maitland exits.*]

Judge. Not for me! I never drink at midday.

Laurel. But my grandmother was telling me this morning you used to glory in your palate!

Judge. We change as we grow older. As you'll find, little girl! [*Looking at her.*] But she *isn't* a little girl!

Laurel. I am sixteen. But backward.

Judge. Bless my soul! What am I to make of that!

Laurel. Nothing. It's too long a story.

Judge. Then you are Olivia's daughter? Shy Olivia.

Laurel [*finger on lips*]. Hush. We don't speak of her.

Judge. She is living, I hope, my dear child?

Laurel. In sin, Judge. Oh . . . [*Enter Mrs. St. Maugham.*]

Mrs. St. Maugham [*coming in on a swirl*]. So you've met her. The little girl of my little girl. No grandmother today. But *Puppy* . . . [*going up to him, laying her hands on his arms*] . . . after twenty years! . . . No longer *young!*

Judge. What do you expect when you measure me by that unsuitable nickname! Am I late? I lost my confounded way.

Mrs. St. Maugham. But you don't drive yourself!

[*Maitland reenters with sherry on tray.*]

Judge. I do. I'm so poor. And much too old to be poor. [*Suddenly, snatching his handkerchief.*] Oh . . . forgive me . . . [*Is about to sneeze.*]

Mrs. St. Maugham. Have you a cold?

Judge. We won't pin it down! A trifle. An allergy. They were threshing in the cornfields. [*Sneezes. Puts on a large*

pair of dark sun spectacles.] I can stand London dust—
but not the country!

Laurel. But now we can't see you!

Judge. You will! Twenty minutes will cheat my old nose that
we are back at the Old Bailey.

[*Exit Maitland, and from now on he brings in the cold dishes
and places them on the sideboard*.]

Mrs. St. Maugham [*helping herself to the sherry*]. Before
we talk of the past . . . how do you find the present?

Judge. Too busy. Too busy. One hasn't time to think one's
getting nearer to God.

Laurel [*to her grandmother. Anxious*.] Have you made it
right with her?

Mrs. St. Maugham [*to Laurel*]. Speak louder. Never whisper.
[*Offers Judge sherry. He refuses. To Judge*.] My Laurel
has a companion. A charming woman. Able—but passionate. At war, just now, with Pinkbell.

Laurel [*still anxious*]. *Grandloo* . . .

Mrs. St. Maugham. The door was closed, Sweet. One is not
at one's best through mahogany. But I heard no sound
of packing.

Judge. Pinkbell . . . *What* it brings back! What incorruptible
ritual! How I remember—after the summer glare of
Piccadilly—the young man that I was crossing your
hall . . . like a pawn across a chessboard.

Mrs. St. Maugham [*low, aside*]. Had you better go and look
for her?

Judge. . . . and how after the first and second footman . . .
one arrived at last at Pinkbell. *He* stood at the foot of
the stairs! The apprehension one had of his sour displeasure . . .

Maitland [*under his breath—to Laurel*]. Not *him*—he's not
meaning! [*Lifting his chin slightly at the ceiling*.]

Judge. *His* severity, his corklike dryness—later on, when I
had to rebuke the public eye, I remembered Pinkbell!
My demeanor on the bench is Pinkbell's.

Maitland [*ready to burst—drawing himself up and letting
out the words like an explosion*]. Everything—*now*—is
at your service—Madame! *On the sideboard*!

Mrs. St. Maugham. Simply. *Simply*. Times have changed,
Maitland! [*Door opens*.] Ah *here* she is! Our Miss
Madrigal! [*To Miss Madrigal who sweeps in, wrapt in
an enigmatic mantle of silence, the temporary dressing
gown of her anger and offense*.] Let me introduce you!

How you have relieved me! [*Judge rises but Madrigal sweeps by with a slight bow and arrives near her own table. To Judge—covering up.*] My right hand. My green hand. The mistress of my garden. [*Slightly aside.*] She has a specialty for the anonymous! [*Louder.*] Some sherry—Miss Madrigal?

Madrigal [*has reached the smaller table and stands behind her chair with her hands on the back of it, her eyes lowered*]. No, thank you.

Mrs. St. Maugham. Then—shall we all sit down? [*Judge follows her to the table. As she seats herself, glances across as though she had noticed the other table for the first time.*] But why this segregation?

Laurel [*promptly*]. The Boss's orders. [*She and Miss Madrigal sit.*]

Judge [*seating himself. To Laurel*]. Are you below the salt? Or are we?

Laurel. Miss Madrigal means this to be the schoolroom.

Mrs. St. Maugham. She is so witty!—Now you can start, Maitland. You can give us your cold chicken. [*To Judge.*] I don't entertain any more. The fight's over. Even the table is laid with fragments of forgotten ritual.

Judge. Faith is handed down that way.

Mrs. St. Maugham. When Pinkbell is dead we shall not know why we use two glasses for one bottle.

Maitland. And what about the wine, Ma'am?

Laurel. The Judge doesn't drink.

Mrs. St. Maugham. And I have such a bottle of Chablis on the ice for you!

Judge. Alcohol in the middle of the day disperses the old brains I try to keep together.

Laurel [*leaning across*]. But aren't *we* to have any!

Mrs. St. Maugham. If we get flushed, Laurel, and too much at our ease . . .

Laurel. I think that will be nice . . .

Mrs. St. Maugham. The reverse, alas, is the truth. But bring it, Maitland. Bring the bottle . . . [*Exit Maitland. To Miss Madrigal.*] . . . and after lunch shall we show the Judge our roses? [*To Judge.*] Miss Madrigal has soil-magic! [*Leaning over again to Miss Madrigal.*] Things grow for *you*—during the night.

Laurel [*as Madrigal doesn't answer*]. You mustn't talk to us. We're invisible.

Judge. But you have ears?

Laurel [*nodding*]. We overhear.

Mrs. St. Maugham. You'll overhear the flavor of the past.
Life was full of great rules then. And we high
women were terrible. Would you have youth back, Puppy?

Judge. No. For a man youth *isn't* the triumph.

Mrs. St. Maugham. I'd have it back if I could—even life's
reverses! Wouldn't you, Miss Madrigal?

Madrigal [*high and sharp*]. You have spilled the salt, Laurel.

Mrs. St. Maugham. I was asking . . . do you think grief
tastes more sharply than pleasure on the palate?

Madrigal [*startled*]. I beg your pardon . . .

Mrs. St. Maugham. You can do better than that, Miss
Madrigal!

Madrigal. I have not the give and take [*into her plate*] of
ordinary conversation.

[*Enter Maitland, carrying a bottle.*]

Mrs. St. Maugham. Show it to me, Maitland. [*He shows it
to her.*] Now open it.

[*He takes it to the sideboard.*]

Judge [*looking round as Maitland draws the cork*]. In that
case . . . after luncheon you'll have to let me close
my eyes!

Mrs. St. Maugham. What—sleep in the daytime!

Judge. That shocks you? In my job old age is part of the
trappings!

Mrs. St. Maugham. One gets old—all the same.

Judge. Judges don't age. Time decorates them. You should
come and hear me! Learned and crumpled like a rose
leaf of knowledge I snuffle and mumble. I sham deaf.
I move into court with the red glory of a dried saint
carried in festival . . .

Laurel [*to Maitland*]. Maitland . . . psst . . . *this* is what you
missed!

Judge. What?

Laurel. Maitland and I want to know.

Mrs. St. Maugham [*warningly*]. *And*—Miss Madrigal? Talk
is a partaking. Not a usurping.

Laurel. But it's *Maitland* who collects the Notable Trial
Series!

Judge. Maitland?

Maitland [*shamed*]. Maitland is myself, m'lord.

Laurel. We want to know—then . . . in plainer language—
how you will enter court tomorrow!

Judge. In ermine. In scarlet. With a full-bottomed wig.

Magnificent! Seeing me now as I am—[*Taking off his sun glasses.*] You wouldn't know me!

[*A wine glass falls, broken, to the ground.*]

Madrigal. Oh!

Mrs. St. Maugham. What's the matter?

Laurel. She broke the glass.

Madrigal. My hand knocked it.

Mrs. St. Maugham. Maitland will get you another. Another glass, please, Maitland.

Maitland. There are no more on the sideboard.

Mrs. St. Maugham. There are plenty in the pantry.

Laurel. Oh—*don't* make him leave the room while the Judge is talking.

Mrs. St. Maugham. I forgot! [*To Judge.*] Maitland has been in prison, Puppy.

Judge [*to Maitland*]. Have you indeed?

Maitland. Five years, m'lord.

Judge [*blandly*]. I hope not too unpleasant?

Maitland. It's given me a fascination and a horror, m'lord, if you can understand. A little stage-struck.

Judge. Dear me, I hope that's not the usual effect. It's supposed to be a deterrent.

Maitland [*waving the bottle a little wildly*]. Yes and no. Yes and no. It's hard to explain.

Mrs. St. Maugham. Don't try. Take my second glass and give some wine to Miss Madrigal.

Laurel. When she had one she wasn't offered any.

Maitland. She doesn't drink, Madam.

Mrs. St. Maugham. One's palate is reborn every morning! Fill the glass!

Madrigal. I am not used to wine . . .

Mrs. St. Maugham. One must dissemble!

Madrigal. . . . but today I will have some.

[*Maitland pours for Miss Madrigal.*]

Mrs. St. Maugham [*meaningfully*]. It helps one to hold up one's end—at a table.

Laurel [*holding out her glass*]. And mine! Fill mine! Oh, Judge—go *on!*

Judge. With what?

Laurel. With tomorrow.

[*Maitland stops to pick small bits of broken glass and to do so leaves bottle on Madrigal's table. From then on Madrigal fills her own glass from time to time.*]

Mrs. St. Maugham. Heavens, Laurel! Talk is a thoroughbred! One does not say "go on"—as if it were a donkey!

Judge. First I am driven to church to pray.

Laurel. To pray?

Judge. I pray against bias. And against vanity.

Madrigal [*low*]. And—*for charity?*

Judge [*smiling*]. That's outside my job. [*To Madrigal.*] I am sorry . . . I have forgotten how they call you?

Madrigal. The name is Madrigal.

Judge. I ignore the heart, Miss Madrigal, and satisfy justice. [*Then to Mrs. St. Maugham.*] Every little line on my face is written by law, not life.

Mrs. St. Maugham. Oh—to be bound up again, Puppy, as you are! To be involved . . . to be back in the hurly-burly . . .

Judge. My life's not the hurly-burly! That's for the counsel! I'm the old creature with the memory! I have to remember the things they *said* they said—but didn't. I have to decide according to dry facts—when appealed to in a passion.

Laurel. But tomorrow, Judge! *Tomorrow!*

Mrs. St. Maugham. Stop badgering the Judge, Laurel!

Judge [*indulgently*]. No! Let her be! On to the law courts! At the gate my trumpeters knock three times. Then blow for my admittance. In a little room behind the court I change my great wig for a small one.

Laurel [*breathless*]. Then . . . ?

Judge [*histrionic for her amusement*]. Then—garbed and toffed with medieval meanings, obscured by ritual, carrying the gloves of justice and the cap of death—on a hollow knock—*I go in.*

Laurel. . . . and the *prisoner* . . .

Mrs. St. Maugham [*warning finger, smiling*]. The judge deserves a halt! One *cannot* just ask the next question! Applaud . . . enlarge the arena . . .

Laurel. But I want to ask a question!

Mrs. St. Maugham. Not yet! I am trying to weave in . . . Oh whoever invented *two* tables! Can't one *join* them?

Judge. Not across fifty years. Not the Past and the Present!

Laurel [*fuming with impatience*]. But can I ask the Judge . . .

Mrs. St. Maugham. Ask then! And don't leave our friend out of everything!

Laurel. I don't know how to *include* her—when I want to ask my own question!

Mrs. St. Maugham. Ask Miss Madrigal . . .

Laurel. But it's the *Judge* I'm asking! Judge—aren't you going to try a murderer tomorrow!

Judge. That is *not* a subject for discussion.

Mrs. St. Maugham. You *see!* You *see* how stiff he can be! You see the resemblance!

Judge. To whom?

Mrs. St. Maugham [*delighted*]. To Pinkbell!

Laurel. But here, today, you are *alone* with us! No one will quote you! [*Pleadingly.*] And we are mad on murder!

Judge. Murder is a sordid thing.

Laurel. Oh—you don't think so! Murder cracks open the lives of people you don't know—like cracking open a walnut! Murder is a crisis! *What* must have gone before to make it so! Isn't it true that to you, Judge, everything is told for the first time?

Judge. In principle.

Laurel. But Miss Madrigal says that the Judge isn't even interested! That he sleeps.

Madrigal. I said he *seemed* to sleep.

Judge. With one eye open. Like a tiger.

Mrs. St. Maugham [*to Madrigal*]. Have you been to a trial, then?

Laurel. She *has.* She told me.

Mrs. St. Maugham. You defeat my purpose! Let her answer.

Judge [*to Madrigal, politely*]. Have you heard me on the bench, Miss Madrigal?

Madrigal. When I spoke to Laurel of judges it was in a general sense. [*Pause.*] But I heard you give a judgment.

Judge. I hope it was a good one. [*No answer.*] I trust it was one of my better days.

Madrigal. I think, if I remember, that I would not have come to your conclusion.

Mrs. St. Maugham [*to Judge*]. Miss Madrigal has such answers to life! [*To Madrigal, in quite a different tone*]. But *that* was a strange one.

Judge. Well, a judge does not always get to the bottom of a case.

Madrigal. No. It takes the pity of God to get to the bottom of things.

Mrs. St. Maugham. That's enough!

Madrigal [*overriding*]. You must forgive me. *You* insisted. [*Holding up her glass with a smile.*] It has removed the inhibitions.

Mrs. St. Maugham. Bring the coffee on!

Laurel [*to Judge*]. When it's a murderer—what do you feel?

Mrs. St. Maugham. What should he feel, Laurel! Judges see prisoners by the million!

Laurel [*overriding*]. But you've got to say, haven't you, whether the man's to live or die? Do you suffer?

Madrigal. Nobody will suffer. They all go into a dream together!

Laurel [*turning*]. Even the prisoner?

Madrigal. The prisoner thinks he is at the judgment seat of justice. A place where all motives are taken into account.

Laurel. And isn't it?

Madrigal. No.

[*Mrs. St. Maugham rings.*]

Laurel. But Judge, while he listens—if the truth is quite different—does he never cry out?

Judge. He may write notes to his counsel.

Laurel. Miss Madrigal says that when all has gone against him . . .

Madrigal [*wildly*]. I am quoted enough! . . . .

Laurel. . . . that after the verdict—when he is asked "Have you anything to say?" . . .

Madrigal. The prisoner is punch-drunk! And says nothing.

Judge. Not always. Some have said remarkable things. There comes to my mind a woman. . . . Have you the trial, Maitland, of Connie Dolly Wallis?

Laurel. Of *whom*? [*Laurel seizes flap of Maitland's pocket.*]

Maitland [*stammering, disengaging himself*]. I . . . I haven't all the volumes, m'lord. I haven't that one.

Judge. It was not one of my successes. But you should read it for what the woman said when she stood before me. It was just before I sentenced her. [*Tilting his head back, looking at the ceiling, fingering his chin thoughtfully with his fingers.*] Fine eyes, she had. I think I should remember them. A tall woman with a face like an eagle. "What I have been listening to in court," she said, "is not my life. It is the shape and shadow of my life. With the accidents of truth taken out of it."

Laurel. What was she tried for, Judge?

Judge. Murder.

Madrigal. I remember the case. [*Looking at the Judge.*] A liar! A pathological imaginer! [*Going high.*] A girl who lied! And lied! And when she told the truth it didn't save her!

Judge [*reacts—leaning forward*]. Have you been to many trials?

Madrigal. One trial. One. But it isn't the duplication—that makes the impression! It's the first time . . . the first time . . .

[*Crash! Cricket ball.*]

Mrs. St. Maugham. Quick, Maitland! *It's the fishmonger's boy! . . . the fishmonger's boy . . . [Racing to the front door ahead of Maitland.]* Catch him! [*They exit. Judge and Madrigal are left facing each other from the tables. Laurel stands looking from one to the other.*]

Laurel [*to Judge*]. Did they hang her? [*Judge rises and looks at Madrigal.*] Did they hang her?

                Curtain comes down as she speaks.

Twenty minutes after luncheon.

The two tables have been cleared. The Judge is alone, seated deep in thought. Offstage at the sound of a door closing he leans his head back and covers his face with a large handkerchief. Beside him are a small tray, glass and carafe.

Laurel enters from door right.

Madrigal is seen about to enter from garden, but seeing Laurel she draws back. Throughout this scene, until her entry she is seen sporadically (at director's discretion), partly masked by a shrub. She is anxious and waiting obviously for the Judge to be free and alone. It is not the intention that she overhear.

Laurel [*whisper*]. Judge . . . Judge . . . wake up . . . [*The Judge mumbles behind his handkerchief.*] If you have your teeth out I will turn my back.

Judge [*whipping off his handkerchief*]. My teeth are my own, thank God!

Laurel. What have you been thinking of—under that hand-kerchief?

Judge. I am an old man—trying to sleep, Laurel.

Laurel [*urgent*]. What did she *do*?

Judge. Who?

Laurel. In that case you were speaking of.

Judge. In my days young girls didn't pester old judges about murder.

Laurel. You are old-fashioned.

Judge. You will be old-fashioned one day. It's more shocking than getting old.

Laurel. Who died—that they should arrest her?

Judge. Her step-sister.

Laurel [*seating herself on stool at his feet*]. How was it done? And why? Was it jealousy?

Judge [*struggling to his feet and moving away*]. If you are going to sit down I am going to stand up.

Laurel [*swiveling round and following him with her eyes*].
  Was she hanged?

Judge. Who? What are you saying?

Laurel. I was asking you about the case you were mentioning.

Judge [*shortly*]. She was reprieved. There was a doubt.

Laurel. Yours?

Judge [*as shortly*]. Not mine. Enough has been said, I think.

Laurel. Where do they go—all your murderers—when they
  don't go to the gallows?

Judge. One doesn't—mercifully—know.

Laurel. Do you remember them?

Judge. In some strange way they are catalogued. As I get
  older they don't always come to hand.

Laurel. But one would know them by their peculiar
  habits . . .

Judge. Perhaps. Some mark might lie upon them.

Laurel. If they took their country walks—for instance—
  back and forth—up and down—wearing out the carpet
  —in their bedroom—

Judge. What?

Laurel. —with a habit—like a sailor's—of walking in a con-
  fined space—might it be that Judge?

[*Enter Mrs. St. Maugham softly so as not to disturb the
  Judge. She sees Laurel.*]

Mrs. St. Maugham. Laurel! He was to sleep, child! And now
  you have disturbed him.

Laurel. I think he was disturbed already! [*Exits.*]

Mrs. St. Maugham [*murmuring as she crosses the room*].
  My *original*! . . . so elegant and gentle . . . [*Taking her
  spectacle case from the wall bracket.*] What do you
  think of her?

Judge. I am not fond of young girls.

Mrs. St. Maugham. You are not? You used to be! It was
  unfortunate about her companion, but your fault,
  Puppy, for not drinking the wine at luncheon!

Judge. How did you discover her?

Mrs. St. Maugham. I advertised. I took a chance and was
  justified. Miss Madrigal came to me like rain from
  heaven.

Judge. With references?

Mrs. St. Maugham. I never listen to what one woman says
  of another. References are a want of faith in one's own
  judgment! Finish your sleep, Puppy! Since you must
  have it. [*Exit. Enter Madrigal.*]

Madrigal. I am sorry to disturb you . . .

Judge. On the contrary.

Madrigal. . . . of course you think . . . this is not where I
ought to be. There would be no difficulty . . . I have
private means. . . . But it's an understandable job . . .
so fitted to me . . . [*Suddenly.*] Do you believe in God?
I thought God had given it to me! [*As his eyes are fixed
on her. After a pause, desperately.*] Why don't you say
something!

Judge. I had hoped you would be gone by now. I must say—
the coincidences at luncheon in retrospect are distaste-
ful!

Madrigal. So now what will you do?

Judge. I am an old man, Miss Madrigal, and very learned.
I don't know.

Madrigal [*ironically*]. Judge—I can't wait seven hours . . .
twice! You sent me to see my maker on a Tuesday—
but that was altered. I have done what they call "time."
It was a lifetime. I don't know what *you* can do to me!
What can you do to me?

Judge. I do not presume to judge you twice.

Madrigal. Oh, you would come to the same conclusion!
Cleverer minds than mine could not convince you! But
I learned in nine days that innocence is not enough.
There's nothing to gain by talking! You came here by
accident . . .

Judge. I wish I hadn't.

Madrigal. What can it be to you?

Judge. Embarrassment. [*Angry.*] And now you have planted
me with human perplexity . . . and ethical perplexity.
It's most unpleasant!

Madrigal. I could have slipped away . . .

Judge. There are worse solutions! Don't you think you might
have chosen anything but this! . . . old friends . . .
and a child to consider.

Madrigal. It's the child I'm considering! She needs me. When
I came here I thought I had met myself again! But I
can't stay here to be a sad piece of news—a curiosity!
If I stay—will you tell them who I am?

Judge. Connie Dolly Wallis—what the devil am I to do with
you?

Madrigal. The name is Madrigal.

Judge. Of course you had to take a name.

Madrigal. It's more than a name to me.

Judge. What I mean goes deeper. Crime, Miss Madrigal, is a flaw in the character.

Madrigal. I come of a stock—who in some insensate way—*cannot* accept defeat! My father was cashiered. And after forty years of appeals—reinstated. My grandfather died upright, on his feet. He said God wouldn't give a fallen general houseroom. For fifteen years, and alone, I have hammered out what I am! I did not know I was as dogged as any of them!

Judge. But even conceding . . .

Madrigal. You need concede nothing to solitude! It is a teacher!

Judge. You were a girl of considerable feeling if I remember.

Madrigal. Not now. I am burnt out, white—like the moon, lunar!

Judge. Are you not—if I may gently say so—somewhat a stranger to life?

Madrigal. The girl I was! She was the stranger!

Judge. You have greatly changed.

Madrigal. At our last meeting I died. It alters the appearance.

Judge. Dear me. Oh deary me . . . As if there were not quite enough—this week ahead of me.

Madrigal. You would have been going. Why not leave?

Judge. Because I belong to a guild of men—who feel responsibility. And a deep distaste for situations.

Madrigal. What shall you do?

Judge. Don't *badger* me! [*Suddenly.*] What's the matter?

Madrigal [*putting her hand over her eyes*]. It is that . . . after being so long *unknown* . . . it makes my head swim to be *known* . . .

[*Olivia enters.*]

Olivia. Judge! I remember you! You used to be so kind to me when I was little! What was that odd name Mother had for you? *Puppy?* I used to wonder at it.

Judge. You were a silent little girl.

Olivia. Yes, I was silent. I have come rather suddenly to fetch my daughter . . .

Madrigal. To fetch her!

Olivia. Oh—we met before—do you remember—

Judge [*quickly interrupting*]. I have to go—can my car be of use, Miss Madrigal? [*Low.*] It would be simple.

Olivia [*breaking in*]. Oh, don't go—don't go! I'm so glad you are here! It's so lucky.

Judge. Lucky?

Olivia. For me. For with you here I shall put things better.

Judge [*takes out his watch and looks at it*]. I ought to go. I am not good out of my setting.

Olivia. Surely *you* are not afraid of life?

Judge. On the contrary—the law has made me nervous of life.

Olivia. No, Judge! *Please* stay! It's the influence of a stranger. With a third person in the room my mother hears reason better.

Mrs. St. Maugham [*catapulting into the room*]. Don't count on it, Olivia! [*Forestalling.*] I *got* your letter!

Olivia. But you don't read them. You never did! We've had our orders. We leave tonight for Cyprus.

Mrs. St. Maugham. Cyprus! Whoever heard of it! It flashed in history and is gone forever! Disraeli—Bismarck—I can't remember! See what comes of marrying an army officer!

[*Laurel makes her entry from the garden, stands in the archway, silent.*]

Olivia. Laurel!

Laurel. Have you come alone?

Mrs. St. Maugham. We have a guest! No drama!

Laurel. You haven't been in four years.

Olivia [*glance at mother*]. But *now* I have come for you! Oh —as I drove down here—all the hedges and the telegraph posts were saying—Laurel . . .

Laurel. Are you going to have a baby?

Olivia. Yes.

Laurel. So there's no room for me!

Olivia. There's room! There's always been room! A heart isn't a house—with a room for each person! I can't wait any longer! Come just as you are . . .

Madrigal. I can pack her things!

Laurel. What are you up to, Boss!

Mrs. St. Maugham. You are so kind! But there's no need for packing!

Laurel. Did you speak without thinking?

Madrigal. No.

Laurel. But I've told you what she is! I've told you . . .

Madrigal. And do you think I have believed you?

Olivia. There's a seat taken on the plane tonight . . .

Laurel. And fly with you? Have you thought of the risk?

Olivia. On the plane? One doesn't think of that.

Laurel. The risk that—if you take me—I might murder my

   stepsister!

Judge. Are you mad?

Laurel. They say so.

Madrigal. Don't give her the triumph of your attention.

Mrs. St. Maugham. Laurel always uses wild words instead
  of weeping! Give her time to recover! [*To Olivia.*] I
  knew—when you came in like that—we should have
  trouble with her!

Madrigal. You have missed your effect, Laurel. The moment
  is passing. Would you care to let it go?

Mrs. St. Maugham. *Now* what are you saying!

Madrigal. . . . and your mother is waiting!

Laurel. The sky's the limit, Boss! The sky's the limit!

Madrigal. No time for games.

Laurel. I mean—no limit! I can say anything!

Judge. I would not.

Laurel. Shall I go on?

Judge. No.

Laurel. Shall I?

Madrigal. If you want your scene—take it.

Laurel. How calm you are!

Mrs. St. Maugham. Miss Madrigal has the calm of a woman
  in a million!

Laurel. She has the calm of a woman who has been a long
  time . . . alone.

Madrigal. So we are in for it?

Laurel. No. It can be played on the edge still.

Madrigal. An edge is sharp! One must come down one side
  or the other . . .

Mrs. St. Maugham. You see . . . they are always at some
  amusing invention. They're inseparable. What game,
  my poppet?

Laurel. A game that two can play.

[*Enter Maitland.*]

Laurel. Maitland! Look! It's my mother!

Maitland. I know it's your mother.

Mrs. St. Maugham. Must the whole house be gathered!

Maitland. I came for the coffee tray.

Mrs. St. Maugham. Oh, no, you didn't! You came for
  curiosity!

Laurel. Maitland! Wait, Maitland! How did you know?

Maitland. She has been before . . .

Laurel. How deep you are! I did not know that . . .

Maitland. But I am loyal to Madame. [*Goes off fast.*]

Mrs. St. Maugham. Loyalty! Loyalty died with Queen Victoria! Disregarded in my own house! Disregarded! I am talking to you, Olivia.

Olivia. Each time I came you promised you would tell her.

Mrs. St. Maugham. I had my own reasons! You never would listen! You were never like other girls! The Judge will remember—though daughters forget everything—You remember, Puppy, how I tried with her?

Judge. I remember only the result. The shy and gentle daughter.

Olivia. Thank you, Judge. But I am not staying any longer! I want to go . . .

Mrs. St. Maugham. . . . But you'll not take Laurel! I have a special knowledge of her! To me she is like a porcelain on a shelf—cracked in some marvelous way for the better!

Olivia. My mother uses words in her special fashion! For a phrase—she would make capital of anything!

Mrs. St. Maugham. Charming—for a mother to hear! And in front of an old friend! If—at a luncheon party— you want to have out the damage of a lifetime . . .

Madrigal. Let's have it!

Mrs. St. Maugham. What!

Madrigal. I beg your pardon.

Mrs. St. Maugham. Were you objecting?

Madrigal. Yes. I think the wine has cut the caution.

[*The Judge motions Mrs. St. Maugham to stop.*]

Mrs. St. Maugham. Don't gesture at me, Puppy!

Judge. Anything may precipitate . . .

Mrs. St. Maugham. What?

Madrigal. Anything!

Judge. Will you come into another room—and I will advise you?

Madrigal. No. Your advice is foreseen! That I must leave here—but it is the *child* who must leave! Laurel must go, Mrs. St. Maugham, go with her mother.

Mrs. St. Maugham. You take a great liberty!

Madrigal. Yes, now I have a sense of liberty.

Mrs. St. Maugham. That is not what I meant!

Madrigal. No, but it is what I mean!

Mrs. St. Maugham. This girl of special soil! Transplant her?

Madrigal. You have not a green thumb, Mrs. St. Maugham, with a plant or a girl. This is a house where nothing good can be made of her!

Mrs. St. Maugham. My house!

Madrigal. Your house! Why even your garden is demented! By the mercy of God you do not keep an animal!

Mrs. St. Maugham. You are mad! You are a monster!

Madrigal. No, I am a woman who has lost touch with things. With indulgence. With excuses, with making merry over bad things. The light—and the shade—has been hammered out of me. I am as humorless as a missionary.

Judge. Why complicate life? The past is over.

Madrigal. If the past is useful, I shall not hesitate to use it. What I have been has long been done with—[*To Laurel.*] What you are is yet to come. This is an end to your fancy life.

Mrs. St. Maugham. Stop the woman, Puppy! Stop her!

Olivia. But Miss Madrigal has something to say!

Judge. No, she hasn't.

Madrigal. Oh! I am not inexperienced. You must allow me a certain bias.

Judge. Have a care!

Madrigal. I am beyond caring!

Laurel. Boss, Boss, don't go too far!

Madrigal. Don't drive me to it! Who else can tell you that when your moment comes when truth might serve you —you will not make it sound.

Laurel. But everybody knows about me! They *know* what happened!

Madrigal. They know what you have told them! Shall we now deprive your grandmother of your famous seduction?

Mrs. St. Maugham. At what a moment!

Olivia [*turning to her mother*]. But is that what she said? Is that what you have believed?

Madrigal. Wait! Let the child tell you.

Laurel. You were not there!

Madrigal. I did not need to be there. The story can be read backwards! What newspaper did the cook take in, I wonder.

Olivia. A child of twelve!

Madrigal. An only child is never twelve! [*Crossing to Laurel.*] Do you cry?

Laurel. No.

Madrigal. I should cry.

Laurel. I am not near crying.

Madrigal. I should cry—with relief—that your mother

wants you! You told me you were looking for which
is you. Find the right one! [*Pause.*] Be careful! Even
a mother can't wait forever.

Olivia. But why did she pretend? Why was it done?

Madrigal. Odd things are done for love.

[*Laurel runs to door, halts and turns at door.*]

Olivia [*half crossing to her*]. Give it up, Laurel! It isn't worth
going on.

Laurel [*to Madrigal*]. Has it got to be the truth?

Madrigal [*half smiling*]. One can lie. . . . But truth is more
interesting!

Laurel. . . . and you get better and better at spotting it! [*Taking her mother's hand.*] You win, Boss!

[*They exit.*]

Madrigal [*calling after them through the open door*]. Your
blue linen dress is folded in the top drawer. *Look* for
your yellow striped one . . .

Mrs. St. Maugham [*gripping tooth and nail to the behavior
of a hostess, mincingly forcing out the tin clatter of the
words. To the Judge*]. What a *precipitation*—of melo-
drama—your visit's fallen on! [*Glancing at the door
—flame beginning to run in her tone.*] Blood is thicker
than water I had thought but it appears not!

Judge. My dear—my dear old friend. . . .

Mrs. St. Maugham. If you were on your *knees* you wouldn't
stop me! [*Turning on Madrigal.*] That was a black
patch, Miss Madrigal! If there's a straw to be lit—
you've set a match to it! What collusion behind my
back! [*To Judge.*] You've been a witness to it!

Judge [*edging to the door*]. You would be better talking
alone, I think . . .

Mrs. St. Maugham. Stay where you are, Puppy! Men are
such cowards! In the name of discretion or a cool head
or some such nonsense—they leave one in the lurch. . . .

Judge. So *much* better . . . better not say anything!

Mrs. St. Maugham. There's an undependability in high-
minded men! They sit—*objective!* When they should
be burning beside one! But—when things become *personal . . . what would you say if your clerk put your
wig on!*

Judge [*unhappily*]. I should reflect at length, I expect, and
decide on inaction.

Mrs. St. Maugham. So you would! [*Turning.*] But *I've* been
robbed of my granddaughter!

Madrigal [*calmly*]. If you face facts, Mrs. St. Maugham, you are tired of her.

Mrs. St. Maugham [*faintly*]. Be a man, Puppy! Put her out! Put her out in the street for me!

[*The Judge makes an unhappy movement of recoil.*]

Mrs. St. Maugham [*with mounting passion*]. The flaming impudence! The infamy! [*Panting.*] And I—*lavish! Trusting* . . . leaning . . . *But I've been leaning on a demon!* In your heart—every penny should have scalded you! *I've been betrayed!* Don't talk to me of wages! You'll see none of them!

Judge [*to Madrigal*]. Perhaps this is where I may be of some use?

Madrigal [*smiling gently*]. No, Judge. Not now. Fifteen years ago you might have been.

Mrs. St. Maugham [*starting forward*]. Do you dare to speak! What are these innuendoes?

Judge [*low. To Madrigal*]. Least said, soonest mended.

Mrs. St. Maugham. Hints—since lunch—have been flying like gnats from side to side of the room! [*Getting to her feet.*] Nobody tells me—in plain English—anything! *Have you two met before then?*

Madrigal [*matter of fact*]. I was once sentenced to death by the Judge here.

Mrs. St. Maugham [*for a second silenced*]. Ah.

Judge [*simultaneously*]. Ill-advised. Ill-advised.

Mrs. St. Maugham [*with a retake of energy*]. Oh! . . . If I were not seventy—this would revive me! To *death!* . . . But there you *are!*

Madrigal. Those who still live—have to be somewhere.

Mrs. St. Maugham. If it were true . . . it's *outrageous*. And if I start putting two and three together—Good heavens, *how can you be living at all!*

Judge. There was a doubt.

Mrs. St. Maugham. What I doubt is my senses! The thing's impossible! Either I don't believe it—or it's quite private! Besides if it were true it would be—*most* inconvenient! Oh . . . I would like the situation annulled! And the conversation put back . . .

Judge. To where?

Mrs. St. Maugham. To where it hadn't happened! And at the interview—*how dared you*—I let pass—so many excellent applicants in favor of you!

Madrigal [*mildly*]. No—really—it was not so.

Mrs. St. Maugham [*struck by another thought*]. . . . and the references! The *references* I had . . . I am *amazed!* You must have *forged* them!

Madrigal. I gave you none.

Mrs. St. Maugham. Why?

Madrigal [*simply*]. I had none.

Judge [*explaining mildly*]. This lady came to you out of prison.

Mrs. St. Maugham. I would have thought a university. Oh —you have been most satisfactory I *thought*—but *now* —a light is thrown! I remember replies—which now I see to be insolences! I can smell backwards a dozen indisciplines! I'm growing more and more thunderstruck! Prison . . . !

Madrigal. But—

Mrs. St. Maugham. Don't speak to me, if you please! You who come out of God knows what ancient Publicity! Blazing—from heaven knows what lurid newspapers! A Headline! A felon! How can you *lunch* with me, Puppy, and *know* such things! Oh I'm dumbfounded! What's more, I've been defrauded! Go! Pack your bags! Pack your bags! Out of the house with you!

[*Enter Maitland, on a light wind of impatience.*]

Maitland. I can't wait. . . . I *can't* wait forever! [*To Mrs. St. Maugham, who is practically collapsed.*] Is she . . . who we think she is!

Mrs. St. Maugham [*in a faint groan*]. She is.

Maitland [*turning radiantly to Madrigal*]. Oh . . . Miss . . . Oh . . . Madame.

[*Madrigal gives tiny bow.*]

Mrs. St. Maugham [*practically "out"—but terrible*]. Heavens! What an anticlimax! What veneration! One would think the woman was an actress!

Maitland. When one is a humble man one can't express it. I think it is—to *think*—that after such a gale she is with us.

Mrs. St. Maugham [*feebly*]. That's enough, Maitland.

Maitland [*backing toward the door*]. To have stood one's life before the judge here . . . if you'll pardon me, m'lord, even though you eat your lunch like other men—[*Turning sharply as the door opens.*] Here's the nurse! All in a dither . . .

Nurse [*rushing in. Stopping short at sight of guests*]. Mrs. St. Maugham . . .

Mrs. St. Maugham [*in a daze*]. We have friends now. It can wait, Nurse.

Nurse. Mr. Pinkbell is dead.

Mrs. St. Maugham [*still dazed*]. You can go, Nurse. I'll attend to it later. [*Nurse, aghast, backs to the door.*] I say we have *friends*, Nurse!

[*Nurse exits in horrified flounce.*]

Judge. But . . . *good* heavens . . . Pinkbell!

Mrs. St. Maugham [*dazed*]. He is in expert hands.

Maitland. But the poor old bastard . . . He has passed *over!*

Mrs. St. Maugham. Is *that* what she said?

Maitland. They've downed him—stiff as a rod. He hasn't tomorrow . . . [*Struck by a worse thought.*] He hasn't the *rest of today!*

Mrs. St. Maugham. Dead . . . and my past goes with him . . .

Judge. Dear me, dear me. I am shocked. First to know he is alive. Then to learn that he isn't.

Mrs. St. Maugham [*musing*]. When I was a young woman he educated me . . . my manner with distinguished foreigners. . . . He saw to my Ascots. He bought my wine for me. Is there an afterlife, Puppy?

Judge [*starting to go, gathering up his spectacle case, etc. Smiling*]. I don't give judgments easily. But in *this* life you will miss him.

Mrs. St. Maugham. Alas, no. [*Getting up, crossing room to him.*] Shall you come again, Puppy? When the excitement of your week is over?

Judge [*shaking his head*]. Too much happens in this house —for an old man.

Mrs. St. Maugham. I am coming with you to your car. Everyone—accusing everyone—has been tiring. Stay with her, Maitland, I shan't be long. Keep an eye on her. [*Exits past Judge.*]

Judge. Good-bye, Miss Madrigal [*Turns back from door*]. After all . . . have you liked the life here?

Madrigal. It has a hollow quality which soothes me.

Judge. But what shall you do?

Madrigal. I shall continue to explore—the astonishment of living!

Judge [*as he turns away—to himself*]. No man's infallible. [*He exits.*]

Maitland [*in eager excitement, directly the door is closed*]. Can I come where you're going? I will serve you. We could throw our five and fifteen years away from us!

In the dustbin!

Madrigal. Not mine! Not *my* fifteen years! I value them!
They made me.

Maitland [*ecstatic*]. Ah—that's the strength I hanker after!
That's what I've been missing! I was born to worship
the stars! But I've never known *which* stars . . . [*spreads
his arms wide*] . . . when the whole heaven's full of
them! [*Mrs. St. Maugham comes in. On the same high
note.*] I wish to give my notice!

Mrs. St. Maugham [*crossing the room*]. Again! You choose
such odd moments!

Maitland. I wish to accompany Miss Madrigal!

Mrs. St. Maugham. Where to?

Maitland. Where she's going.

Mrs. St. Maugham. Yet *now* you have it all your own way,
Maitland.

Maitland [*wincing, glancing up at the ceiling*]. Don't say
that!

Mrs. St. Maugham. I'll talk to you later . . . I must go up . . .
[*As she leaves, to herself.*] . . . stiff as a rod . . . the poor
old bastard . . . [*Exits.*]

Madrigal [*instantly turning to Maitland and talking in clear
articulated haste like someone leaving important messages they have hardly time to deliver*] . . . thin out the
seedlings—as I showed you . . . the lilac wants pruning
. . . and the rock-rose and the pasque flower . . .

Maitland [*trying to interrupt*]. But . . .

Madrigal [*rapidly, in desperate haste, glancing once at Pinkbell's door in fear of being interrupted*]. . . . tie in the
wild grape! Cut the heads on the moss rose . . .

Maitland. But . . .

Madrigal [*taking no notice*]. . . . the asphodel and the dew
plant . . .

Maitland. But what's to become of my decision!

Madrigal [*in irritated despair that he doesn't listen*]. Oh—
don't give notice so often! It's a fidgety habit!

[*Enter Olivia and Laurel.*]

Maitland. You look a proper daughter!

[*Enter Mrs. St. Maugham.*]

Mrs. St. Maugham. Leave us, Maitland! [*He exits.*] Well,
Laurel . . . now you have a mother! It's not so rare!
Every kitten has one!

Laurel [*looking from Mrs. St. Maugham to Madrigal*].
Grandloo . . .

Mrs. St. Maugham [*still rather sharp from several reasons . . . that she has been beaten in battle, also that Madrigal is in the room and she doesn't want Laurel near her*]. Don't begin badly! Where are your gloves? [*With a dryness that really is to cover the fact she may show emotion. Her hand up to ward her off.*] No good-byes! I'm too old for them . . .

Laurel. Grandloo . . .

Olivia. Go to the car, darling.

Mrs. St. Maugham. Begin by obeying. [*Laurel exits.*] Well, Olivia. What are you going to do with her? Teach her the right things? After I've taught her the wrong ones?

Olivia. You're like an old Freethinker—who finds he has a son a clergyman!

Mrs. St. Maugham. Is that so dreadful?

Olivia. No . . . but to you inscrutable. [*Toward door, then turning.*] Why did you want her?

Mrs. St. Maugham [*caught off-guard*]. Is it a crime to want to be remembered? [*Dryly.*] The Pharaohs built the Pyramids for that reason.

Olivia [*at door, quietly*]. The thoughts of a *daughter* are a kind of memorial.

Mrs. St. Maugham. Is that an obituary?

Olivia [*wryly*]. Only to the past, Mother. [*Exit Olivia.*]

Mrs. St. Maugham [*rushing energetically to window*]. Leave her hair long! It gives her the choice later! [*A pause; then louder.*] Keep her bust high! [*Then slowly back into room. To Madrigal.*] What do women do—in my case?

Madrigal [*looking back at her*]. They garden.

Mrs. St. Maugham. But it seems I am not very good at that either! Are your things packed?

Madrigal [*coldly*]. I am a light-footed traveler.

Mrs. St. Maugham [*holding out the catalogue*]. Before you go will you point out the white crinum? [*She hands it to her. Madrigal takes it and looks down it. Watching her.*] You, who have an impertinent answer to everything—is there an afterlife?

Madrigal [*stooping over a table and marking the catalogue without looking up*]. Certainly.

Mrs. St. Maugham [*surprised*]. You say—"certainly"?

Madrigal [*leaving catalogue open on the table*]. One does not sit alone for fifteen years without coming to conclusions.

Mrs. St. Maugham. Is there . . . affection in it? [*Picks up catalogue.*]

Madrigal. But you have been living all this while without affection! Haven't you noticed it?

Mrs. St. Maugham [*for a moment there is no answer. Mrs. St. Maugham seems to be reading the catalogue as she stands. She turns and comes back toward Madrigal, reading aloud*]. . . . "very rare . . . from the High Andes of Bolivia. Jasmine-like tubular flowers."

Madrigal. Don't waste your time. They are beyond you.

Mrs. St. Maugham [*not raising her head*]. It speaks wonderfully of the Uvularia.

Madrigal. When will you learn you live on chalk?

Mrs. St. Maugham [*in exactly same tone*]. I have made such a muddle of the heart. Will Olivia forgive me?

Madrigal. It is pointless to wonder. You have no choice how she will sum up. [*Pause. Quietly.*] She will live longer.

Mrs. St. Maugham [*dryly*]. Am I to die unloved?

Madrigal. If necessary. *I* was prepared to do it.

Mrs. St. Maugham [*suddenly sitting down, looking at the ceiling and letting the catalogue fall in her lap*]. The Unicorn Root . . . [*She is really saying this because she is going to say something else. It's to gain time for herself.*]

Madrigal. . . . needs a sheltered spot. You haven't one.

Mrs. St. Maugham [*slowly, to the ceiling*]. If you stay here —you can grow windbreaks . . . [*Suddenly, bringing her head down.*] I must know one thing!

Madrigal. What?

Mrs. St. Maugham [*her face agleam with human curiosity*]. Did you do it?

Madrigal [*unperturbed and calm*]. What learned men at the top of their profession couldn't find out in nine days— why should *you* know?

Mrs. St. Maugham [*looking down at the catalogue, after a second's pause*]. . . . the Dierama . . . the Wand Flower. . . .

Madrigal [*moving over to her*]. It won't grow on chalk. But if *I* stay with you—[*putting her hand almost tenderly on Mrs. St. Maugham's shoulder*]—and we work together . . . with potash—and a little granular peat . . . We can *make* it do so.

                                                          Curtain

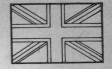

Robert Bolt **A Man For All Seasons**

A PLAY IN TWO ACTS

Sir Thomas More

> *More* is a man of an angel's wit and singular learning;
> I know not his fellow. For where is the man of that
> gentleness, lowliness, and affability? And as time re-
> quireth a man of marvellous mirth and pastimes; and
> sometimes of as sad gravity: a man for all seasons.

—ROBERT WHITTINTON

> He was the person of the greatest virtue these islands
> ever produced.

—SAMUEL JOHNSON

A Modern Man
For All Seasons

BY ROBERT BOLT

A man for all Seasons is a good man. I don't mean morally good (though no doubt he'd be that too), but good in the sense that a good car is good, or a good plow, or a good knife. Good for what it's *for*. A good knife is a sharp knife because a knife is for cutting. But what is a man for? We don't know, so we can't say what kind of man is a good one.

It's such a long time since we did know what a man was for that we seem to have concluded it's a silly question to ask. It may be. But certainly every other question is silly until it is answered.

The use of these cars, plows, knives, bombs and other gadgets is a human use. Only human beings use them. And to know what they are for without knowing what we are for is like living in the upstairs of a house which lacks its first story. Just that precarious condition is our condition now, I think.

The Existentialists (Frenchmen are quick at this kind of thing) say this whole desire for a mental dwelling is misguided and impossible. Like it or lump it, they say, men have no home and must learn to live in the open, exposed to wind, rain and starlight, pelted by meteors, transfixed by cosmic rays and generally suffering without surprise whatever meaningless arrangements matter may fall into.

Compared to this view of our position, ordinary pessimism is a matter for cap and bells. It commands respect. Courage always does. Moreover it is logically watertight.

Indeed my only objection to the Existentialist view of our position is that it *is* a view of our position, not a position that anybody actually occupies. As a view it's an exact definition of our position. As a position it's an exact definition of immediate insanity. Or so it seems to me. Of course that may be just the measure of my own timidity.

The philosophic mental dwelling which Man needs—or which I say he needs—is some picture of himself from which he can recognize himself and find what he is for. Other ages, more fortunate in this than ours, have had such a picture. Other individuals, more fortunate in this than me, still do. For example, some of my best friends are Christians.

Christians know what Man is for: he is for saving his soul. They have a picture of the ideal man: the Christian saint.

Some other of my friends are Marxists. They too know what Man is for: he is for bringing about the classless state. They have a picture of the ideal man: the revolutionary proletarian.

Some others yet again are crude materialists (though only the best of them would say so). They know what Man is for: he is for getting rich (not very rich, just rich). They have a picture of the ideal man—the Success (unhampered by guilt, attending to his appetites).

But I am neither Christian nor Marxist, nor hope much for Success. I have no picture of the ideal man and ought to be content with that; but I am not.

And so I'm thrown back on admiring mere actual qualities in merely actual men without inquiring at all deeply why. And asked to describe a man for our own short Season I thought to take a random handful of obviously admirable men—say Schweitzer, Einstein, Gandhi, Lenin, Hammerskjöld—and by putting down my reasons for admiring them to provide the reader with materials for a composite profile of a man for himself. But this won't answer, because their particular virtues won't combine, and none of their virtues is sufficient by itself.

Take Schweitzer. He is powered by charity, traditionally the senior virtue. Small wonder that when we cast around for a good name to pronounce, our tongues fall gratefully on his.

His own life in Art and Thought was happy. But his attention was held by the world's suffering. When he was thirty-eight the contrast became unendurable, his own happiness impermissible. He left Europe and music for Africa and leprosy.

To load your own shoulders with the world's suffering and walk on like this is just possibly all right if your shoulders are herculean as his are. But it's dangerously like stoicism. By various means we have made that load so heavy that most of us would be squashed flat by it before we'd gone a single step. And Heaven knows steps have got to be taken in the Sixties, if we're to live to see the Seventies.

Einstein now. Ptolemy and Copernicus merely moved the center of the universe. Einstein showed it had none, an intellectual leap of such appalling courage that most of us are still in fact left gaping on the higher bank. In his person he was simple and modest, in his opinions always on the side of kindness, always against the bullies. Intellectual genius and personal sweetness together make up wisdom, and Einstein is our name for that.

But it was Einstein who, in August, 1939, urged President Roosevelt to produce the atomic bomb. And this makes him responsible (not solely responsible, but responsible). How could such an admirable man come to be responsible for such a dreadful thing?

He knew himself to be a very important scientist, but thought himself of no particular importance as a man. The humility is venerable, but the split is disastrous. The idea that when a man puts on a white laboratory coat he ceases to be himself seems to me medieval. Yet that is the central idea of our day and age, the idea that the works of science don't come under moral judgment.

Thus we say the atom bomb is not evil in itself, that it depends on how it is used. You might as well say that a thumbscrew is not evil in itself. There is no way of using a thumbscrew that isn't evil. There is no way of using the bomb that isn't evil. A thumbscrew is for inflicting pain. The bomb is for indiscriminate slaughter. And the idea that the inventors of the bomb were serving science and that not they but science is responsible, has no more ordinary substance in it than a dispute on the sex of angels.

The Man for our season would have to know about science. Perhaps he'd have to be a scientist. But he would be a man first, last, all the time, and would not leave his manhood with all its hampering confusion at the door of his laboratory.

Gandhi is the evidence we offer for up-to-date saintliness. Passive Disobedience is a simple idea and many men have had it but Gandhi made it work. In an age when there is so much tyranny, and force has become unusably dangerous, what could nourish hope more richly than this, to contest your enemy's Evil with your Good, and win?

But for Gandhi the contest was a rigged one. The British occupation of India was only half-heartedly tyrannical. When Indians lay down on railway tracks in British India

the trains perforce were stopped. This gave the Indians a
victory—and the British a problem. But in a thoroughgoing
tyranny the train would have driven on. It wouldn't happen
twice.

Great credit to Gandhi and his followers for their victory,
but some credit also to my doubtful countrymen for their
defeat.

And now the tyrants have no doubt. If Good is to meet
Evil now, it must be nakedly and no holds barred. What
then?

Of course if the *whole population* lay down on the rails,
not Stalin nor Hitler could keep the trains in motion. But
what country has a whole population of heroes? We know
the amount of naked evil in the world; where are we to
find that much naked good?

Gandhi would reply that you can't always have exactly
as much Good as you really want. Well, in the presence of
a man like that I will take off my hat—and my shoes too,
but my Man for this season will start more cautiously with
the Good we've already got.

Lenin was a genius of action, like Napoleon and Caesar.
No objective historian of our century is ever going to deny
that he was a big man. I think he was a good man too. Take
it that he was a good man for the sake of my argument.

Lenin was followed by Stalin. Like everybody else today
I'm sufficiently a Marxist to believe such accidents aren't
really accidental. I mean there must have been something
in the reign of Lenin that made the reign of Stalin historically probable if not inevitable. What was it?

I think it was sheer impatience, plus this same doctrine
of historical inevitability. In Czarist Russia any liberal-
minded man had good reasons for impatience. The leaders
of underprivileged people are always impatient. Good.
I'm glad that they're impatient. They're impatient because
they're forward looking and generous minded.

But how does a forward-looking, generous-minded man,
even if impatient, prepare the way for a cruel and repressive
man? If such a man begins to *act* ruthlessly, that is cruelly,
then he has suppressed the generosity that made him impatient in the first place. In the name of what can a man be
turned in a circle like this?

In the name of History, in Lenin's case. He believed the
Historical Process was embodied in the Working Class. He
believed the Working Class was embodied in the Communist

Party. He believed the Communist Party was embodied in its Central Committee. He knew from experience that the Central Committee was embodied in himself. So he himself was the embodiment of History. And a man will do things in the name of History which he would never do for himself.

Thus it was that Lenin created the police state that Stalin used. And after Stalin probably many others. A democracy is like a living plant, troublesome, messy, needing attention, but a police state is like a block of stone and will endure of itself. And once individual liberty is dead (shot through the skull in a cellar or peacefully passing away during sleep), it won't come to life when it's wanted.

Our Man then would share Lenin's conviction that something could be done to better the world, but he would know that he was not the embodiment of History, or anything but just himself, with no more sanction to commit a crime than any other man. He would have all the moral squeamishness of the Western liberal without his sick conviction that nothing really can be done.

And that brings me to Mr. Hammerskjöld. His praises we all have been sadly singing: his utter integrity, his predilection for the company of creative men, his equal concern for the persons of the eminent and lowly, his industry, his erudition, his analytic mind.

What makes him specially relevant to our purpose, though, is that his burning sense of duty ran in harness with the modesty of his aspirations.

He shuttled indefatigably between the roaring dinosaurs, the only human being there, one sometimes felt, conversing with each in its own strange language, able to understand the bits of sense within the reverberated and indignant bellowings of each, and returning with it tactfully translated to the others: his modest conviction that since all men want to live, there must be a way for them to avoid killing themselves. He was the perfect official in the world's most important office.

But an official by his nature must finally do what he's told. He can facilitate, not initiate. And initiative, real, disturbing initiative is needed on that scene. It seems that Hammerskjöld was one of those fine and very attractive spirits born to be the servants of much lesser men. And what's the good of that?

Even so I dimly feel that he comes nearest to the Man we want, though on a less heroic scale than the others.

Indeed I don't think we want, don't think we can afford a Hero. It seems that, if we can negotiate the next fifty years or so, many of our present problems will be solved. It's a big "if," but the prize is proportionate. Meanwhile, the times are critical. A Captain of Fate, an epoch-making specialist in one particular virtue, rocks the boat to one side or the other. I think we want not captains but a full crew of moderate men. *But:*

"Moderate" will not in them mean slothful, or devitalized as it often does today. On the contrary they will be moderate, these Men, because they are complete.

As near as I can get to it, it's this: one virtue practiced to the uttermost produces wonders. But lacking its opposite virtue it carries the lack with it and prepares for a swing of the pendulum. It can even have the effect of vice.

On the other hand, a virtue countered by its opposite obviously can't be practiced to the uttermost. And I do see that if the pulls are equal as well as opposite, the Man in whom they operate is reduced to the still center. And thus it is that a man can claim to have his virtues in a state of perfect balance when in fact he's merely stagnant.

The difference between a man who functions from the still center and merely stagnant man is one of mere vitality. There is something in a healthy man that makes him act.

Our Man then will have the love of life (his own life too —he'd make a most unwilling martyr). But this crude vitality, which he shares with bacteria and chickweed, is in him informed with all these pulls and counterpulls we've been considering. He will be a complex creature, troubled, knowing, wary, worldly-wise, never nearer to the truth than when he's nearest laughing at himself (never using laughter as a get-out though), often tired. An exhausting business being a man; after seventy years or so we die of it. But it seems after all that the Man we want is just a man: without the capital M.

The Common Man: Late middle age. He wears from head to foot black tights which delineate his pot-bellied figure. His face is crafty, loosely benevolent, its best expression that of base humor.

Sir Thomas More: Late forties. Pale, middle-sized, not robust. But the life of the mind in him is so abundant and debonair that it illuminates the body. His movements are open and swift but never wild, having a natural moderation. The face is intellectual and quickly delighted, the norm to which it returns serious and compassionate. Only in moments of high crisis does it become ascetic—though then freezingly.

Richard Rich: Early thirties. A good body unexercised. A studious unhappy face lit by the fire of banked-down appetite. He is an academic hounded by self-doubt to be in the world of affairs and longing to be rescued from himself.

Duke of Norfolk: Late forties. Heavy, active, a sportsman and soldier held together by rigid adherence to the minimal code of conventional duty. Attractively aware of his moral and intellectual insignificance, but also a great nobleman, untouchably convinced that his acts and ideas are important because they are his.

Alice More: Late forties. Born into the merchant class, now a great lady; she is absurd at a distance, impressive close to. Overdressed, coarsely fashioned, she worships society; brave hot-hearted, she worships her husband. In consequence, troubled by and defiant toward both.

Margaret More: Middle twenties. A beautiful girl of ardent moral fineness; she both suffers and shelters behind a reserved stillness which it is her father's care to mitigate.

Cardinal Wolsey: Old. A big decayed body in scarlet. An almost megalomaniac ambition unhappily matched by an excelling intellect, he now inhabits a lonely den of self-indulgence and contempt.

Thomas Cromwell: Late thirties. Subtle and serious; the face expressing not inner tension but the tremendous outgoing will of the Renaissance. A self-conceit that can cradle gross crimes in the name of effective action. In short, an intellectual bully.

Chapuys: Sixties. A professional diplomat and lay ec-
clesiastic dressed in black. Much on his dignity as a
man of the world, he in fact trots happily along a mental
footpath as narrow as a peasant's.

Chapuys' Attendant: An apprentice diplomat of good
family.

William Roper: Early thirties, a stiff body and an im-
mobile face. Little imagination, moderate brain, but an
all-consuming rectitude which is his cross, his solace,
and his hobby.

The King: Not the Holbein Henry, but a much younger
man, clean-shaven, bright-eyed, graceful and athletic.
The Golden Hope of the New Learning throughout
Europe. Only the levity with which he handles his absolute power forehadows his future corruption.

A Woman: Middle fifties. Self-opinionated, self-right-
eous, selfish, indignant.

Cranmer: Late forties. Sharp-minded, sharp-faced. He
treats the Church as a job of administration, and theol-
ogy as a set of devices, for he lacks personal religiosity.

The set is the same throughout but capable of varied
lightings, as indicated. Its form is finally a matter for
the designer, but to some extent is dictated by the action of the play. I have visualized two galleries of flattened Tudor arches, one above the other, able to be
entered from off-stage. A flight of stairs leading from
the upper gallery to the stage. A projection which can
suggest an alcove or closet, with a tapestry curtain to
be drawn across it. A table and some chairs, sufficiently heavy to be congruous indoors or out.

The costumes are also a matter for the designer, but I
have visualized no exact reproductions of the elaborate
style of the period. I think plain colors should be used,
thus scarlet for the Cardinal, gray for More, gold for
the King, green for the Duke, blue for Margaret, black
and pinstripe for the administrators Rich and Cromwell, and so on.

When the curtain rises, the set is in darkness but for a single spot on the Common Man, who sits on a big property basket.

Common Man [*rises*]. It is perverse! To start a play made up of Kings and Cardinals in speaking costumes and intellectuals with embroidered mouths, with me.

If a King or a Cardinal had done the prologue he'd have had the right materials. And an intellectual would have shown enough majestic meanings, colored propositions, and closely woven liturgical stuff to dress the House of Lords! But this!

Is this a costume? Does this say anything? It barely covers one man's nakedness! A bit of black material to reduce Old Adam to the Common Man.

Oh, if they'd let me come on naked, I could have shown you something of my own. Which would have told you without words——! Something I've forgotten . . . Old Adam's muffled up [*Backing towards the basket.*] Well, for a proposition of my own, I need a costume. [*Takes out and puts on the coat and hat of Steward.*] Matthew! The Household Steward of Sir Thomas More! [*Lights come up swiftly on set. He takes from the basket five silver goblets, one larger than the others, and a jug with a lid, with which he furnishes the table. A burst of conversational merriment off; he pauses and indicates head of stairs.*] There's company to dinner. [*He pours a cup of wine.*] All right! A Common Man! A Sixteenth-Century Butler! [*He drinks from the cup.*] All right—the Six—[*He breaks off, agreeably surprised by the quality of the liquor, regards the jug respectfully and drinks again from jug.*] The Sixteenth Century is the Century of the Common Man. [*He puts down the jug.*] Like all the other centuries. And that's my proposition. [*During the last part of the speech, voices are heard off. Now, enter, at the head of the stairs, Sir Thomas More.*]

Steward. That's Sir Thomas More.

More. The wine please, Matthew?

Steward. It's there, Sir Thomas.

More [*looking into the jug*]. Is it good?

Steward. Bless you, sir! I don't know.

More [*mildly*]. Bless you too, Matthew.

[*Enter Rich at the head of the stairs.*]

Rich [*enthusiastically pursuing an argument*]. But every man has his price!

More. No-no-no—

Steward [*contemptuously*]. Master Richard Rich.

Rich. But yes! In money too.

More [*with gentle impatience*]. No no no.

Rich. Or pleasure. Titles, women, bricks-and-mortar, there's always something.

More. Childish.

Rich. Well, in suffering, certainly.

More [*interested*]. Buy a man with suffering?

Rich. Impose suffering, and offer him—escape.

More. Oh. For a moment I thought you were being profound. [*He gives a cup to Rich.*]

Rich [*to Steward*]. Good evening, Matthew.

Steward [*snubbing*]. 'Evening, sir.

Rich. No, not a bit profound; it then becomes a purely practical question of how to make him suffer sufficiently.

More. Mm . . . [*He takes him by the arm and walks with him.*] And . . . who recommended you to read Signor Machiavelli? [*Rich breaks away laughing—a fraction too long. More smiles.*] No, who? [*More laughter*]. . . . Mm?

Rich. Master Cromwell.

More. Oh . . . [*He goes back to the wine jug and cups.*] He's a very able man.

Rich. And so he is!

More. Yes, I say he is. He's very able.

Rich. And he will do something for me, he says.

More. I didn't know you knew him.

Rich. Pardon me, Sir Thomas, but how much do you know about me?

More. Whatever you've let me know.

Rich. I've let you know everything!

More. Richard, you should go back to Cambridge; you're deteriorating.

Rich. Well, I'm not used . . . ! D'you know how much I have
    to show for seven months' work—

More. Work?

Rich. Work! Waiting's work when you wait as I wait,
    hard . . . ! For seven months, that's two hundred days,
    I have to show: the acquaintance of the Cardinal's
    outer doorman, the indifference of the Cardinal's
    inner doorman, and the Cardinal's chamberlain's hand
    in my chest . . . ! Oh—also one half of a Good Morning
    delivered at fifty paces by the Duke of Norfolk. Doubt-
    less he mistook me for someone.

More. He was very affable at dinner.

Rich. Oh, everyone's affable *here* . . . [*More is pleased.*]
    Also, of course, the friendship of Sir Thomas More.
    Or should I say acquaintance?

More. Say friendship.

Rich. Well, there! "A friend of Sir Thomas and still no office?
    There must be something wrong with him."

More. I thought we said friendship . . . [*He considers; then.*]
    The Dean of St. Paul's offers you a post; with a house,
    a servant and fifty pounds a year.

Rich. What? What post?

More. At the new school.

Rich [*bitterly disappointed*]. A teacher!

More. A man should go where he won't be tempted. Look,
    Richard, see this. [*He hands him a silver cup.*] Look . . .
    Look . . .

Rich. Beautiful.

More. Italian . . . Do you want it?

Rich. Why?

More. No joke; keep it; or sell it.

Rich. Well—Thank you, of course. Thank you! Thank you!
    But—

More. You'll sell it, won't you?

Rich. Well—I—Yes, I will.

More. And buy, what?

Rich [*with sudden ferocity*]. Some decent clothes!

More [*with sympathy*]. Ah.

Rich. I want a gown like yours.

More. You'll get several gowns for that I should think. It
    was sent to me a little while ago by some woman. Now
    she's put a lawsuit into the Court of Requests. It's a
    bribe, Richard.

Rich. Oh . . . [*Chagrined.*] So you give it away, of course.

More. Yes!

Rich. To me?

More. Well, I'm not going to keep it, and you need it. Of course—if you feel it's contaminated . . .

Rich. No, no. I'll risk it.

[*They both smile.*]

More. But, Richard, in office they offer you all sorts of things. I was once offered a whole village, with a mill, and a manor house, and heaven knows what else—a coat of arms, I shouldn't be surprised. Why not be a teacher? You'd be a fine teacher. Perhaps even a great one.

Rich. And if I was, who would know it?

More. You, your pupils, your friends, God. Not a bad public, that . . . Oh, and a *quiet* life.

Rich [*laughing*]. *You* say that!

More. Richard, I was commanded into office; it was inflicted on me . . . [*Rich regards him.*] Can't you believe that?

Rich. It's hard.

More [*grimly*]. Be a teacher.

Norfolk [*enters at the head of the stairs*]. It was magnificent!

Steward [*to audience*]. The Duke of Norfolk. Earl Marshal of England.

Norfolk. I tell you he stooped from the clouds! [*Breaks off; irritably.*] Alice!

[*Alice enters instantly at the head of the stairs.*]

Alice [*irritably*]. Here!

Steward [*to audience*]. Lady Alice. My master's wife.

Norfolk. I tell you he stooped—

Alice. He didn't—

Norfolk. Goddammit, he did—

Alice. Couldn't—

Norfolk. He *does*—

Alice. Not possible—

Norfolk. But *often*—

Alice. Never.

Norfolk. Well, damn my soul.

More [*to Margaret, who has appeared on the gallery*]. Come down, Meg.

Steward [*soapy; to audience*]. Lady Margaret, my master's daughter; lovely, really lovely.

Alice [*glances suspiciously at Steward*]. Matthew, get about your business. [*Steward exits.*] We'll settle this, my lord,

we'll put it to Thomas. Thomas, no falcon could stoop
     from a cloud, could it?

More. I don't know, my dear; it sounds unlikely. I have seen
     falcons do some very splendid things.

Alice. But how could he stoop from a cloud? He couldn't
     see where he was going.

Norfolk. You see, Alice—you're ignorant of the subject; a
     real falcon don't *care* where he's going! [*He takes some
     wine.*] Thank you, Thomas. Anyway, I'm talking to
     Meg. [*A sportsman's story.*] 'Twas the very first cast
     of the day, Meg; the sun was behind us. And from side
     to side of the valley like the roof of a tent was solid
     mist—

Alice. Oh, mist.

Norfolk. Well, mist is cloud, isn't it?

Alice. No.

Rich. The opinion of Aristotle is that mists are an exhalation
     of the earth whereas clouds—

Norfolk. He stooped five hundred feet! Like that! Like an
     Act of God, isn't he, Thomas?

More. He's tremendous.

Norfolk [*to Alice*]. Tremendous.

Margaret. Did he kill the heron?

Norfolk. Oh, the *heron* was *clever*. [*Very evidently discred-
     itable.*] It was a royal stoop though. [*Slyly.*] If you could
     ride, Alice, I'd show you.

Alice [*hotly*]. I can ride, my lord!

More. No, no, you'll make yourself ill.

Alice. And I'll bet—twenty-five—no, thirty shillings I see
     no falcon stoop from no cloud!

Norfolk. Done.

More. Alice—you can't ride with *them.*

Alice. God's body, Thomas, remember who you are. Am I
     a city wife?

More. No indeed, you've just lost thirty shillings, I think;
     there *are* such birds. And the heron got home to his
     chicks, Meg, so everything was satisfactory.

Margaret [*smiling*]. Yes.

More. What was that of Aristotle's, Richard?

Richard. Nothing, Sir Thomas—'twas out of place.

Norfolk [*to Rich*]. I've never found much use in Aristotle
     myself, not practically. Great philosopher, of course.
     Wonderful mind.

Rich. Exactly, Your Grace!

Norfolk [*suspicious*]. Eh?

More. Master Rich is newly converted to the doctrines of Machiavelli.

Rich. Oh *no* . . . !

Norfolk. Oh, the Italian. Nasty book, from what I hear.

Margaret. Very practical, Your Grace.

Norfolk. You read it? Amazing girl, Thomas, but where are you going to find a husband for her?

More [*More and Meg exchange a glance*]. Where indeed?

Rich. The doctrines of Machiavelli have been largely mistaken, I think; indeed, properly apprehended, he has no doctrine. Master Cromwell has the sense of it I think when he says—

Norfolk. You know Cromwell?

Rich. . . . Slightly, Your Grace.

Norfolk. The Cardinal's Secretary.

[*Exclamations of shock from More, Margaret and Alice.*]

Alice. Never—it can't be.

Margaret. The Cardinal's—it's impossible.

More. Not possible!

Norfolk. It's a fact.

More. When, Howard?

Norfolk. Two, three days.

[*They move about uneasily.*]

Alice. A *farrier's* son?

Norfolk. Well, the Cardinal's a butcher's son, isn't he?

Alice. It'll be up quick and down quick with Master Cromwell.

[*Norfolk grunts*]

More [*quietly*]. Did you know this?

Rich. No!

Margaret. Do you *like* Master Cromwell, Master Rich?

Alice. He's the only man in London if he does!

Rich. I think I do, Lady Alice!

More [*pleased*]. Good . . . Well, you don't need *my* help now.

Rich. Sir Thomas, if only you knew how much, much rather I'd yours than his!

[*Enter Steward, who gives a letter to More, who opens it and reads.*]

More. Talk of the Cardinal's Secretary and the Cardinal appears. He wants me. Now.

Alice. At this time of the night?

More [*mildly*]. The King's business.

Alice. The Queen's business.

Norfolk. More than likely, Alice, more than likely.

More [*cuts in sharply*]. What's the time?

Steward. Eleven o'clock, sir.

More. Is there a boat?

Steward. Waiting, sir.

More [*to Alice and Margaret*]. Go to bed. You'll excuse me, Your Grace? Richard? Now you'll go to bed . . .

[*The More family, as a matter of routine, put their hands together.*]

More, Alice, Margaret. Dear Lord, give us rest tonight, or if we must be wakeful, cheerful. Careful only for our soul's salvation. For Christ's sake. Amen.

More. And bless our Lord the King.

Alice and Margaret. And bless our Lord the King.

All. Amen.

[*And then immediately a brisk leave-taking: More moving off below, the others mounting the stairs.*]

More. Howard, are *you* at Richmond?

Norfolk. No, down the river.

More. Then good night! [*He sees Rich disconsolate.*] Oh, Your Grace, here's a young man desperate for employment. Something in the clerical line.

Norfolk. Well, if you recommend him.

More. No. I don't recommend him; but I point him out. [*Moving off.*] He's at the New Inn. Can you take him there?

Norfolk [*to Rich; mounting the stairs*]. All right, come on.

Rich. My Lord.

Norfolk. We'll hawk at Hounslow, Alice.

Alice. Wherever you like. [*Alice and Margaret follow Norfolk*]

Rich [*at foot of the stairs*]. Sir Thomas! . . . [*More turns.*] Thank you.

More. Be a teacher. [*Moving off again.*] Alice! The ground's hard at Hounslow!

Norfolk. Eh? [*Delighted roar.*] That's where the Cardinal crushed his bum!

More, Norfolk, Alice, Rich. Good night! Good night! [*They process off along the gallery.*]

More [*softly*]. Margaret.

Margaret. Yes?

More. Go to bed.

[*Margaret exits above, More exits below. After a moment*

Rich walks swiftly back, picks up the goblet and is going off with it.]

Steward [*takes goblet*]. Eh!

Rich. What—Oh . . . It's a gift, Matthew. Sir Thomas gave it to me. [*Steward regards it silently.*] He gave it to me.

Steward [*returns it*]. Very nice present, sir.

Rich [*beginning to leave with it*]. Yes. Good night, Matthew.

Steward. Sir Thomas has taken quite a fancy to you, sir.

Rich. Er, here— [*Gives him some money and goes.*]

Steward. Thank you, sir . . . [*To audience.*] That one'll come to nothing. [*Begins packing props into basket. Pauses with a cup in hand.*] My master Thomas More would give anything to anyone. Some say that's good and some say that's bad, but I say he can't help it—and that's bad . . . because some day someone's going to ask him for something that he wants to keep; and he'll be out of practice. [*Puts a cloth, papers, pen and ink, and candles on the table.*] There must be something that he wants to keep. That's only common sense.

[*Enter Wolsey. He sits at the table and immediately commences writing, watched by Common Man, who then exits. Enter More.*]

Wolsey [*writing*]. It's half-past one. Where've you been?

[*A bell strikes one.*]

More. One o'clock, Your Grace. I've been on the river.

[*Wolsey writes in silence while More waits standing.*]

Wolsey [*still writing, pushes paper across the table*]. Since you seemed so violently opposed to the dispatch for Rome, I thought you'd like to look it over.

More [*touched*]. Thank you, Your Grace.

Wolsey. Before it goes.

More [*smiles*]. Your Grace is very kind. [*He takes it and reads.*] Thank you.

Wolsey. Well, what d'you think of it? [*He is still writing.*]

More. It seems very well phrased, Your Grace.

Wolsey [*permits himself a chuckle*]. The devil it does! [*He sits back.*] And apart from the style, Sir Thomas?

More [*crisply*]. It's addressed to Cardinal Campeggio.

Wolsey. Yes?

More. Not to our ambassador.

Wolsey. Our ambassador's a ninny.

More [*a smile*]. Your Grace appointed him.

Wolsey [*treats it at the level of humor, mock exasperation*].

Yes I need a *ninny* in Rome! So that I can write to Cardinal Campeggio!

More [*won't respond; with aesthetic distaste—not moral disapproval*]. It's devious.

Wolsey. It's a devious situation!

More. There must be something simple in the middle of it. [*Again this is not a moral dictum; it is said rather wistfully, as something he is beginning to doubt.*]

Wolsey [*after a pause, rather gently.*] I believe you believe that. [*Briskly.*] You're a constant regret to me, Thomas. If you could just see facts flat on, without that horrible moral squint; with just a little common sense, you could have been a statesman.

More [*after a little pause*]. Oh, Your Grace flatters me.

Wolsey. Don't frivol . . . Thomas, are you going to help me?

More [*hesitates, looks away*]. If Your Grace will be specific.

Wolsey. Ach, you're a plodder! Take you altogether, Thomas, your scholarship, your experience, what are you? [*A single trumpet calls, distant, frosty and clear. Wolsey gets up and goes and looks from the window.*] Come here. [*More joins him.*] The King.

More. Yes.

Wolsey. Where has he been? D'you know?

More. I, Your Grace?

Wolsey. Oh, spare me your discretion. He's been to play in the mud again.

More [*coldly*]. Indeed.

Wolsey. Indeed! Indeed! Are you going to oppose me? [*Trumpet sounds again. Wolsey visibly relaxes.*] He's gone in . . . [*He leaves the window.*] All right, we'll plod. The King wants a son; what are you going to do about it?

More [*dry murmur*]. I'm very sure the King needs no advice from me on what to do about it.

Wolsey [*from behind, grips his shoulder fiercely*]. Thomas, we're alone. I give you my word. There's no one here.

More. I didn't suppose there was, Your Grace.

Wolsey. Oh. Sit down! [*He goes to the table, sits, signals More to sit. More unsuspectingly obeys. Then, deliberately loud.*] Do you favor a change of dynasty, Sir Thomas? D'you think two Tudors is sufficient?

More [*starting up in horrified alarm*]. For God's sake, Your Grace—

Wolsey. Then the King needs a son; I repeat, what are you going to do about it?

More [*steadily*]. I pray for it daily.

Wolsey [*softly*]. God's death, he means it . . . That thing out there's at least fertile, Thomas.

More. But she's not his wife.

Wolsey. No, Catherine's his wife and she's as barren as a brick. Are you going to pray for a miracle?

More. There *are* precedents.

Wolsey. Yes. All right. Good. Pray. Pray by all means. But in addition to prayer there is effort. My effort's to secure a divorce. Have I your support or have I not?

More [*sits*]. A dispensation was granted so that the King might marry Queen Catherine, for state reasons. Now we are to ask the Pope to—dispense with his dispensation, also for state reasons?

Wolsey. I don't *like* plodding, Thomas, don't make me plod longer than I have to—Well?

More. Then clearly all we have to do is approach His Holiness and ask him.

[*The pace becomes rapid.*]

Wolsey. I think we might influence His Holiness' answer—

More. Like this? [*Indicating the dispatch.*]

Wolsey. Like that and in other ways—

More. I've already expressed my opinion on this—

Wolsey. Then, good night! Oh, your conscience is your own affair; but you're a statesman! Do you *remember* the Yorkist Wars?

More. Very clearly.

Wolsey. Let him die without an heir and we'll have them back again. Let him die without an heir and this "peace" you think so much of will go out like that! [*He extinguishes the candle.*] Very well then . . . England needs an heir; certain measures, perhaps regrettable, perhaps not— [*Pompous.*] There is much in the Church that *needs* reformation, Thomas— [*More smiles.*] All right, regrettable! But necessary, to get us an heir! Now explain how you as Councilor of England can obstruct those measures for the sake of your own, private, conscience.

More. Well . . . I believe, when statesmen forsake their own private conscience for the sake of their public duties . . . they lead their country by a short route to chaos.

[*During this speech he relights the candle with another.*] And we shall have my prayers to fall back on.

Wolsey. You'd like that, wouldn't you? To govern the country by prayers?

More. Yes, I should.

Wolsey. I'd like to be there when you try. Who *will?* [*He half lifts the chain from his shoulders.*] Who will put his neck in this—after me? You? Tunstall? Suffolk?

More. Tunstall for me.

Wolsey. Aye, but for the King. What about my Secretary, Master Cromwell?

More. Cromwell!

Wolsey. You'd rather do it yourself?

More. Me rather than Cromwell.

Wolsey. Then come down to earth, Thomas. [*He looks away.*] And until you do, bear in mind you have an enemy!

More [*wishing to make sure, quietly*]. Where, Your Grace?

Wolsey [*looks back at him, hard-faced, harsh; for the first time we see this is a carnivore*]. Here, Thomas.

More. As Your Grace pleases.

Wolsey. As God wills!

More. Perhaps, Your Grace. [*Mounting stairs.*]

Wolsey. More! You should have been a cleric!

More [*amused, looking down from gallery.*] Like yourself, Your Grace?

[*Exit More. Wolsey is left staring, then exits through the lower arches with candle, taking most of the light from the stage as he does so. But the whole rear of the stage is now patterned with webbed reflections thrown from brightly moonlit water, so that the structure is thrown into black relief, while a strip of light descends along the front of the stage, which is to be the acting area for the next scene. An oar and a bundle of clothing are lowered into this area from above. Enter Common Man; he unties the bundle and begins to don the coat and hat of Boatman.*]

More [*off*]. Boat! Boat! [*Approaching.*] Boat!

Boatman [*donning coat and hat*]. Here, sir!

More [*off*]. A boatman please!

Boatman. Boat here, sir! [*He seizes the oar. Enter More.*]

More [*peering*]. Boatman?

Boatman. Yes, sir. [*To audience, indicating oar.*] A boatman.

More. Take me home.

Boatman [*pleasantly*]. I was just going home myself, sir.

More. Then find me another boat.

Boatman. Bless you, sir—that's all right. [*Comfortably.*] I expect you'll make it worth my while, sir.

Cromwell [*stepping from behind an arch*]. Boatman, have you a license?

Boatman. Eh? Bless you, sir, yes; I've got a license.

Cromwell. Then you know that the fares are fixed—[*Turns to More. Exaggerated pleasure.*] Why, it's Sir Thomas!

More. Good morning, Master Cromwell. You work very late.

Cromwell. I'm on my way to the Cardinal.

More [*recollecting*]. Ah yes, you are to be felicitated. Good morning, Master *Secretary*. [*He smiles politely.*]

Cromwell [*smiling*]. Yes.

More. If it *is* felicity to be busy in the night.

Cromwell. It is.

More. Felicitations then.

[*They exchange a dry little bow.*]

Cromwell. You have just left him, I think.

More. Yes, I have.

Cromwell. You left him . . . in his laughing mood, I hope?

More. On the whole I would say not. No, not laughing.

Cromwell. Oh, I'm sorry. [*Backing to exit.*] I am one of your *multitudinous* admirers, Sir, Thomas. A penny ha'penny to Chelsea, Boatman. [*Exit Cromwell.*]

Boatman. The coming man they say, sir.

More. Do they? Well, where's your boat?

Boatman. Just along the wharf, sir.

[*They are going when Chapuys and his Attendant enter.*]

Chapuys. Sir Thomas More!

More. Signor Chapuys? You're up very late, Your Excellency.

Chapuys [*significantly*]. So is the Cardinal, Sir Thomas.

More [*closing up*]. He sleeps very little.

Chapuys. You have just left him, I think.

More. You are correctly informed. As always.

Chapuys. I will not ask you the subject of your conversation . . . [*He waits.*]

More. No, of course not.

Chapuys. Sir Thomas, I will be plain with you . . . plain, that is, so far as the diplomatic decencies permit. [*Loudly.*] My master Charles, the King of Spain! [*Pulls More aside; discreetly.*] My master Charles, the King of Spain, feels himself concerned in anything concerning his blood relations. He would feel himself insulted by any insult offered to his mother's sister! I refer, of course, to Queen Catherine. [*He regards More keenly.*] The King of Spain would feel himself insulted by any insult offered to Queen Catherine.

More. His feeling would be natural.

Chapuys [*consciously shy*]. Sir Thomas, may I ask if you and the Cardinal parted, how shall I say, amicably?

More. Amicably . . . Yes.

Chapuys [*a shade indignant*]. In agreement?

More. Amicably.

Chapuys [*warmly*]. Say no more, Sir Thomas; I understand.

More [*a bit worried*]. I hope you do, Your Excellency.

Chapuys. You are a good man.

More. I don't see how you deduce that from what I told you.

Chapuys [*holds up a hand*]. A nod is as good as a wink to a blind horse. I understand. You are a good man. [*He turns to exit.*] Dominus vobiscum. [*Chapuys exits. More looks after him.*]

More [*abstracted*]. . . . spiritu tuo . . .

Boatman [*mournful; he is squatting on the ground*]. Some people think boats stay afloat on their own, sir, but they don't; they cost money. [*More is abstractedly gazing over the audience.*] Take anchor rope, sir, you may not believe me, for a little skiff like mine, but it's a penny a fathom. [*More is still abstracted.*] And with a young wife, sir, as your know . . .

More [*abstracted*]. I'll pay what I always pay you . . . The river looks very black tonight. They say it's silting up, is that so?

Boatman [*joining him*]. Not in the middle, sir. There's a channel there getting deeper all the time.

More. How is your wife?

Boatman. She's losing her shape, sir, losing it fast.

More. Well, so are we all.

Boatman. Oh yes, sir; it's common.

More [*going*]. Well, take me home. [*Exit More.*]

Boatman. That I will, sir! [*Crossing to the basket and pulling it out.*] From Richmond to Chelsea, a penny halfpenny . . . [*He goes for the tablecloth.*] From Chelsea to Richmond, a penny halfpenny. From Richmond to Chelsea, it's a quiet float downstream, from Chelsea to Richmond, it's a hard pull upstream. And it's a penny halfpenny either way. Whoever makes the regulations doesn't row a boat. [*Puts the cloth into the basket, takes out slippers.*] Home again.

[*Lighting changes to More's house. More enters, sits wearily. He takes off hat, half takes off coat but is too tired. A bell chimes three. Steward kneels to put on his slippers for him.*]

More. Ah, Matthew . . . Is Lady Alice in bed?

Steward. Yes, sir.

More. Lady Margaret?

Steward. No, sir. Master Roper's here.

More [*surprised*]. At this hour? . . . Who let him in?

Steward. He's a hard man to keep out, sir.

More. Where are they?

[*Margaret and Roper enter.*]

Margaret. Here, Father.

More. Thank you, Matthew. [*Steward exits. More, regarding them; resignedly.*] Good morning, William. It's a little early for breakfast.

Roper [*stolidly*]. I haven't come for breakfast, sir.

[*More looks at him and sighs.*]

Margaret. Will wants to marry me, Father.

More. Well, he can't marry you.

Roper. Sir Thomas, I'm to be called to the Bar.

More [*warmly*]. Oh, congratulations, Roper!

Roper. My family may not be at the palace, sir, but in the City—

More. The Ropers were advocates when the Mores were selling pewters; there's nothing wrong with your family. There's nothing wrong with your fortune—there's nothing wrong with you—[*sourly*] except you need a clock—

Roper. I can buy a clock, sir.

More. Roper, the answer's "no." [*Firmly.*] And will be "no" so long as you're a heretic.

Roper [*firing*]. That's a word I don't like, Sir Thomas!

More. It's not a likable word. [*Coming to life.*] It's not a likable thing!

[*Margaret is alarmed, and from behind More tries to silence Roper.*]

Roper. The Church is heretical! Doctor Luther's proved that to my satisfaction!

More. Luther's an excommunicate.

Roper. From a heretic Church! Church? It's a shop—Forgiveness by the florin! Job lots now in Germany! . . . Mmmm, and divorces.

More [*expressionless*]. Divorces?

Roper. Ah, half England's buzzing with that.

More. "Half England." The Inns of Court may be buzzing, England doesn't buzz so easily.

Roper. It will. And is that a Church? Is that a Cardinal? Is that a Pope? Or Antichrist! [*More looks up angrily. Margaret signals frantically.*] Look, what I know I'll say!

Margaret. You've no sense of the *place!*

More [*rueful*]. He's no sense of the time.

Roper. I—

[*But More gently holds up his hand and he stops.*]

More. Listen, Roper. Two years ago you were a passionate Churchman; now you're a passionate—Lutheran. We must just pray that when your head's finished turning, your face is to the front again.

Roper. Don't lengthen your prayers with *me*, sir!

More. Oh, one more or less . . . Is your horse here?

Roper. No, I walked.

More. Well, take a horse from the stables and get back home.

[*Roper hesitates.*] Go along.

Roper. May I come again?

[*More indicates Margaret.*]

Margaret. Yes. Soon.

Roper. Good night, sir. [*Roper exits.*]

Margaret. Is that final, Father?

More. As long as he's a heretic, Meg, that's absolute. [*Warmly.*] Nice boy . . . Terribly strong principles though. I thought I told you to go to bed.

Margaret. Yes, why?

More [*lightly*]. Because I intended you to *go* to bed. You're very pensive.

Margaret. You're very gay. Did the Cardinal talk about the divorce?

More. Mm? You know I think we've been on the wrong track with Will—It's no good arguing with a Roper—

Margaret. Father, did he?

More. Old Roper was just the same. Now let him think he's going *with* the current and he'll turn round and start swimming in the opposite direction. What we want is a really substantial attack on the Church.

Margaret. We're going to get it, aren't we?

More. Margaret, I'll not have you talk treason . . . And I'll
    not have you repeat lawyer's gossip. I'm a lawyer my-
    self and I know what it's worth.

Alice [*off. Indignant and excited*]. Thomas!

More. Now look what you've done.

[*Alice enters at the head of the stairs in her nightgown.*]

Alice. Young Roper! I've just seen young Roper! On *my*
    horse.

More. He'll bring it back, dear. He's been to see Margaret.

Alice. Oh—why you don't beat that girl!

More. No, no, she's full of education—and it's a delicate
    commodity.

Alice. Mm! And more's the pity!

More. Yes, but it's there now and think what it cost. [*He
    sneezes.*]

Alice [*pouncing*]. Ah! Margaret—hot water.

[*Exit Margaret.*]

More. I'm sorry you were awakened, chick.

Alice. I wasn't sleeping very deeply. Thomas—what did
    Wolsey want?

More [*innocently*]. Young Roper asked me for Margaret.

Alice. What! Impudence!

More. Yes, wasn't it?

Alice. Old fox! What did he want, Thomas?

More. He wanted me to read a dispatch.

Alice. Was that all?

More. A Latin dispatch.

Alice. Oh! You don't want to talk about it?

More [*gently*]. No.

[*Enter Margaret with a cup, which she takes to More.*]

Alice. Norfolk was speaking for you as Chancellor before
    he left.

More. He's a dangerous friend then. Wolsey's Chancellor,
    God help him. We don't want another. [*Margaret takes
    the cup to him; he sniffs it.*] I don't want this.

Alice. Drink it. Great men get colds in the head just the same
    as commoners.

More. That's dangerous, leveling talk, Alice. Beware of the
    Tower.

Alice. Drink it!

More [*rises*]. I will, I'll drink it in bed.

[*They move to the stairs and ascend, talking.*]

Margaret. Would you want to be Chancellor?

More. No.

Margaret. That's what I said. But Norfolk said if Wolsey fell—

More [*no longer flippant*]. If Wolsey fell, the splash would swamp a few small boats like ours. There will be no new Chancellors while Wolsey lives.

[*They exit above. The light is dimmed there and a bright spot descends below. Into this bright circle is thrown a great red robe and the Cardinal's hat. The Common Man enters and roughly piles them into his basket. He then takes from his pocket a pair of spectacles and from the basket a book.*]

Common Man [*reading*]. "Whether we follow tradition in ascribing Wolsey's death to a broken heart, or accept Professor Larcomb's less feeling diagnosis of pulmonary pneumonia, its effective cause was the King's displeasure. He died at Leicester on 29 November, 1530, while on his way to the Tower under charge of High Treason.

"England's next Lord Chancellor was Sir Thomas More, a scholar and, by popular repute, a saint. His scholarship is supported by his writings; saintliness is a quality less easy to establish. But from his willful indifference to realities which were obvious to quite ordinary contemporaries, it seems all too probable that he had it." [*Exit Common Man. As he goes, lights come up and a screen is lowered depicting Hampton Court. Cromwell is sitting halfway up the stairs. Rich enters.*]

Cromwell. Rich! [*Rich stops, sees him, and smiles willingly.*] What brings you to Hampton?

Rich. I came with the Duke last night, Master Cromwell. They're hunting again.

Cromwell. It's a kingly pastime, Master Rich. [*Both smile.*] I'm glad you found employment. You're the Duke's Secretary, are you not?

Rich [*flustered*]. My work is mostly secretarial.

Cromwell [*as if making an effort of memory*]. Or is it his librarian you are?

Rich. I do look after His Grace's library, yes.

Cromwell. Oh. Well, that's something. And I don't suppose you're bothered much by His Grace—in the library? [*Rich smiles uncertainly.*] It's odd how differently men's fortunes flow. My late master, Wolsey, died in disgrace, and here I am in the King's own service. There you are in a *comparative* backwater—yet the new Lord Chancellor's an old friend of yours. [*He looks at Rich directly.*]

Rich [*uncertain*]. He isn't really my *friend.* . . .

Cromwell. Oh, I thought he was. [*He gets up, prepares to go.*]

Rich. In a sense he is.

Cromwell [*reproachful*]. Well, I always understood he set you up in life.

Rich. He recommended me to the Duke.

Cromwell. Ah yes. Are you very attached to His Grace's library, or would you be free to accept an office?

Rich [*suspicious*]. Have you offices in gift?

Cromwell [*deprecating*]. I am listened to by those who have.

Rich. Master Cromwell—what *is* it that you do for the King?

[*Enter Chapuys.*]

Chapuys [*roguish*]. Yes, *I* should like to know that, Master Cromwell.

Cromwell. Ah, Signor Chapuys. You've met His Excellency, Rich? [*He indicates Chapuys.*] The Spanish Ambassador. [*He indicates Rich.*] The Duke of Norfolk's librarian.

Chapuys. But how should we introduce *you*, Master Cromwell, if we had the happiness?

Cromwell. Oh, sly! Do you notice how sly he is, Rich? Well, I suppose you would call me [*he suddenly turns*] "The King's Ear" . . . [*A deprecating shrug.*] It's a useful organ, the ear. But in fact it's even simpler than that. When the King wants something done, I do it.

Chapuys. Ah. [*Mock interest.*] But then why these Justices, Chancellors, Admirals?

Cromwell. Oh, *they* are the constitution. Our ancient, English constitution. I merely do things.

Chapuys. For example, Master Cromwell. . . .

Cromwell [*admiring*]. O-oh—beware these professional diplomats. Well now, for example; next week at Deptford we are launching the *Great Harry*—one thousand tons, four masts, sixty-six guns, and overall length of one hundred and seventy-five feet; it's expected to be very effective—all this you probably know. However, you may not know that the King himself will guide her down the river; yes, the King himself will be her pilot. He will have assistance, of course, but he himself will be her pilot. He will have a pilot's whistle upon which he will blow, and he will wear in every respect a common pilot's uniform. Except for the material, which will be cloth of gold. These innocent fancies require more preparation than you might suppose and someone has to do it. [*He spreads his hands.*] Meanwhile, I do prepare myself for higher things. I stock my mind.

Chapuys. Alas, Master Cromwell, don't we all? This ship for instance—it has fifty-six guns by the way, not sixty-six and only forty of them heavy. After the launching, I understand, the King will take his barge to Chelsea.

[*Cromwell's face darkens during this speech.*]

Cromwell [*sharply*]. Yes—

Chapuys. To—

Cromwell. Sir Thomas More's.

Chapuys [*sweetly*]. Will you be there?

Cromwell. Oh no—they'll talk about the divorce. [*It is Chapuys' turn to be shocked. Rich draws away uneasily.*] The King will ask him for an answer.

Chapuys [*ruffled*]. He has given his answer!

Cromwell. The King will ask him for another.

Chapuys. Sir Thomas is a good son of the Church!

Cromwell. Sir Thomas is a man.

[*Enter Steward. Both Cromwell and Chapuys look towards him sharply, then back at one another.*]

Chapuys [*innocently*]. Isn't that his Steward now?

Cromwell. I believe it is. Well, good day, Your Excellency.

Chapuys [*eagerly*]. Good day, Master Cromwell. [*He expects him to go.*]

Cromwell [*standing firm*]. Good day.

[*And Chapuys has to go. Cromwell walks aside with furtive and urgent beckonings to Steward to follow. Rich follows but hangs off. Meanwhile Chapuys and his Attendant have gone behind screen, beneath which their legs protrude clearly.*]

Steward [*conspiratorially*]. Sir, Sir Thomas doesn't talk about it. [*He waits but Cromwell remains stony.*] He doesn't talk about it to his wife, sir. [*He waits again.*]

Cromwell. This is worth nothing.

Steward [*significantly*]. But he doesn't talk about it to Lady Margaret—that's his daughter, sir.

Cromwell. So?

Steward. So he's worried, sir . . . [*Cromwell is interested.*] Frightened . . . [*Cromwell takes out a coin but pauses suspiciously*.] Sir, he goes *white* when it's mentioned!

Cromwell [*hands him the coin*]. All right.

Steward [*looks at the coin; reproachfully*]. Oh, *sir!*

Cromwell [*waves him away*]. Are you coming in my direction, Rich?

Rich [*still hanging off*]. No no.

Cromwell. I think you should, you know.

Rich. *I* can't tell you anything!

[*Exit Cromwell and Rich in separate directions. Chapuys and Attendant come from behind screen.*]

Chapuys [*beckons Steward*]. Well?

Steward. Sir Thomas rises at six, sir, and prays for an hour and a half.

Chapuys. Yes?

Steward. During Lent, sir, he lived entirely on bread and water.

Chapuys. Yes?

Steward. He goes to confession twice a week, sir. Parish priest. Dominican.

Chapuys. Ah. He is a true son of the Church.

Steward [*soapy*.] That he is, sir.

Chapuys. What did Master Cromwell want?

Steward. Same as you, sir.

Chapuys. No man can serve two masters, Steward.

Steward. No indeed, sir; I serve *one*. [*He pulls to the front an enormous cross until then hanging at his back on a length of string—a caricature of the ebony cross worn by Chapuys*.]

Chapuys. Good, simple man. Here. [*Gives him a coin. Going.*] Peace be with you.

Steward. And with you, sir.

Chapuys. Our Lord watch you.

Steward. You too, sir. [*Exit Chapuys and Attendant.*] That's a very religious man.

[*Enter Rich.*]

Rich. Matthew! What does Signor Chapuys want?

Steward. I've no idea, sir.

Rich [*gives him a coin*]. What did you tell him?

Steward. I told him that Sir Thomas says his prayers and goes to confession.

Rich. Why that?

Steward. That's what he wanted to know, sir. I mean I could have told him any number of things about Sir Thomas —that he has rheumatism, prefers red wine to white, is easily seasick, fond of kippers, afraid of drowning. But that's what he wanted to know, sir.

Rich. What did he say?

Steward. He said that Sir Thomas is a good churchman, sir.

Rich [*going*]. Well, that's true, isn't it?

Steward. I'm just telling you what he said, sir. Oh, uh, Master Cromwell went that way, sir.

Rich [*furious*]. Did I ask you which way Master Cromwell went? [*Rich exits in opposite direction.*]

Steward [*to audience, thoughtfully*]. The great thing's not to get out of your depth . . . What I can tell them's common knowledge! But now they've given money for it and everyone wants value for his money. They'll make a secret of it now to prove they've not been bilked . . . They'll make it a secret by making it dangerous . . . Mm . . . Oh, when I can't touch the bottom I'll go deaf, blind and dumb. [*He holds out coins.*] And that's more than I *earn* in a fortnight!

[*A fanfare of trumpets; the rear of the stage becomes a source of glittering blue light; Hampton Court is hoisted out of sight, and a rosebay is lowered. As the fanfare ceases, Norfolk, Alice, Margaret, erupt onto the stage.*]

Alice [*with chain of office which she puts on table. Distressed*]. No sign of him, my lord!

Norfolk. God's body, Alice, he must be found.

Alice [*to Meg*]. He *must* be in the house!

Margaret. He's *not* in the house, Mother!

Alice. Then he must be here in the garden!

[*They "search" among the screens.*]

Norfolk. He takes things too far, Alice.

Alice. Do I not know it?

Norfolk. It will end badly for him!

Alice. I know that too!

[*They "notice" the Steward.*]

Norfolk. Where's your master?

Margaret. Matthew! Where's my father? } [*Together.*]

Alice. Where is Sir Thomas?

[*Fanfare, shorter but nearer.*]

Norfolk [*despairing*]. Oh, my God.

Alice. Oh, Jesus!

Steward. My lady—the King?

Norfolk. Yes, fool! [*Threatening.*] And if the King arrives and the Chancellor's not here—

Steward. Sir, my lady, it's not *my* fault!

Norfolk [*quietly displeased*]. Lady Alice, Thomas'll get no good of it. This is not how Wolsey made himself great.

Alice [*stiffly*]. Thomas has his own way of doing things, my lord!

Norfolk [*testily*]. Yes yes, Thomas is unique; but where *is* Thomas?

[*Steward swings onstage a small Gothic door. Plainsong is heard. All run to the door. Norfolk opens it.*]

Alice. Thomas!

Steward. Sir!

Margaret. Father!

Norfolk [*indignantly*]. My Lord Chancellor! [*More enters through the doorway. He blinks in the light. He is wearing a cassock; he shuts the door behind him.*] What sort of fooling is this? Does the King visit you every day?

More. No, but I go to vespers most days.

Norfolk. He's here!

More. But isn't this visit *meant* to be a surprise?

Norfolk [*grimly*]. For you, yes, not for him.

Margaret. Father . . . [*She indicates his cassock.*]

Norfolk. Yes—d'you propose to meet the King disguised as a parish clerk? [*They fall upon him to drag the cassock over his head.*] A parish clerk, my Lord Chancellor! You dishonor the King and his office!

More [*appearing momentarily from the folds of the cassock*]. The service of God is not a dishonor to any office. [*The cassock is pulled off.*] Believe me, my friend, I do not belittle the honor His Majesty is doing me. [*Briskly.*] Well! That's a lovely dress, Alice; so's that, Margaret. [*He looks at Norfolk.*] I'm a dowdy bird, aren't I? [*Looks at Alice.*] Calm yourself. [*Steward swings the door offstage.*] Alice, we're all ready now. [*He turns about and we see that his gown is caught up behind him revealing his spindly legs in long hose laced up at the thighs.*]

Alice. Thomas!

[*Margaret laughs.*]

More. What's the matter? [*He turns around again and his womenfolk pursue him to pull down the gown while Norfolk throws his hands in the air. Expostulation, explanation, exclamation overlap in a babble.*]

Norfolk. By God, you can be harebrained!

Margaret. Be still!

Alice. Oh, Thomas! Thomas!

[*Margaret spies chain of office, brings it to More.*]

Norfolk. What whim possessed you—

More. 'Twas not a whim!

Alice. Your second-best stockings!

Margaret [*offering the chain*]. Father—

More [*refusing*]. No, no, no, no—

Norfolk. Oh, enough's enough!

More. Haven't you done—

[*Fanfare—at the end of which Henry, in a cloth of gold, runs out of the sunlight halfway down the steps and blows a blast on his pilot's whistle. All kneel. In the silence he descends slowly to their level, blowing softly.*]

More. Your Majesty does my house more honor than I fear my household can bear.

Henry. No ceremony, Thomas! No ceremony! [*They rise.*] A passing fancy—I happened to be on the river. [*Holds out a shoe, proudly.*] Look, mud.

More. We do it in better style, Your Grace, when we come by the road.

Henry. Oh, the road! There's the road for me, Thomas, the river; *my* river . . . By heaven, what an evening! Lady Alice, I fear we come upon you unexpectedly.

Alice [*shocked*]. Oh no, Your Grace—[*remembering*] that is yes, but we are ready for you—ready to entertain Your Grace, that is.

More. This is my daughter Margaret, sir. She has not had the honor to meet Your Grace.

[*She curtsies low.*]

Henry [*looking her over*]. Why, Margaret, they told me you were a scholar.

[*Margaret is confused.*]

More. Answer, Margaret.

Margaret. Among women I pass for one, Your Grace.

[*Norfolk and Alice exchange approving glances.*]

Henry. Antiquone modo Latine loqueris, an Oxoniensi?

(Is your Latin the old Latin, or Oxford Latin?)

Margaret. Quem me docuit pater, Domine.

(My father's Latin, Sire.)

Henry. Bene. Optimus est. Graecamne linguam quoque te docuit?

(Good. That is the best. And has he taught you Greek too?)

Margaret. Graecam me docuit non pater meus sed mei

patris amicus, Johannes Coletus, Sancti Pauli Decanus.
In litteris Graecis tamen, non minus quam Latinis, ars
magistri minuitur discipuli stultitia.
(Not my father, Sire, but my father's friend, John
Colet, Dean of St. Paul's. But it is with the Greek as
it is with the Latin; the skill of the master is lost in
the pupil's lack of it.) [*Her Latin is better than his; he
is not altogether pleased.*]

Henry. Ho! [*He walks away from her, talking; she begins
to rise from her curtsy; More gently presses her down
again before King Henry turns.*] Take care, Thomas:
"too much learning is a weariness of the flesh, and
there is no end to the making of books." [*Back to Margaret.*] Can you dance, too?

Margaret. Not well, Your Grace.

Henry. Well, *I* dance superlatively! [*He plants his leg before
her face.*] That's a dancer's *leg,* Margaret! [*She has the
wit to look straight up and smile at him. All good
humor, he pulls her to her feet, sees Norfolk grinning
the grin of a comrade.*] Hey, Norfolk? [*Indicates Norfolk's leg with much distaste.*] Now *that's* a wrestler's
leg. But I can throw him. [*Seizes Norfolk.*] Shall I show
them, Howard? [*Norfolk is alarmed for his dignity. To
Margaret.*] Shall I?

Margaret [*looking at Norfolk; gently*]. No, Your Grace.

Henry [*releases Norfolk; seriously*]. You are gentle. [*To
More, approvingly.*] That's good. [*To Margaret.*] You
shall read to me. [*Margaret is about to demur.*] No no,
you shall read to me. Lady Alice, the river's given me
an appetite.

Alice. If Your Grace would share a very simple supper.

Henry. It would please me to. [*Preparing to lead off, sees
Margaret again.*] I'm something of a scholar too, Margaret, did you know?

Margaret. All the world knows Your Grace's book, asserting the seven sacraments of the Church.

Henry. Ah yes. Between ourselves, your father had a hand
in that; eh, Thomas?

More. Here and there, Your Grace. In a minor capacity.

Henry [*looking at him*]. He seeks to shame me with his
modesty . . . [*Turns to Alice.*] On second thought we'll
follow, Lady Alice, Thomas and I will follow. [*He
waves them off. They bow, withdraw to the steps and*

start up.] Wait! [*Raises whistle to lips.*] Margaret, are
you fond of music?

Margaret. Yes, Your Grace.

Henry [*beckons her to him; holds out whistle*]. Blow. [*She
is uncertain.*] Blow. [*She does.*] Louder! [*She does and
at once music is heard without, stately and oversweet.
Expressions of pleasure all around.*] I brought them
with me, Lady Alice; take them in! [*Exit all but More
and Henry. The music begins to recede.*] Listen to this,
Thomas. [*He walks about, the auditor, beating time.*]
Do you know it?

More. No, Your Grace, I—

Henry. Sh! [*More is silent; Henry goes on with his listening.*]
. . . I launched a ship today, Thomas.

More. Yes, Your Grace, I—

Henry. Listen, man, listen . . . [*A pause.*] . . . The *Great
Harry* . . . I steered her, Thomas, under sail.

More. You have many accomplishments, Your Grace.

Henry [*holds up a finger for silence. A pause*]. A great experience. [*More keeps silent.*] . . . A great experience,
Thomas.

More. Yes, Your Grace.

[*The music is growing fainter.*]

Henry. I am a fool.

More. How so, Your Grace?

Henry [*a pause, during which the music fades to silence*].
What else but a fool to live in a Court, in a licentious
mob—when I have friends, with gardens.

More. Your Grace—

Henry. No courtship, no ceremony, Thomas. Be seated. You
are my friend, are you not?

[*More sits.*]

More. Your Majesty.

Henry [*eyes lighting on the chain on the table by More*].
And thank God I have a friend for my Chancellor.
[*Laughingly, but implacably, he takes up the chain and
lowers it over More's head.*] Readier to be friends, I
trust, than he was to be Chancellor.

More. My own knowledge of my poor abilities—

Henry. I will judge of your abilities, Thomas . . . Did you
know that Wolsey named you for Chancellor?

More. Wolsey!

Henry. Aye, before he died. Wolsey named you and Wolsey
was no fool.

More. He was a statesman of incomparable ability, Your
　　Grace.

Henry. Was he? Was he so? [*He rises.*] Then why did he
　　fail me? Be seated—it was villainy then! Yes, villainy.
　　I was right to break him; he was all pride, Thomas; a
　　proud man; pride right through. And he failed me!
　　[*More opens his mouth.*] He failed me in the one thing
　　that mattered! The one thing that matters, Thomas,
　　then or now. And why? He wanted to be Pope! Yes,
　　he wanted to be the Bishop of Rome. I'll tell you some-
　　thing, Thomas, and you can check this for yourself—
　　it was never merry in England while we had Cardinals
　　amongst us. [*He nods significantly at More, who lowers
　　his eyes.*] But look now—[*Walking away.*]—I shall for-
　　get the feel of that . . . great tiller under my hands . . .
　　I took her down to Dogget's Bank, went about and
　　brought her up in Tilbury Roads. A man could sail
　　clean round the world in that ship.

More [*with affectionate admiration*]. Some men could, Your
　　Grace.

Henry [*offhand*]. Touching this matter of my divorce,
　　Thomas: have you thought of it since we last talked?

More. Of little else.

Henry. Then you see your way clear to me?

More. That you should put away Queen Catherine, Sire?
　　Oh, alas [*he thumps the chair in distress*] as I think of it
　　I see so clearly that I can *not* come with Your Grace
　　that my endeavor is not to think of it at all.

Henry. Then you have not thought enough . . . ! [*With real
　　appeal.*] Great God, Thomas, why do you hold out
　　against me in the desire of my heart—the very wick
　　of my heart?

More [*draws up his sleeve, baring his arm*]. There is my
　　right arm. [*A practical proposition.*] Take your dagger
　　and saw it from my shoulder, and I will laugh and be
　　thankful, if by that means I can come with Your Grace
　　with a clear conscience.

Henry [*uncomfortably pulls at the sleeve*]. I know it, Thomas,
　　I know. . . .

More [*rises, formally*]. I crave pardon if I offend.

Henry [*suspiciously*]. Speak then.

More. When I took the Great Seal your Majesty promised
　　not to pursue me on this matter.

Henry. Ha! So I break my word, Master More! No no, I'm

joking . . . I joke roughly . . . [*He wanders away.*] I often think I'm a rough fellow . . . Yes, a rough young fellow. [*He shakes his head indulgently.*] Be seated . . . That's a rosebay. We have one like it at Hampton—not so red as that though. Ha—I'm in an excellent frame of mind. [*Glances at the rosebay.*] Beautiful. [*Reasonable, pleasant.*] You must consider, Thomas, that I stand in peril of my soul. It was no marriage; she was my brother's widow. Leviticus: "Thou shalt not uncover the nakedness of thy brother's wife." Leviticus, Chapter Eighteen, Verse Sixteen.

More. Yes, Your Grace. But Deuteronomy—

Henry [*triumphant*]. Deuteronomy's ambiguous!

More [*bursting out*]. Your Grace, I'm not fit to meddle in these matters—to me it seems a matter for the Holy See—

Henry [*reprovingly*]. Thomas, Thomas, does a man need a Pope to tell him when he's sinned? It was a sin, Thomas; I admit it; I repent. And God has punished me; I have no son . . . Son after son she's borne me, Thomas, all dead at birth, or dead within the month; I never saw the hand of God so clear in anything . . . I have a daughter, she's a good child, a well-set child—But I have no son. [*He flares up.*] It is my bounden *duty* to put away the Queen, and all the Popes back to St. Peter shall not come between me and my duty! How is it that you cannot see? Everyone else does.

More [*eagerly*]. Then why does Your Grace need my poor support?

Henry. Because you are honest. What's more to the purpose, you're known to be honest . . . There are those like Norfolk who follow me because I wear the crown, and there are those like Master Cromwell who follow me because they are jackals with sharp teeth and I am their lion, and there is a mass that follows me because it follows anything that moves—and there is you.

More. I am sick to think how much I must displease Your Grace.

Henry. No, Thomas, I respect your sincerity. Respect? Oh, man, it's water in the desert . . . How did you like our music? That air they played, it had a certain—well, tell me what you thought of it.

More [*relieved at this turn; smiling*]. Could it have been Your Grace's own?

Henry [*smiles back*]. Discovered! Now I'll never know your
   true opinion. And that's irksome, Thomas, for we artists, though we love praise, yet we love truth better.
More [*mildly*]. Then I will tell Your Grace truly what I
   thought of it.
Henry [*a little disconcerted*]. Speak then.
More. To me it seemed—delightful.
Henry. Thomas—I chose the right man for Chancellor.
More. I must in fairness add that my taste in music is reput-
   edly deplorable.
Henry. Your taste in music is excellent. It exactly coincides
   with my own. Ah music! Music! Send them back
   without me, Thomas; I will live here in Chelsea and
   make music.
More. My house is at Your Grace's disposal.
Henry. Thomas, you understand me; we will stay here to-
   gether and make music.
More. Will Your Grace honor my roof after dinner?
Henry [*walking away, blowing moodily on his whistle*]. Mm?
   Yes, I expect I'll bellow for you. . . .
More. My wife will be more—
Henry. Yes, yes. [*He turns, his face set.*] Touching this other
   business, mark you, Thomas, I'll have no opposition.
More [*sadly*]. Your Grace?
Henry. No opposition, I say! No opposition! Your con-
   science is your own affair; but you are my Chancellor!
   There, you have my word—I'll leave you out of it. But
   I don't take it kindly, Thomas, and I'll have no opposi-
   tion! I see how it will be; the bishops will oppose me.
   The full-fed, hypocritical "Princes of the *Church*"! Ha!
   As for the Pope! Am I to burn in Hell because the
   Bishop of Rome, with the King of Spain's knife to his
   throat, mouths me Deuteronomy? Hypocrites! They're
   all hypocrites! Mind they do not take you in, Thomas!
   Lie low if you will, but I'll brook no opposition—no
   noise! No words, no signs, no letters, no pamphlets—
   Mind that, Thomas—no writings against me!
More. Your Grace is unjust. I am Your Grace's loyal minister. If I cannot serve Your Grace in this great matter
   of the Queen—
Henry. I have no Queen! Catherine is not my wife and no
   priest can make her so, and they that say she is my
   wife are not only liars . . . but traitors! Mind it, Thomas!

More. Am I a babbler, Your Grace? [*But his voice is un-steady.*]

Henry. You are stubborn . . . [*Wooingly.*] If you could come with me, you are the man I would soonest raise—yes, with my own hand.

More [*covers his face*]. Oh, Your Grace overwhelms me!

[*A complicated chiming of little bells is heard.*]

Henry. What's that?

More. Eight o'clock, Your Grace.

Henry [*uneasily eying More*]. Oh, lift yourself up, man—have I not promised? [*More braces.*] Shall we eat?

More. If Your Grace pleases. [*Recovering.*] What will Your Grace sing for us?

Henry. Eight o'clock you said? Thomas, the tide will be changing. I was forgetting the tide. I'd better go.

More [*gravely*]. I'm sorry, Your Grace.

Henry. I must catch the tide or I'll not get back to Richmond till . . . No, don't come. Tell Norfolk. [*He has his foot on the stairs when Alice enters above.*] Oh, Lady Alice, I must go. [*Alice descends, her face serious.*] I want to catch the tide. To tell the truth, Lady Alice, I have forgotten in your haven here how time flows past outside. Affairs call me to court and so I give you my thanks and say good night. [*He mounts.*]

More and Alice [*bowing*]. Good night, Your Grace.

[*Exit Henry, above.*]

Alice. What's this? You crossed him.

More. Somewhat.

Alice. Why?

More [*apologetic*]. I couldn't find the other way.

Alice [*angrily*]. You're too nice altogether, Thomas!

More. Woman, mind your house.

Alice. I *am* minding my house!

More [*taking in her anxiety*]. Well, Alice. What would you want me to do?

Alice. Be ruled! If you won't rule him, be ruled!

More [*quietly*]. I neither could nor would rule my King. [*Pleasantly.*] But there's a little . . . little, area . . . where I must rule myself. It's very little—less to him than a tennis court. [*Her face is still full of foreboding; he sighs.*] Look; it was eight o'clock. At eight o'clock, Lady Anne likes to dance.

Alice [*relieved*]. Oh?

More. I think so.

Alice [*with irritation*]. And *you* stand between them!

More. I? What stands between them is a sacrament of the Church. I'm less important than you think, Alice.

Alice [*appealing*]. Thomas, stay friends with him.

More. Whatever can be done by smiling, you may rely on me to do.

Alice. You don't know *how* to flatter.

More. I flatter very well! My recipe's beginning to be widely copied. It's the basic syrup with just a soupçon of discreet impudence.

Alice [*still uneasy*]. I wish he'd eaten here. . . .

More. Yes—we shall be living on that "simple supper" of yours for a fortnight. [*She won't laugh.*] Alice . . . [*She won't turn.*] Alice . . . [*She turns.*] Set your mind at rest —this [*tapping himself*] is not the stuff of which martyrs are made.

[*Enter above, quickly, Roper.*]

Roper. Sir Thomas!

More [*winces*]. Oh, no. . . .

[*Enter after Roper, Margaret.*]

Alice. Will Roper—what do you want?

Margaret. William, I told you not to!

Roper. I'm not easily "told," Meg.

Margaret. I *asked* you not to.

Roper. Meg, I'm full to here! [*Indicates his throat.*]

Margaret. It's not convenient!

Roper. Must everything be made convenient? I'm not a convenient man, Meg—I've got an inconvenient conscience! [*Margaret gestures helplessly to More.*]

More [*laughs*]. Joshua's trumpet. One note on that brass conscience of yours and my daughter's walls are down.

Roper [*descending*]. You raised her, sir.

More [*a bit puzzled*]. How long have you been here? Are you in the King's party?

Roper. No, sir, I am *not* in the King's party! [*Advancing.*] It's of that I wish to speak to you. My spirit is perturbed.

More [*suppressing a grin*]. It is, Will? Why?

Roper. I've been offered a seat in the next Parliament. [*More looks up sharply.*] Ought I to take it?

More. No . . . Well that depends. With your views on Church Reform I should have thought you could do yourself a lot of good in the next Parliament.

Roper. My views on the Church, I must confess—since last we met my views have somewhat modified. [*More and*

Margaret exchange a smile.] I modify nothing concerning the *body* of the Church—money-changers in the temple must be scourged from thence—with a scourge of fire if that is needed! But an attack on the Church herself! No, I see behind that an attack on God—

More. Roper—

Roper. The Devil's work!

More. Roper!

Roper. To be done by the Devil's ministers!

More. For heaven's sake remember my office!

Roper. Oh, if you stand on your office—

More. I don't stand on it, but there are certain things I may not hear!

Roper. Sophistication. It is what I was told. The Court has corrupted you, Sir Thomas; you are not the man you were; you have learned to study your "convenience"; you have learned to flatter!

More. There, Alice, you see? I have a reputation for it.

Alice. God's Body, young man, if I was the Chancellor I'd have you whipped!

[*Enter Steward.*]

Steward. Master Rich is here, Sir Thomas.

[*Rich follows him closely.*]

Rich. Good evening, sir.

More. Ah, Richard?

Rich. Good evening, Lady Alice. [*Alice nods, noncommittally.*] Lady Margaret.

Margaret [*quite friendly but very clear*]. Good evening, Master Rich.

[*A pause.*]

More. Do you know—[*indicates Roper*] William Roper, the younger?

Rich. By reputation, of course.

Roper. Good evening, Master—

Rich. Rich.

Roper. Oh. [*Recollecting something.*] Oh.

Rich [*quickly and hostilely*]. You have heard of me?

Roper [*shortly*]. Yes.

Rich [*excitedly*]. In what connection? I don't know what you can have heard—[*He looks about; hotly.*] I sense that I'm not welcome here! [*He has jumped the gun; they are startled.*]

More [*gently*]. Why, Richard, have you done something that should make you not welcome?

Rich. Why, do you suspect me of it?

More. I shall begin to.

Rich [*drawing closer to him and speaking hurriedly*]. Cromwell is asking questions. About you. About you particularly. [*More is unmoved.*] He is continually collecting information about you!

More. I know it. [*Steward begins to slide out.*] Stay a minute, Matthew.

Rich [*pointing*]. That's one of his sources!

More. Of course; that's one of my servants.

Rich [*hurriedly, in a low voice again*]. Signor Chapuys, the Spanish Ambassador—

More. —collects information too. That's one of his functions. [*He looks at Rich very gravely.*]

Rich [*voice cracking*]. You look at me as though I were an enemy!

More [*putting out a hand to steady him*]. Why, Richard, you're shaking.

Rich. I'm adrift. Help me.

More. How?

Rich. Employ me.

More. No.

Rich [*desperately*]. Employ me!

More. No!

Rich [*moves swiftly to exit; turns*]. I would be steadfast!

More. Richard, you couldn't answer for yourself even so far as tonight.

[*Rich exits. All watch him; the others turn to More, their faces alert.*]

Roper. Arrest him.

Alice. Yes!

More. For what?

Alice. He's dangerous!

Roper. For libel; he's a spy.

Alice. He is! Arrest him!

Margaret. Father, that man's bad.

More. There is no law against that.

Roper. There is! God's law!

More. Then God can arrest him.

Roper. Sophistication upon sophistication!

More. No, sheer simplicity. The law, Roper, the law. I know what's legal not what's right. And I'll stick to what's legal.

Roper. Then you set man's law above God's!

More. No, far below; but let me draw your attention to a fact
—I'm *not* God. The currents and eddies of right and
wrong, which you find such plain sailing, I can't navi-
gate. I'm no voyager. But in the thickets of the law, oh,
there I'm a forester. I doubt if there's a man alive who
could follow me there, thank God. . . . [*He says this
last to himself.*]

Alice [*exasperated, pointing after Rich*]. While you talk,
he's gone!

More. And go he should, if he was the Devil himself, until
he broke the law!

Roper. So now you'd give the Devil benefit of law!

More. Yes. What would you do? Cut a great road through
the law to get after the Devil?

Roper. I'd cut down every law in England to do that!

More [*roused and excited*]. Oh? [*Advances on Roper.*] And
when the last law was down, and the Devil turned round
on you—where would you hide, Roper, the laws all
being flat? [*He leaves him.*] This country's planted thick
with laws from coast to coast—man's laws, not God's—
and if you cut them down—and you're just the man to
do it—d'you really think you could stand upright in the
winds that would blow then? [*Quietly.*] Yes, I'd give
the Devil benefit of law, for my own safety's sake.

Roper. I have long suspected this; this is the golden calf; the
law's your god.

More [*wearily*]. Oh, Roper, you're a fool, God's my god. . . .
[*Rather bitterly.*] But I find him rather too [*very bitterly*]
subtle . . . I don't know where he is nor what he wants.

Roper. My god wants service, to the end and unremitting;
nothing else!

More [*dryly*]. Are you sure that's God? He sounds like
Moloch. But indeed it may be God—And whoever
hunts for me, Roper, God or Devil, will find me hiding
in the thickets of the law! And I'll hide my daughter
with me! Not hoist her up the mainmast of your sea-
going principles! They put about too nimbly! [*Exit
More. They all look after him. Margaret touches
Roper's hand.*]

Margaret. Oh, that was harsh.

Roper [*turning to her; seriously*]. What's happened here?

Alice [*still with her back to them, her voice strained*]. He
can't abide a fool, that's all! Be off!

Roper [*to Margaret*]. Hide you. Hide you from what?

Alice [*turning, near to tears*]. He said nothing about hiding me, you noticed! I've got too fat to hide, I suppose!

Margaret. You know he meant us both.

Roper. But from what?

Alice. I don't know. I don't know if he knows. He's not said one simple, direct word to me since this divorce came up. It's not God who's gone subtle! It's him!

[*Enter More, a little sheepish. He goes to Roper.*]

More [*kindly*]. Roper, that was harsh: your principles are— [*he can't resist sending him up*] excellent—the very best quality. [*Roper bridles. Contritely.*] No, truly now, your principles are fine. [*Indicating the stairs, to all.*] Look, we must make a start on all that food.

Margaret. Father, can't you be plain with us?

More [*looks quickly from daughter to wife. Takes Alice's hand*]. I stand on the wrong side of no statute, and no common law. [*Takes Meg's hand too.*] I have not disobeyed my sovereign. I truly believe no man in England is safer than myself. And I want my supper. [*He starts them up the stairs and goes to Roper.*] We shall need your assistance, Will. There's an excellent Burgundy— if your principles permit.

Roper. They don't, sir.

More. Well, have some water in it.

Roper. Just the water, sir.

More. My poor boy.

Alice [*stopping at the head of the stairs, as if she will be answered.*] Why does Cromwell collect information about you?

More. I'm a prominent figure. Someone somewhere's collecting information about Cromwell. Now no more shirking; we must make a start. [*Shepherding Roper up the stairs.*] There's a stuffed swan if you please. [*Alice and Margaret exit above.*] Will, I'd trust *you* with my life. But not your principles. [*They mount the stairs.*] You see, we speak of being anchored to our principles. But if the weather turns nasty you up with an anchor and let it down where there's less wind, and the fishing's better. And "Look," we say, "Look, I'm anchored!" [*Laughing, inviting Roper to laugh with him.*] "To my principles!" [*Exit above, More and Roper. Enter Common Man pulling the basket. From it he takes an inn sign, which he hangs in the alcove. He inspects it.*]

Common Man. "The Loyal Subject" . . . [*To audience.*] A

pub. [*Takes from the basket and puts on a jacket, cap and napkin.*] A publican. [*Places two stools at the table, and on it mugs and a candle, which he lights.*] Oh, he's a deep one, that Sir Thomas More . . . Deep . . . It takes a lot of education to get a man as deep as that . . . [*Straight to audience.*] And a deep nature to begin with too. [*Deadpan.*] The likes of me can hardly be *expected* to follow the process of a man like that. . . . [*Slyly.*] Can we? [*He inspects the pub.*] Right, ready. [*He goes right.*] Ready, sir!

[*Cromwell enters, carrying a bottle.*]

Cromwell. Is this a good place for a conspiracy, innkeeper?

Publican [*woodenly*]. You asked for a private room, sir.

Cromwell [*looking round*]. Yes, I want one without too many little dark corners.

Publican. I don't understand you, sir. Just the four corners as you see.

Cromwell [*sardonically*]. You don't understand me.

Publican. That's right, sir.

Cromwell. Do you know who I am?

Publican [*promptly*]. No, sir.

Cromwell. Don't be too tactful, innkeeper.

Publican. I don't understand, sir.

Cromwell. When the likes of you *are* too tactful, the likes of me begin to wonder who's the fool.

Publican. I just don't understand you, sir.

Cromwell [*puts back his head and laughs silently*]. The master statesman of us all. "I don't understand." [*Looks at Publican almost with hatred.*] All right. Get out. [*Exit Publican. Cromwell goes to the exit. Calling.*] Come on. [*Enter Rich. He glances at the bottle in Cromwell's hand and remains cautiously by the exit.*] Yes, it may be that I am a little intoxicated. [*Leaves Rich standing.*] But not with alcohol, I've a strong head for that. With success! And who has a strong head for success? None of us gets enough of it. Except Kings. And they're born drunk.

Rich. Success? What success?

Cromwell. Guess.

Rich. Collector of Revenues for York.

Cromwell [*amused*]. You do keep your ear to the ground, don't you? No.

Rich. What then?

Cromwell. Sir Thomas Paget is—retiring.

Rich. Secretary to the Council!

Cromwell. 'Tis astonishing, isn't it?

Rich [*hastily*]. Oh no—I mean—one sees, it's logical.

Cromwell. No ceremony, no courtship. Be seated. [*Rich starts to sit.*] As His Majesty would say. [*Rich jumps up —is pulled down, laughs nervously and involuntarily glances round.*] Yes; see how I trust you.

Rich. Oh, I would never repeat or report a thing like that—

Cromwell [*pouring the wine*]. What kind of thing would you repeat or report?

Rich. Well, nothing said in friendship—may I say "friendship"?

Cromwell. If you like. D'you believe that—that you would never repeat or report anything et cetera?

Rich. Yes!

Cromwell. No, but seriously.

Rich. Why, yes!

Cromwell [*puts down the bottle. Not sinister, but rather as a kindly teacher with a promising pupil*]. Rich, seriously.

Rich [*pauses, then bitterly*]. It would depend what I was offered.

Cromwell. Don't say it just to please me.

Rich. It's true. It would depend what I was offered.

Cromwell [*patting his arm*]. Everyone knows it; not many people can say it.

Rich. There are *some* things one wouldn't do for anything. Surely.

Cromwell. Mm—that idea's like these life lines they have on the embankment: comforting, but you don't expect to have to use them. [*Briskly.*] Well, congratulations!

Rich [*suspiciously*]. On what?

Cromwell. I think you'd make a good Collector of Revenues for York Diocese.

Rich [*gripping himself*]. Is it in your gift?

Cromwell. It will be.

Rich [*with conscious cynicism*]. What do I have to do for it?

Cromwell. Nothing. [*He lectures.*] It isn't like that, Rich. There are no rules. With rewards and penalties—so much wickedness purchases so much worldly prospering—[*Rises. He breaks off and stops, suddenly struck.*] Are you sure you're not religious?

Rich. Almost sure.

Cromwell. Get sure. [*Resumes pacing up steps.*] No, it's not like that, it's much more a matter of convenience, administrative convenience. The normal aim of administration is to keep steady this factor of convenience—and Sir Thomas would agree. Now normally when a man wants to change his woman, you let him if it's convenient and prevent him if it's not—normally indeed it's of so little importance that you leave it to the priests. But the constant factor is this element of convenience.

Rich. Whose convenience?

[*Cromwell stops.*]

Cromwell [*sits*]. Oh, ours. But everybody's too. However, in the present instance the man who wants to change his woman is our Sovereign Lord, Harry, by the Grace of God, the Eighth of that name. Which is a quaint way of saying that if he wants to change his woman he will. [*He rises and walks back towards Rich.*] So *that* becomes the constant factor. And our job as administrators is to make it as convenient as we can. I say "our" job, on the assumption that you'll take this post at York I've offered you? [*Makes Rich move over.*]

Rich. Yes . . . yes, yes. [*But he seems gloomy.*]

Cromwell [*sits. Sharply*]. It's a bad sign when people are depressed by their own good fortune.

Rich [*defensively*]. I'm not depressed!

Cromwell. You look depressed.

Rich [*hastily buffooning*]. I'm lamenting. I've lost my innocence.

Cromwell. You lost that some time ago. If you've only just noticed, it can't have been very important to you.

Rich [*much struck*]. That's true! Why that's true, it can't!

Cromwell. We experience a sense of release, do we, Master Rich? An unfamiliar freshness in the head, as of open air?

Rich [*takes the wine*]. Collector of Revenues isn't bad!

Cromwell. Not bad for a start. [*He watches Rich drink.*] Now our present Lord Chancellor—*there's* an innocent man.

Rich [*indulgently*]. The odd thing is—he *is*.

Cromwell [*looks at him with dislike*]. Yes, I say he is. [*With the light tone again.*] The trouble is, his innocence is tangled in this proposition that you can't change your woman without a divorce, and can't have a divorce unless the Pope says so. And although his present Holiness is—judged even by the most liberal standards—a

strikingly corrupt old person, yet he still has this word
"Pope" attached to him. And from this quite meaningless circumstance I fear some degree of . . .

Rich [*pleased, waving his cup*]. . . . Administrative inconvenience.

Cromwell [*nodding as to a word-perfect pupil*]. Just so.
[*Deadpan.*] This goblet that he gave you, how much was
it worth? [*Rich looks down. Quite gently.*] Come along,
Rich, he gave you a silver goblet. How much did you
get for it?

Rich. Fifty shillings.

Cromwell. Could you take me to the shop?

Rich. Yes.

Cromwell. Where did he get it? [*No reply. Rich puts the cup
down.*] It was a gift from a litigant, a woman, wasn't it?

Rich. Yes.

Cromwell. Which court? Chancery? [*Takes the bottle; re-
strains Rich from filling his glass.*] No, don't get drunk.
In which court was this litigant's case?

Rich. Court of Requests.

Cromwell [*grunts, his face abstracted. Becoming aware of
Rich's regard, he smiles.*] There, that wasn't too painful,
was it?

Rich [*laughing a little and a little rueful*]. No!

Cromwell [*spreading his hands*]. That's all there is. And
you'll find it easier next time.

Rich [*looks up briefly, unhappily*]. What application do they
have, these tidbits of information you collect?

Cromwell. None at all, usually.

Rich [*stubbornly, not looking up*]. But sometimes.

Cromwell. Well, there *are* these men—you know—"upright," "steadfast," men who want themselves to be the
constant factor in the situation; which, of course, they
can't be. The situation rolls forward in any case.

Rich [*still stubbornly*]. So what happens?

Cromwell [*not liking his tone, coldly*]. If they've any sense
they get out of its way.

Rich. What if they haven't any sense?

Cromwell [*still coldly*]. What, none at all? Well, then they're
only fit for Heaven. But Sir Thomas has plenty of sense;
he could be frightened.

Rich [*looks up, his face nasty*]. Don't forget he's an innocent, Master Cromwell.

Cromwell. I think we'll finish there for tonight. After all, he is the Lord Chancellor. [*Going.*]

Rich. You wouldn't find him easy to frighten! [*Cromwell exits. He calls after him.*] You've mistaken your man this time! He doesn't know how to be frightened!

Cromwell [*returning. Rich rises at his approach*]. Doesn't know how to be frightened? Why, then he never put his hand in a candle . . . Did he? [*And seizing Rich by the wrist he holds his hand in the candle flame.*]

Rich [*screeches and darts back, hugging his hand in his armpit, regarding Cromwell with horror*]. You enjoyed that! [*Cromwell's downturned face is amazed. Triumphantly.*] You enjoyed it!

Curtain

The scene is as for start of Act One. When the curtain rises the stage is in darkness save for a spot, in which stands the Common Man. He carries the book, a place marked by his finger, and wears his spectacles.

Common Man. The interval started early in the year 1530 and it's now the middle of May, 1532. [*Explanatory.*] Two years. During that time a lot of water's flowed under the bridge, and one of the things that have come floating along on it is . . . [*Reads.*] "The Church of England, that finest flower of our Island genius for compromise; that system, peculiar to these shores, the despair of foreign observers, which deflects the torrents of religious passion down the canals of moderation." That's very well put. [*Returns to the book, approvingly.*] "Typically, this great effect was achieved not by bloodshed but by simple Act of Parliament. Only an unhappy few were found to set themselves against the current of their times, and in so doing to court disaster. For we are dealing with an age less fastidious than our own. Imprisonment without trial, and even examination under torture, were common practice."

[*Lights rise to show More, seated, and Roper, standing. Exit Common Man. Roper is dressed in black and wears a cross. He commences to walk up and down, watched by More. A pause.*]

More. Must you wear those clothes, Will?

Roper. Yes, I must.

More. Why?

Roper. The time has come for decent men to declare their allegiance!

More. And what allegiance are those designed to express?

Roper. My allegiance to the Church.

More. Well, you *look* like a Spaniard.

Roper. All credit to Spain then!

More. You wouldn't last six months in Spain. You'd have been burned alive in Spain, during your heretic period.

Roper. I suppose you have the right to remind me of it. [*Points accusingly.*] That chain of office that *you* wear is a degradation!

More [*glances down at it*]. I've told you. If the bishops in Convocation submitted this morning, I'll take it off ... It's no degradation. Great men have worn this.

Roper. When d'you expect to hear from the bishops?

More. About now. I was promised an immediate message.

Roper [*recommences pacing*]. I don't see what difference Convocation can make. The Church is already a wing of the Palace, is it not? The King is already its "Supreme Head"! Is he not?

More. No.

Roper [*startled*]. You are denying the Act of Supremacy!

More. No, I'm not; the Act states that the King—

Roper. —is Supreme Head of the Church in England— [*underlining the words*] "so far as the law of God allows." How far the law of God does allow it remains a matter of opinion, since the Act doesn't state it.

Roper. A legal quibble.

More. Call it what you like, it's there, thank God.

Roper. Very well; in your opinion how far does the law of God allow this?

More. I'll keep my opinion to myself, Will.

Roper. Yes? I'll tell you mine—

More. Don't! If your opinion's what I think it is, it's High Treason, Roper! [*Enter Margaret above, unseen.*] Will you remember you've a wife now! And may have children!

Margaret. Why must he remember that?

Roper. To keep myself "discreet."

Margaret [*smiling*]. Then I'd rather you forgot it.

More [*unsmiling*]. You are either idiots, or children.

[*Enter Chapuys, above.*]

Chapuys [*very sonorously*]. Or saints, my lord!

Margaret. Oh, Father, Signor Chapuys has come to see you.

More [*rising*]. Your Excellency.

Chapuys [*strikes pose with Margaret and Roper*]. Or saints, my lord; or saints.

More [*grins maliciously at Roper*]. That's it of course— saints! Roper—turn your head a bit—yes, I think I do

detect a faint radiance. [*Reproachfully*.] You should
have told us, Will.

Chapuys. Come come, my lord; you too at this time are not
free from some suspicion of saintliness.

More [*quietly*]. I don't like the sound of that, Your Excellency. What do you require of *me*? What, Your Excellency?

Chapuys [*awkward beneath his sudden keen regard*]. May I
not come simply to pay my respects to the English
Socrates—as I see your angelic friend Erasmus calls
you.

More [*wrinkles nose*]. Yes, I'll think of something presently
to call Erasmus. [*Checks*.] Socrates! I've no taste for
hemlock, Your Excellency, if that's what you require.

Chapuys [*with a display of horror*]. Heaven forbid!

More [*dryly*]. Amen.

Chapuys [*spreads hands*]. Must I require anything? [*Sonorously*.] After all, we are brothers in Christ, you and I!

More. A characteristic we share with the rest of humanity.
You live in Cheapside, Signor. To make contact with a
brother in Christ you have only to open your window
and empty a chamber-pot. There was no need to come
to Chelsea. [*Chapuys titters nervously. Coldly*.] William.
The Spanish Ambassador is here on business. Would
you mind?

[*Roper and Margaret begin to go.*]

Chapuys [*rising, unreal protestations*]. Oh no! I protest!

More. He is clearly here on business.

Chapuys. No; but really, I protest! [*It is no more than token:
when Roper and Margaret reach head of stairs he calls*.]
Dominus vobiscum filii mei!

Roper [*pompously*]. Et cum spiritu tuo, excellencis! [*Exit
Roper and Margaret*.]

Chapuys [*approaching More, thrillingly*]. And how much
longer shall we hear that holy language in these shores?

More [*alert, poker-faced*]. 'Tisn't "holy," Your Excellency;
just old.

[*Chapuys sits with the air of one getting down to brass tacks*.]

Chapuys. My lord, I cannot believe you will allow yourself
to be associated with the recent actions of King Henry!
In respect of Queen Catherine.

More. Subjects are associated with the actions of Kings willynilly.

Chapuys. The Lord Chancellor is not an ordinary subject.

He bears responsibility [*He lets the word sink in; More shifts.*] for what is done.

More [*agitation begins to show through*]. Have you considered that what has been done badly, might have been done worse, with a different Chancellor.

Chapuys [*mounting confidence, as More's attention is caught*]. Believe me, Sir Thomas, your influence in these policies has been much searched for, and where it has been found it has been praised—*but* . . . There comes a point, does there not? . . .

More. Yes. [*Agitated.*] There does come such a point.

Chapuys. When the sufferings of one unfortunate lady swell to an open attack on the religion of an entire country that point has been passed. Beyond that point, Sir Thomas, one is not merely "compromised," one is in truth corrupted.

More [*stares at him*]. What do you want?

Chapuys. Rumor has it that if the Church in Convocation has submitted to the King, you will resign.

More [*looks down and regains composure*]. I see. [*Suavely.*] Supposing rumor to be right. Would you approve of that?

Chapuys. Approve, applaud, admire.

More [*still looking down*]. Why?

Chapuys. Because it would show one man—and that man known to be temperate—unable to go further with this wickedness.

More. And that man known to be Chancellor of England too.

Chapuys. Believe me, my lord, such a signal would be seen—

More. "Signal"?

Chapuys. Yes, my lord; it would be seen and understood.

More [*now positively silky*]. By whom?

Chapuys. By half of your fellow countrymen! [*Now More looks up sharply.*] Sir Thomas, I have just returned from Yorkshire and Northumberland, where I have made a tour.

More [*softly*]. Have you indeed?

Chapuys. Things are very different there, my lord. There they are ready.

More. For what?

Chapuys. Resistance!

More [*softly, as before*]. Resistance by what means? [*Suddenly his agitation must find expression, if only physical. He is galvanized from his seat and as he suddenly stops, with his back to Chapuys, More's face is electrically alert. Chapuys hears the excitement in.*] By force of arms?

Chapuys [*almost sure the fish is hooked, leaning forward but playing it cool*]. We are adjured by St. Paul to don the arms of God when the occasion warrants.

More. Metaphorical arms. The breastplate of righteousness and the helmet of salvation. Do you mean a metaphorical resistance? [*Indignation and fear make his voice vibrate with the excitement of enthusiasm.*]

Chapuys [*intones*]. "He shall flee the *iron* weapons, and the bow of steel shall strike him through."

More [*there is a pause while his agile mind scans the full frightening implications of this for himself; it is almost with a start of recollection that he remembers to answer Chapuys at all*]. I see.

[*Enter Roper, above, excited.*]

Roper. Sir Thomas! [*More looks up angrily.*] Excuse me, sir —[*Indicates off.*] His Grace the Duke of Norfolk— [*More and Chapuys rise. Roper excitedly descends.*] It's all over, sir, they've—

[*Enter Norfolk above, Alice and Margaret, below.*]

Norfolk. One moment, Roper, I'll do this! Thomas—[*Sees Chapuys.*] Oh. [*He stares at Chapuys hostilely.*]

Chapuys. I was on the point of leaving, Your Grace. Just a personal call. I have been trying . . . er, to borrow a book . . . but without success—you're sure you have no copy, my lord? Then I'll leave you. [*Bowing.*] Gentlemen, ladies. [*Going up the stairs, he stops unnoticed as Roper speaks.*]

Roper. Sir Thomas—

Norfolk. I'll do it, Roper! Convocation's knuckled under, Thomas. They're to pay a fine of a hundred thousand pounds. And . . . we've severed the connection with Rome.

More [*smiling bitterly*]. "The connection with Rome" is nice. [*Bitterly.*] "The connection with Rome."

Roper [*addressing Norfolk, but looking at More*]. Your Grace, this is quite certain, is it?

Norfolk. Yes. [*More puts his hand to his chain. Chapuys exits. All turn.*] Funny company, Thomas?

More. It's quite unintentional. He doesn't mean to be funny. [*He fumbles with the chain.*] Help me with this.

Norfolk. Not I.

Roper [*takes a step forward. Then, subdued*]. Shall I, sir?

More. No thank you, Will. Alice?

Alice. Hell's fire—God's Blood and Body, *no!* Sun and moon, Master More, you're taken for a wise man! Is this wisdom—to betray your ability, abandon practice, forget your station and your duty to your kin and behave like a printed book!

More [*listens gravely; then*]. Margaret, will you?

Margaret. If you want.

More. There's my clever girl.

[*She takes it from his neck.*]

Norfolk. Well, Thomas, why? Make me understand—because I'll tell you now, from where I stand, this looks like cowardice!

More [*excited and angry*]. All right I will—this isn't "Reformation," this is war against the Church! . . . [*Indignant.*] Our King, Norfolk, has declared war on the Pope—because the Pope will not declare that our Queen is not his wife.

Norfolk. And is she?

More [*with cunning*]. I'll answer that question for one person only, the King. Aye, and that in private too.

Norfolk [*contemptuously*]. Man, you're cautious.

More. Yes, cautious. I'm not one of your hawks.

Norfolk [*walks away and turns*]. All right—we're at war with the Pope! The Pope's a Prince, isn't he?

More. He is.

Norfolk. And a bad one?

More. Bad enough. But the theory is that he's also the Vicar of God, the descendant of St. Peter, our only link with Christ.

Norfolk [*sneering*]. A tenuous link.

More. Oh, tenuous indeed.

Norfolk [*to the others*]. Does this make sense? [*No reply; they look at More.*] You'll forfeit all you've got—which includes the respect of your country—for a theory?

More [*hotly*]. The Apostolic Succession of the Pope is— [*Stops; interested.*] . . . Why, it's a theory, yes; you can't see it; can't touch it; it's a theory. [*To Norfolk, very rapidly but calmly.*] But what matters to me is not whether it's true or not but that I believe it . . . I trust I make myself obscure?

Norfolk. Perfectly.

More. That's good. Obscurity's what I have need of now.

Norfolk. Thomas. This isn't Spain, you know.

More [*looks at him, takes him aside; in a lowered voice*]. Have I your word that what we say here is between us and has no existence beyond these walls?

Norfolk [*impatiently*]. Very well.

More [*almost whispering*]. And if the King should command you to repeat what I have said?

Norfolk. I should keep my word to you!

More. Then what has become of your oath of obedience to the King?

Norfolk [*indignant*]. You lay traps for me!

More [*now grown calm*]. No, I show you the times.

Norfolk. Why do you insult me with these lawyer's tricks?

More. Because I am afraid.

Norfolk. And here's your answer. The King accepts your resignation very sadly; he is mindful of your goodness and past loyalty, and in any matter concerning your honor and welfare he will be your good lord. So much for your fear.

More [*flatly*]. You will convey my humble gratitude.

Norfolk. I will. Good day, Alice. [*Going.*] I'd rather deal with you than your husband.

More [*complete change of tone; briskly professional*]. Oh, Howard! [*He stops him.*] Signor Chapuys tells me he's just made a "tour" of the North Country. He thinks we shall have trouble there. So do I.

Norfolk [*stolid*]. Yes? What kind of trouble?

More. The Church—the old Church, not the new Church— is very strong up there. I'm serious, Howard, keep an eye on the border this next spring; and bear in mind the Old Alliance.

Norfolk [*looks at him*]. We will. We do . . . As for the Spaniard, Thomas, it'll perhaps relieve your mind to know that one of Secretary Cromwell's agents made the tour with him.

More. Oh. [*A flash of jealousy.*] Of course if Master Cromwell has matters in hand—

Norfolk. He has.

More. Yes, I can imagine.

Norfolk. But thanks for the information. [*Going upstairs.*] It's good to know you still have . . . some vestige of patriotism.

More [*angrily*]. That's a remarkably stupid observation, Norfolk!

[*Norfolk exits.*]

Alice. So there's an end of you. What will you do now—sit by the fire and make goslings in the ash?

More. Not at all, Alice, I expect I'll write a bit. [*He woos them with unhappy cheerfulness.*] I'll write, I'll read, I'll think. I think I'll learn to fish! I'll play with my grand-children—when son Roper's done his duty. [*Eagerly.*] Alice, shall I teach you to read?

Alice. No, by God!

More. Son Roper, *you're* pleased with me I hope?

Roper [*goes to him; moved*]. Sir, you've made a noble gesture.

More [*blankly*]. A gesture? [*Eagerly.*] It wasn't possible to continue, Will. I was not *able* to continue. I would have if I could! I make no gesture! [*Apprehensive, looks after Norfolk.*] My God, I hope it's understood I make no gesture! [*He turns back to them.*] Alice, you don't think I would do this to you for a gesture! *That's* a gesture! [*Thumbs his nose.*] *That's* a gesture! [*Jerks up two fingers.*] I'm no street acrobat to make gestures! I'm practical!

Roper. You belittle yourself, sir, this was not practical; [*resonantly*] this was moral!

More. Oh, now I understand you, Will. Morality's *not* practical. Morality's a gesture. A complicated gesture learned from books—that's what you say, Alice, isn't it? . . . And you, Meg?

Margaret. It *is*, for most of us, Father.

More. Oh no, if you're going to plead humility! Oh, you're cruel. I have a cruel family.

Alice. Yes, you can fit the cap on anyone you want, I know that well enough. If there's cruelty in this house, I know where to look for it.

Margaret. No, Mother!

Alice. Oh, you'd walk on the bottom of the sea and think yourself a crab if he suggested it! [*To Roper.*] And you! You'd dance him to the Tower—You'd dance him to the block! Like David with a harp! Scattering hymn books in his path! [*To More.*] Poor silly man, d'you think they'll *leave* you here to learn to fish?

More [*straight at her*]. If we govern our tongues they will! Now listen, I have a word to say about that. I have

made no statement. I've resigned, that's *all*. On the
King's Supremacy, the King's divorce which he'll now
grant himself, the marriage he'll then make—have you
heard me make a statement?

Alice. No—and if I'm to lose my rank and fall to housekeep-
ing I want to know the reason; so make a statement now.

More. No—[*Alice exhibits indignation.*] Alice, it's a point
of law! Accept it from me, Alice, that in silence is my
safety under the law, but my silence must be absolute,
it must extend to you.

Alice. In short you don't trust us!

More. A man would need to be half-witted not to trust you
—but—[*Impatiently.*] Look—[*He advances on her.*]
I'm the Lord Chief Justice, I'm Cromwell, I'm the
King's Head Jailer—and I take your hand [*He does so.*]
and I clamp it on the Bible, on the Blessed Cross
[*clamps her hand on his closed fist*] and I say: "Woman,
has your husband made a statement on these matters?"
Now—on peril of your soul remember—what's your
answer?

Alice. No.

More. And so it must remain. [*He looks around at their
grave faces.*] Oh, it's only a life line, we shan't have to
use it but it's comforting to have. No, no, when they
find I'm silent they'll ask nothing better than to leave
me silent; you'll see.

[*Enter Steward.*]

Steward. Sir, the household's in the kitchen. They want to
know what's happened.

More. Oh. Yes. We must speak to them. Alice, they'll mostly
have to go, my dear. [*To Steward.*] But not before we've
found them places.

Alice. We can't find places for them all!

More. Yes, we can; yes, we can. Tell them so.

Alice. God's death, it comes on us quickly. . . . [*Exit Alice,
Margaret with the chain, and Roper.*]

More. What about you, Matthew? It'll be a smaller household now, and for you I'm afraid, a smaller wage. Will
you stay?

Steward. Don't see how I could then, sir.

More. You're a single man.

Steward [*awkwardly*]. Well, yes, sir, but I mean I've got my
own—

More [*quickly*]. Quite right, why should you? . . . I shall miss you, Matthew.

Steward [*with man-to-man jocosity*]. No-o-o. You never had much time for me, sir. You see through *me*, sir, I know that. [*He almost winks.*]

More [*gently insists*]. I shall miss you, Matthew; I shall miss you. [*Exit More. Steward snatches off his hat and hurls it to the floor.*]

Steward. Now, damn me, isn't that them all over! [*He broods, face downturned.*] Miss? . . . He . . . Miss? . . . *Miss* me? . . . What's *in* me for *him* to miss? . . . [*Suddenly he cries out like one who sees a danger at his very feet.*] Wo-AH! [*Chuckling.*] We-e-eyup! [*To audience.*] I nearly fell for it. [*He walks away.*] "Matthew, will you kindly take a cut in your wages?" "No, Sir Thomas, I will not." That's it and [*fiercely*] that's all of it! [*Falls to thought again. Resentfully.*] All right, so he's down on his luck! I'm sorry. I don't mind saying that: I'm sorry! Bad luck! If I'd any good luck to spare he could have some. I wish we could *all* have good luck, *all* the time! I wish we had wings! I wish rainwater was beer! But it isn't! . . . And what with not having wings but walking—on two flat feet; and good luck and bad luck being just exactly even stevens; and rain being water—don't you complicate the job by putting things in me for me to miss! [*He takes off his steward's coat, picks up his hat; draws the curtain to the alcove. Chuckling.*] I did, you know. I nearly fell for it. [*Exit Common Man. Norfolk and Cromwell enter to alcove.*]

Norfolk. But he makes no noise, Mr. Secretary; he's silent, why not leave him silent?

Cromwell [*patiently*]. Not being a man of letters, Your Grace, you perhaps don't realize the extent of his reputation. This "silence" of his is bellowing up and down Europe! Now may I recapitulate: He reported the Spaniard's conversation to you, informed on the Spaniard's tour of the North Country, warned against a possible rebellion there.

Norfolk. He did!

Cromwell. We may say then, that he showed himself hostile to the hopes of Spain.

Norfolk. That's what I *say*!

Cromwell [*patiently*]. Bear with me, Your Grace. Now if he opposes Spain, he supports us. Well, surely that follows? [*Sarcastically*.] Or do you see some third alternative?

Norfolk. No no, that's the line-up all right. And I may say Thomas More—

Cromwell. Thomas More will line up on the right side.

Norfolk. Yes! Crank he may be, traitor he is not.

Cromwell [*spreading his hands*]. And with a little pressure, he can be got to say so. And that's all we need—a brief declaration of his loyalty to the present administration.

Norfolk. I still say let sleeping dogs lie.

Cromwell [*heavily*]. The King does not agree with you.

Norfolk [*glances at him, flickers, but then rallies*]. What kind of "pressure" d'you think you can bring to bear?

Cromwell. I have evidence that Sir Thomas, during the period of his judicature, accepted bribes.

Norfolk [*incredulous*]. What! Goddammit, he was the only judge since Cato who *didn't* accept bribes! When was there last a Chancellor whose possessions after three years in office totaled one hundred pounds and a gold chain.

Cromwell [*rings hand bell and calls*]. Richard! It is, as you imply, common practice, but a practice may be common and remain an offense; this offense could send a man to the Tower.

Norfolk [*contemptuously*]. I don't believe it.

[*Enter a Woman and Rich, who motions her to remain and approaches the table, where Cromwell indicates a seat. Rich has acquired self-importance.*]

Cromwell. Ah, Richard. You know His Grace, of course.

Rich [*respectful affability*]. Indeed yes, we're *old* friends.

Norfolk [*savage snub*]. Used to look after my books or something, didn't you?

Cromwell [*clicks his fingers at Woman*]. Come here. This woman's name is Catherine Anger; she comes from Lincoln. And she put a case in the Court of Requests in— [*consults a paper*.]

Woman. A property case, it was.

Cromwell. Be quiet. A property case in the Court of Requests in April, 1526.

Woman. And got a wicked false judgment!

Cromwell. And got an impeccably correct judgment from our friend Sir Thomas.

Woman. No, sir, it was not!

Cromwell. We're not concerned with the judgment but the

gift you gave the judge. Tell this gentleman about that. The judgment, for what it's worth, was the right one.

Woman. No, sir! [*Cromwell looks at her; she hastily addresses Norfolk.*] I sent him a cup, sir, an Italian silver cup I bought in Lincoln for a hundred shillings.

Norfolk. Did Sir Thomas accept this cup?

Woman. I sent it.

Cromwell. He did accept it, we can corroborate that. You can go. [*She opens her mouth.*] Go!

[*Exit Woman.*]

Norfolk [*scornfully*]. Is that your witness?

Cromwell. No; by an odd coincidence this cup later came into the hands of Master Rich here.

Norfolk. How?

Rich. He gave it to me.

Norfolk [*brutally*]. Can you corroborate that?

Cromwell. I have a fellow outside who can; he was More's steward at that time. Shall I call him?

Norfolk. Don't bother, I know him. When did Thomas give you this thing?

Rich. I don't exactly remember.

Norfolk. Well, make an effort. Wait! I can tell you! I can tell you—it was that spring—it was that night we were there together. You had a cup with you when we left; was that it? [*Rich looks to Cromwell for guidance but gets none.*]

Rich. It may have been.

Norfolk. Did he often give you cups?

Rich. I don't suppose so, Your Grace.

Norfolk. That was it then. [*New realization.*] And it was April! The April of twenty-six. The very month that cow first put her case before him! [*Triumphantly.*] In other words, the moment he knew it was a bribe, he got rid of it.

Cromwell [*nodding judicially*]. The facts will bear that interpretation, I suppose.

Norfolk. Oh, this is a horse that won't run, Master Secretary.

Cromwell. Just a trial canter, Your Grace. We'll find something better.

Norfolk [*between bullying and pleading*]. Look here, Cromwell, I want no part of this.

Cromwell. You have no choice.

Norfolk. What's that you say?

Cromwell. The King particularly wishes you to be active in the matter.

Norfolk [*winded*]. He has not told me that.

Cromwell [*politely*]. Indeed? He told me.

Norfolk. But *why*?

Cromwell. We feel that, since you are known to have been a friend of More's, your participation will show that there is nothing in the nature of a "persecution," but only the strict processes of law. As indeed you've just demonstrated. I'll tell the King of your loyalty to your friend. If you like, I'll tell him that you "want no part of it," too.

Norfolk [*furious*]. Are you threatening me, Cromwell?

Cromwell. My *dear* Norfolk . . . This isn't Spain.

[*Norfolk stares, turns abruptly and exits. Cromwell turns a look of glacial coldness upon Rich.*]

Rich. I'm sorry, Secretary, I'd forgotten he was there that night.

Cromwell [*scrutinizes him dispassionately; then*]. You must try to remember these things.

Rich. Secretary, I'm sincerely—

Cromwell [*dismisses the topic with a wave and turns to look after Norfolk*]. Not such a fool as he looks, the Duke.

Rich [*Civil Service simper*]. That would hardly be possible, Secretary.

Cromwell [*straightening his papers, briskly*]. Sir Thomas is going to be a slippery fish, Richard; we need a net with a finer mesh.

Rich. Yes, Secretary?

Cromwell. We'll weave one for him, shall we, you and I?

Rich [*uncertainly*]. I'm only anxious to do what is correct, Secretary.

Cromwell [*smiling at him*]. Yes, Richard, I know. [*Straight-faced.*] You're absolutely right, it must be done by law. It's just a matter of finding the right law. Or making one. Bring my papers, will you? [*Exit Cromwell. Enter Steward.*]

Steward. Could we have a word now, sir?

Rich. We don't require you after all, Matthew.

Steward. No, sir, but about . . .

Rich. Oh yes. . . . Well, I begin to need a steward, certainly; my household is expanding . . . [*Sharply.*] But as I remember, Matthew, your attitude to me was some-times—disrespectful! [*The last word is shrill.*]

Steward [*with humble dignity*]. Oh. Oh, I must contradict you there, sir; that's your imagination. In those days, sir, you still had your way to make. And a gentleman in that position often imagines these things. Then when he's reached his proper level, sir, he stops thinking about them. [*As if offering tangible proof.*] Well—I don't think you find people "disrespectful" nowadays, do you, sir?

Rich. There may be something in that. Bring my papers. [*Going, he turns at the exit and anxiously scans Steward's face for signs of impudence.*] I'll permit no breath of insolence!

Steward [*the very idea is shocking*]. I should hope not, sir. [*Exit Rich.*] Oh, I can manage this one! He's just my size! [*Lighting changes so that the set looks drab and chilly.*] Sir Thomas More's again. Gone down a bit. [*Exit Common Man. Enter Chapuys and Attendant, cloaked. Alice enters above wearing a big coarse apron over her dress.*]

Alice. My husband is coming down, Your Excellency.

Chapuys. Thank you, madam.

Alice. And I beg you to be gone before he does!

Chapuys [*patiently*]. Madam, I have a Royal Commission to perform.

Alice. Aye. You said so. [*Alice exits.*]

Chapuys. For sheer barbarity, commend me to a good-hearted Englishwoman of a certain class. . . . [*Wraps cloak about him.*]

Attendant. It's very cold, Excellency.

Chapuys. I remember when these rooms were warm enough.

Attendant [*looking about*]. "Thus it is to incur the enmity of a King."

Chapuys. A heretic King. [*Looking about.*] Yes, Sir Thomas is a good man.

Attendant. Yes, Excellency, I like Sir Thomas very much.

Chapuys. Carefully, carefully.

Attendant. It *is* uncomfortable dealing with him, isn't it?

Chapuys [*smilingly patronizing*]. Goodness can be a difficulty.

Attendant [*somewhat shocked*]. Excellency?

Chapuys [*recovers instantly his official gravity*]. In the long run, of course, *all* good men everywhere are allies of Spain. No good man cannot be, and no man who is not can be good. . . .

Attendant. Then he is really for us.

Chapuys [*still graciously instructing*]. He is opposed to Cromwell, is he not?

Attendant [*smiling back*]. Oh, yes, Excellency.

Chapuys [*as a genteel card player, primly triumphant, produces the ace of trumps*]. If he's opposed to Cromwell, he's for us. [*No answer; a little more sharply.*] There's no third alternative?

Attendant. I suppose not, Excellency.

Chapuys [*rides him down, tried beyond all bearing*]. Oh—I wish your mother had chosen some other career for you. You've no political sense whatever! [*Enter More.*] Sir Thomas! [*Goes to him, solemnly and affectionately places hands on his shoulders, gazing into his eyes.*] Ah, Sir Thomas, in a better state this threadbare stuff will metamorphose into shining garments, these dank walls to walls of pearl, this cold light to perpetual sunshine. [*He bends upon More a melancholy look of admiration.*]

More [*as yet quite friendly, smiles quizzically*]. It sounds not unlike Madrid . . . ?

Chapuys [*throws up his hands delightedly*]. Even in times like this, even now, a pleasure to converse with you.

More [*chuckles a little, takes Chapuys by the wrist, waggles it a little and then releases it as though to indicate that pleasantries must now end*]. Is this another "personal" visit, Chapuys, or is it official?

Chapuys. It falls between the two, Sir Thomas.

More [*reaching the bottom of stairs*]. Official then.

Chapuys. No, I have a personal letter for you.

More. From whom?

Chapuys. My master, the King of Spain. [*More puts his hands behind his back.*] You will take it?

More. I will not lay a finger on it.

Chapuys. It is in no way an affair of State. It expresses my master's admiration for the stand which you and Bishop Fisher of Rochester have taken over the so-called divorce of Queen Catherine.

More. I have taken no stand!

Chapuys. But your views, Sir Thomas, are well known—

More. My views are much guessed at. [*Irritably.*] Oh come, sir, could you undertake to convince [*grimly*] King Harry that this letter is "in no way an affair of State"?

Chapuys. My dear Sir Thomas, I have taken extreme precautions. I came here very much incognito. [*A self-indulgent chuckle.*] Very nearly in disguise.

More. You misunderstand me. It is not a matter of your precautions but my duty, which would be to take this letter immediately to the King.

Chapuys [*flabbergasted*]. But, Sir Thomas, your views—

More [*with the heat of* fear *behind it*]. Are well known you say. It seems my loyalty to my King is less so!

Chapuys [*glibly*]. "Render unto Caesar the things which *are* Caesar's—[*he raises a reproving finger*] but unto God—"

More. Stop! [*He walks about, suppressing his agitation, and then as one who excuses a display of bad manners.*] Holy writ is holy, Excellency.

[*Enter Margaret bearing before her a huge bundle of bracken. The entry of the bracken affords him a further opportunity to collect himself.*]

Margaret. Look, Father! [*She dumps it.*] Will's getting more.

More. Oh, well done! [*This is not whimsy; they're cold and their interest in fuel is serious.*] Is it dry? [*He feels it expertly.*] Oh it is. [*Sees Chapuys staring; laughs.*] It's bracken, Your Excellency. We burn it. [*Enter Alice.*] Alice, look at this.

Alice [*eying Chapuys*]. Aye.

More [*crossing to Chapuys*]. May I? [*Takes the letter to Alice and Margaret.*] This is a letter from the King of Spain; I want you to see it's not been opened. I have declined it. You see the seal has not been broken? [*Returning it to Chapuys.*] I wish I could ask you to stay, Your Excellency—the bracken fire is a luxury.

Chapuys [*with a cold smile*]. One I must forgo. [*Aside to Attendant.*] Come. [*Crosses to exit, pauses.*] May I say I am sure my master's admiration will not be diminished. [*Bows, noncommittally.*] Ladies.

More. I'm gratified.

Chapuys [*bows to them, the ladies curtsy*]. The man's utterly unreliable. [*Exit Chapuys and Attendant.*]

Alice [*after a little silence kicks the bracken*]. "Luxury"! [*She sits wearily on the bundle.*]

More. Well, it's a luxury while it lasts . . . There's not much sport in it for you, is there? [*She neither answers nor looks at him from the depths of her fatigue. After a moment's hesitation he braces himself.*] Alice, the money from the bishops. I can't take it. I wish—oh, heaven, how I wish I could! But I can't.

Alice [*as one who has ceased to expect anything*]. I didn't
think you would.

More [*reproachfully*]. Alice, there *are* reasons.

Alice. We couldn't come so deep into your confidence as to
know these reasons why a man in poverty can't take
four thousand pounds?

More [*gently but very firmly*]. Alice, this isn't poverty.

Alice. D'you know what we shall eat tonight?

More [*trying for a smile*]. Yes, parsnips.

Alice. Yes, parsnips and stinking mutton! [*Straight at him.*]
For a knight's lady!

More [*pleading*]. But at the worst, we could be beggars, and
still keep company, and be merry together!

Alice [*bitterly*]. Merry!

More [*sternly*]. Aye, merry!

Margaret [*her arm about her mother's waist*]. *I* think you
should take that money.

More. Oh, don't you see? [*He sits by them.*] If I'm paid by
the Church for my writings—

Alice. This had nothing to do with your writings! This was
charity pure and simple! Collected from the clergy high
and low!

More. It would *appear* as payment.

Alice. You're not a man who deals in appearances!

More [*fervently*]. Oh, am I not though. . . . [*Calmly.*] If the
King takes this matter any further, with me or with
the Church, it will be very bad, if I even appear to
have been in the pay of the Church.

Alice [*sharply*]. Bad?

More. If you will have it, dangerous.

Margaret. But you don't write against the King.

More [*rises*]. I write! And that's enough in times like these!

Alice. You said there *was* no danger!

More. I don't think there is! And I don't want there to be!

[*Enter Roper carrying a sickle.*]

Roper [*steadily*]. There's a gentleman here from Hampton
Court. You are to go before Secretary Cromwell. To
answer certain charges.

[*Alice rises and Margaret, appalled, turns to More.*]

More [*after a silence, rubs his nose*]. Well, that's all right.
We expected that. [*He is not very convincing.*] When?

Roper. Now.

Alice [*exhibits distress*]. Ah—

More. Alice, that means nothing; that's just technique . . . Well, I suppose "now" means now.

[*Lighting changes, darkness gathering on the others, leaving More isolated in the light.*]

Margaret. Can I come with you?

More. Why? No. I'll be back for dinner. I'll bring Cromwell to dinner, shall I? It'd serve him right.

Margaret. Oh, Father, don't be witty!

More. Why not? Wit's what's in question.

Roper [*quietly*]. While we are witty, the Devil may enter us unawares.

More. He's not the Devil, son Roper, he's a lawyer! And my case is watertight!

Alice. They say he's a very penetrating lawyer.

More. What, Cromwell? Pooh, he's a pragmatist—and that's the only resemblance he has to the Devil, son Roper; a pragmatist, the merest plumber.

[*Exit Alice, Margaret, Roper, in darkness. Lights come up. Enter Cromwell, bustling, carrying a file of papers.*]

Cromwell. I'm sorry to invite you here at such short notice, Sir Thomas; good of you to come. [*Draws back curtain from alcove, revealing Rich seated at a table, with writing materials.*] Will you take a seat? I think you know Master Rich?

More. Indeed yes, we're old friends. That's a nice gown you have, Richard.

Cromwell. Master Rich will make a record of our conversation.

More. Good of you to tell me, Master Secretary.

Cromwell [*laughs appreciatively; then*]. Believe me, Sir Thomas—no, that's asking too much—but let me tell you all the same, you have no more sincere admirer than myself. [*Rich begins to scribble.*] Not yet, Rich, not yet. [*Invites More to join him in laughing at Rich.*]

More. If I might hear the charges?

Cromwell. Charges?

More. I understand there are certain charges.

Cromwell. Some ambiguities of behavior I should like to clarify—hardly "charges."

More. Make a note of that will you, Master Rich? There are no charges.

Cromwell [*laughing and shaking head*]. Sir Thomas, Sir Thomas . . . You know it amazes me that you, who were once so effective *in* the world and are now so

much retired from it, should be opposing yourself to
the whole movement of the times? [*He ends on a note
of interrogation.*]

More [*nods*]. It amazes me too.

Cromwell [*picks up and drops a paper; sadly*]. The King is
not pleased with you.

More. I am grieved.

Cromwell. Yet do you know that even now, if you could
bring yourself to agree with the Universities, the Bishops, and the Parliament of this realm, there is no
honor which the King would be likely to deny you?

More [*stonily*]. I am well acquainted with His Grace's generosity.

Cromwell [*coldly*]. Very well. [*Consults the paper.*] You have
heard of the so-called Holy Maid of Kent—who was
executed for prophesying against the King?

More. Yes, I knew the poor woman.

Cromwell [*quickly*]. You sympathize with her?

More. She was ignorant and misguided; she was a bit mad,
I think. And she has paid for her folly. Naturally I
sympathize with her.

Cromwell [*grunts*]. You admit meeting her. You met her—
and yet you did not warn His Majesty of her treason.
How was that?

More. She spoke no treason. Our conversation was not political.

Cromwell. My dear More, the woman was notorious! Do
you expect me to believe that?

More. Happily there are witnesses.

Cromwell. You wrote a letter to her?

More. Yes, I wrote advising her to abstain from meddling
with the affairs of Princes and the State. I have a copy
of this letter—also witnessed.

Cromwell. You have been cautious.

More. I like to keep my affairs regular.

Cromwell. Sir Thomas, there is a more serious charge—

More. Charge?

Cromwell. For want of a better word. In the May of 1526
the King published a book. [*He permits himself a little
smile.*] A theological work. It was called *A Defence of
the Seven Sacraments.*

More. Yes. [*Bitterly.*] For which he was named "Defender
of the Faith," by His Holiness the Pope.

Cromwell. By the Bishop of Rome. Or do you insist on
"Pope"?

More. No, "Bishop of Rome" if you like. It doesn't alter his
authority.

Cromwell. Thank you, you come to the point very readily;
what *is* that authority? As regards the Church in Europe; [*approaching*] for example, the Church in England. What exactly *is* the Bishop of Rome's authority?

More. You will find it very ably set out and defended, Master
Secretary, in the King's book.

Cromwell. The book published under the King's name would
be more accurate. You wrote that book.

More. I wrote no part of it.

Cromwell. I do not mean you actually held the pen.

More. I merely answered to the best of my ability certain
questions on canon law which His Majesty put to me.
As I was bound to do.

Cromwell. Do you deny that you *instigated* it?

More. It was from first to last the King's own project. This
is trivial, Master Cromwell.

Cromwell. I should not think so if I were in your place.

More. Only two people know the truth of the matter. Myself
and the King. And, whatever he may have said to you,
he will not give evidence to support this accusation.

Cromwell. Why not?

More. Because evidence is given on oath, and he will not
perjure himself. If you don't know that, you don't yet
know him.

[*Cromwell looks at him viciously.*]

Cromwell [*goes apart; formally*]. Sir Thomas More, is there
anything you wish to say to me concerning the King's
marriage with Queen Anne?

More [*very still*]. I understood I was not to be asked that
again.

Cromwell. Evidently you understood wrongly. These
charges—

More [*with a sudden, contemptuous sweep of his arm*]. They
are terrors for children, Master Secretary—an empty
cupboard! To frighten children in the dark, not me.

Cromwell [*it is some time now since anybody treated him
like this, and it costs him some effort to control his
anger, but he does and even manages a little smile as
one who sportingly admits defeat*]. True . . . true, Sir

Thomas, very apt. [*Then coldly.*] To frighten a man, there must be something *in* the cupboard, must there not?

More [*made wary again by the tone*]. Yes, and there is nothing in it.

Cromwell. For the moment there is this: [*picks up a paper and reads*] "I charge you with great ingratitude. I remind you of many benefits graciously given and ill received. I tell you that no King of England ever had nor could have so villainous a servant nor so traitorous a subject as yourself." [*During this, More's face goes ashen and his hand creeps up to his throat in an unconscious gesture of fear and protection. Cromwell puts down the paper and says.*] The words are not mine, Sir Thomas, but the King's. Believe that.

More. I do. [*He lowers his hands, looks up again, and with just a spark of his old impudence.*] I recognize the style. So I am brought here at last.

Cromwell. Brought? You brought yourself to where you stand now.

More. Yes—Still, in another sense—I was brought.

Cromwell. Oh, yes. You may go home now. [*After a fractional hesitation, More goes, his face fearful and his step thoughtful, and he pauses uncertainly as Cromwell calls after him.*] For the present. [*More carries on, and exits.*] I don't like him so well as I did. There's a man who raises the gale and won't come out of the harbor.

Rich [*a covert jeer*]. Do you still think you can frighten him?

Cromwell. Oh, yes.

Rich [*given pause*]. What will you do?

Cromwell. We'll put something in the cupboard.

Rich [*now definitely uneasy*]. What?

Cromwell [*as to an importunate child*]. Whatever's necessary. The King's a man of conscience and he wants either Sir Thomas More to bless his marriage or Sir Thomas More destroyed.

Rich [*shakily*]. They seem odd alternatives, Secretary.

Cromwell. Do they? That's because you're not a man of conscience. If the King destroys a man, that's proof to the King that it must have been a bad man, the kind of man a man of conscience *ought* to destroy—and of course a bad man's blessing's not worth having. So either will do.

Rich [*subdued*]. I see.

Cromwell. Oh, there's no going back, Rich. I find we've made ourselves the keepers of this conscience. And it's ravenous. [*Exit Cromwell and Rich. Enter More. Common Man enters, removes a cloth, hears More, shakes head, exits.*]

More [*calling*]. Boat! . . . Boat! . . . . [*To himself.*] Oh, come along, it's not as bad as that. . . . [*Calls.*] Boat! [*Enter Norfolk. He stops. Turning, pleased.*] Howard! . . . I can't get home. They won't bring me a boat.

Norfolk. Do you blame them?

More. Is it as bad as that?

Norfolk. It's every bit as bad as that!

More [*gravely*]. Then it's good of you to be seen with me.

Norfolk [*looking back, off*]. I followed you.

More [*surprised*]. Were *you* followed?

Norfolk. Probably. [*Facing him.*] So listen to what I have to say: You're behaving like a fool. You're behaving like a crank. You're not behaving like a gentleman—All right, that means nothing to you; but what about your friends?

More. What about them?

Norfolk. Goddammit, you're dangerous to know!

More. Then don't know me.

Norfolk. There's something further. . . . You must have realized by now there's a . . . policy, with regards to you. [*More nods.*] The King is using me in it.

More. That's clever. That's Cromwell. . . . You're between the upper and the nether millstones then.

Norfolk. I am!

More. Howard, you must cease to know me.

Norfolk. I do know you! I wish I didn't but I do!

More. I mean as a friend.

Norfolk. You *are* my friend!

More. I can't relieve you of your obedience to the King, Howard. You must relieve yourself of our friendship. No one's safe now, and you have a son.

Norfolk. You might as well advise a man to change the color of his hair! I'm fond of you, and there it is! You're fond of me, and there it is!

More. What's to be done then?

Norfolk [*with deep appeal*]. Give in.

More [*gently*]. I can't give in, Howard—[*A smile.*] You might as well advise a man to change the color of his eyes. I can't. Our friendship's more mutable than *that*.

Norfolk. Oh, that's immutable, is it? The one fixed point
in a world of changing friendships is that Thomas More
will not give in!

More [*urgent to explain*]. To me it *has* to be, for that's
myself! Affection goes as deep in me as you think, but
only God is love right through, Howard; and *that's* my
self.

Norfolk. And who are you? Goddammit, man, it's dispro-
portionate! *We're* supposed to be the arrogant ones,
the proud, splenetic ones—and we've all given in! Why
must you stand out? [*Quietly and quickly.*] You'll break
my heart.

More [*moved*]. We'll do it now, Howard: part, as friends,
and meet as strangers. [*He attempts to take Norfolk's
hand.*]

Norfolk [*throwing it off*]. Daft, Thomas! Why d'you want
to take your friendship from me? For friendship's sake!
You say we'll meet as strangers and every word you've
said confirms our friendship!

More [*takes a last affectionate look at him*]. Oh, that can be
remedied. [*Walks away, turns; in a tone of deliberate
insult.*] Norfolk, you're a fool.

Norfolk [*starts; then smiles and folds his arms*]. *You* can't
place a quarrel; you haven't the style.

More. Hear me out. You and your class have "given in"—
as you rightly call it—because the religion of this country means nothing to you one way or the other.

Norfolk. Well, that's a foolish saying for a start; the nobility
of England has always been—

More. The nobility of England, my lord, would have snored
through the Sermon on the Mount. But you'll labor
like Thomas Aquinas over a rat-dog's pedigree. Now
what's the name of those distorted creatures you're all
breeding at the moment?

Norfolk [*steadily, but roused towards anger by More's tone*].
An artificial quarrel's not a quarrel.

More. Don't deceive yourself, my lord, we've had a quarrel
since the day we met, our friendship was but sloth.

Norfolk. You can be cruel when you've a mind to be; but
I've always known that.

More. What's the name of those dogs? Marsh mastiffs? Bog
beagles?

Norfolk. Water spaniels!

More. And what would you do with a water spaniel that was
  afraid of water? You'd hang it! Well, as a spaniel is
  to water, so is a man to his own self. I will not give in
  because I oppose it—*I* do—not my pride, not my
  spleen, nor any other of my appetites but *I* do— *I!*
  [*More goes up to him and feels him up and down like
  an animal. Margaret's voice is heard, well off, calling
  her father. More's attention is irresistibly caught by
  this; but he turns back determinedly to Norfolk.*] Is
  there no single sinew in the midst of this that serves no
  appetite of Norfolk's but is just Norfolk? There is!
  Give *that* some exercise, my lord!

Margaret [*off, nearer*]. Father?

Norfolk [*breathing hard*]. Thomas. . . .

More. Because as you stand, you'll go before your Maker in
  a very ill condition!

[*Enter Margaret, below; she stops, amazed at them.*]

Norfolk. Now steady, Thomas. . . .

More. And he'll have to think that somewhere back along
  your pedigree—a bitch got over the wall!

[*Norfolk lashes out at him; he ducks and winces. Exit Norfolk.*]

Margaret. Father! [*As he straightens up.*] Father, what was
  that?

More. That was Norfolk. [*He looks after him wistfully.
  Roper enters.*]

Roper [*excited, almost gleeful*]. Do you know, sir? Have you
  heard? [*More is still looking off, not answering. To
  Margaret.*] Have you told him?

Margaret [*gently*]. We've been looking for you, Father.

[*More is still looking off.*]

Roper. There's to be a new Act through Parliament, sir!

More [*half-turning, half-attending*]. Act?

Roper. Yes, sir—about the marriage!

More [*indifferently*]. Oh. [*Turning back again. Roper and
  Margaret look at one another.*]

Margaret [*puts a hand on his arm*]. Father, by this Act,
  they're going to administer an oath.

More [*with instantaneous attention*]. An oath! [*He looks
  from one to the other.*] On what compulsion?

Roper. It's expected to be treason!

More [*very still*]. What is the oath?

Roper [*puzzled*]. It's about the marriage, sir.

More. But what is the wording?

Roper. We don't need to know the [*contemptuously*] word-ing—we know what it will mean!

More. It will mean what the words say. An oath is *made* of words! It may be possible to take it. Or avoid it. [*To Margaret*.] Have we a copy of the Bill?

Margaret. There's one coming out from the City.

More. Then let's get home and look at it. Oh, I've no boat. [*He looks off again after Norfolk*.]

Margaret [*gently*]. Father, he tried to hit you.

More. Yes—I spoke, slightingly, of water spaniels. Let's get home. [*He turns and sees Roper excited and truculent*.]

Roper. But sir—

More. Now listen, Will. And, Meg, you listen, too, you know I know you well. God made the *angels* to show him splendor—as he made animals for innocence and plants for their simplicity. But Man he made to serve him wittily, in the tangle of his mind! If he suffers us to fall to such a case that there is no escaping, then we may stand to our tackle as best we can, and yes, Will, then we may clamor like champions . . . if we have the spittle for it. And no doubt it delights God to see splendor where He only looked for complexity. But it's God's part, not our own, to bring ourselves to that extremity! Our natural business lies in escaping—so let's get home and study this Bill. [*Exit More, Roper and Margaret. Enter Common Man, dragging a cage. The rear of the stage remains in moonlight. Now descends a rack, which remains suspended*.]

Common Man [*aggrieved. Brings the basket on*]. Now look! . . . I don't suppose anyone enjoyed it any more than he did. Well, not much more. [*Takes from the basket and dons a coat and hat*.] Jailer! [*Shrugs. Pushes basket off and arranges three chairs behind the table*.] The pay scale being what it is they have to take a rather common type of man into the prison service. But it's a job. [*Admits More to jail, turns keys*.] Bit nearer the knuckle than most perhaps, but it's a job like any other job—[*Sits on steps. Enter Cromwell, Norfolk, Cranmer, who sit, and Rich, who stands behind them. More enters the cage and lies down*.] They'd let him out if they could, but for various reasons they can't. [*Twirling keys*.] I'd let him out if I could but I can't. Not without taking up residence in there myself. And he's in there already, so what'd be the point? You know the old adage? "Better a live rat than a dead lion," and that's about it. [*An envelope descends swiftly before him. He opens it and reads.*] "With reference to the old adage: Thomas Cromwell was found guilty of High Treason and executed on 28 July, 1540. Norfolk was found guilty of High Treason and should have been executed on 27 January, 1547, but on the night of 26 January, the King died of syphilis and wasn't able to sign the warrant. Thomas Cranmer"—Archbishop of Canterbury, [*jerking thumb*] that's the other one—"was burned alive on 21 March, 1556." [*He is about to conclude but sees a postscript.*] Oh. "Richard Rich became a Knight and Solicitor-General, a Baron and Lord Chancellor, and died in his bed." So did I. And so, I hope, will all of you. [*He goes to More and rouses him.*] Wake up, Sir Thomas.

More [*rousing*]. What, again?

Jailer. Sorry, sir.

More [*flops back*]. What time is it?

Jailer. One o'clock, sir.

More. Oh, this is iniquitous!

Jailer [*anxiously*]. Sir.

More [*sitting up*]. All right. [*Putting on slippers.*] Who's there?

Jailer. The Secretary, the Duke, and the Archbishop.

More. I'm flattered. [*He stands, claps hand to hip.*] Ooh!

[*Preceded by Jailer he limps across the stage; he has aged and is pale, but his manner, though wary, is relaxed; while that of the Commission is bored, tense, and jumpy.*]

Norfolk [*looks at him*]. A seat for the prisoner. [*While Jailer brings a stool from under the stairs and More sits on it, Norfolk rattles off.*] This is the Seventh Commission to inquire into the case of Sir Thomas More, appointed by His Majesty's Council. Have you anything to say?

More. No. [*To Jailer.*] Thank you.

Norfolk [*sitting back*]. Master Secretary.

Cromwell. Sir Thomas— [*He breaks off.*] Do the witnesses attend?

Rich. Secretary.

Jailer. Sir.

Cromwell [*To Jailer*]. Nearer! [*He advances a bit.*] Come where you can hear! [*Jailer takes up stance by Rich. To More.*] Sir Thomas, you have seen this document before?

More. Many times.

Cromwell. It is the Act of Succession. These are the names of those who have sworn to it.

More. I have, as you say, seen it before.

Cromwell. Will you swear to it?

More. No.

Norfolk. Thomas, we must know plainly—

Cromwell [*throws down document*]. Your Grace, *please!*

Norfolk. Master Cromwell!

[*They regard one another in hatred.*]

Cromwell. I beg Your Grace's pardon.

[*Sighing, rests his head in his hands.*]

Norfolk. Thomas, we must know plainly whether you recognize the offspring of Queen Anne as heirs to His Majesty.

More. The King in Parliament tells me that they are. Of course I recognize them.

Norfolk. Will you swear that you do?

More. Yes.

Norfolk. Then why won't you swear to the Act?

Cromwell [*impatiently*]. Because there is more than that *in* the Act.

Norfolk. Is that it?

More [*after a pause*]. Yes.

Norfolk. Then we must find out what it is in the Act that he objects to!

Cromwell. Brilliant. [*Norfolk rounds on him.*] God's wounds!

Cranmer [*hastily*]. Your Grace—May I try?

Norfolk. Certainly. I've no pretension to be an expert in police work.

[*During the next speech Cromwell straightens up and folds arms resignedly.*]

Cranmer [*clears his throat fussily*]. Sir Thomas, it states in the preamble that the King's former marriage, to the Lady Catherine, was unlawful, she being previously his brother's wife and the—er—"Pope" having no authority to sanction it. [*Gently.*] Is that what you deny? [*No reply.*] Is that what you dispute? [*No reply.*] Is that what you are not sure of? [*No reply.*]

Norfolk. Thomas, you insult the King and His Council in the person of the Lord Archbishop!

More. I insult no one. I will not take the oath. I will not
  tell you why I will not.

Norfolk. Then your reasons must be treasonable!

More. Not "must be"; may be.

Norfolk. It's a fair assumption!

More. The law requires more than an assumption; the law
  requires a fact.

[*Cromwell looks at him and away again.*]

Cranmer. I cannot judge your legal standing in the case; but
  until I know the *ground* of your objections, I can only
  guess your spiritual standing too.

More [*for a second furiously affronted; then humor over-
  takes him*]. If you're willing to guess at that, Your
  Grace, it should be a small matter to guess my objections.

Cromwell [*quickly*]. You do have objections to the Act?

Norfolk [*happily*]. Well, we know *that*, Cromwell!

More. You don't, my lord. You may *suppose* I have objections. All you *know* is that I will not swear to it. From
  sheer delight to give you trouble it might be.

Norfolk. Is it material why you won't?

More. It's most material. For refusing to swear, my goods
  are forfeit and I am condemned to life imprisonment.
  You cannot lawfully harm me further. But if you were
  right in supposing I had reasons for refusing and right
  again in supposing my reasons to be treasonable, the
  law would let you cut my head off.

Norfolk [*he has followed with some difficulty*]. Oh yes.

Cromwell [*an admiring murmur*]. Oh, well done, Sir Thomas.
  I've been trying to make that clear to His Grace for
  some time.

Norfolk [*hardly responds to the insult; his face is gloomy
  and disgusted*]. Oh, confound all this. . . . [*With real
  dignity.*] I'm not a scholar, as Master Cromwell never
  tires of pointing out, and frankly I don't know whether
  the marriage was lawful or not. But damn it, Thomas,
  look at those names. . . . You know those men! Can't
  you do what I did, and come with us, for fellowship?

More [*moved*]. And when we stand before God, and you
  are sent to Paradise for doing according to your conscience, and I am damned for not doing according to
  mine, will you come with me, for fellowship?

Cranmer. So those of us whose names are there are damned,
  Sir Thomas?

More. I don't know, Your Grace. I have no window to look
 into another man's conscience. I condemn no one.

Cranmer. Then the matter is capable of question?

More. Certainly.

Cranmer. But that you owe obedience to your King is not
 capable of question. So weigh a doubt against a certainty—and sign.

More. Some men think the Earth is round, others think it
 flat; it is a matter capable of question. But if it is flat,
 will the King's command make it round? And if it is
 round, will the King's command flatten it? No, I will
 not sign.

Cromwell [*leaping up, with ceremonial indignation*]. Then
 you have more regard to your own doubt than you
 have to his command!

More. For myself, I have no doubt.

Cromwell. No doubt of what?

More. No doubt of my grounds for refusing this oath.
 Grounds I will tell to the King alone, and which you,
 Master Secretary, will not trick out of me.

Norfolk. Thomas—

More. Oh, gentlemen, can't I go to bed?

Cromwell. You don't seem to appreciate the seriousness of
 your position.

More. I defy anyone to live in that cell for a year and not
 appreciate the seriousness of his position.

Cromwell. Yet the State has harsher punishments.

More. You threaten like a dockside bully.

Cromwell. How should I threaten?

More. Like a Minister of State, with justice!

Cromwell. Oh, justice is what you're threatened with.

More. Then I'm not threatened.

Norfolk. Master Secretary, I think the prisoner may retire
 as he requests. Unless you, my lord—

Cranmer [*pettishly*]. No, I see no purpose in prolonging the
 interview.

Norfolk. Then good night, Thomas.

More [*hesitates*]. Might I have one or two more books?

Cromwell. You have books?

More. Yes.

Cromwell. I didn't know; you shouldn't have.

More [*turns to go, pauses. Desperately*]. May I see my family?

Cromwell. No! [*More returns to cell.*].Jailer!

Jailer. Sir!

Cromwell. Have you ever heard the prisoner speak of the King's divorce, or the King's Supremacy of the Church, or the King's marriage?

Jailer. No, sir, not a word.

Cromwell. If he does, you will of course report it to the Lieutenant.

Jailer. Of course, sir.

Cromwell. You will swear an oath to that effect.

Jailer [*cheerfully*]. Certainly, sir!

Cromwell. Archbishop?

Cranmer [*laying the cross of his vestment on the table*]. Place your left hand on this and raise your right hand —take your hat off—Now say after me: I swear by my immortal soul—[*Jailer, overlapping, repeats the oath with him*]—that I will report truly anything said by Sir Thomas More against the King, the Council or the State of the Realm. So help me God. Amen.

Jailer [*overlapping*]. So help me God. Amen.

Cromwell. And there's fifty guineas in it if you do.

Jailer [*looks at him gravely*]. Yes, sir. [*He goes.*]

Cranmer [*hastily*]. That's not to tempt you into perjury, my man!

Jailer. No, sir! [*At exit he pauses; to audience.*] Fifty guineas isn't tempting; fifty guineas is alarming. If he'd left it at swearing. . . . But fifty—That's serious money. If it's worth that much now it's worth my neck presently. [*With decision.*] I want no part of it. They can sort it out between them. I feel my deafness coming on. [*Exit Jailer. The Commission rises.*]

Cromwell. Rich!

Rich. Secretary?

Cromwell. Tomorrow morning, remove the prisoner's books.

Norfolk. Is that necessary?

Cromwell [*suppressed exasperation*]. Norfolk. With regards this case, the King is becoming impatient.

Norfolk. Aye, with you.

Cromwell. With all of us. [*He walks over to the rack.*] You know the King's impatience, how commodious it is!

[*Norfolk and Cranmer exit. Cromwell is brooding over the instrument of torture.*]

Rich. Secretary!

Cromwell [*abstracted*]. Yes. . . .

Rich. Sir Redvers Llewellyn has retired.

Cromwell [*not listening*]. Mm. . . .

Rich [*goes to the other end of the rack and faces him. With some indignation*]. The Attorney-General for Wales. His post is vacant. You said I might approach you.

Cromwell [*contemptuous impatience*]. Oh, not *now*. . . . [*Broods.*] He must submit, the alternatives are bad. While More's alive the King's conscience breaks into fresh stinking flowers every time he gets from bed. And if I bring about More's death—I plant my own, I think. There's no other good solution! He must submit! [*He whirls the windlass of the rack, producing a startling clatter from the ratchet. They look at each other. He turns it again slowly, shakes his head and lets go.*] No; the King will not permit it. [*He walks away.*] We have to find some gentler way.

[*The scene change commences as he says this, and exit Rich and Cromwell. From night it becomes morning, cold gray light from off the gray water. Enter Jailer and Margaret.*]

Jailer. Wake up, Sir Thomas! Your family's here!

More [*starting up. A great cry*]. Margaret! What's this? You can visit me? [*Thrusts his arms through the cage.*] Meg. Meg. [*She goes to him. Then horrified.*] For God's sake, Meg, they've not put *you* in here?

Jailer [*reassuringly*]. No-o-o, sir. Just a visit; a short one.

More [*excited*]. Jailer, jailer, let me out of this.

Jailer. Yes, sir. I'm allowed to let you out.

More. Thank you. [*Goes to the door of the cage, gabbling while Jailer unlocks it.*] Thank you, thank you. [*He comes out. He and she regard each other; then she drops into a curtsy.*]

Margaret. Good morning, Father.

More [*ecstatic, wraps her to him*]. Oh, good morning—Good morning. [*Enter Alice, supported by Roper. She, like More, has aged and is poorly dressed*]. Good morning, Alice. Good morning, Will.

[*Roper is staring at the rack in horror. Alice approaches More and peers at him technically.*]

Alice [*almost accusatory*]. Husband, how do you do?

More [*smiling over Margaret*]. As well as need be, Alice. Very happy now. Will?

Roper. This is an awful place!

More. Except it's keeping me from you, my dears, it's not so bad. Remarkably like any other place.

Alice [*looks up critically*]. It drips!

More. Yes. Too near the river.

[*Alice goes apart and sits, her face bitter.*]

Margaret [*disengages from him, takes basket from her mother*]. We've brought you some things. [*Shows him. There is constraint between them*]. Some cheese. . . .

More. Cheese.

Margaret. And a custard. . . .

More. A custard!

Margaret. And, these other things. . . . [*She doesn't look at him.*]

Roper. And a bottle of wine. [*Offering it.*]

More. Oh. [*Mischievously.*] Is it good, son Roper?

Roper. I don't know, sir.

More [*looks at them, puzzled*]. Well.

Roper. Sir, come out! Swear to the Act! Take the oath and come out!

More. Is this why they let you come?

Roper. Yes. . . . Meg's under oath to persuade you.

More [*coldly*]. That was silly, Meg. How did you come to do that?

Margaret. I wanted to!

More. You want me to swear to the Act of Succession?

Margaret. "God more regards the thoughts of the heart than the words of the mouth." Or so you've always told me.

More. Yes.

Margaret. Then say the words of the oath and in your heart think otherwise.

More. What is an oath then but words we say to God?

Margaret. That's very neat.

More. Do you mean it isn't true?

Margaret. No, it's true.

More. Then it's a poor argument to call it "neat," Meg. When a man takes an oath, Meg, he's holding his own self in his own hands. Like water. [*He cups his hands.*] And if he opens his fingers *then*—he needn't hope to find himself again. Some men aren't capable of this, but I'd be loath to think your father one of them.

Margaret. In any State that was half good, you would be raised up high, not here, for what you've done already. It's not your fault the State's three-quarters bad. Then if you elect to suffer for it, you elect yourself a hero.

More. That's very neat. But look now. . . . If we lived in a State where virtue was profitable, common sense would make us good, and greed would make us saintly. And we'd live like animals or angels in the happy land that *needs* no heroes. But since in fact we see that avarice, anger, envy, pride, sloth, lust and stupidity commonly profit far beyond humility, chastity, fortitude, justice and thought, and have to choose, to be human at all ... why then perhaps we *must* stand fast a little—even at the risk of being heroes.

Margaret [*emotionally*]. But in reason! Haven't you done as much as God can reasonably *want*?

More. Well ... finally ... it isn't a matter of reason; finally it's a matter of love.

Alice [*hostile*]. You're content, then, to be shut up here with mice and rats when you might be home with us!

More [*flinching*]. Content? If they'd open a crack that wide [*between finger and thumb*] I'd be through it. [*To Margaret.*] Well, has Eve run out of apples?

Margaret. I've not yet told you what the house is like, without you.

More. Don't, Meg.

Margaret. What we do in the evenings, now that you're not there.

More. Meg, have done!

Margaret. We sit in the dark because we've no candles. And we've no talk because we're wondering what they're doing to you here.

More. The King's more merciful than you. He doesn't use the rack.

[*Enter Jailer.*]

Jailer. Two minutes to go, sir. I thought you'd like to know.

More. Two minutes!

Jailer. Till seven o'clock, sir. Sorry. Two minutes. [*Exit Jailer.*]

More. Jailer! [*Seizes Roper by the arm.*] Will—go to him, talk to him, keep him occupied—[*Propelling him after Jailer.*]

Roper. How, sir?

More. Anyhow! Have you got any money?

Roper [*eagerly*]. Yes!

More. No, don't try and bribe him! Let him play for it; he's got a pair of dice. And talk to him, you understand! And take this—[*he hands him the wine*] and mind you share it—do it properly, Will! [*Roper nods vigorously and exits.*] Now listen, you must leave the country. All of you must leave the country.

Margaret. And leave you here?

More. It makes no difference, Meg; they won't let you see me again. [*Breathlessly, a prepared speech under pressure.*] You must all go on the same day, but not on the same boat; different boats from different ports—

Margaret. After the trial, then.

More. There'll be no trial, they have no case. Do this for me, I beseech you?

Margaret. Yes.

More. Alice? [*She turns her back.*] Alice, I command you!

Alice [*harshly*]. Right!

More [*looks into the basket*]. Oh, this is splendid; I know who packed this.

Alice [*harshly*]. I packed it.

More. Yes. [*He eats a morsel.*] You still make superlative custard, Alice.

Alice. Do I?

More. That's a nice dress you have on.

Alice. It's my cooking dress.

More. It's very nice anyway. Nice color.

Alice [*turns; quietly*]. By God, you think very little of me. [*Mounting bitterness.*] I know I'm a fool. But I'm no such fool as at this time to be lamenting for my dresses! Or to relish complimenting on my custard!

More [*regarding her with frozen attention. He nods once or twice*]. I am well rebuked. [*He holds out his hands*] Al—

Alice. No! [*She remains where she is, glaring at him.*]

More [*he is in great fear of her*]. I am faint when I think of the worst that they may do to me. But worse than that would be to go with you not understanding why I go.

Alice. I don't!

More [*just hanging on to his self-possession*]. Alice, if you can tell me that you understand, I think I can make a good death, if I have to.

Alice. Your death's no "good" to me!

More. Alice, you must tell me that you understand!

Alice. I don't! [*She throws it straight at his head.*] I don't believe this had to happen.

More [*his face is drawn*]. If you say that, Alice, I don't see how I'm to face it.

Alice. It's the truth!

More [*gasping*]. You're an honest woman.

Alice. Much good may it do me! I'll tell you what I'm afraid
   of: that when you've gone, I shall hate you for it.

More [*turns from her, his face working*]. Well, you mustn't,
   Alice, that's all. [*Swiftly she crosses the stage to him;
   he turns and they clasp each other fiercely.*] You
   mustn't, you—

Alice [*covers his mouth with her hand*]. Ss-s-sh. . . . As for
   understanding, I understand you're the best man that
   I ever met or am likely to; and if you go—well, God
   knows why I suppose—though as God's my witness
   God's kept deadly quiet about it! And if anyone wants
   my opinion of the King and his Council they've only to
   ask for it!

More. Why, it's a lion I married! A lion! A lion! [*He breaks
   away from her, his face shining.*] Say what you may—
   this custard's very good. It's very, very good. [*He puts
   his face in his hands; Alice and Margaret comfort him;
   Roper and Jailer erupt onto the stage above, wrangling
   fiercely.*]

Jailer. It's no good, sir! I know what you're up to! And it
   can't be done!

Roper. Another minute, man!

Jailer [*descending; to More*]. Sorry, sir, time's up!

Roper [*gripping his shoulder from behind*]. For pity's sake!

Jailer [*shaking him off*]. Now don't do that, sir! Sir Thomas,
   the ladies will have to go now!

More. You said seven o'clock!

Jailer. It's seven now. You must understand my position, sir.

More. But one more minute!

Margaret. Only a little while—give us a little while!

Jailer [*reprovingly*]. Now, miss, you don't want to get me
   into trouble.

Alice. Do as you're told. Be off at once!

[*The first stroke of seven is heard on a heavy, deliberate bell,
   which continues, reducing what follows to a babble.*]

Jailer [*taking Margaret firmly by the upper arm*]. Now come
   along, miss; you'll get your father into trouble as well
   as me. [*Roper descends and grabs him.*] Are you ob-
   structing me, sir? [*Margaret embraces More and dashes
   up the stairs and exits, followed by Roper. Taking Alice
   gingerly by the arm.*] Now, my lady, no trouble!

Alice [*throwing him off as she rises*]. Don't put your muddy hand on me!

Jailer. Am I to call the guard then? Then come on!

[*Alice, facing him, puts foot on bottom stair and so retreats before him, backwards.*]

More. For God's sake, man, we're saying goodbye!

Jailer. You don't know what you're asking, sir. You don't know how you're watched.

Alice. Filthy, stinking, gutter-bred turnkey!

Jailer. Call me what you like, ma'am; you've got to go.

Alice. I'll see you suffer for this!

Jailer. You're doing your husband no good!

More. Alice, goodbye, my love!

[*On this, the last stroke of the seven sounds. Alice raises her hand, turns, and with considerable dignity, exits. Jailer stops at the head of the stairs and addresses More, who, still crouching, turns from him, facing audience.*]

Jailer [*reasonably*]. You understand my position, sir, there's nothing I can do; I'm a plain, simple man and just want to keep out of trouble.

More [*cries out passionately*]. Oh, Sweet Jesus! These plain, simple men!

[*Immediately music, portentous and heraldic, is heard. Bars, rack and cage are flown swiftly upwards. The lighting changes from cold gray to warm yellow, re-creating a warm interior. Small coat of arms comes down and hangs, followed by large coat of arms above stairs, then two medium coats of arms. Then the largest coat of arms appears. During this the Jailer takes off jailer's coat, throws it off, takes off the small chair and moves armchair to the center. Moves the table under the stairs. He brings on the jury bench, takes hats from the basket and puts them on poles with a juryman's hat, takes jailer's hat off head and puts it on a pole. Seven are plain gray hats, four are those worn by the Steward, Boatman, Innkeeper and Jailer. And the last is another of the plain gray ones. He takes a portfolio from the basket and puts it on the table, and pushes basket into a corner. He then brings on two throne chairs. While he is still doing this, and just before coats of arms have finished their descent, enter Cromwell. He ringingly addresses the audience as soon as the music ends.*]

Cromwell [*indicating descending props*].

What Englishman can behold without Awe
The Canvas and the Rigging of the Law!

[*Brief fanfare.*]

Forbidden here the galley-master's whip—
Hearts of Oak, in the Law's Great Ship!

[*Brief fanfare. To Common Man who is tiptoeing discreetly off-stage.*] Where are you going?

Common Man. I've finished here, sir.

Cromwell. You're the Foreman of the Jury.

Common Man. Oh no, sir.

Cromwell. You are John Dauncey. A general dealer?

Common Man [*gloomily*]. Yes, sir?

Cromwell [*resuming his rhetorical stance*]. Foreman of the Jury. Does the cap fit?

Common Man [*puts on the gray hat. It fits*]. Yes, sir.

Cromwell.

So, now we'll apply the good, plain sailor's art,
And fix these quicksands on the Law's plain chart!

[*Several narrow panels, orange and bearing the monogram "HR VIII" in gold letters, are lowered. Renewed, more prolonged fanfare; during which enter Cranmer and Norfolk, who sit on throne chairs. On their entry More and Foreman rise. As soon as the fanfare is finished Norfolk speaks.*]

Norfolk [*takes refuge behind a rigorously official manner*]. Sir Thomas More, you are called before us here at the Hall of Westminster to answer charge of High Treason. Nevertheless, and though you have heinously offended the King's Majesty, we hope if you will even now forthink and repent of your obstinate opinions, you may still taste his gracious pardon.

More. My lords, I thank you. Howbeit I make my petition to Almighty God that He will keep me in this, my honest mind, to the last hour that I shall live. . . . As for the matters you may charge me with, I fear, from my present weakness, that neither my wit nor my memory will serve to make sufficient answers. . . . I should be glad to sit down.

Norfolk. Be seated. Master Secretary Cromwell, have you the charge?

Cromwell. I have, my lord.

Norfolk. Then read the charge.

Cromwell [*formally*]. That you did conspire traitorously and maliciously to deny and deprive our liege lord Henry

of his undoubted certain title, Supreme Head of the
Church in England.

More [*with surprise, shock, and indignation*]. But I have
never denied this title!

Cromwell. You refused the oath tendered to you at the
Tower and elsewhere—

More [*again shocked and indignant*]. Silence is not denial.
And for my silence I am punished, with imprisonment.
Why have I been called again? [*At this point he is
sensing that the trial has been in some way rigged.*]

Norfolk. On a charge of High Treason, Sir Thomas.

Cromwell. For which the punishment is *not* imprisonment.

More. Death . . . comes for us all, my lords. Yes, even for
Kings he comes, to whom amidst all their Royalty and
brute strength he will neither kneel nor make them any
reverence nor pleasantly desire them to come forth, but
roughly grasp them by the very breast and rattle them
until they be stark dead! So causing their bodies to be
buried in a pit and sending *them* to a judgment . . .
whereof at their death their success is uncertain.

Cromwell. Treason enough here!

Norfolk. The death of Kings is not in question, Sir Thomas.

More. Nor mine, I trust, until I'm proven guilty.

Norfolk [*leaning forward urgently*]. Your life lies in your
own hand, Thomas, as it always has.

More [*absorbs this*]. For our own deaths, my lord, yours and
mine, dare we for shame enter the Kingdom with ease,
when Our Lord Himself entered with so much pain?
[*And now he faces Cromwell, his eyes sparkling with
suspicion.*]

Cromwell. Now, Sir Thomas, you stand upon your silence.

More. I do.

Cromwell. But, Gentlemen of the Jury, there are many kinds
of silence. Consider first the silence of a man when he
is dead. Let us say we go into the room where he is
lying; and let us say it is in the dead of night—there's
nothing like darkness for sharpening the ear; and we
listen. What do we hear? Silence. What does it betoken,
this silence? Nothing. This is silence, pure and simple.
But consider another case. Suppose I were to draw a
dagger from my sleeve and make to kill the prisoner
with it, and suppose their lordships there, instead of crying out for me to stop or crying out for help to stop me,
maintained their silence. That *would* betoken! It would

betoken a willingness that I should do it, and under the
law they would be guilty with me. So silence can, according to circumstances, speak. Consider, now, the
circumstances of the prisoner's silence. The oath was
put to good and faithful subjects up and down the
country and they had declared His Grace's title to be
just and good. And when it came to the prisoner he refused. He calls this silence. Yet is there a man in this
court, is there a man in this country, who does not
know Sir Thomas More's opinion of the King's title?
Of course not! But how can that be? Because this silence betokened—nay, this silence *was* not silence at all
but most eloquent denial.

More [*with some of the academic's impatience for a shoddy
line of reasoning*]. Not so, Master Secretary, the maxim
is "qui tacet consentire." [*Turns to Common Man.*] The
maxim of the law is [*very carefully*] "Silence gives con-
sent." If, therefore, you wish to construe what my
silence "betokened," you must construe that I con-
sented, not that I denied.

Cromwell. Is that what the world in fact construes from it?
Do you pretend that is what you *wish* the world to construe from it?

More. The world must construe according to its wits. This
Court must construe according to the law.

Cromwell. I put it to the Court that the prisoner is perverting
the law—making smoky what should be a clear light
to discover to the Court his own wrongdoing! [*Cromwell's official indignation is slipping into genuine anger
and More responds.*]

More. The law is not a "light" for you or any man to see by;
the law is not an instrument of any kind. [*To the Foreman.*] The law is a causeway upon which, so long as
he keeps to it, a citizen may walk safely. [*Earnestly
addressing him.*] In matters of conscience—

Cromwell [*smiling bitterly*]. The conscience, the conscience. . . .

More [*turning*]. The word is not familiar to you?

Cromwell. By God, too familiar! I am very used to hear it in
the mouths of criminals!

More. I am used to hear bad men misuse the name of God,
yet God exists. [*Turning back.*] In matters of conscience, the loyal subject is more bounden to be loyal *to*
his conscience than to any other thing.

Cromwell [*breathing hard; straight at More*]. And so provide a noble motive for his frivolous self-conceit!

More [*earnestly*]. It is not so, Master Cromwell—very and pure necessity for respect of my own soul.

Cromwell. Your own self, you mean!

More. Yes, a man's soul is his self!

Cromwell [*thrusts his face into More's. They hate each other and each other's standpoint*]. A miserable thing, whatever you call it, that lives like a bat in a Sunday School! A shrill incessant pedagogue about its own salvation—but nothing to say of your place in the State! Under the King! In a great native country!

More [*not untouched*]. Is it my place to say "good" to the State's sickness? Can I help my King by giving him lies when he asks for truth? Will you help England by populating her with liars?

Cromwell [*backs away. His face stiff with malevolence*]. My lords, I wish to call [*he raises his voice*] Sir Richard Rich! [*Enter Rich. He is now splendidly official, in dress and bearing; even Norfolk is a bit impressed.*] Sir Richard. [*Indicating Cranmer.*]

Cranmer [*proffering Bible*]. I do solemnly swear . . .

Rich. I do solemnly swear that the evidence I shall give before the Court shall be the truth, the whole truth, and nothing but the truth.

Cranmer [*discreetly*]. So help me God, Sir Richard.

Rich. So help me God.

Norfolk. Take your stand there, Sir Richard.

Cromwell. Now, Rich, on twelve March, you were at the Tower?

Rich. I was.

Cromwell. With what purpose?

Rich. I was sent to carry away the prisoner's books.

Cromwell. Did you talk with the prisoner?

Rich. Yes.

Cromwell. Did you talk about the King's Supremacy of the Church?

Rich. Yes.

Cromwell. What did you say?

Rich. I said to him. "Supposing there was an Act of Parliament to say that I, Richard Rich, were to be King, would not you, Master More, take me for King?" "That I would," he said, "for then you would be King."

Cromwell. Yes?

Richard. Then he said—

Norfolk [*sharply*]. The prisoner?

Rich. Yes, my lord. "But I will put you a higher case," he said. "How if there were an Act of Parliament to say that God should not be God?"

More. This is true; and then you said—

Norfolk. Silence! Continue.

Rich. I said, "Ah, but I will put you a middle case. Parliament has made our King Head of the Church. Why will you not accept him?"

Norfolk [*strung up*]. Well?

Rich. Then he said Parliament had no power to do it.

Norfolk. Repeat the prisoner's words!

Rich. He said, "Parliament has not the competence." Or words to that effect.

Cromwell. He denied the title?

Rich. He did.

[*All look to More, but he looks to Rich.*]

More. In good faith, Rich, I am sorrier for your perjury than my peril.

Norfolk. Do you deny this?

More. Yes! My lords, if I were a man who heeded not the taking of an oath, you know well I need not to be here. Now I will take an oath! If what Master Rich has said is true, then I pray I may never see God in the face! Which I would not say were it otherwise for anything on earth.

Cromwell [*to Foreman, calmly, technically*]. That is not evidence.

More. Is it probable—is it probable—that after so long a silence on this, the very point so urgently sought of me, I should open my mind to such a man as that?

Cromwell [*to Rich*]. Do you wish to modify your testimony?

Rich. No, Secretary.

More. There were two other men! Southwell and Palmer!

Cromwell. Unhappily, Sir Richard Southwell and Master Palmer are both in Ireland on the King's business. [*More gestures helplessly.*] It has no bearing. I have their deposition here in which the Court will see they state that being busy with the prisoner's books they did not hear what was said. [*Hands deposition to Foreman, who examines it with much seriousness.*]

More. If I had really said this is it not obvious he would instantly have called these men to witness?

Cromwell. Sir Richard, have you anything to add?

Rich. Nothing, Mr. Secretary.

Norfolk. Sir Thomas?

More [*looking at Foreman*]. To what purpose? I am a dead man. [*To Cromwell.*] You have your desire of me. What you have hunted me for is not my actions, but the thoughts of my heart. It is a long road you have opened. For first men will disclaim their hearts and presently they will have no hearts. God help the people whose Statesmen walk your road.

Norfolk. Then the witness may withdraw.

[*Rich crosses the stage, watched by More.*]

More. I *have* one question to ask the witness. [*Rich stops.*] That's a chain of office you are wearing. [*Reluctantly Rich faces him.*] May I see it? [*Norfolk motions him to approach. More examines the medallion.*] The red dragon. [*To Cromwell.*] What's this?

Cromwell. Sir Richard is appointed Attorney-General for Wales.

More [*looking into Rich's face, with pain and amusement*]. For Wales? Why, Richard, it profits a man nothing to give his soul for the whole world . . . But for Wales!

[*Exit Rich, stiff-faced, but infrangibly dignified.*]

Cromwell. Now I must ask the Court's indulgence! I have a message for the prisoner from the King. [*Urgently.*] Sir Thomas, I am empowered to tell you that even now—

More. No no, it cannot be.

Cromwell. The case rests! [*Norfolk is staring at More.*] My lord!

Norfolk. The jury will retire and consider the evidence.

Cromwell. Considering the evidence it shouldn't be necessary for them to retire. [*Standing over Foreman.*] Is it necessary?

Foreman [*shakes his head*]. No, sir!

Norfolk. Then is the prisoner guilty or not guilty?

Foreman. Guilty, my lord!

Norfolk [*leaping to his feet; all rise save More*]. Prisoner at the bar, you have been found guilty of High Treason. The sentence of the Court—

More. My lord! [*Norfolk breaks off. More has a sly smile. From this point to end of play his manner is of one who has fulfilled all his obligations and will now consult no interest but his own.*] My lord, when *I* was practicing

the law, the manner was to ask the prisoner *before*
pronouncing sentence, if he had anything to say.

Norfolk [*flummoxed*]. Have you anything to say?

More. Yes. [*He rises; all others sit.*] To avoid this I have
taken every path my winding wits would find. Now that
the Court has determined to condemn me, God
knoweth how, I will discharge my mind . . . concerning
my indictment and the King's title. The indictment is
grounded in an Act of Parliament which is directly
repugnant to the Law of God. The King in Parliament
cannot bestow the Supremacy of the Church because
it is a Spiritual Supremacy! And more to this the im-
munity of the Church is promised both in Magna Carta
and the King's own Coronation Oath!

Cromwell. Now we plainly see that you *are* malicious!

More. Not so, Master Secretary! [*He pauses, and launches,
very quietly, ruminatively, into his final stock-taking.*]
I am the King's true subject, and pray for him and all
the realm . . . I do none harm, I say none harm, I think
none harm. And if this be not enough to keep a man
alive, in good faith I long not to live . . . I have, since
I came into prison, been several times in such a case
that I thought to die within the hour, and I thank Our
Lord I was never sorry for it, but rather sorry when it
passed. And therefore, my poor body is at the King's
pleasure. Would God my death might do him some
good . . . [*With a great flash of scorn and anger.*]
Nevertheless, it is not for the Supremacy that you have
sought my blood—but because I would not bend to the
marriage! [*Immediately the scene change commences,
while Norfolk reads the sentence.*]

Norfolk. Prisoner at the bar, you have been found guilty on
the charge of High Treason. The sentence of the Court
is that you shall be taken from this Court to the Tower,
thence to the place of execution, and there your head
shall be stricken from your body, and may God have
mercy on your soul! [*The trappings of justice are flown
upwards. Norfolk and Cranmer exit with chairs. The
lights are dimmed save for three areas: spots, left,
center, and right front, and a black arch cutout is
lowered. Through this arch—where the ax and the
block are silhouetted against a light of steadily increasing brilliance—comes the murmur of a large crowd,
formalized almost into a chant. The Foreman doffs cap,*

*and as Common Man he removes the prisoner's chair
and the two benches. Cromwell pushes the table off,
takes a small black mask from basket and puts it on
Common Man. The Common Man thus becomes the
traditional Headsman. He ascends the stairs, sets up
the block from its trap, gets the ax and then straddles
his legs. At once the crowd falls silent. Exit Cromwell,
dragging basket. Norfolk joins More in the center spot.
Cranmer takes his position on the rostrum. The Woman
goes under the stairs.]* I can come no further, Thomas.
[Proffering a goblet.] Here, drink this.

More. My Master had easel and gall, not wine, given him to
drink. Let me be going.

Margaret. Father! *[She runs to him in the center spot and
flings herself upon him.]* Father! Father, Father, Father,
Father!

More. Have patience, Margaret, and trouble not thyself.
Death comes for us all; even at our birth—*[he holds her
head and looks down at it for a moment in recollection]*
—even at our birth, death does but stand aside a little.
And every day he looks towards us and muses somewhat to himself whether that day or the next he will
draw nigh. It is the law of nature, and the will of God.
[He disengages from her. Dispassionately.] You have
long known the secrets of my heart.

[Margaret exits with Norfolk.]

Woman. Sir Thomas! *[He stops.]* Remember me, Sir
Thomas? When you were Chancellor, you gave a false
judgment against me. Remember that now.

More. Woman, you see how I am occupied. *[With sudden
decision goes to her in the left spot. Crisply.]* I remember your matter well, and if I had to give sentence now
I assure you I should not alter it. You have no injury;
so go your way; and content yourself; and trouble me
not! *[She exits. He walks swiftly to the stairs, then
stops, realizing that Cranmer, carrying his Bible, has
followed him. Quite kindly.]* I beseech Your Grace,
go back. *[Offended, Cranmer does so. The lighting is
now complete, i.e., darkness save for three areas of
light, the one at cutout arch now dazzlingly brilliant.
When More gets to head of stairs by the Headsman, he
turns to Headsman.]* Friend, be not afraid of your
office. You send me to God.

Cranmer [*envious rather than waspish*]. You're very sure of
    that, Sir Thomas. [*He exits.*]

More [*takes off his hat, revealing the gray disordered hair*].
    He will not refuse one who is so blithe to go to him.
    [*Kneeling. Immediately is heard a harsh roar of kettle-
    drums. There is total blackout at head of the stairs,
    while the drums roar. Then the drums cease.*]

Headsman [*bangs the trap down, in the darkness*]. Behold—
    the head—of a traitor!

[*The lights come up.*]

Common Man [*comes to the center of the stage, having taken
    off his mask*]. I'm breathing . . . Are you breathing too?
    . . . It's nice, isn't it? It isn't difficult to keep alive,
    friends—just don't *make* trouble—or if you must make
    trouble, make the sort of trouble that's expected. Well,
    I don't need to tell you that. Good night. If we should
    bump into one another, recognize me. [*He exits.*]

                                 Curtain.

Ann Jellicoe **The Knack**

A COMEDY

To Roger and Keith

Ann Jellicoe

BY JOHN RUSSELL TAYLOR

Ann Jellicoe is certainly exotic, and perhaps unique, among the younger dramatists in that her prime ambition initially was to be a director, and her first full-length play, *The Sport of My Mad Mother,* was, in fact, written first and foremost as a means, she hoped, of strengthening her hand when it came to the practical realization of this ambition. Her experience up to writing this play, which won third prize in the *Observer* drama competition of 1956 (along with *A Resounding Tinkle* and an Australian play), had, in fact, been largely in the field of direction: born in Middlesborough in 1928, she studied at the Central School of Speech and Drama, then worked in repertory and travelled before joining the staff in 1952. During her two years as staff producer at the Central School she was responsible for many student productions, and since leaving has frequently returned to direct, mainly productions of plays by modern English writers (her productions of *The Hole* and *Live Like Pigs* in particular were far superior to their original professional productions). In 1952 she founded and ran for two years an open-stage theatre club, the Cockpit Theatre, directing many plays there, including an early one-act indiscretion of her own, which she now prefers to forget, in which according to her own account she fell prey to the contemporary vogue for the verse-plays of Christopher Fry, with disastrous consequences.

In 1956, wanting if possible to break into the professional theatre as a director, she began work upon *The Sport of My Mad Mother,* not fully understanding then that no one is looked upon more askance in the theatre than an author, particularly a new, young author, who wants to direct his (or even more startlingly *her*) own plays. However, the play won its *Observer* prize, was accepted for production on the strength of this by the English Stage Company, and staged with the help of a grant from Schweppes. Ann Jellicoe and George Devine shared the direction, and the play was a complete commercial disaster; from the critics

it received slightly more approval than from playgoers, but
on the whole not very much. Even so, one or two critics
recognized that Ann Jellicoe was trying, not yet with complete success admittedly, to do something quite new in the
English theatre: to make her play primarily something
which happened in front of its audience and made its effect
as a totality, rather than a piece of neatly carpentered literary craftsmanship which would "read well" and work only
by way of its dialogue's appeal to the mind.

The script of *The Sport of My Mad Mother,* in fact,
makes very little sense just read cold: it is simply the short
score from which a full orchestral sound can be conjured
by a skilled musician, or the scenario for a ballet waiting for
a composer to write the music and a choreographer to stage
it; it is, not surprisingly considering the circumstances of
its writing, "director's theatre" to the nth degree, clearly seen
by the author mainly as an *aide-mémoire* in the transference
of her initial conception from the stage of her own mind to
a real, physical stage. Consequently when staged it makes
extraordinary demands on the playgoer schooled in the
traditional techniques of the English stage: he expects the
play he sees to be, in effect, written mainly for the ear, with
the eye required to act on its own just once in a while,
when it may note a bit of business and aid the mind to deduce some logical significance for it. But here is a play
which assaults (the word is used advisedly) both eye and
ear, and makes very little appeal to the intellect at all.

It is about a group of teddy-boys, whose behavior
throughout is instinct with a purely arbitrary spirit of violence, one or two outsiders who become involved mysteri-
ously with them (Caldaro, a young American; Dodo, a
retarded 13-year-old) and Greta, their spiritual leader, a
legendary figure of destruction and in the end, when she
gives birth to a child, of creation too, who corresponds pre-
sumably to Kali, the Indian goddess of creation and destruction who is the "mad mother" of the title ("All creation is
the sport of my mad mother Kali"). Much of the dialogue,
most of it, in fact, is almost entirely incantatory in effect,
with a minimum of analysable sense; just enough to create
the atmosphere of menace and violence always on the point
of being unleashed, without ever defining the nature and
purpose (if any) of either too exactly. Quite a lot of the
"dialogue" indeed, is merely sound—cries and ejaculations,
repeated monosyllables shorn of any associative effect and

used entirely for their tonal qualities. On the page it looks as intimidating and uncommunicative as the hieroglyphs of some unknown tongue; in the theatre it all surges over and around one, a strange, disturbing pattern of sights and sounds which produces a corresponding series of emotional reactions from which gradually a total picture of a violent, instinctive way of life emerges: it is about people who are for the most part inarticulate and uncommunicative, and instead of trying to externalize their emotions and reactions in necessarily stilted and artificial words it creates in the theatre a sort of symbolic equivalent of the mental climate in which they live and thrusts us willy-nilly into it.

But it can do this only so long as we abandon ourselves to the experience instead of stopping to question it. As soon as we deliberately extract ourselves from participation in what is happening and ask what any particular line or section *means*, we are lost and the play is lost to us. In an interview in the *New Theatre Magazine*, published by members of the drama faculty of Bristol University, Ann Jellicoe herself put all this very clearly:

> I think the word "meaning" shows exactly what is wrong with people's attitudes. If they were to ask "What is the play about?" it would be a better approach. This is a new kind of play, which demands a new approach. Most playgoers today are not used to taking anything direct in the theatre. What they do is transform it into words and put it through their brain. For instance, there is a scene in my play where Caldaro is knocked out, and the Teds stand him on his feet, wrap him up in newspaper, cavort round him, chanting until they get to a pitch of ecstasy when they tear the newspaper off him. Now in this action there are hardly any words that make sense—there is nothing which your intellect can take in. If you sit watching and say "What does this mean? What does this mean?" you're not going to get anywhere; but if you allow yourself to be excited by the visual action and the gradual crescendo of noise underlining this, you may begin to appreciate what it's about. . . .
>
> You see, so many plays tell you what is happening the whole time. People don't act angry; they tell you they're angry. Now, my play is about incoherent people—people who have no power of expression, of

analysing their emotions. They don't know why they're afraid; they don't even know that they are afraid. So they have to compensate for their fear by attacking someone else; they're insecure and frustrated, and they have to compensate for that by being big, and violent. And all this is directly shown, instead of being explained; if you're content to watch it without thinking all the time "What is the meaning?" so that you don't even see or hear, you're so busy thinking—then you will get what it's about.

The Sport of My Mad Mother might well appeal to a variety of people for a variety of reasons, but the Girl Guides Association is about the last body one would expect to find its attitudes, its tone or its style palatable. Yet shortly after it was produced Ann Jellicoe was commissioned by them to write a show for staging at the Empire Pool, Wembley, the only conditions being that it should be "of interest to youth," have a "positive ending," make room for some foreign guides, and have a cast of about 800 girls, 100 boys, and possibly some adults. (The most likely explanation of the commission seems to be that they had heard she wrote "interesting plays about teenagers.") Her imagination fired by the possibilities inherent in the form of presentation, she decided to accept the commission and produce something personal which at the same time satisfied all these conditions. The result, *The Rising Generation,* was rejected out of hand by the committee, even after complete rewriting and conventionalization, but the original text was later published in *Ark,* the magazine of the Royal College of Art.

From this it emerges as by far the most interesting and imaginative work ever written in the simple but spectacular form of the youth pageant (though that, admittedly, is not saying very much). It is a story about intolerance and totalitarian rule, told in parable form, though a parable, surely, little calculated to appeal to the Girl Guide ideal: it postulates a conspiracy by the monstrous regiment of women, headed by Mother, "an enormous woman half-masked with a padded headdress and shoes," to dominate the world and exterminate men. Men are banished and expunged from history; girls at school have to repeat religiously "Shakespeare was a woman. Milton was a woman. The Black Prince was a woman. Robin Hood, she was a

woman. King John was a woman. Newton was a woman";
while their teacher firmly indoctrinates them: "Men are
black. Men are thick. Men are tall. Men are strong. Men
will tear you, beat you, eat you. When you're older, you will
know." But finally the girls get together with the boys to
rebel against the tyrannical domination of Mother, and
though she puts into operation her final threat, the Bomb,
they survive and as the show ends the whole vast arena is
transformed into a flying saucer to carry them all to a new
life somewhere in space. Throughout, the piece not only
says something, and says it clearly enough to "appeal to
youth," but it also uses the wide open spaces of the Empire
Pool and its resources brilliantly: the spotlit pursuit of the
boy Stephen, the triumphal progress of Mother, her op-
ponents held at bay by a battalion of charladies with flaming
mops, and the great final transformation could hardly fail
to make their effect. It was perhaps too much to expect the
Girl Guides Association to see the singular merits of *The
Rising Generation*, but by refusing it they rejected the
most interesting work they are ever likely to receive in
response to a commission, and incidentally deprived the
7,000 Guides who fill the Empire Pool every night when
such a show is on of a strikingly effective piece of spectacular entertainment, to put it no higher.

If *The Rising Generation* suggests in some ways a re-
handling of themes from *The Sport of My Mad Mother* in a
rather different context, Ann Jellicoe's next play, *The
Knack*, staged by the English Stage Company at the Arts,
Cambridge, in 1961, shows a complete departure in subject
matter, allied with a remarkable consistency in form and
style. We might have imagined that the style employed in
The Sport of My Mad Mother applied only to the completely inarticulate and nonintellectual who could not be
got at in dramatic terms any other way, but even from the
New Theatre Magazine interview we should have known
better, for there Ann Jellicoe generalizes her views on
dramatic expression like this:

> When I write a play I am trying to communicate
> with the audience. I do this by every means in my
> power—I try to get at them through their eyes, by
> providing visual action; I try to get at them through
> their ears, for instance by noises and rhythm. These
> are not loose effects; they are introduced to communi-

cate with the audience directly through their senses, to reinforce the total effect of the play, and they are always geared to character and situation. The theatre is a medium which works upon people's imagination and emotion—not merely their intellect. And I am trying to use every possible effect that the theatre can offer to stir up the audience—to get at them through their emotions. . . . I write this way because—the image that everybody has of the rational, intellectual and intelligent man—I don't believe it's true. I think people are driven by their emotions, and by their fears and insecurities.

The Knack might be a direct illustration of this statement: it is a comedy about, as far as can be seen, normally intelligent, articulate people caught at precisely the point where the image of rational, intelligent man breaks down just because they are completely ruled by their emotions, their fears and insecurities. The subject of these feelings, naturally enough, is sex—where else is the normally civilized man more subject to noncivilized, indeed anticivilized, influences? The situation is classically simple. Three men, Tolen, Tom, and Colin, live in one house: Tolen has more than enough sex, being a living demonstration of sexual determination, stamina, and resilience: Tom, having one supposes struck a fairly happy balance, is not violently involved; and Colin, their landlord, does not get anything like enough and worries about it. Into their lives comes an innocent—at least she seems to be an innocent—called Nancy, and a tussle for her develops between Tolen, who sees her as yet another scalp for his belt, and Colin (though their conflict only slowly develops, and at one stage Colin is happy to let Tolen seduce Nancy while he takes notes on technique). Colin is to some extent in a one-up position because he is landlord, but Tolen has the advantage of him in the enviable field of sexual experience, and while Nancy is out of the room being sick after a fainting fit Tolen tries to play off his advantage against Colin's, offering to take Colin into a girl-sharing arrangement he is negotiating with a friend if in return Colin will throw out Tom, whose ironic and unpredictable presence he finds irksome, in favor of the other womanizer. Their plans are swept aside, however, by Nancy's vociferous assertions upon recovery that she was raped while unconscious—by Colin. Colin and

Tolen have a violent row on the point, Tolen saying Colin couldn't, Colin saying he didn't but he could; finally Tolen leaves and Colin and the girl are left together under the friendly eye of Tom. . . .

That is what happens—what *happens,* not for the most part what is *said.* Whole sections of the text make no noticeable sense in themselves, because it is always what is going on, and what the audience apprehends from participating in what is going on, that counts. Often the dialogue is simply a series of disjointed *non sequiturs* or uncomprehending repetitions, and in one key scene, where Colin and Tom gradually draw Nancy into their fantasy that the bed in the room is actually a piano, of "pings" and "plongs" variously distributed and extending virtually uninterrupted over some three pages of the script. The most remarkable quality of the play, in fact, is the sheer drive of the action, physical and emotional, right through its three acts in one unbroken movement; in the theatre not only does the play not demand rationization on the part of its audience but, unlike *The Sport of My Mad Mother,* which is by comparison sometimes uncertain and immature (the last act in particular fails to cap the previous two conclusively), it positively forbids it: the spectator is carried along irresistibly by the verve and ebullience of the play, and at the end, even if he does not know what, stage by stage, it means, he certainly knows vividly what it is about.

In the five years between *The Sport of My Mad Mother* and *The Knack* Ann Jellicoe has matured and developed extraordinarily as a dramatist while continuing obstinately to plough her solitary furrow (her translation, during that time, of two Ibsen plays, *Rosmersholm* and *The Lady from the Sea,* has had no noticeable effect on her writing). Her plays are quiet unlike anyone else's, and even in a generation of dramatists distinguished above all else for their sure grasp of practical theatre her work stands out by virtue of its complete command of theatrical effect. Her plays are difficult to stage, undeniably, since they depend so completely on their theatrical qualities and the sensitivity and accuracy with which the director can cover the bare framework of mere words with the intricately organized architecture fully drawn out in the creator's head. But once staged, and staged well, they infinitely repay the trouble; one only hopes it will not be another five years before she chooses again to face some director with such a challenge.

Tom. Smallish in size. Vigorous, balanced, strong and sensitive in his movements. He speaks with a great range of pitch, pace and volume and with immense energy and vitality.

Colin. Tall and uncoordinated. Explodes into speech and talks jerkily, flatly, haltingly. Basically a strong and intelligent man, but unsure of himself. Gets very angry with himself.

Tolen. Once an unpromising physical specimen he has developed himself by systematic physical exercise. His body is now much as he would like it to be. He appears strong, well-built, full of rippling muscle. All his movements are a conscious display of this body. He almost always speaks with a level, clipped smoothness and a very considered subtlety of tone.

Nancy. Aged about seventeen. Potentially a beautiful girl but her personality, like her appearance, is still blurred and unformed. She wears an accordion-pleated skirt.

The acting area should be as close to the audience as possible.

*A room. The room is in the course of being painted by Tom.
The distribution of the paint is determined by the way the
light falls. There is a window up left in the back wall and
another down right. The paint is darkest where the shadows
are darkest and light where they are most light. The painting
is not smooth, pretty or finished, but fierce and determined.
Onstage there is a stepladder, a divan, two simple wooden
chairs; a pair of chest expanders hangs from the door (down
left). Curtain up. Tom onstage. Enter Colin.*

Colin. Er . . . I . . . er . . .
Tom. Fabulous. It's fabulous. It's fantastic.
[*Pause.*]
Colin. Er . . .
Tom. Is it dry yet?
Colin. Where?
Tom. Anywhere.
[*Colin tries.*]
Colin. Getting on.
Tom. Good.
[*Pause.*]
Colin. I . . . er . . .
Tom. I hate that divan. [*Pause.*] More white there perhaps.
    More white. [*Pause.*] Here. How does the light fall?
Colin. Eh?
Tom. The light. Get with it. White where it's light, black
    where it's dark, grey in between.
[*Pause.*]
Colin. Oh yes . . . yes.
Tom. Yes? Good. More white. [*He takes a brush of black
    paint and paints.*] Blast. [*He gets a rag, looks at wall,
    considers it and then starts working black paint with
    rag.*] Yes? Yes? [*Pause.*] Yes?

Colin. It's not in the system.

Tom. Eh?

Colin. White where it's light, black where it's dark.

Tom. It's nice. I like it.

Colin. You're so messy. Everything's messed. It's so badly done.

Tom. I'm not, I'm not a decorator. It looks different, yes?

Colin. Different?

Tom. Yes.

Colin. To what?

Tom. To before I moved in. [*Pause.*] He won't like it.

Colin. Who won't?

Tom. It'll annoy him. It'll annoy Tolen. It'll enrage him.

Colin. The house doesn't belong to Tolen.

Tom. He'll say it's childish.

Colin. It's my house. I rent it, so it's mine. [*Pause.*] There's a lot of stuff in the passage.

Tom. Ha ha! Because Tolen didn't think of it first.

Colin. The passage is all bunged up. I want to bring my bed downstairs.

Tom. What's Tolen's first name?

Colin. He says he hasn't got one.

Tom. Not got one?

Colin. He never uses it. I want to bring my bed . . .

Tom. If he never uses it . . .

Colin. . . . My bed downstairs.

Tom. He must have it.

Colin. I want to bring my bed—

Tom. Well bring it down! What?

Colin. I can't get it out of the front door.

Tom. You want to bring your bed—

Colin. There's too much stuff in the passage.

Tom. I put the stuff in the passage.

Colin. There's a chest of drawers behind the front door. You can't get out.

Tom. Or in. Where's Tolen?

Colin. Out. [*Pause.*] Seeing a girl.

Tom. Oh.

Colin. There's too much stuff in the passage.

Tom. Why do you want to bring your bed downstairs?

Colin. The wardrobe and the chest of drawers. We'll bring them in here.

Tom. What!

Colin. Temporarily.

Tom. No.

Colin. So I can get the bed through the front door.

Tom. We'll bring the bed in here and take it out through the window.

[*Slight pause.*]

Colin. You only put the wardrobe outside while you were painting.

Tom. I don't want it back. The room's so beautiful.

Colin. But you must be practical—

Tom. This blasted thing—

Colin. You've got to sit—

Tom. The bottom's falling out.

Colin. You've got to sleep—

Tom. Chairs!

Colin. You can't sleep on the floor. Chairs?

Tom. On the floor. Sleep on it! I think I'll put the mattress on the floor!

Colin. What!

Tom. Yes! The mattress on the floor. An empty—an empty beautiful room! What an angle! Look! Upwards? What an idea! [*Colin sinks bewildered on to a chair.*] You marvel, you! [*Seizes Colin's chair.*] On the wall! Out of the way! Off the floor! I'll hang them on the wall!

Colin. Oh no!

Tom. Oh yes! [*Throws mattress on floor.*] Help! You! Come on! Help me! Help me! Colin! My God, what a splendid idea!

Colin. There's too much stuff in the passage.

Tom. Put it in the basement.

Colin. We haven't got a basement.

Tom. Give it to Tolen! Put it in Tolen's room! Yes! Come on, help me! Oh! A beautiful empty room! Why do you want to bring your bed downstairs?

Colin. Getting another.

Tom. Oh?

Colin. A bigger one. Six foot.

[*Pause.*]

Tom. Let's get this shifted.

Colin. Hadn't we better bring mine in first?

Tom. Into the basement. Give it to Tolen.

[*Noise, off, of motor-bike which shudders to a stop outside the front door.*]

Colin. We haven't got a basement.

Tom. Tolen. That's his motor-bike.

[*Sound of somebody trying front door.*]

Colin. It's Tolen. He can't get in. [*Shouting.*] Be with you.

[*Exit Tom and Colin with divan. Enter Tolen through window upstage. Colin appears at window and disappears.*]

Colin [*off*]. Not there.

Tom [*off*]. What?

Colin [*off*]. He's disappeared.

Tom [*off*]. That's odd. [*Enter Tom through door followed by Colin.*]

Colin. Oh there you . . .

Tolen. Your windows are rather dirty.

Tom. Let's wash them.

Colin. I——I've got some Windolene. [*Exit Colin.*]

Tom. What's that?

Colin [*off*]. For cleaning windows. [*Pause. Reenter Colin with Windolene which he hands to Tom.*]

Tom [*reading label*]. Wipe it on Windolene, Wipe it off window clean. [*Tom wipes some of the Windolene on the bottom half of the window.*]

Tolen. Washing with clean water and then polishing with newspaper would have less electrostatic action.

Colin. Oh?

Tolen. Would repel dirt more efficiently.

[*Tom starts to experiment with the various shapes he can make.*]

Tolen. Now you must do the top half, Tom.

[*Tom hoists the bottom half of the window up and crosses to window D.R. and puts on the Windolene there.*]

Tolen. You do realize, Tom, that in order to clean the window, you have to wipe off the Windolene? [*Pause.*] The white stuff has to be polished off the window.

Tom. Let's get that bed down, shall we, Colin?

Colin. You can't leave that stuff on.

Tom. Oh?

Tolen. You can't leave it on. "Wipe on sparingly with a damp cloth and wipe off immediately."

Tom. It's as good as net curtains, only better.

Colin. Net curtains?

Tom. You should paint your windows white, Tolen. White reflects heat. You'll be O.K. when the bomb drops. [*Exit Tom.*]

Colin. What? What did you say?

Tom [*off*]. O.K. when the bomb drops. O.K. when the . . .

Colin. Net curtains? [*Exit Colin. Pause. Tolen is about to exit when he hears bumps, crashes and yells, off. This resolves into dialogue*]:

Colin [*off*]. It won't go round.

Tom [*off*]. It will.

Colin [*off*]. It won't. Take it apart.

Tom [*off*]. What?

Colin [*off*]. Take it to bits.

Tom [*off*]. Oh, all right.

Colin [*off*]. Can you take the head?

Tom [*off*]. The what?

Colin [*off*]. The head! Hold the head! The head!

Tom [*off*]. Help!

Colin [*off*]. Eh?

Tom [*off*]. Help! Help!

Colin [*off*]. Mind the plaster. [*Crash, off.*] Oh!

Tom [*off*]. You're so houseproud. [*Enter Colin with head of bed. Colin is about to lean head against wall.*] Not where it's wet! Fool! [*Colin leans head against step-ladder. Crash, off.*] Help! Help! I'm stuck! [*Laughing.*] I'm stuck! The foot!

Colin. The what?

Tom [*off*]. The foot!

Colin. Your foot! [*Exit Colin.*]

Tom [*off*]. Of the bed.

[*Banging and crashing, off, with various imprecations. Enter Colin with foot of bed.*]

Tolen. Have there been any telephone calls?

Colin. Eh?

Tolen. I'm expecting a couple of girls to telephone.

Colin. There was a Maureen and er—a Joan.

Tolen. Joan? Joan who? [*Colin is nonplussed.*] Never mind, she'll telephone again. [*Pause.*] I was afraid it was the barmaid at the "Sun."

Colin. Alice?

[*Enter Tom.*]

Tolen. She took me into the little back room this morning.

Tom. What about Jimmy?

Tolen. Probably at Chapel.

Tom. On Saturday?

Tolen. She said he was at Chapel. Beyond that bead curtain you know, there's a room full of silver cups. Cases of them. And a large pink sofa in the middle. I never knew Jimmy was a sporting man.

Colin. Who was the other one?

Tolen. The other?

Colin. The one you were expecting to telephone.

Tolen. Girl I met in a telephone kiosk. [*Exit Tolen. Small crash, off. Reenter Tolen.*]

Tolen. Colin, would you mind moving that bed? I would like to get up to my room.

Colin. Oh, the base. Sorry.

Tom. Can't you climb over?

[*Exit Colin. Crashing sounds, off. Reenter Colin.*]

Colin [*to Tom*]. Give me a hand, will you?

Tom. Why can't Tolen?

Colin. Eh?

Tom. It's him that wants to get upstairs.

Colin. Oh, er . . . [*Exit Colin. Reenter dragging base.*]

Tom. Mind the paint. [*Tom helps Colin onstage with bed.*]

Tolen. Why are you bringing your bed downstairs, Colin?

Colin. Getting a new one.

Tolen. Oh?

Colin. A bigger one—six foot.

Tolen. Oh, like mine.

Colin. I—er—I thought—I thought I'd like another one. You know—er—bigger. Just—just in case, you know. I thought I'd like a bigger—another bed—more comfortable. [*Pause.*] I could always put my married cousins up.

[*Long pause.*]

Tolen. Have you got a girl yet, Colin?

Colin. No.

Tolen. Carol left six months ago, didn't she?

Colin. Mm.

Tom. Have you got a girl yet, Colin?

Colin. No.

Tom. Got a woman?

Colin. No.

Tom. You haven't, have you.

Colin. No.

Tom. You haven't!

Colin. No.

Tom. You haven't! You haven't! You fool! Why d'you want another bed?

Colin. Mind my bed!

Tom. His bed! Colin's bed!

Colin. It's not strong.

Tom [*through the bars*]. Grr! Grr!

Colin. Hey! Stop! Stop it!

Tom. It creaks! It runs! It spins! Watch it! Yahoo!

Colin. You'll—

Tom. Poop—poop—

Colin. I say—

Tom. Poop poop poop poop—

Colin. Stop it. Stop it.

Tom. Poop poop, look out!

Colin. Stop stop—ow!

[*Everything collapses. Tom and Colin are enmeshed in the bed and stepladder.*]

Colin. You—you—you nit.

[*Pause.*]

Tolen. Did you put turpentine in the white?

Tom. Eh?

Tolen. The white paint. Did you put turpentine in the white?

Tom. Yes.

Tolen. It'll go yellow.

Colin. What?

Tolen. The white paint will go yellow.

Colin. Yellow!

Tolen. Yes.

Colin. I never knew that.

Tolen. The turpentine thins the white lead in the paint and the linseed oil seeps through and turns the white yellow.

Colin. Oh. D'you think we should do it again?

[*Tom is pulling at the chest expanders.*]

Tom. Peter left these, wasn't it nice of him?

[*Pause. A girl passes the window. Tolen starts to exit through window.*]

Colin. Where are you going? Where—[*Exit Tolen.*] How does he do it?

Tom. He's beginning to wear out my window. Let's move the chest of drawers so he can come in through the front door. He doesn't actually do them in the street, you know.

Colin. Doesn't he?

Tom. He makes his contact and stashes them up for later. He's enlarging his collection.

Colin. How does he meet them?

Tom. Your bed's in the way. What are we going to do with this bed? What you going to do with it?

Colin. Oh that. Oh—what's the use? [*Tom lugs part of the bed across and leans it against Colin.*] What's Tolen got that I haven't got? Maureen says Tolen's got sexy ankles. [*Tom brings up another piece and leans it against Colin.*] Are my ankles sexy?

Tom. What are you going to do with this bed?

Colin. Thought I'd take it round to Copp Street.

Tom. Copp Street?

Colin. To the junk yard.

Tom. To sell?

Colin. I thought so.

Tom. For money?

Colin. Why not?

Tom. O.K. We'll take it round to Copp Street. How far is it to Copp Street?

Colin. Twenty minutes.

Tom. Twenty! [*Long pause.*] Put it back in your room.

[*Pause. Colin shakes his head. Pause. Tom opens his mouth to speak.*]

Colin [*interrupting*]. Not in the passage.

[*Pause.*]

Tom. Can't you just stand there? You look quite nice really. [*Slight pause.*]

Colin. Put it together.

Tom. No.

Colin. If we put it together it'll stand by itself.

Tom. No.

Colin. On its own feet.

Tom. I can't bear it.

[*Pause.*]

Colin. Take the foot. [*Tom does so listlessly.*] And the head. [*Tom does so.*]

Tom. How can you sleep on this? I'd think I was at the zoo.

Colin. How d'you get a woman? How can I get a girl?

[*They start to put the bed together.*]

Tom. Do you know why the Duck-billed Platypus can't be exported from Australia—or do I mean platipi?

Colin. How can I get a woman?

Tom. You think this is going to be a silly story, don't you.

Colin. Well?

Tom. Because they eat their own weight in worms every day and they starve to death in one and a half hours or something. It's rather a nice object. It's not a nice bed but it's not a bad object. Yes. Look. It's rather nice. [*Colin picks up mattress.*] No.

Colin. But—

Tom. No.

Colin. But a mattress naturally goes on a bed.

Tom. It's not a bed. It's an object. More than that, it's wheeled traffic. Mm. Not much room, is there? I must get those chairs off the floor. Put the mattress in the passage.

Colin. It's more comfy on the bed.

Tom. Oh, very well. [*Tom experiments with the bed.*]

Colin. Why is Tolen so sexy?

[*Tolen passes the window and tries the front door. Enters by window.*]

Tom. You were very quick. Did she repulse you?

Tolen. No. I'm seeing her later.

Tom. Next time I'll time you.

Tolen. Next time come and watch me.

[*Tom takes the chest expanders and tries them a few times.*]

Tom. I'm getting pretty good. Whew! I can do ten of these. Whew! It's awful!

Tolen. I can do twenty—but then . . .

Tom. Let's see you.

[*Tolen indicates he is below bothering to use his energy.*]

Colin. I can do twenty as well.

Tom. Let's see you. [*Colin takes the chest expanders and starts.*] He's bending his elbows, it's easier that way.

Colin. Four.

Tom. Tolen.

Tolen. Yes, Tom?

Tom. Do you think it's a good idea for Colin to buy a six-foot bed?

Tolen. Where's he buying it?

Colin. Nine. [*Pause.*] Catesby's.

Tom. Plutocrat.

Tolen. Heal's would have been better.

Colin. Twelve. Eh?

Tolen. Heal's have more experience with beds.

Colin. Expensive. Fourteen.

Tolen. They may be more expensive, but they have more experience. You pay for their greater experience.

Tom. Yes, but do you think it's a good idea, a sound idea, ethically, for Colin to buy a six-foot bed when he hasn't got a woman?

Tolen. Rory McBride has an eight-foot bed.

Tom. Don't stop! You have to keep it up the whole time. You're not allowed to stop. How sexy is Rory McBride? Who is he anyway?

Colin. D'you think—?

Tom. Don't stop!

Colin. D'you think—?

Tom. What?

Colin. I ought to get an eight-foot bed? [*Colin stops.*]

Tom. How many?

Colin. Twenty-four. [*Staggering.*] Where's the bed?

Tom. You mean the object.

[*Colin collapses on the bed. A girl is seen to pass the window. Exit Tolen through window.*]

Colin. Where's he gone?

Tom. A girl passed by and he went after her.

[*Pause.*]

Colin. You got a cigarette?

Tom. I thought you didn't smoke.

Colin. Have you got a cigarette?

Tom. No. [*Pause.*] Listen, Colin, I've had a new idea for you. For teaching children about music.

Colin. Oh—

Tom. Listen! My idea about the chalk—was it a good one?

Colin. It was all right.

Tom. Did you use it or not? Did you?

Colin. All right. All right. Just tell me.

Tom. Tolen could help, blast him.

Colin. How?

Tom. He's a musician. You need his advice. But don't let that bastard near the kids, he'll bully them. Now listen, I been thinking about this. You got a piano? Well, have you? Golly the bleeding school wouldn't be furnished without a piano.

Colin. We've got one.

Tom. Good. Listen, I been thinking about this. Teaching's so intellectual and when it's not intellectual, it's bossy, or most of it. The teachers tell the kids everything and all they get is dull little copycats, little automata; dim, limited and safe—

Colin. Oh, get on.

Tom. You get the piano and you get the kids and you say it's a game see? "Right," you say, "You're not to look at the keys, 'cos that's cheating."

Colin. Not look—

Tom. If they look at each other playing, they'll just copy each other. Now, don't put your own brain between them and the direct experience. Don't intellectualize. Let them come right up against it. And don't talk about music, talk about noise.

Colin. Noi—

Tom. What else is music but an arrangement of noises? I'm serious. "Now," you say, "one of you come out here and make noises on the piano." And finally one of them will come out and sort of hit the keys, bang, bang. "Right," you say, "now someone come out and make the same noise."

Colin. Eh?

Tom. The same noise. That's the first step. They'll have to *listen* to see they hit in the same place—and they can do it more or less 'cos they can sort of—you know—clout it in the middle bit. So next you get them all going round the piano in a circle, all making the same noise, and they'll love that. When they get a bit cheesed, you develop it. "O.K.," you say, "let's have another noise."

Colin. I don't see the point, I mean—

Tom. Now listen, this way they'll find out for themselves, give them a direct experience and they'll discover for themselves—all the basic principles of music and they won't shy away—they won't think of it as culture, it'll be pop to them. Listen! You, goon, moron, you don't like Bartok, do you?

Colin. No.

Tom. Don't be so pleased with yourself. You don't understand it, your ear's full of Bach, it stops at Mahler. But after a few lessons like this, you play those kids Schoenberg, you play them Bartok. They'll know what he's doing. I bet they will! It'll be rock'n roll to them. My God, I ought to be a teacher! My God I'm a genius!

Colin. What about Tolen?

Tom. What about him?

Colin. You said he could help.

Tom. To borrow his gramophone records.

Colin. He never lends them, he never lets anyone else touch them. [*Pause*.] It's a good idea.

Tom. Good.

Colin. Thanks. [*Pause*.] Why do you say Tolen is a bastard?

Tom. Be careful. He only dazzles you for one reason. Really,

Colin, sex, sex, sex: that's all we ever get from you.

Colin. It's all right for you and Tolen.

Tom. We're all of us more or less total sexual failures.

Colin. Tolen isn't a sexual failure.

Tom. He needs it five hours a day, he says.

Colin. Then he can't be a sexual failure. [*Pause.*] He can't be a sexual failure. [*Pause.*] He can't be a sexual failure having it five hours a day. [*Pause.*] Can he?

[*Long pause.*]

Tom. I don't like that wall. There's something wrong with that wall. It's not right.

Colin. Can he?

[*Nancy appears outside behind the window up left and looks about her.*]

Tom. Hm. Colin—

Colin. Can he?

Tom. Colin.

[*Nancy vanishes.*]

Colin. What?

Tom. Oh nothing. What do you think about that wall?

Colin. Blast the wall! Blast the bloody wall! [*Nancy reappears outside the window.*] Oh . . . oh . . . oh . . .

Tom. Speak to her.

Colin. I—I—

Tom. Ask her the time. Ask her to lend you sixpence.

Colin. I—I—you.

Tom. Eh?

Colin. You—please.

Tom. I can't do it for you.

Colin. Oh—[*Colin turns away. Pause. Nancy vanishes. Long pause.*]

Tom. What do you think about that wall?

Colin. What? Oh . . . it's . . . it's . . . [*Colin does something violent. Pause. Enter Tolen through window.*]

Tom. Someone was riding your motor-bike.

Tolen. What? [*Exit Tolen through window.*]

Colin. Who was riding his motor-bike?

[*Reenter Tolen through window.*]

Tom. I swear someone was riding your motor-bike. [*Pause.*] Well?

Tolen. Well?

Tom. How long did you take this time?

Tolen. Did you time me?

Tom. Did you time yourself?

Colin. How long did you take?

Tolen. Not more than about ten minutes—

Colin. Ten minutes! Only ten minutes!

Tolen. Really, Colin, do you think I'm so clumsy, so vulgar as to do it in the street? I'm meeting her . . .

Tom. Ten minutes! Ten minutes from door to door? From start to finish? From hello to good-bye?

Colin. Ten minutes.

Tom. Ten Tolen! Ten! Ten minutes! Ten whole minutes! What! No! You're slipping, man! You're sliding! You're letting us down! Ten. You can do better than that. Faster man! Faster! Faster! Faster!

Colin. Eh?

Tom. Give him a drink of water. Listen, Tolen. Three! Three! Three! D'you hear? Dreams I got for you, Tolen. Dreams and plans I got for you. Four minutes! Get it down to four minutes. Four minutes from start to finish—like the four-minute mile.

Colin. Eh?

Tom. Heroic! Think! A new series in the Olympic Games!

Colin. Is he joking?

Tom. And then, Tolen, by discipline, by training, by application: three minutes fifty-nine seconds! Three minutes fifty-five! Three minutes fifty! And then—one day— one unimaginable day: three minutes! Three minutes from start to finish!

Colin. Is it nicer, faster?

Tom. Nice? Nice? Nice? That's not the point. My God! I'm disappointed in you, Tolen, My God I am! Yes! I am! A man with every advantage, every opportunity, every accoutrement—God's gift to woman! And think of those women Tolen: waiting to be satisfied—their need, Tolen, their crying need—[*weeping*]. And with the capacity, with the capacity for, with the capacity for spreading yourself around. [*Pause while Tom regains control.*]

Tolen. I think you're mad.

Tom. Ah, Tolen, never mind. Relax. I see what you mean. I'm a man, too. I understand. Yes, I do. Yes, yes I do. [*Slight pause.*] You couldn't do it. [*Slight pause.*] You couldn't keep it up. You couldn't keep up the pace. [*Tolen appears slightly restive.*] Nobody could. It's too much. It's too fast. It's not human, it's superhuman. No, no, let's forget it. Let's be generous. I understand.

[*Pause.*] Wait! Here's what I propose. Here's what I suggest. One in three! One in three in your own time! Yes, Tolen, every third one as long as you like. [*Tolen yawns and climbs on the bed.*] He's tired. He's weary. He's overdone it. Poor chap. He's tired. Poor bloke. Quick, quick. Blankets! Brandy! Pills! Pillows! Nurses! Stretchers! Doses! Nurses! Horlicks! Nurses! Hot water bottles! Nurses! Nurses! Nurses! Nurses! Have a piece of barley sugar. [*Nancy appears at window. Tolen takes notice. Nancy disappears.*] Save yourself! Control yourself! Give yourself a chance!

Tolen. A bit too provincial.

Colin. What?

Tolen. That girl.

[*Pause.*]

Tom [*really wanting to know*]. How can you tell she's provincial?

Tolen. Of course, Tom, you will not appreciate that the whole skill, the whole science, is in the slowness: the length of time a man may take. The skill is in the slowness. Of course, Tom, I don't expect you can appreciate this. There is little skill, Tom, and no subtlety in the three-minute make. However——

Colin. It's better slower?

Tolen. However, if I wished, Tom, if I wanted, you do realize that I could do it in about eighty-five seconds.

Tom. Yes.

Colin. Tolen.

Tolen. Yes, Colin?

Colin. Will you——I mean——will you show me——[*pause*] how ——[*pause*]?

Tolen. You mean how I get women?

Colin. Yes.

Tolen. I can tell you what I know intellectually, Colin, what my experience has been. But beyond that it's a question of intuition. Intuition is, to some degree, inborn, Colin. One is born with an intuition as to how to get women. But this feeling can be developed with experience and confidence, in certain people, Colin, to some degree. A man can develop the knack. First you must realize that women are not individuals but types. No, not even types, just women. They want to surrender but they don't want the responsibility of surrendering. This is one reason why the man must dominate. On the other hand there are no set rules. A man must be infinitely subtle; must use his intuition, a very subtle intuition. If you feel it necessary in order to get the woman you must even be prepared to humiliate yourself, to grovel, to utterly abase yourself before the woman—I mean only in cases of extreme necessity, Colin. After all, what does it matter? It's just part of getting her. Once you've got her it's the woman that grovels. Finally, Colin, the man is the master.

For you must appreciate, Colin, that people like to be dominated. They like to be mastered. They ask to be relieved of the responsibility of deciding for themselves. It's a kindness towards people to relieve them of responsibility. In this world, Colin, there are the masters and there are the servants. Very few men are real men, Colin, are real masters. Almost all women are servants. They don't want to think for themselves, they want to be dominated.

First you must establish contact. Of course you won't find that as easy as I do. I'm not referring to touch, tactile communication, that comes later. I mean the feeling between you. You are aware of the girl, the girl is aware of you, a vibration between you . . .

Colin. Just a minute.

Tolen. Yes?

Colin. I just want to get it straight.

Tolen. Take your time.

[*Pause.*]

Colin. I don't see what you mean by contact.

Tolen. Very difficult to explain. Tom, can you explain?

Tom. No.

Tolen. Once you feel it, Colin, you will know it next time. Having established this basis of contact, then you work to break down her resistance, to encourage surrender. Flattery is useful; if a woman is intelligent make her think she's pretty, if she's pretty make her think she's beautiful. Never let them think, never let them see you are clever or intellectual. Never be serious with a woman. Once you let a woman start thinking, the whole process takes infinitely more time. Keep her laughing, keep her talking; you can judge by her laughter, by the way she laughs, how you're getting on.

Perhaps it might be useful to consider what is the right food.

Colin. The right food?

Tolen. Food is of the utmost importance. Food is of the essence. One's body needs protein and energy-giving substance. I find with my perhaps unusual sexual demands that my body requires at least twice the normal daily intake of protein.

Colin. Protein?

Tolen. Cheese, eggs, milk, meat. I drink about four pints of milk a day—Channel Island milk. And eat about a pound of steak. It needn't be the most expensive, the cheaper cuts have the same food value. For instance, skirt.

Tom. Skirt?

Tolen. Skirt.

Colin. Skirt. Cheese, eggs, milk, meat, skirt. Got a pencil, Tom.

Tolen. Skirt is meat.

Colin. Oh.

Tom. Don't you see what you're doing to this growing lad? He hasn't got a woman, now he'll go and eat himself silly on milk and meat. Stoke up the fire and block up the chimney. Listen, Colin, suppose this was a piano.

Tolen. A what?

Colin. Shut up.

Tom. A piano. Plonk, plonk, plonk.

Tolen. It's a bed.

Tom. It's not, it's a piano, listen.

Colin. I want Tolen to tell me—

Tom. Shut up, he's told you enough. A piano, plonk. Now supposing you couldn't—

Colin. Listen, Tolen—

Tom. Supposing you couldn't see my hand—

Colin. Shut up.

Tom. I play—C sharp, F and A—

Colin. Tolen—[*Nancy passes window.*] I want—listen to me. I want to hear what—I want to hear what Tolen has to say. Listen—listen to me. I want to hear wh-what Tolen has to say. So *what* you think it's b-bad for me to listen to Tolen. You're not in charge of me. I am and I'm sick of myself, I'm absolutely sick, and here I am stuck with myself. I want to hear what Tolen has to say— [*Nancy reappears at window.*] I want to hear what Tolen has to say. So *what* I want to hear, I want to hear what—

[*Nancy taps at window. Pause.*]

Nancy. Do you know where I can find the Y.W.C.A.?

[*Pause.*]

Tom. The what?

Nancy. The Y.W.C.A.

[*Pause.*]

Tom. Come on in. Come in by the front door. [*Exit Tom.*]

Nancy. Oh thanks. Thanks very much.

[*Sound of weighty object being moved. Enter Nancy carrying a holdall and a carrier bag and Tom carrying a large suitcase.*]

Nancy. Hullo.

Tolen. Hullo.

Nancy. Hullo.

Colin. Oh, hullo.

[*Pause.*]

Tom. Well, has anyone seen it?

Colin. Seen what?

Tom. Seen what?

Nancy. The Y.W.C.A.

Tom. The Y.W.C.A.

Colin. Oh, the Y.W.C.A.

Tom. Yes.

Colin. No.

[*Pause.*]

Tom. Would you like to sit down?

Nancy. Well, thanks, but—but well, thanks. [*She sits.*]

Tom. Would you like a cup of tea or something?

Nancy. Oh, well, no thanks, really.

Tom. No trouble, it's no trouble. I'll put the kettle on. [*Exit Tom.*]

Tolen. Did he say he'd put a kettle on? He's not boiled a kettle since he came here.

Tom [*off*]. Colin!

Colin. Yes?

Tom [*off*]. How do you turn the gas on? [*Pause. Tolen now pursues the intention of teasing Nancy and making her uncomfortable. He succeeds. If possible achieve this without words. But if necessary insert line: Tolen: "Bit short in the neck. Nice hair though." Enter Tom.*] How do you turn— [*Pause.*] What do you think of our piano?

Nancy. What?

Tom. Our piano: Do you like it? Our piano?

Nancy. What piano?

Tom. This piano.

Nancy. Piano?

Tom. Yes.

Nancy. That's not a piano.

Tom. Yes it is, it's a piano.

Nancy. It's a bed.

Tom. It's a piano, honest, listen: ping!

Nancy. It's a bed.

Tom. It's a piano, isn't it, Colin?

Colin. Eh?

Tom. This is a piano.

Colin. Piano?

Tom. Piano.

Colin. Oh yes, a piano. Ping.

Nancy. It's a bed.

Tom [*using the edge of the bed as keyboard*]. Ping [*high*]
        ping [*low*]. Ping [*running his finger right down: glis-
        sando*] pi-i-i-i-i-ng.

Colin [*middle*]. Ping.

Nancy. It's a bed.

Tom. Bechstein.

Nancy. Bechstein?

Tom [*high*] ping. [*Medium high*] ping. [*Medium low*] ping.
        [*Low*] ping.

Nancy. It's a bed.

Tom [*1st 3 bars "Blue Danube" starting low*]. Ping ping ping
        ping ping.

Nancy. It's a bed.

Colin. Rosewood.

Tom [*4th and 5th bars B.D.*]. Ping ping ping ping.

Nancy. It's a bed.

Tom [*6th, 7th, 8th bars B.D.*]. Ping ping ping ping ping
        ping ping.

Colin [*taking over 9th bar*]. Ping ping.

Tom, Colin [*together playing chords in unison 10–13th
        bars*]. Ping ping ping ping ping
        Ping ping
        Ping ping
        Ping ping ping ping ping
        Ping ping.

Nancy [*tentative, taking over*]. Ping ping.

Tom, Colin [*gently encouraging Nancy who joins in 17th,
        18th, 19th bars B.D.*].

    Ping ping ping ping ping
    Ping ping
    Ping ping.
    [*All three letting go with great rich chords.*]
    Ping ping ping ping ping
    Ping ping
    Ping ping
    Ping ping ping ping ping
    Ping ping ping ping
    Ping ping ping ping ping ping.

Nancy. Ping.
Colin. Ping.
Nancy. Ping.
Colin. Ping.
Nancy. Ping.
Colin. Plong.
Nancy. Plong.
Colin. Plong plong.
Nancy. Ping plong.
Colin. Plong.
Nancy. Ping.
Colin. Ping.
Nancy. Plong.
[*Pause.*]
Colin. Plong.
[*Pause.*]
Nancy. Plong.
[*Pause.*]
Colin. Plong.
Tolen. Why be so childish about a bed?

[*Author's Note: All the above could be rearranged or im-
    provised to suit different actors and different produc-
    tions provided the sequence of events is clear:
    1. Tom and Colin charm Nancy into entering into the
    game.
    2. Tom retires leaving Colin and Nancy getting on
    rather well, a growing relationship which Tolen inter-
    rupts.*]

[*Long pause.*]
Tom. Would anyone like to know how they train lions to
    stand on boxes? [*Pause.*] Would you like to know how

they train lions to stand on boxes? First we must have a box. [*Taking bucket.*] That will do. Now this marks the limit of the cage—the edge, the bars.

Tolen. Must you be so childish?

Tom. Childlike. The trainer takes his whip. Whip? Whip? We'll do without a whip. Now a lion. I must have a lion . . . Tolen, you'd make a good lion. No? O.K. Colin.

Colin. No.

Tom. Come on, be a lion.

Colin. No.

Tom. Go on, can't you roar? The trainer taking the box in his left hand, and the whip—imagine the whip—in his right, advances on the lion and drives him backward against the cage bars, yes? Now. There is a critical moment when the lion must leap at the attacker otherwise it will be too late, see? Right. The trainer can recognize the critical moment. So, at the moment when the lion rears to attack, the trainer draws back and the lion, no longer threatened, drops his forepaws and finds himself standing on the box. Do this a few times and you've trained a lion to stand on a box.

[*Pause.*]

Colin. How does the box get there?

Tom. What?

Colin. You've still got it in your hand.

Tom. The trainer puts it there.

Colin. When?

[*Pause.*]

Tom. Let's try. You come and be lion.

Colin. No.

Tom. All right, I'll be lion. [*He tries a roar or two.*] Whew! It makes you feel sexy. [*He tries again.*]

Colin. I'd like to be lion.

Tom. All right.

Colin. I wonder if I could roar into something.

Tom. Eh?

Colin. It would help the resonance. [*He roars into bucket.*]

Tom. That's the lion's box.

Colin. Sounds marvellous inside. [*Colin sees Nancy's carrier bag. He picks it up.*]

Tom. Hey, you can't touch that.

Colin. Eh?

Nancy. Oh, that's all right.

[*Colin empties contents, including a copy of* Honey *magazine. Puts carrier bag on his head and goes round roaring.*]

Tom. Yes! Yes! Yes! Yes! Yes!

[*Colin roars at Tom who roars back, then at Nancy. Nancy laughs, half scared, half excited. Colin roars at her and she runs away. Colin gropes around for her, but she evades him, laughing.*]

Tom. You should wear a carrier bag more often.

Colin. Just a minute. [*Colin takes the bag off his head and makes holes for eyes. Replaces bag. Roars again after Nancy. Tolen takes off belt he wears and cracks it like a whip.*]

Tolen. I'll be trainer.

Tom. Eh? Very well.

Tolen. Ready? [*Pause. Tolen advances on Colin cracking his "whip" and getting a sweet pleasure from the identification. Colin roars, Tolen gets more excited.*]

Tolen. Back—back you—back you—back—back you beast you—beast you beast you back back!

[*Nancy gets mixed up between them. She screams and exits. Tolen picks up* Honey. *Pause.*]

Tom. Just think what you could do with a real whip, Tolen. Or a Sjambok. Think of that.

Colin [*taking off carrier bag*]. What's happened? Has she gone?

Tom. She left her suitcases.

End of Act One

The room is very peaceful. Tom is painting gently and thinking about his paint. Colin has the carrier bag on his head and is feeling free and experimental. Anything the actor may improvise is probably best, but Colin might feel like some exotic bird: standing on one leg, hopping, crowing; possibly using the chest expanders in some unconventional way. After a long pause.

Tom. What do you think?

[*Pause.*]

Colin. Not thinking.

[*Pause.*]

Tom. Eh?

[*Pause.*]

Colin. Not thinking.

Tom. Look!

Colin. Oh.

Tom. A . . . [*pause*]. This place soothes me.

[*Pause. Colin takes off the carrier bag.*]

Colin. I remember the first time I saw this street.

Tom. Northam Street?

Colin. These mean streets [*pause*]—the feeling of space in these streets—it's fantastic. [*Pause.*] When they're empty they're sort of—splendid, a sort of—crumbling splendour [*pause*] and a feeling of—in winter, on a hazy, winter day a—a—a—romantic! And in summer hot and—listless. And at weekends, summer and the sun shining and children dashing about and mothers talking—you know, gossiping and men cleaning motorbikes and [*getting excited*] they can be forbidding, threatening—I mean—you know—if the light's flat and darkish,—no sun—just flat and lowering, it's stupendous! And early morning—early autumn—I've walked through these streets all alone, you know, all by myself

—so quiet so . . . so . . . [*Telephone rings, off.*] It'll be for him. It'll be for Tolen. [*Colin replaces carrier bag on his head and picks up a magazine. Exit Tom. Telephone stops ringing. Pause. Nancy appears at the window, she doesn't see Colin. Nancy climbs through the window and goes towards the suitcases. Colin sees Nancy. Nancy sees Colin and is transfixed. Pause. Enter Tolen through window. Pause. Tolen whips off his belt. Nancy darts away hysterical. There is a maelstrom of movement during which the bed gets overturned, Nancy is caught behind it and Colin and Tolen are covering all the exits. Enter Tom through door. Pause.*]

Tom. Colin, take that carrier bag off your head.

Colin. Eh?

Tom. Take it off. [*Colin removes carrier bag.*] Shall we get the bed straight? [*Tom goes to the foot of the bed.*] Tolen? [*Tom and Colin put bed right.*] You not found the Y.W.C.A.?

Nancy. No.

Tom. What's the address?

Nancy. I've got it here. [*She hands him a scrap of paper.*]

Tom. Martin's Grove W.2. Where's Martin's Grove?

Colin. I don't know. I'll get the street map. [*Exit Colin. Pause.*]

Nancy. Thanks.

Tolen. That's all right.

Nancy. Oh, thanks.

Tolen. Don't mention it.

[*Enter Colin with map.*]

Tom. How does it work?

Colin. Index.

Tom. Eh?

Colin. Back.

Tom. I see.

Tolen. Just come off the train, have you?

Nancy. Yes.

Colin. James Park, James Square, turn over, and again. Ah. Mapperton, Marlow.

Tolen. Is it the—

Tom. Martin's Grove W.2. J4.73. What's that?

Colin. Page seventy-three.

Tolen. Is it the first time you've been here?

Nancy. Here?

Tolen. In London?

Nancy. Oh yes.

[*Tolen and Nancy laugh.*]

Colin. Square J above, 4 across.

Tom. What tiny print.

Tolen. You've got Chinese eyebrows.

Nancy. Eh?

Tolen. Chinese eyebrows. Very clear arch. Very delicate.

Nancy. Have I?

Tolen. Have you got a mirror, I'll show you.

Nancy. Oh.

Colin. Turn it the other way.

Tom. Eh?

Colin. Round. That's it.

Tolen. See? Very pretty.

Nancy. Oh.

Tom. Here. [*Pause.*] Here it is.

Nancy. Eh? Oh, thanks.

Tom. Not far. Five minutes. [*Nancy is occupied with Tolen.*]
    We'll take you. We'll take you there.

Nancy. Oh. Oh thanks. [*Pause.*] Well perhaps I ought to—

Tolen. What's your name?

Nancy. Nancy, Nancy Jones. What's yours?

Tolen. Tolen.

Nancy. Tolen? Tolen what?

Tolen. Tolen.

Nancy. Tolen, oh I see, like Capucine.

Tolen. I beg your pardon?

Nancy. Capucine.

Tolen. Capucine?

Nancy. Like Capucine. Nothing Capucine, Capucine noth-
    ing.

Tolen. Please would you tell me what you mean?

Nancy. You not seen her? She's an actress. She acts.

Tolen. On television?

Nancy. In the films. Is it your Christian name or your sur-
    name? [*Pause.*] Well, is it? Is it your surname or your
    Christian name?

Tolen. It's my surname.

Nancy. What's your Christian name?

Tolen. I never use my first name. I have no first name.

Nancy. What is it?

Tolen. I prefer not to use it.

Nancy. Why?

Tolen. I don't use it. I have no first name. I never use my first name. [*Tolen moves away. Pause. Tolen returns to near Nancy. Nancy shifts uncomfortably.*] What's the matter? Is anything wrong? Is anything the matter with you?

Nancy. No.

Tolen. Why are you so nervous?

Nancy. I'm not.

Tolen. You look nervous.

Nancy. Me nervous? Do I?

Tolen. Yes.

Nancy. Oh—

Tolen. Yes?

Nancy. Nothing.

Tolen. What's the matter?

Nancy. It's—it's—

Tolen. Well?

Nancy. It's—

Tolen. You are nervous, aren't you? Very nervous. Why don't you take your coat off?

Nancy. I don't want to.

Tolen. My dear, you take it off.

Nancy. I don't want to.

Tolen. Why don't you want to?

Nancy. No. [*Exit Colin.*] It's—it's—

Tolen. Yes?

[*Pause.*]

Nancy. You're looking at me.

Tolen. Am I?

Nancy. Yes.

Tolen. How am I looking?

Nancy. I don't know, I—

Tolen. How am I looking?

Nancy. I—

Tolen. Well?

Nancy. I feel—

Tolen. What?

Nancy. I don't know, I—

Tolen. You feel funny, don't you—go on, tell me—go on— tell me—tell me.

[*Nancy moves away. Tolen laughs.*]

Tom. What's the most frightening building in London?

Tolen. It depends what you mean by frightening.

Tom. Break it up, Tolen.

Tolen. What I do is my affair, not yours.

Tom. She doesn't know a thing.

Tolen. She knows what she wants, or rather what she will want.

Tom. I don't think you're the right person to give a girl her first experience.

Tolen. She's an independent human being. Why should you say what's good for her? How old are you, Nancy?

Nancy. Seventeen.

Tolen. There you are. [*Pause.*] Anyway, she's not really my type. I've had sufficient for today. I'm merely amusing myself. It's more subtle.

Tom. You know what happens to young girls alone in London, don't you?

Nancy. Yes—no—I—

Tom. You'd better find a Catholic Girls' Refuge.

Nancy. I'm not a Catholic.

Tom. You'll find the address in any ladies lavatory in any railway station.

Nancy. Oh—I—

Tolen. How do you know?

Nancy. I think I ought to go—I—

[*Enter Colin with tea things including milk in a bottle.*]

Colin. That damned stuff in the passage. You'll have to move it.

Tom. I'm not having it in here.

Colin. I'm not having it in the passage.

Tom. I'm not having it in here.

Colin. When you take a furnished room, you take the furniture as well.

Tom. Not that furniture.

Colin. What's wrong with the furniture?

Tom. I'm not having it in here. Put it on the bed. Take it to Copp Street.

Colin. It's my furniture, you're not selling my furniture.

Tom. You're selling your bed.

Colin. You're not selling my furniture.

Tom. We'll put it on the top landing.

Tolen. Outside my room? I think not.

Tom. Inside your room.

Colin. Oh. Let's have some tea. [*They start pouring out tea.*]

Tolen. What's the most frightening building in London?

Colin. Great Ormond Street Hospital for Children.

[*Pause.*]

Tom. What's that?

Colin. Great Ormond Street Hospital for Children.

Nancy. That's nice. It's true. That's a nice thing to say.

Colin. Oh? Do you think so?

[*Tolen touches Nancy.*]

Tom. Do you know how the elephant got the shape it is? Well, there was once a little piggy animal, see? With two great big front teeth that stuck out. However, there are certain advantages in being big—you know, you can eat off trees and things—like horses—

Tolen. For you this is remarkably incoherent.

Tom. Thanks. So this animal got big and it grew an enormous great long jaw so it could scoop up the vegetation. An enormous jaw, seven foot long—imagine! As big as a door! Now. A seven-foot jaw involves certain difficulties in getting the food from the front of your jaw to the back . . .

Tolen. Biscuits?

Tom. It had to use its upper lip to shovel the garbage along.

Colin. Aren't there some chocolate?

Tom. I ate them. Well, the creature's upper lip began to grow. It grew so big it began to do all the work and the creature didn't bother to use its seven-foot jaw. Now, as you know, any organ not in constant use atrophies so the jaw began to shrivel. [*To Tolen.*] Not that you need . . .

Nancy. Tea?

Tom. *But* the two front teeth—

Nancy. More tea?

Tom. Remained. So you are left with an animal having an extraordinarily long upper jaw and two big front teeth. You're left with an elephant. No problem at all. Yes I would, please.

[*Tolen touches Nancy's arm.*]

Nancy. D'you like it? It's new.

Tolen. You should paint that wall straight away or it'll patch up.

Tom. What?

Tolen. It will dry blotchy.

Tom. Yes. That's a good idea. Yes!

Tolen. You wanted to see me?

Colin. Eh?

Tolen. That's right.

Colin. Wanted to see you?

Tolen. You will.

Colin. What d'you—

Tolen. Watch this.

Colin. What do you mean?

Tom. In cold blood, Colin. In cold blood.

Tolen. I'll show you how.

Tom. Nancy! [*Angry.*] You should go when you're told.

[*Tolen takes a copy of* Honey *and lies on the bed.*]

Nancy. Would you like something behind your head?

Tolen. There is a pillow in the passage.

[*Nancy exits, returns with pillow.*]

Tolen. Why don't you look at me?

Nancy. I can't.

Tolen. Why can't you?

Nancy. I'll—I'll—

Tolen. What?

Nancy. I'll laugh.

Tolen. Why?

Nancy. You'll make me laugh.

Tolen. Why?

Nancy. You will.

Tolen. Will I?

Nancy. Yes.

Tolen. Will I?

Nancy. Yes.

Tolen. Look at me, laugh! Go on! Look at me, laugh, look
at me, go on, look at me, laugh, look at me, look at me.
[*She laughs. She stops laughing. He might kiss her.*]

Nancy. No, no.

Colin. Ha!

Tolen. You idiot. Fool.

[*Pause.*]

Tom. Do you like my room?

Nancy. What?

Tom. My room.

Nancy. What! It's not much. There's not much to sit on.

Tom. Sit on the piano.

Nancy [*irritated*]. Aw!

Tom. They clutter up the place so I really must get them
on the wall.

Nancy. What?

Tom. The chairs. On the wall.

Nancy. What? Oh, it doesn't matter.

Tom. To get them off the floor. Have I said anything to upset you, Tolen?

Tolen. Nothing you said could possibly upset me. [*Pause.*] Why do you try and find rational reasons for your childish impulses?

Tom. Do I disturb you?

Tolen. You make me smile.

Tom. Ooh! He's annoyed. Oh yes, he's annoyed. Be careful or you might lose control. Ah well. Back to work. Pass me another cup of tea, Nancy.

Nancy. What?

Tom. Get me another cup of tea, there's a dear.

Nancy. What do you think I am?

Tom. Oh. [*Pause.*] Sorry.

Nancy. Oh all right. [*She pours out tea for Tom.*]

Tom. Thanks.

Nancy [*to Tolen*]. Do you want some?

Tolen. No. [*Nancy pours out tea for herself. Long pause.*] All right. She's all yours.

Colin. Eh?

Tolen. You have a try.

Colin. What? Me?

Tolen. Yes.

[*Long pause.*]

Colin. Has Cardiff got big docks?

Nancy. What?

Colin. Has Cardiff got big d-docks?

Nancy. Why ask me?

Colin. Welsh. I mean—aren't you—don't you come from Wales?

Nancy. No.

Colin. It was the name—Jones.

Nancy. Where d'you say the Y.W. was?

Colin. Oh, it's in Martin's Grove. You have to take a 27 bus, get off at the top of Church Street and walk down on the left until—

Nancy. It far?

Colin. Pardon?

Nancy. Is is far?

Colin. No, not very.

Nancy. Good. I'm going.

Colin. What?

Nancy. I'm off. I said I'm going. And as for you. As for you

Mr. Mr. Mr. only one name. Mr. no name. As for you. As for you. As for you . . . [*Tolen laughs.*] That's my *Honey*. Give me my *Honey*.

Colin. I'll take you. I said I'll take you there.

Tolen. You want your magazine? [*She retreats. Tolen follows her. She cannot retreat farther. She slaps him. He kisses her.*] See? It's not difficult.

[*Nancy bursts into tears.*]

Tom. Well that's that. I need this room, Tolen.

Tolen. Expecting someone?

Tom. Maybe.

Tolen. Man or woman? [*Pause.*] Are you a homosexual?

Tom. No. [*Pause.*] Thanks all the same.

[*Exit Tolen.*]

Colin. Why do you like annoying him?

Tom. He was annoyed, wasn't he? He's softening up. Ha ha! Now he'll play gramophone records and make telephone calls. Really Colin, what a mess, suppose the Queen were to come. Oh this wall, this sickening, everlasting wall, it's enormous, it goes on for ever. I'm fed up with it. Here. [*Gives Colin a brush.*]

Colin. Eh? What's this for?

[*Tom gives Nancy a brush.*]

Tom. Only the end bit, the plain bit, the uncreative bit, the bit that don't need genius.

Colin. You want us to paint the wall?

Tom. The white bit, the boring bit. I'm sick of it.

Colin. You're so damned lazy.

Tom. Attack it. Attack it.

Colin. And messy.

Nancy. Yes! Yes! you yes! [*She attacks wall.*] You ha ha! Yes [*mumbling between her teeth*]. Yes! Um hm um hm!

Tom. A dear girl. A darling girl. There. That's right. [*Exit Tom.*]

Colin. Here?

Tom [*off*]. Here?

Colin. The end.

Tom [*off*]. The window end?

Colin. Yes.

Tom [*entering*]. That's right. [*Enter Tom with a sheet which he ties round Nancy. She takes her jacket off and gives it to him.*]

Tom. Ah yes, that's nice. Faster, serfs! [*Pause.*] Elephants.

[*Pause.*] The Indians keep elephants like we keep cows.
—I was wondering how big an elephant's udder was.
My God, imagine it swishing around. Do you know,
in Walt Disney's early films there were cows and the
censor cut the udders out so he put brassieres on them,
imagine! . . . Jersey cows wear brassieres, it's true.
Jersey cows wear brassieres. Something wrong here,
cows shouldn't need brassieres. Human beings need
them because they stand upright. They used to go on
all fours, so they hung downwards—vertically—now
they stand upright and it puts on this terrible strain . . .
[*Nancy is laughing.*] All right, all right. It's true.

Colin. Oh—

Tom. Eh?

Colin. I wish you wouldn't show off.

Tom [*to Nancy*]. Hi! [*To Colin.*] I don't show off.

Colin. You do.

Tom [*restraining Nancy*]. Colin wishes I wouldn't show off.

Colin. Well you do show off.

Tom. I don't.

Colin. You do. Stop slapping it.

Nancy. I like splashing.

Colin. It's splashing.

Nancy. So what?

Colin. It's dripping.

Nancy. I don't care. I don't care.

Colin. Don't get so excited.

Nancy. You're talking. I hear you.

Colin. Look at her. Look at her.

Tom. I see her.

Nancy. So what.

Tom [*shepherding Nancy to a bit of wall away from his careful painting*]. Watch it—yes—there's a—and now—that's right—more left.

Nancy. What's the difference between an elephant and a pillar box?

Colin. They can neither of them ride a bicycle.

Nancy. You knew!

Colin. What? What?

Nancy. I can reach higher than you.

Colin [*holding up his arm*]. Heard it before.

Nancy. Yes, I can.

Tom. I don't show off.

Colin. What? No, you can't.

Nancy. I can.

Colin. You can't.

Tom. I do—

Nancy. I can—

Tom. —sometimes—

Nancy. —look—

Colin. You don't—I mean—

Nancy. I can reach higher than you—

Colin. Ouch!

Nancy. What?

Colin. It's all run up my elbow. Oh.

Tom. You're dripping everywhere. There's a cloth in the kitchen.

[*Exit Colin. Telephone rings, off. Pause. Enter Tolen.*]

Tolen. It's for you.

Tom. Man or woman?

Tolen. Woman.

[*Exit Tom. Pause. Tolen moves to help Nancy off with sheet. She avoids him.*]

Tolen. No one's going to rape you.

Nancy. Oh!

Tolen [*laughing*]. Girls never get raped unless they want it.

Nancy. Oh!

Tolen. I'm sorry about—what happened.

Nancy. That's—

Tolen. It was clumsy—very—

Nancy. That's all right.

Tolen. It was because they were here—the clumsiness I mean—

Nancy. Was it?

Tolen. In a way, in a way.

Nancy. Oh.

Tolen. Don't you believe me?

Nancy. I don't know—I—

Tolen. Please—

Nancy. I—

Tolen. Please believe me.

Nancy. It doesn't matter.

Tolen. It does matter, it matters very much. [*Pause.*] It matters very much to me. [*Pause.*] How sweet you are. Such a sweet face, such sweetness. [*Pause. He kisses her.*] Ssh . . . ssh . . . Come . . . come up . . . come upstairs . . .

Nancy. Oh . . . oh . . .

Tolen. Come up to my room . . .

Nancy. Oh . . . oh . . . no . . .

Tolen. You like music? I've got some records upstairs . . . I'll play you some records.

[*Enter Colin.*]

Colin. Well, let's get on—oh— . . . Where are you going? Are you going out? To find the Y.W.? I'll come too.

Tolen. What?

Colin. I'll come as well.

Tolen. Where?

Colin. To find it.

Tolen. What?

Colin. The Y.W.

[*Pause.*]

Tolen. Why don't you go?

Colin. Eh?

Tolen. Why don't you go look for the Y.W.?

Colin. Well, you're coming aren't you? [*Tolen is exasperated.*] Well—you—

Nancy. Oh—

Colin. Oh come on—

Nancy. I don't think I—

Colin. Oh please—

Nancy. What about the cases?

Colin. The cases?

Nancy. I can't go without them.

Colin. He'll look after them.

Nancy. Who will?

Colin. He will.

Tolen. Me?

Nancy. Where are you going?

Tolen. I'm going out.

Nancy. I'd like a walk.

Colin. So would I.

Nancy. What about the cases?

Colin. You stay here.

Tolen. Why should I?

Colin. You could stay here.

Tolen. Why should I?

Colin. You could look after the cases.

Tolen. He can.

Colin. Who can?

Tolen. Tom can.

Colin. He's upstairs. Can't they stay here?

Nancy. I need them at the Y.W.

[*Tolen moves away. Nancy follows.*]

Colin. Let's go look for the Y.W.

Nancy. Are you coming?

Tolen. To the Y.W.?

Colin. Well, let's you and me go.

Nancy. Well—

Colin. Well—

Nancy. I don't think I really—

Colin. You said you did.

Nancy. Did I?

Colin. Yes.

Nancy. What about the cases?

Tolen. Why don't you carry them?

Colin. Me?

Tolen. If you're going to the Y.W., why don't you carry them?

Colin. Let's go for a walk.

Nancy. What about the cases?

Tolen. You carry them.

Colin. She!

Tolen. Yes.

Colin. She can't carry them.

Tolen. She's already carried them. She carried them here.

Colin. She can't carry them.

Tolen. You carry them.

Colin. I want both hands free.

[*Pause. Enter Tom. Tolen starts to exit.*]

Nancy. Where you going?

Tolen. Oh, anywhere. D'you want to?

Nancy. D'you want me to?

Tolen. If you want to.

Colin. Are you going to the Y.W.?

Tolen. Maybe.

Colin. I'll come too.

Tolen. What about the cases?

[*Colin picks up the cases.*]

Colin. I'll come too.

[*Tolen and Nancy exit.*]

Tom. Stay with them, Colin.

Colin. Eh?

Tom. Stick with them.

[*Exit Colin. Tolen and Nancy are seen to pass window, followed soon after by Colin. Exit Tom. Heavy dragging and banging off. Enter Tom looking very pleased with himself, takes bed to bits and drags it off. More banging. Enter Tom exhausted. Drinks milk. Exits with tray. Re-enters and resumes painting. Tolen and Nancy pass window. Door is tried, off. Tolen and Nancy enter through window. Both are laughing a good deal.]*

Tolen. That door blocked again?

Tom. Been moving a few things.

Tolen. And if you push it under—ooops! *[Nancy laughs]* and over—ooops! *[Nancy laughs.]*

[Enter Colin through window.]

Tom. You look very seasick.

Colin. Shut up. *[Colin thrusts carrier bag on his head. Nancy is pretty hysterical. Tolen works her up, kissing and laughing. Tom intensifies the atmosphere by beating a rhythm on bed or stepladder, possibly using mouth music as well.]*

Tolen. We'll go and listen to those gramophone records. *[Exit Tolen and Nancy. Tom stops beating. Pause Large crash, off. Enter Tolen.]*

Tolen. Who put that stuff on the stairs?

Tom. Oh, are the stairs blocked?

Tolen. I can't get up to my room.

Tom. Oh, can't you?

[Enter Nancy.]

Nancy. Why's the wardrobe on the stairs—and the bed—the stairs are blocked . . . *[Tolen grabs her.]* Oh! You're hurting me!

Tom. Stop. Stop that.

Nancy. Let me go! Let me go! Let me go! *[She escapes but not before Tolen has hurt and thoroughly frightened her.]* Don't touch me! *[Tom and Colin attempt to comfort her but they only excite her more.]* Keep off! Keep off! D'you hear? Keep away! Don't touch me! You—you—you—don't touch me! You don't touch me. All right? All right? . . . Now, now then, now . . . what's—what's up? What is it, eh? Yes? What you—what you want with me?—what you want—What you trying on, eh? What you trying to do? What is it, eh? What you want—you—you—you . . . Mr. Smart! Mr. Smartie! You think you're—You think you're—You think you're pretty clever. You think you're all right. . . . You do, don't you, Mr. Smartie! Mr. Tight Trousers! Mr. Tight Trousers! Mr. Narrow Trousers! You

think you're the cat's—you think you're . . . I'll show
you . . . I'll show you, Mr. Tight Trousers. Just you
don't come near me, d'you hear? Just you don't come
near me—come near me, d'you hear? Come near me!
I'll show you, Mr. Tight Trousers! Tight Trousers! Yes!
Yes! Come near me! Come near me! Come near me!
Come! Come! Come! Come! Come! [*Tolen laughs and
walks away. Nancy moans and collapses. Colin somehow catches her as she falls.*]

Colin. She's fainted!

Tom. Lucky there was someone to catch her.

End of Act Two

Before the curtain rises there is a loud banging and crashing, mixed with shouts and cries.

Curtain up.

Colin is holding Nancy like a sack of potatoes. Tom and Tolen are just finishing putting up the bed.

Tom. Give it a bash! And so—oops! A bedmaker, that's you Tolen, a master bedwright. O.K. Has she come round yet?

Colin. Come round?

Tom. Is she still out?

Colin. Out?

Tom. Oh, he's a thick one. This way.

Colin. I'm not thick, she's heavy.

Tom. Don't drop her. Now we've got this out of the passage, Tolen, you can go upstairs to bed. We'll put her here to rest. Sling her over. . . . Not like that!

Colin. You said sling.

Tom. She's in a faint, fainted, can't defend herself.

[*They get Nancy on the bed.*]

Nancy. Oh . . . oh dear . . . oh dear . . . I do feel . . . I think I'm going to be—

Tom. Sick? [*Nancy nods.*] Not here. [*Colin holds out bucket. Tom dashes to door and opens it.*] Bathroom. [*Exit Nancy followed by Tom. Pause. Tolen goes to door. Opens it and listens a moment, then closes door and bolts it.*]

Colin. What are you doing?

Tolen. I don't want to be interrupted, Colin. I have something I wish to discuss with you.

Colin. Oh, I see. . . . But this is Tom's room.

Tolen. This is your room, Colin, your room. You are the landlord. The house belongs to you. It's for you to say whose room this is, Colin. Who lives here.

Colin. Oh, yes—er—

Tolen. There is something I would like to discuss with you, Colin. An idea I had.

Colin. Oh?

Tolen. You know that you need help, Colin. You do know that, don't you?

Colin. Mm.

Tolen. Now tell me, Colin, how many women have you had?

Colin. Mm . . .

Tolen. Two women. Only two. And you were late starting weren't you, Colin? Very late. Not until last year. And Carol left you how many months ago?

Colin. Mm . . .

Tolen. Six months ago. That's right, isn't it. Two women in two years. Some of us have more women in two days. I have a suggestion to make to you, Colin. A suggestion which you will find very interesting and which will help you very much. [*Pause.*] Now as you know, Colin, I have a number of friends. *Men.* And they can help you Colin, as I can help you. I am thinking particularly of Rory McBride.

Colin. Oh.

Tolen. Rory McBride is a man, Colin, a clever man, a gifted man, a man I can respect. He knows a great many things, Colin. Rory McBride was doing things at thirteen that you haven't ever done, Colin; things that you don't even know about.

Colin. What sort of things?

Tolen. In a moment, Colin. First I will tell you my suggestion. Now, as you know, I have a number of regular women, Colin. Women I regularly make. And Rory McBride has a number of regular women too. Perhaps not quite as many as I have, but several. Now. Quite recently, Rory and I were talking—comparing notes— and we decided it would be a good idea if we saw each other more often . . . if even we were to live near each other.

Colin. Oh?

Tolen. Yes, Colin . . . perhaps in the same house . . . and that we would share our women.

Colin. Oh!

Tolen. After I have had a woman, Rory can have her, and if I want I can have Rory's. Of course Rory realizes that it may, in a sense, be dangerous for him. He may lose a few of his women. However, Rory is well aware that, in the long run, he will profit by the arrangement; he will learn much, Colin, from the women who have been with me.

Colin [*agreeing*]. Mm.

Tolen. Now this is the suggestion I have to make. I would consider allowing you to come in on this arrangement.

Colin. Oh!

Tolen. Yes, Colin. I would allow you to come in with Rory and me, share our women. I think you would learn a great deal, Colin.

Colin. Oh yes.

Tolen. It would be a privilege for you, a great privilege.

Colin. Oh, yes, I see that.

Tolen. I'm sure Rory will he will agree. [*Pause.*] Now agree to this, Colin. I will ask him.

Colin. Do you think he will?

Tolen. If I ask him, Colin, he will agree. [*Pause.*] Now what I suggest, Colin, is that Rory moves into this house.

Colin. Mm?

Tolen. In here.

Colin. Oh . . .

Tolen. What's the matter, Colin?

Colin. But there's no room. There's you and me and—

Tolen. There is this room, Colin. The room you let to Tom. [*Pause.*] Remember this is your room. You are the landlord. Rory could have this room and . . . [*Tom yells, off, and bangs door.*] Rory McBride has a Chinese girl, Colin, slinky, very nice, do very well for you.

Colin. Chinese?

Tolen. It's only a question of experience. Of course you'll never be quite so—

Colin. Good as—

Tolen. Me, but—

Colin. But still—

Tolen. Oh yes, I don't doubt—

Colin. You really think—

Tolen. Certainly!

Colin. Chinese!

[*Enter Tom through window.*]

Tom. What the hell d'you think you're doing? Why d'you bloody lock the door, Tolen? You bloody remember this is my room. [*He unbolts door.*]

Tolen. Oh no, Tom, this is Colin's room.

Tom. Eh? What's going on here? [*Small crash upstairs.*
   Yelling.] Stop that. What the hell's she up to now?
   Where's her bag? She wants her bleeding bag. I tell you
   she's gone bloody funny like a bleeding windmill.

[*Cry off. Tolen crosses the room.*]

Tolen. Can you not control your women, Tom?

[*Exit Tom. Tolen crosses the room again.*]

Tolen. And a German girl.

Colin. German! [*Colin crosses the room imitating Tolen.*]

Tolen. Hold your head up, Colin. Head up! Don't stick your
   chin out. Keep your belly in. Bend your arms slightly
   at the elbows—not quite so—that's better. They should
   swing freely from your shoulders. . . . Not both together! Keep your head up! Move! Move! Move! Move!
   Feel it coming from your shoulders Colin, from your
   chest! From your gut! From your loin! More loin! More
   gut, man! Loin! Loin! Move! Move! Move! Move!
   Keep your head up! Authority, Colin! Feel it rippling
   through you! Authority! Keep your head up! Authority!
   Authority!

Colin. Authority.

Tolen. Authority! Move! Move! Move! Move! Authority!

Tom [*off*]. You can have a cup of tea and . . .

Nancy [*off*]. Tea!

Tom [*off*]. Tea.

Nancy [*off*]. I won't touch it. [*Enter Nancy wrapped in a
   blanket.*]

Tom [*entering*]. For God's sake make her some tea.

Nancy. I won't touch it. What's that?

Tom. What's what?

Nancy. That.

Tom. We've lugged this thing in here so you can lie down.
   Now lie down.

Nancy. I never asked you to bring it in.

Tom. You—

Nancy. Don't swear. [*Colin walks about the stage.*] You're
   not getting me on that thing again I tell you. Putting
   that thing together again to tempt a girl. Hiding it up
   passages. Stuffing it here and there. What d'you think I
   am? Eh? Eh? Don't you hear? Can't you hear what I
   say? [*Nancy bares her teeth and growls at Colin. He
   is momentarily disconcerted then ignores her and struts
   up and down again.*] An open invitation if you ask me.
   Ask me! Go on ask me! Well somebody ask me . . .

please . . . [*Pause.*] A nasty situation. Dear me, yes. Very nasty, a particularly vicious sense of—criminal, yes, that's it—positively criminal. They ought to be told, somebody should—I shall phone them, phone them—the police, Scotland Yard, Whitehall one two one two [*she catches sight of Colin walking up and down*] one two one two [*she repeats one two one two as often as necessary. Colin picks up the rhythm and they begin to work each other up. Nancy starts to bang the rhythm. Colin stamps about and slaps himself until eventually he hurts himself. Nancy is temporarily assuaged.*]

Tom. That's an interesting movement you've got there, Colin.

Colin. Oh, d'you think so?

Tom. Very interesting.

Colin. Tolen taught it me.

Tom. Oh yes?

Colin. It's got authority.

Tom. Come again?

Colin. Authority.

Tom. Ah. Let's see it again . . . ah.

[*Colin demonstrates, then Tom has a go.*]

Colin. You've got to walk from your gut.

Tom. Eh?

Colin. Your gut.

Tom. Oh I see. I see, I see. Bucket!

Colin. Eh?

Tom. For a helmet. Bucket! Bucket! Jump to it! Don't keep me waiting. Bucket!

Colin. Oh. [*Colin jumps for the bucket, offers it to Tom who puts it on Colin's head.*]

Tom. Now I'll show you what authority's really, Colin. Much more impressive than a carrier—a helmet. Dominating, brutal. [*Tom starts banging a 4/4 rhythm and singing the "Horst Wessel."*] Ra ra ra ra, ra ra ra ra, march! March! March! March! Get on with it! Ra ra ra ra. [*Nancy picks up the 4/4 rhythm and the tune.*] March! Damn you! March! Jams, guns, guts, butter! Jams, guns, guts, butter! Boots! Boots! Boots! Boots! Boots for crushing! Boots for smashing! Sieg heil! Sieg heil! Ha! [*Colin gets rid of the bucket.*] What's the matter? What's up? Don't you like it? I thought you loved it. Tolen loves it, don't you, Tolen? Tolen loves it.

Colin. Tolen doesn't do that.

Tom. Not so loud maybe, but the same general idea. I think it's funnier louder, don't you, Tolen?

Colin. Shut up.

Tom. Just look at Tolen's boots.

[*Pause. Nancy jumps up and down.*]

Nancy. Grrr.

Tom [*disregarding Nancy and speaking to Tolen*]. When I die I could be reincarnated as a sea anemone. It doesn't affect my attitude to death one little bit but it does affect my attitude to sea anemones.

A sea anemone with a crew cut would starve to death. [*Pause.*] Your ears are going red. They're pulsating red and blue. No, I'm exaggerating. One is anyway. The one nearest me. [*Pause.*] That white horse you see in the park could be a zebra synchronized with the railings. [*Tolen moves away. Tom looks very pleased.*]

Nancy. I wouldn't touch it if you made it.

Tom. Eh?

Nancy. I wouldn't.

Tom. Made what?

Nancy. Tea.

Tom [*to Colin*]. You'd better make some.

Colin [*disgruntled*]. Oh.

Tom. Shall I tell you a story? [*Exit Colin.*] I know you'd like to hear about the kangaroo—the kangaroo. You heard me. Did you? Now of course you know that the baby kangaroo lives in its mother's pouch. Don't you. Go on, commit yourself.

Nancy. Oh, all right.

Tom. Don't be so cautious. This one is true and pure. All my stories are true unless I say so. Well, the baby kangaroo is born about two inches long and as soon as it's born it climbs into its mother's pouch—how does it climb? Never mind, it fights its way through the fur . . . [*Colin enters balefully and sets down a tray and exits.*] When it gets inside the pouch the baby kangaroo finds one large, solid nipple. Just one. The baby latches on to this nipple and then it, the nipple, swells and swells and swells until it's shaped something like a door knob in the baby's mouth. And there the baby kangaroo stays for four months, four solid months. What an almighty suck! Isn't that interesting? Doesn't it interest you as a facet of animal behaviour so affecting human be-

haviour? Doesn't it make you marvel at the vast family
of which God made us part? Oh well . . .

[*Pause.*]

Nancy. What happened?

Tom. What happened when?

Nancy. You know when.

Tom. No, I do not.

Nancy. You know when. [*Enter Colin with teapot. Colin
pours out tea in silence. Hands a cup to Tolen, goes
with a cup to Nancy.*] What's that?

Colin. Eh?

Tom. Tea.

Nancy. I'm not having any. I'm not touching it. He's put
something it in.

Colin. Eh?

Tom. Put something in it?

Nancy. Oh yes, he's put something in it.

Tom. Don't be so daft.

Nancy. I'm not touching it.

Tom. But—

Nancy. I'm not.

Tom. What should he put in it? There's absolutely nothing in
it. Nothing at all—look—ugh!—Sugar!

[*Pause.*]

Nancy. I like sugar.

Colin. Two.

Nancy. What?

Colin. Two lumps.

Nancy. I take two.

Colin. I know.

[*Pause. Nancy takes the tea and drinks. Long pause.*]

Nancy. I've been raped. [*Pause.*] I have.

Tolen. I beg your pardon.

Nancy. You heard.

Colin. I didn't.

Nancy. I've been raped.

[*Tolen sneers audibly.*]

Colin. What!

Nancy. I have been—it was just after—when I fainted—
there by the—before I went up with—when I fainted.
I was raped.

[*Tolen sneers.*]

Colin. When she says—

Nancy. I have been, you did—

Colin. Does she mean really—I mean, actually?

Tom. What else?

Nancy. Rape. Rape. I—I've been—

Colin. But—

Nancy. Raped.

Colin. But you haven't.

Nancy. I have.

Colin. No one has—

Nancy. Rape.

Colin. But we've been here all the time, all of us.

Nancy. Huh!

Colin. You know we have.

Tolen. A vivid imagination, that's what's the matter with her.

Nancy. Eh?

Colin. Oh?

Tom. Watch it.

Tolen. Take no notice of her.

Nancy. Eh?

Tolen. Ignore her.

Nancy. What? Rape?

Tom. You be careful, Tolen.

Nancy. Rape! I been—

Tolen. She quite simply wishes to draw attention to herself.

Nancy [*a little unsure*]. Oh?

Tolen. She has fabricated a fantasy that we have raped her.
First because she wants us to take notice of her and
second because she really would like to be raped.

Nancy. Eh?

Colin. Would you mind saying that again?

Tolen. Her saying that we have raped her is a fantasy. She
has fabricated this fantasy because she really does want
to be raped; she wants to be the centre of attention. The
two aims are, in a sense, identical. The fabrication that
we have raped her satisfactorily serves both purposes.

Colin. Oh.

Nancy. What's that word mean? Fabricated?

Tolen. Made it up.

Nancy [*a bit nonplussed*]. Oh no. Oh no. Not that. I know,
oh yes. I'm not having that sort of—I know, oh yes. I'm
the one that knows. You've had your fun and—and—
there! It was there! You've had your fun and now I feel
funny, queer, sick. I know, you're not coping with a—
I'm not a fool you know—I'm not a ninny. . . . No,

no, I didn't make it up . . . fabricated . . . fabricated
. . . fabricated . . .

Tom [*to Tolen*]. What'll you do if she tells everyone you
raped her?

Tolen. What?

Tom. There's a methodist minister lives two doors down.
Suppose she was to yell out of the window? By God
you'd look silly, you'd look right foolish. I'd give a lot
to see that.

Tolen. Are you mad?

Tom [*to Nancy*]. Don't let him off so easily love.

Nancy. Eh?

Tom [*to Tolen*]. What'll you do if she yells down the street?

Nancy. Rape! They done me! Rape! You done me! You did!
Rape! Rape! Rape! Rape! Rape! [*At window.*] Rape!
[*etc., as necessary.*]

Tolen. Shut the window. [*Tolen goes for Nancy.*]

Nancy. Rape! [*Tolen gets her neatly under control and keeps
his hand over her mouth.*]

Tom. Try and keep your dignity on that one.

Colin. Mind she doesn't bite.

Tolen. Shut the window.

[*Colin shuts the window. Tolen releases Nancy.*]

Nancy. You don't want me yelling down the street, do you?

Tolen. We don't want the trivial inconvenience.

Nancy. You're scared they'll hear and lock you up.

Tolen. I do not intend to expose myself to trivial indignities
from petty officials.

Nancy. You're worried. You're scared. You're afraid. I'll
tell. I will tell!

Colin. Eh?

Nancy. The police. The Y.W. I'll report you. That's it. The
lot. Them all. I'll tell them how you raped me—how
you—I'll tell them. The coppers. The Y.W.

Tom. Whew!

Nancy. All the lurid details! All the horrid facts! *News of
the World.* TV. Read all about it! Rape! Rape! Just you
wait! You'll get ten years for this!

Tom. She means it.

Tolen. She's simply drawing attention to herself.

Colin. Means what?

Tom. She means to tell everyone we raped her. Right. [*Putting Tolen on the stop.*] In that case he must rape her.

Colin. Eh?

Tolen. I beg your pardon?

Tom. In that case she must be raped by him.

Nancy. I'm not having it twice.

Tom. You want her to keep quiet.

Tolen. I do not propose to allow her to expose . . .

Tom [*cutting him short*]. Right. You say she's made this up because she really does want to be raped.

Colin. Well?

Tom. If he wants to keep her quiet he must rape her. According to what he says—and he's probably right— that's the only thing will satisfy her.

Colin. If she's raped she'll be the centre of attention, that's it!

Tom. Just so. What do you say?

[*The men are talking about Nancy but, in a sense, have forgotten her. She is resentful.*]

Nancy. Rape!

Tom. What do you say, Tolen?

[*Pause.*]

Tolen. It's your idea. Why don't you rape her?

Tom. I like her yelling down the street.

[*Pause.*]

Tolen. Colin?

Colin. What me? Oh no. I couldn't.

[*Pause.*]

Nancy. Rape!

Tolen. I never yet came to a woman under duress and certainly never because I was forced to it. Because she demanded it. Because I had to buy her silence. I shall not now.

[*Nancy explodes round the room.*]

Nancy. Ray! Ray! Ray! Ray! Ray! [*Continue as long as necessary.*]

Colin. Stop her!

Tolen. Don't let her—

Tom. Whoops! Whoops!

Tolen. Near the—

Colin. What eh?

Tolen. Shut the door!

Colin. Ow!

Tolen. —door!

Tom. Door? Door?

Colin. Door?

[*A chase. Finally Nancy exits down left by mistake. Colin slams door and bolts it.*]

Tolen. The front. The front door. She'll get out the front. Colin!

[*Exit Colin through window. Banging, off, at front door. Reenter Colin.*]

Colin. No, she won't. It's blocked.

[*Pause.*]

Tom. She smashed up the bathroom. She might—

[*Pause.*]

Tolen. My records! [*Tolen throws himself on the door. Enter Nancy barefoot. She wears her pleated skirt thus: her right arm through the placket, the waist band running over her right shoulder and under her left arm. She carries her underclothes, which she scatters gaily.*]

Nancy. Shove you in jug! Put you in jail! One for the road! Long for a stretch! Just you wait! I'll tell!

[*Pause.*]

Tom. That's not how a skirt is usually worn, still it's bigger than a bathing costume.

Colin. It's not a bathing costume.

Nancy. I shall sue you for paternity.

Tom. Now listen, Nancy.

Nancy. All of you.

Tom. Nancy.

Nancy. Don't Nancy me.

Tom [*Nancy ad libs through speech*]. Look love—don't say anything for a minute. Now look, we haven't raped you—but—just a moment—Now listen, everything's happening so fast you must give us a chance to think. I mean you're a reasonable girl, Nancy, an intelligent girl, give us a chance now, just give us a chance like a reasonable, rational, intelligent girl, just let us talk for one moment. No yelling and no dashing off anywhere.

Nancy. It's a trap.

Tom. No it isn't. I promise. It's pax for one minute.

Nancy. All right. I'll give you one minute.

Tom. That's not enough.

Nancy. Two minutes.

Tom. Five.

Nancy. Three.

Tom. Done.

Nancy. Three minutes and no more. Then I'll start yelling again. Lend me a wristwatch.

Tom. Oh very well. Colin!

Nancy. And if you're naughty and cheat I can smash it.

Colin. Oh I say—

Tom. Oh come on, Colin.

[*Colin hands over his watch. Nancy climbs step ladder.*]

[*Author's Note: the following scene falls into four sections.*
    1st section: Introduction to the scene: The three confer.]

Tom. Now, Tolen.

Tolen. The situation is quite clear.

Colin. Not to me it isn't.

Tom. You've got to rape her.

Tolen. Please be quiet, Tom.

Nancy [*while the others confer*]. I've been raped, I've been
    raped, I've been raped, raped, raped, I've been raped,
    I've been raped, I've been raped. I've been raped, I've
    been raped, I've been raped, raped, raped, I've been
    raped, I've been raped, I've been raped.

Tom. Oh go on.

Tolen. An impasse has been reached.

Colin. She believes we've raped her.

Tom. She's convinced herself.

Tolen. She's made it up to draw attention to herself and be-
    cause she wants it.

Tom. She is prepared to report us.

Colin. Yes, yes.

Tom. Tolen doesn't want that.

Colin. No, no.

Tom. But he's not prepared to do the other thing.

Colin. What are we going to do?

[*Pause.*]

Tolen. She must be examined by a competent physician.

Colin. What?

Tolen. A doctor. If she's a virgin—

Tom. Not interfered with—

Tolen. That lets us out!

Colin. What if she's not?

[*Pause.*]

Tom. If she's not a virgin she could say we raped her and
    we'd have a job to prove otherwise.

Tolen. She must be a virgin.

Tom. Why should she be?

Tolen. Well, take a look at her.

Nancy. Two minutes gone. One minute to go.

Tolen. Obviously a virgin.

Tom. I don't see why, it doesn't necessarily follow.

Colin. Follow what?

Nancy. Finished?

Tom. No.

Nancy. Ninety seconds to go.

Colin. Mind the watch.

Nancy. Rape!

Tolen. Don't get so excited, Colin.

Colin. It's my watch.

[*2nd section: Tom begins to enjoy the humour of the situation, and states his attitude; so that Tolen also states his attitude.*]

Tom. Since you take this attitude, there seems no rational course other than to negotiate. Open negotiation.

Tolen. Negotiate!

Tom. Negotiate.

Tolen. Negotiate with a woman. Never.

Tom. Then what is your suggestion?

Tolen. Authority.

Colin. Oh?

Tolen. Authority.

Colin. Ah!

Tolen. In all his dealings with women a man must act with promptness and authority—even, if need be, force.

Colin. Force?

Tom. Force?

Tolen. Force.

[*3rd section: Colin decides that Tolen's attitude is correct.*]

Tom. I cannot agree to force and certainly not to brutality.

Tolen. Never negotiate.

Tom. Calm, calmth.

Nancy. Sixty seconds.

Tolen. Force.

Tom. Negotiate. Parley, parley.

Tolen. Negotiate with a woman—

Tom. Calm.

Tolen. Never! Force!

Colin. He's—

Tolen. Force. Force.
Colin. For—
Tom. Calm, calm, calmth.
Tolen. Force, force. Never negotiate.
Colin. For—for—
Tom. No brutality!
Colin. Force!
Tolen. Never negotiate! Eh?
Colin. Force! Force!
Tom. Oh!
Colin. Force! Force! In dealing with a w-w-w-w—
Nancy. Forty seconds to go!
Colin. —w-woman a man must act with promptness and
    authority.
Tolen. Force.
Colin. Force.

[*4th section: Colin is precipitated into a forceful course of
    action.*]

Tom. Parley, negotiate.
Tolen. Authority.
Tom. Parley.
Tolen. Force.
Colin. Force.
Tom. No, no, parley, parley!
Colin. Force.
Tolen. Force.
Nancy. Twenty.
Tom. Parley, parley.
Tolen. No, no. Force.
Colin. For! For! For! He's right!
Nancy Ten seconds to go.
Colin. Force.
[*The following should tumble across each other as the ex-
    citement mounts.*]
Tolen. Force.
Tom. Parley.
Nancy. Eight.
Colin. Force.
Tolen. Never negotiate.
Tom. Calm.
Colin. He's right, he's absolutely—
Tolen. Force.

Nancy. Four.

Colin. A man—

Nancy. Three.

Colin. Must—

Nancy. Two.

Colin. Use—

Nancy. One.

Colin. Force. [*Slight pause.*] Shut up! Just you shut your—
d'you hear! You're talking through you—Firmness! A
firm hand! Spanking! See who's—I've been here all the
time, d'you hear? All the time. You've not been raped.
You have not. I know. So stop squawking. I know. I've
been here all the time.

Nancy. Ah.

Colin. I've been here all the time. So I can prove, prove,
testify. I have seen nothing. You've not been raped.
I know. I've been here all the time.

Nancy. Ah.

Colin. Come on down now and get them on. Get your clothes
on. Come down, come down you silly little . . . little
messer. You've not been raped, I know. I've been here
all the time.

Nancy. You!

Colin. I've been here all the time!

Nancy. You did it! It was you!

Colin. I been here . . . eh?

Nancy. You! You! You! You! He's it! He did it! He raped
me! He's been here all the time! He says so! He has!
He did it! Yes, he raped me!

Colin. Me!

Nancy. You.

Tom. Him!

Colin. Me!

Nancy. Yes, you. You been here all the time.

Tom. You, she says. She says you did it.

Colin. Me.

Nancy. Yes. You'll get ten years.

Colin. Me, me? Me! Oh no. This is awful. You're making a
terrible mistake.

Nancy. Oh no, not likely.

Colin. Oh, oh you are—tell her someone. Someone, Tolen,
tell—her I didn't. No really, I mean—

Nancy. I got a head on my shoulders.

Colin. I can see that but—

Nancy. That's it, you. You raped me.

Colin. But—but I assure you—I mean—

Nancy. That's him, officer, that's the one.

Colin. No! Tolen—Tom—please. I mean I didn't really I didn't.

Nancy. Clothes!

Colin. Clothes?

Nancy. Tore them off me.

Colin. Tore the—oh no.

Nancy. Scattered.

Colin. No.

Nancy. There they are.

Tom. Clear evidence.

Nancy. That face. You'd never know, they'd never guess.

Colin. Oh, wouldn't they?

Nancy. No girl would ever suspect.

Colin. Oh?

Nancy. But underneath—

Colin. What?

Nancy. Raving with lust.

Colin. Oh no, I mean—

Nancy. Fangs dripping with blood.

Colin. Oh.

Nancy. Bones of countless victims hidden in the basement.

Colin. We haven't got a basement. No! No! I mean I didn't, really I didn't. I didn't rape you—I mean I wouldn't—but well—this is terrible! Me! . . . You really think I did?

Nancy. Of course.

Colin. I mean you really do think I did?

Nancy. Yes.

Colin. You really do!

Nancy. Wait till next Sunday. What's your job?

Colin. Eh? I'm a teacher.

Nancy. Schoolteacher rapes—rapes—rapes—Nancy Jones!

Colin. Oh!

Nancy. Little did the pupils at—at—

Colin. Tottenham Secondary Modern—

Nancy. Tottenham Secondary Modern realize that beneath the handsome exterior of their tall, fair-haired, blue-eyed schoolteacher there lurked the heart of a beast, lusting for the blood of innocent virgins—little did they —You wait till you see the *Sunday Pictorial*.

Colin. Oh, I say, me. Me. Me. Oh I say. Oh. Oh. Do you really think—?

Nancy. What?

Colin. I've got a handsome exterior?

Nancy. Well—rugged perhaps, rather than handsome. And strong.

Colin. Oh.

Nancy. Oh yes, ever so. And lovely hands.

Colin. Oh. Oh. Oh. . . . Are you—are you doing anything tonight?

Nancy. What?

Colin. Are you doing anything tonight?

Nancy. Oh!

Colin. Oh, please, I didn't mean that. I mean I didn't rape you, anyway, I mean, oh well. Look, I mean let's go to the pictures or something or a walk or a drink or anything please. I think you're simply—I mean—Oh golly —do you really think I did? I mean I didn't rape you but I would like to—I mean, I would like to take you to the pictures or something.

Nancy. Well, I don't know it doesn't seem quite—I mean after—

Colin. Oh please—

Nancy. Well—

Colin. The pictures or anything.

Nancy. Would you?

Colin. Oh, yes, I would.

Tolen. This I find all very amusing.

Tom. I thought you might.

Tolen. Hilarious.

Tom. I've always admired your sense of humour.

Colin. Eh?

Tom. Well done. Very good. You're getting on very nicely, Colin. Much better than the great Tolen.

Tolen. That sexual incompetent.

Colin. Eh?

Nancy. He's not incompetent. What's incompetent?

Tom. No good.

Nancy. No good? He's marvellous, he raped me.

Tolen. You have not been raped.

Nancy. I have.

Tolen. You have not been raped and you know it.

Nancy. He raped me.

Tolen. You have not.

Nancy. I have.

Tolen. And certainly not by—

Nancy. Rape.

Tolen. Him. He wouldn't know one end of a woman from the other.

Nancy. Rape, rape.

Tolen. The number of times I've seen him. "Has Cardiff got big docks?" He'll never make it, never.

Colin. What?

Tolen. Granted—

Colin. What did you say?

Nancy. He raped me.

Tolen. Granted he might do better with help—and he needs help. Bow-legged, spavin-jointed, broken-winded, down and out. Look at him.

Colin. Eh?

Nancy. He's rugged.

Tolen. I ask you is it possible—?

Nancy. Handsome.

Tolen. Or likely—?

Nancy. Marvellous, super.

Tolen. It takes him four months hard labour to get a girl to bed.

Nancy. He did, you did, didn't you?

Tolen. That oaf.

Nancy. Go on, tell him.

Colin. Hard labour?

Tolen. You keep out of this.

Nancy. Yes, you shut up.

Tolen. A rapist, oh really.

Nancy. Rape. Rape.

Tolen. That chicken.

Nancy. Rape.

Tolen. How stupid can you get? Too ridiculous.

Nancy. Rape. Rape.

Tolen. Probably impotent.

[*Tom begins to knock a nail into the wall about nine feet above floor level. His banging deliberately punctuates the following.*]

Colin. Why not?

Tolen. What?

Colin. Why not me, pray?

Nancy. Rape. Rape.

Colin. Why not me? [*To Tom.*] Be quiet. [*To Tolen.*] Sexually
    incompetent! Hard labour!

[*Nancy starts to chirrup round the room, Colin while talking
    at the others follows after her.*]

Nancy. Rape pape pape pape pape pape—

[*Tom is banging.*]

Colin [*to Tom*]. Shut up. [*To Tolen.*] Now you listen—

Tom. Rape!

Nancy. R e e e e e e ep.

Colin. All, all I can say is out—out—outrage. Outrage. Out-
    ~rage. [*To Tom.*] Shut up. [*To Tolen.*] Rape, rape, didn't
    I? Couldn't I? I did—I mean I could—[*To Tom.*] Shut
    up. [*To Tolen.*] Now you listen, now get this straight—
    [*To Tom.*] Shut up. [*To Tolen.*] I am not incapable!

Nancy. Pay pay pay pay pay pay pee pee pee pee pee pee.

Colin [*to Nancy*]. Really, I didn't, really, I wouldn't mind—
    [*To Tom.*] Shut up, be quiet. [*To Nancy.*] I'd love to—
    I mean. [*To Tom.*] Shut up! [*Nancy is now keeping up
    an almost permanent yelp. Tom starts on another nail
    in another wall.*] Shut up, shut up. Now get this, get
    this—get—get—shut up—I could've yes. I could've if
    I'd wanted—rape her—shut up—I didn't—you think I
    couldn't—shut up—I—I—Shut! Shut! I'll show you!
    [*Colin starts to chase Nancy round the room. Tom's
    banging covers the chase and stops at the end of it.*]
    Just let me—get her—I'll—I'll show you—I'll—I'll—
    yes I'll—just you I'll show—oh—oh—oh—oh—oh—

Nancy. Oh—oh—oh—oh—

[*A chase with objects.*]

Colin. Oh—oh—oh—oh—

Nancy. Oh—oh—oh—oh—

Tolen. You can't even catch her Colin, can you? Never mind
    rape her. I think you are quite incapable of making a
    woman, Colin. Look, I'll show you.

Colin. If you touch her—I'll kill you!

[*Very long pause. Tolen releases Nancy who goes to Colin.
    A girl passes the window. Tolen laughs gently and then
    exits through window. Tom hoists chair on to the nails
    in the wall.*]

Tom. Ah yes, beautiful. [*Tom hoists second chair on to
    nails.*] Ah, yes. [*Exit Tom.*]

The End

A Study of History   ARNOLD J. TOYNBEE

Abridged by D. C. Somervell

TWO HANDSOME PAPERBACK VOLUMES
IN A BEAUTIFULLY DESIGNED SLIP COVER

Now—Dell presents the long-awaited two-volume abridgement of Toynbee's monumental masterpiece, which *The New York Times* has called, ". . . unquestionably one of the great works of our times."

This remarkably concise abridgement is the work of D. C. Somervell who, with marvelous skill, has retained all of Toynbee's immense depth and breadth of thought. He has managed to preserve not only its texture and atmosphere, but—for the most part—the author's own words.

Two-volume boxed set $1.95

If you cannot obtain copies of this title at your local newsstand, just send the price (plus 10c per copy for handling and postage) to Dell Books, Box 2291, Grand Central Post Office, New York, N.Y. 10017. No postage or handling charge is required on any order of five or more books.

PB-45133-SB
75-50T
c